Kamisama Kiss

Story & Art by

Julietta Suzuki

CHARACTERS

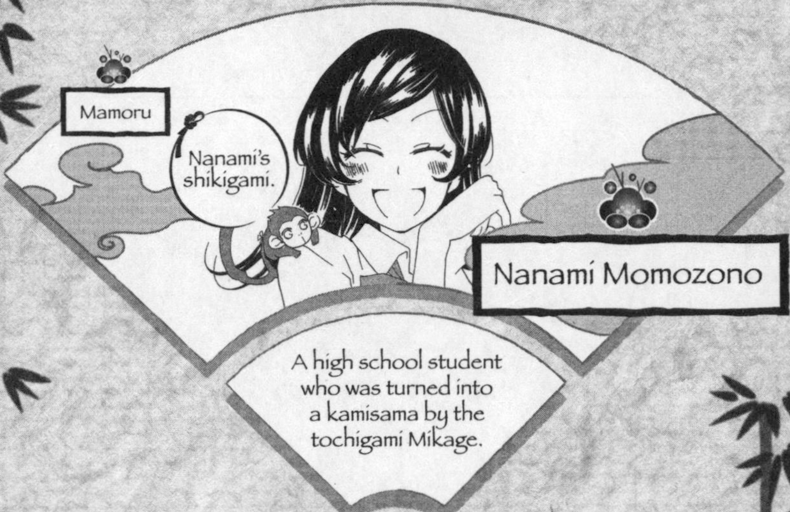
Nanami Momozono
A high school student who was turned into a kamisama by the tochigami Mikage.
Mamoru
Nanami's shikigami.

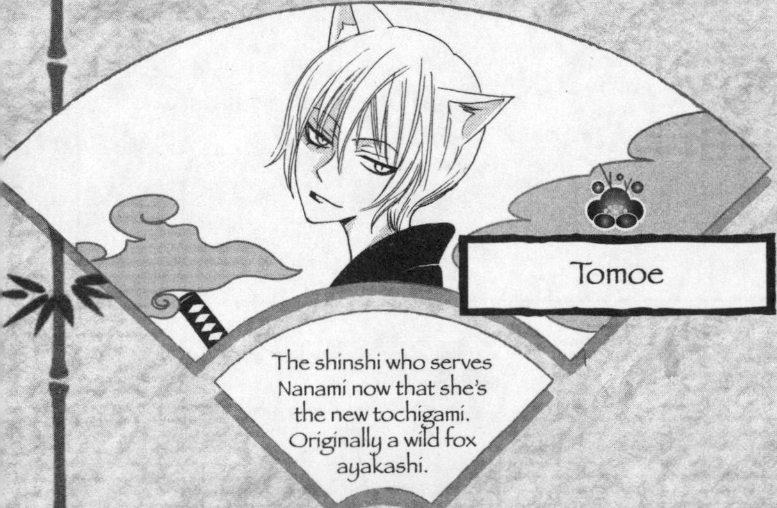
Tomoe
The shinshi who serves Nanami now that she's the new tochigami. Originally a wild fox ayakashi.

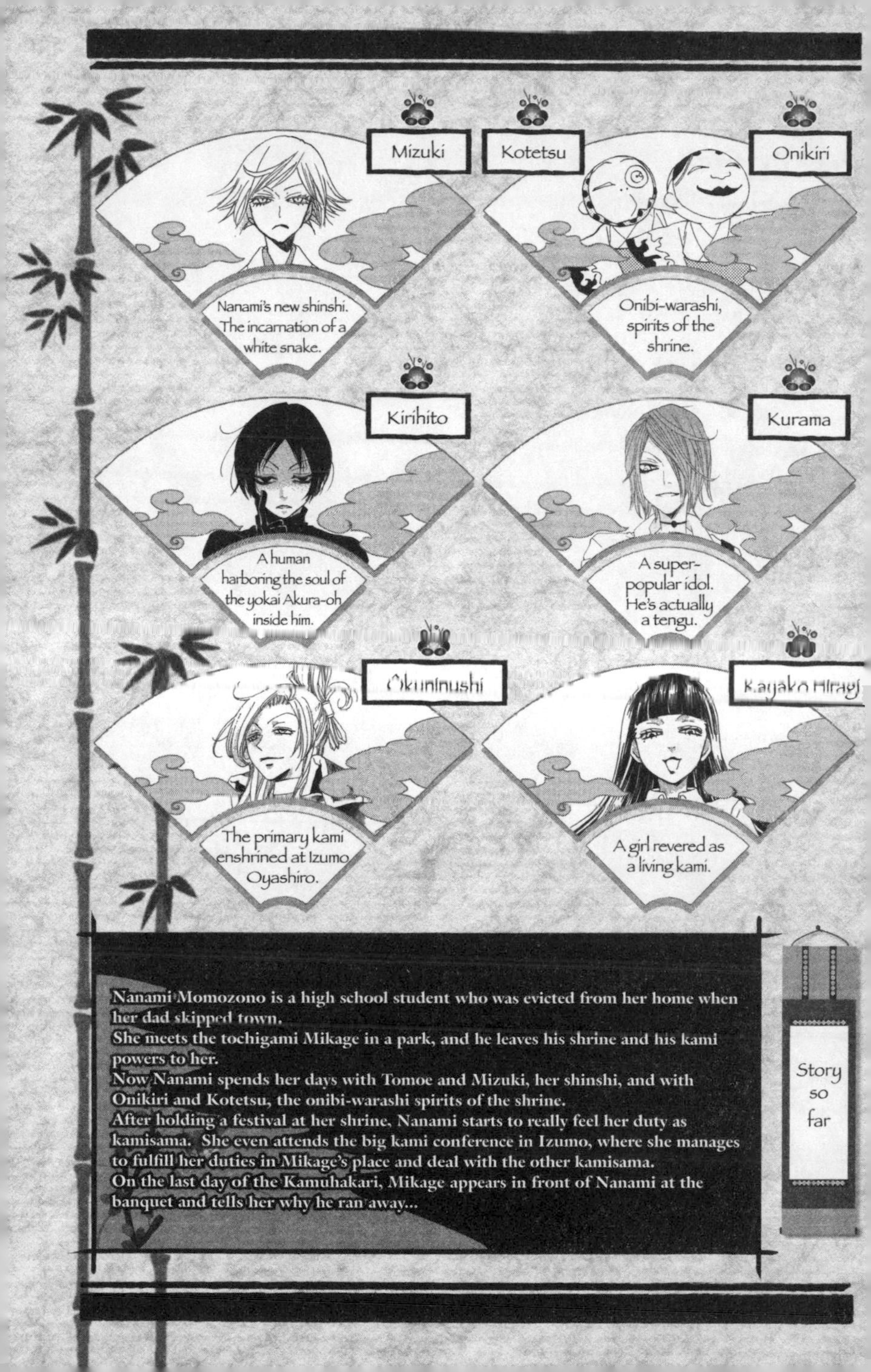

Onikiri
Kotetsu
Onibi-warashi, spirits of the shrine.
Mizuki
Nanami's new shinshi. The incarnation of a white snake.
Kurama
A super-popular idol. He's actually a tengu.
Kirihito
A human harboring the soul of the yokai Akura-oh inside him.
Kayako Hiiragi
A girl revered as a living kami.
Okuninushi
The primary kami enshrined at Izumo Oyashiro.

Story so far

Nanami Momozono is a high school student who was evicted from her home when her dad skipped town.
She meets the tochigami Mikage in a park, and he leaves his shrine and his kami powers to her.
Now Nanami spends her days with Tomoe and Mizuki, her shinshi, and with Onikiri and Kotetsu, the onibi-warashi spirits of the shrine.
After holding a festival at her shrine, Nanami starts to really feel her duty as kamisama. She even attends the big kami conference in Izumo, where she manages to fulfill her duties in Mikage's place and deal with the other kamisama.
On the last day of the Kamuhakari, Mikage appears in front of Nanami at the banquet and tells her why he ran away...

Kamisama Kiss

Volume 9
CONTENTS

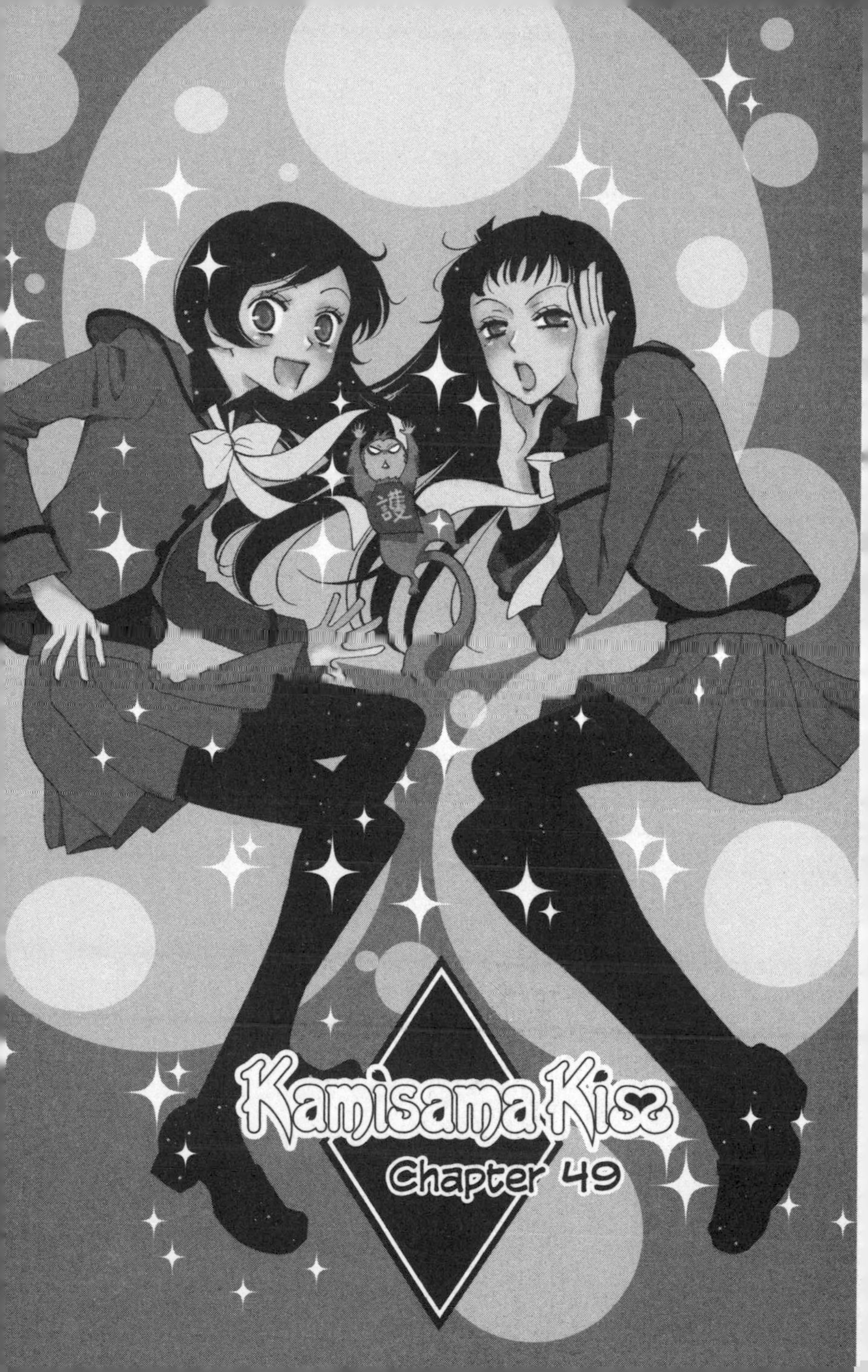
護
Kamisama Kiss
Chapter 49

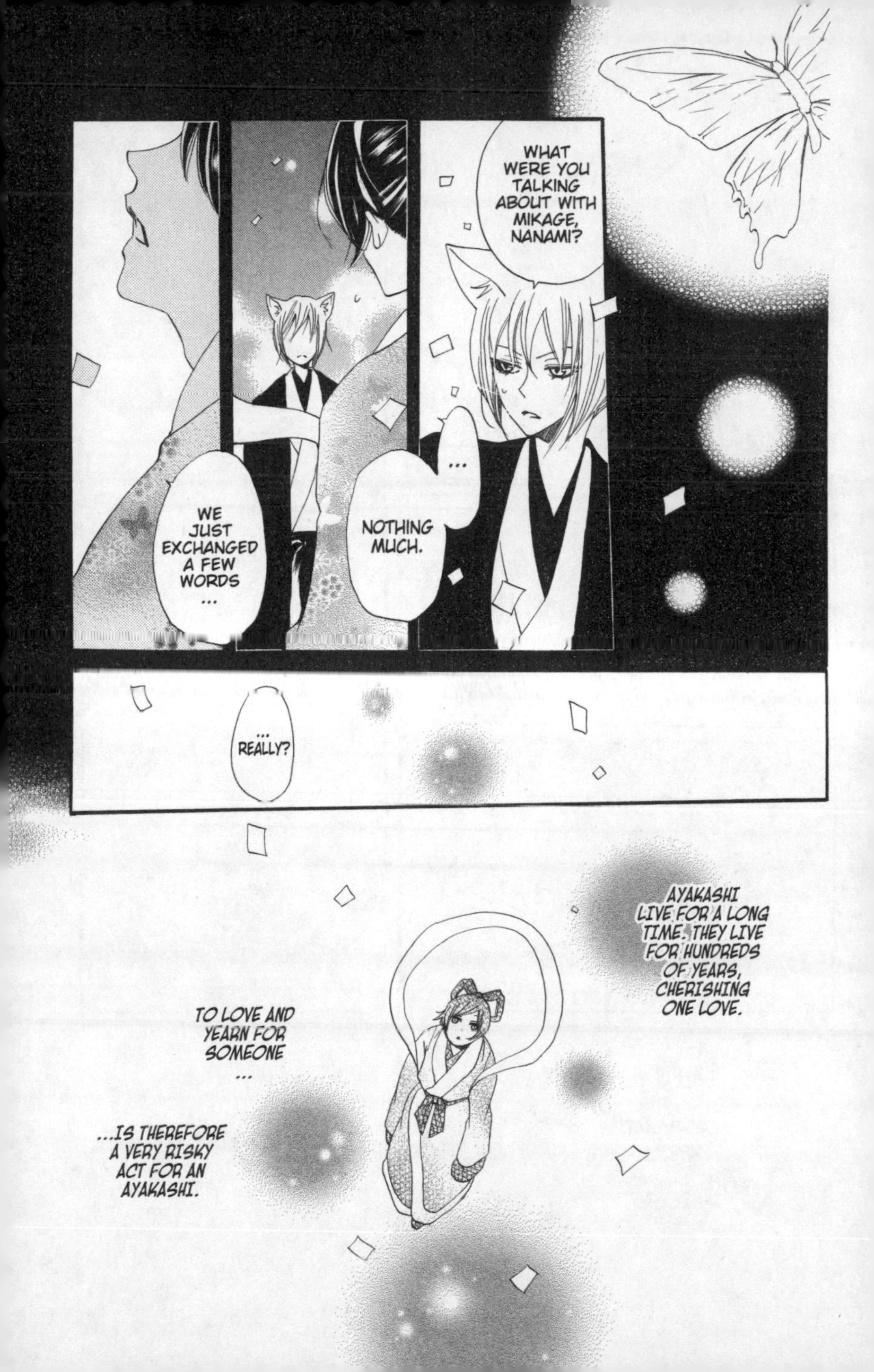
WHAT WERE YOU TALKING ABOUT WITH MIKAGE, NANAMI?
...
NOTHING MUCH.
WE JUST EXCHANGED A FEW WORDS...
...REALLY?
AYAKASHI LIVE FOR A LONG TIME. THEY LIVE FOR HUNDREDS OF YEARS, CHERISHING ONE LOVE.
TO LOVE AND YEARN FOR SOMEONE...
...IS THEREFORE A VERY RISKY ACT FOR AN AYAKASHI.

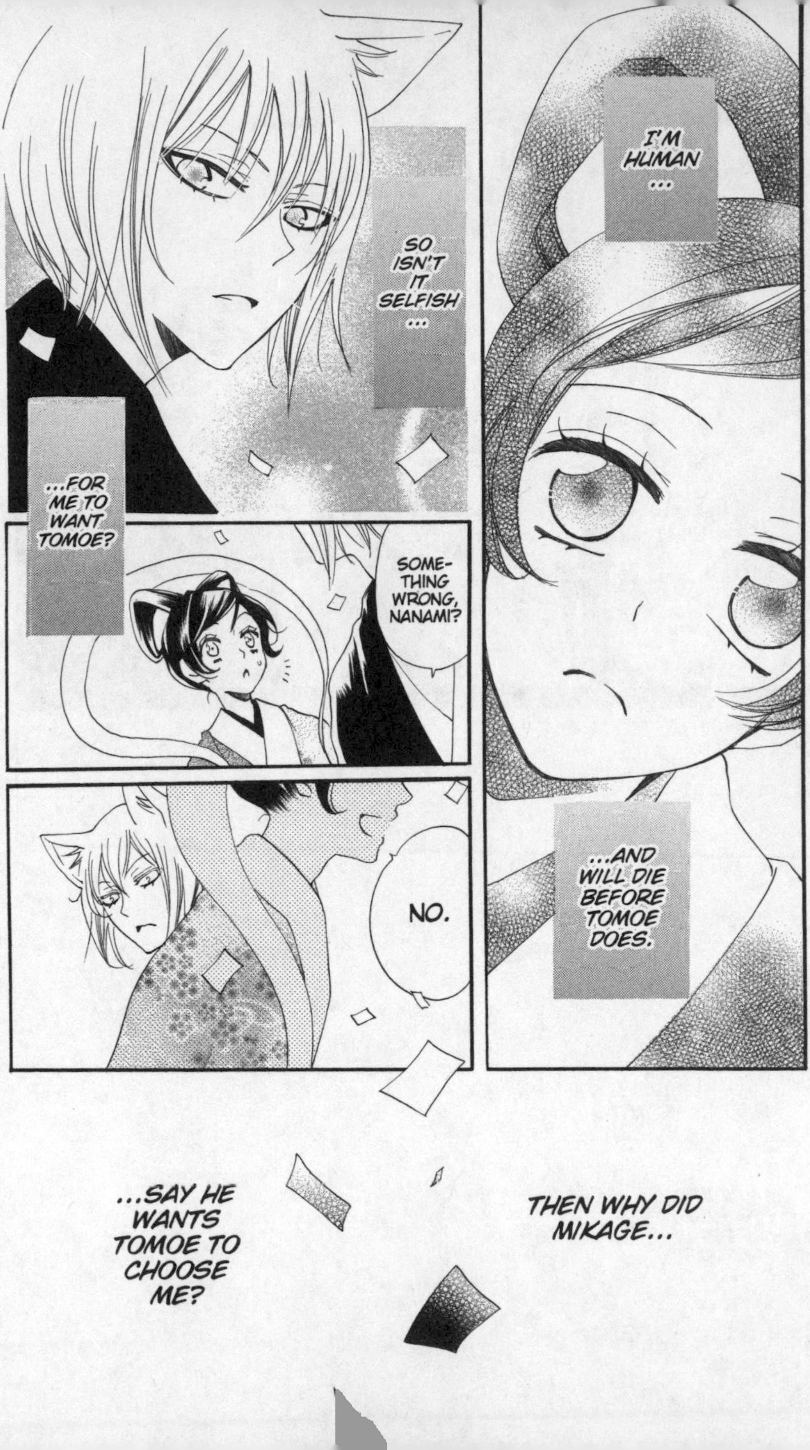
I'M HUMAN...
...AND WILL DIE BEFORE TOMOE DOES.
SO ISN'T IT SELFISH...
...FOR ME TO WANT TOMOE?
SOME-THING WRONG, NANAMI?
NO.
THEN WHY DID MIKAGE...
...SAY HE WANTS TOMOE TO CHOOSE ME?

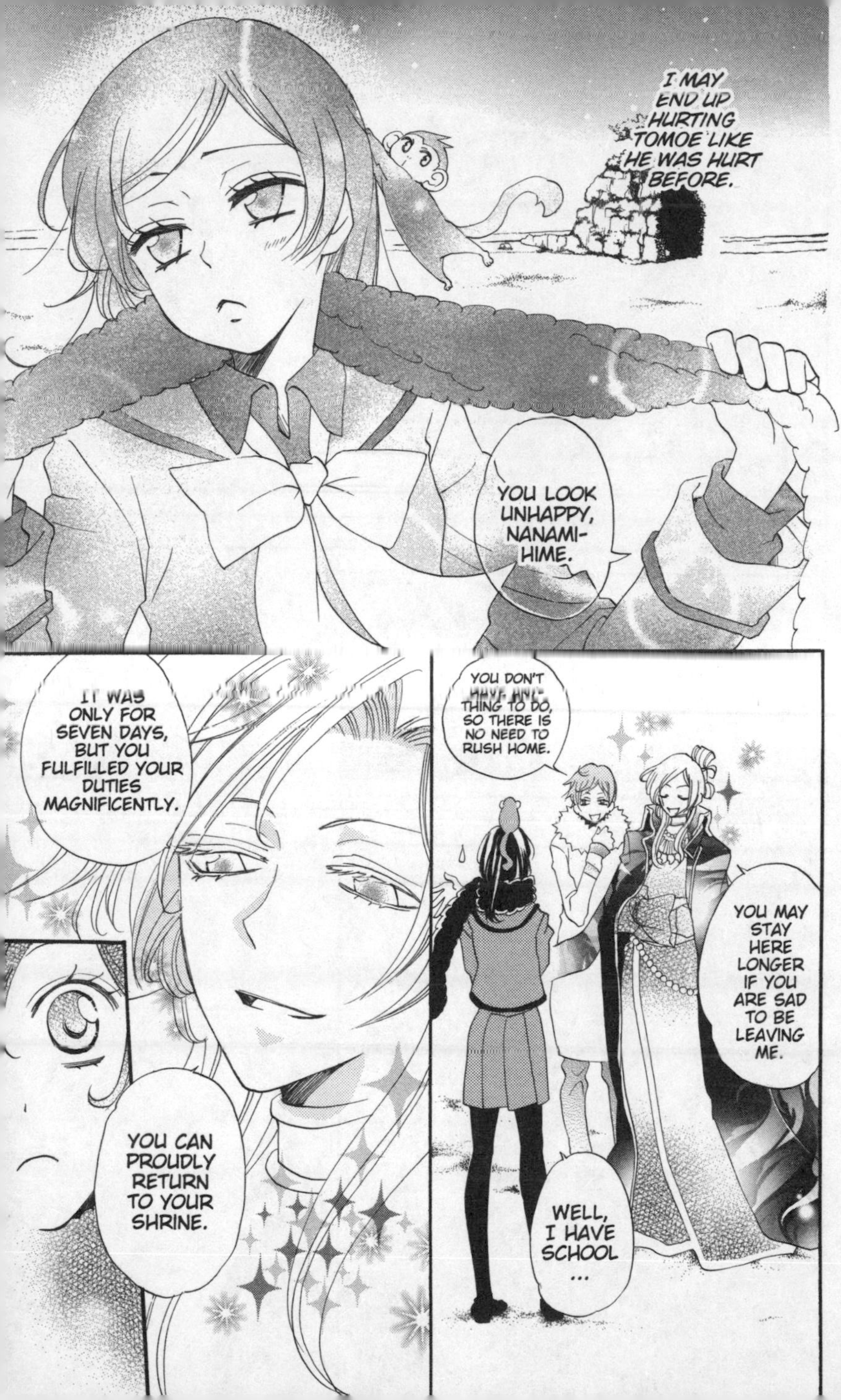
I MAY END UP HURTING TOMOE LIKE HE WAS HURT BEFORE.
YOU LOOK UNHAPPY, NANAMI-HIME.
YOU DON'T HAVE ANYTHING TO DO, SO THERE IS NO NEED TO RUSH HOME.
YOU MAY STAY HERE LONGER IF YOU ARE SAD TO BE LEAVING ME.
WELL, I HAVE SCHOOL ...
IT WAS ONLY FOR SEVEN DAYS, BUT YOU FULFILLED YOUR DUTIES MAGNIFICENTLY.
YOU CAN PROUDLY RETURN TO YOUR SHRINE.

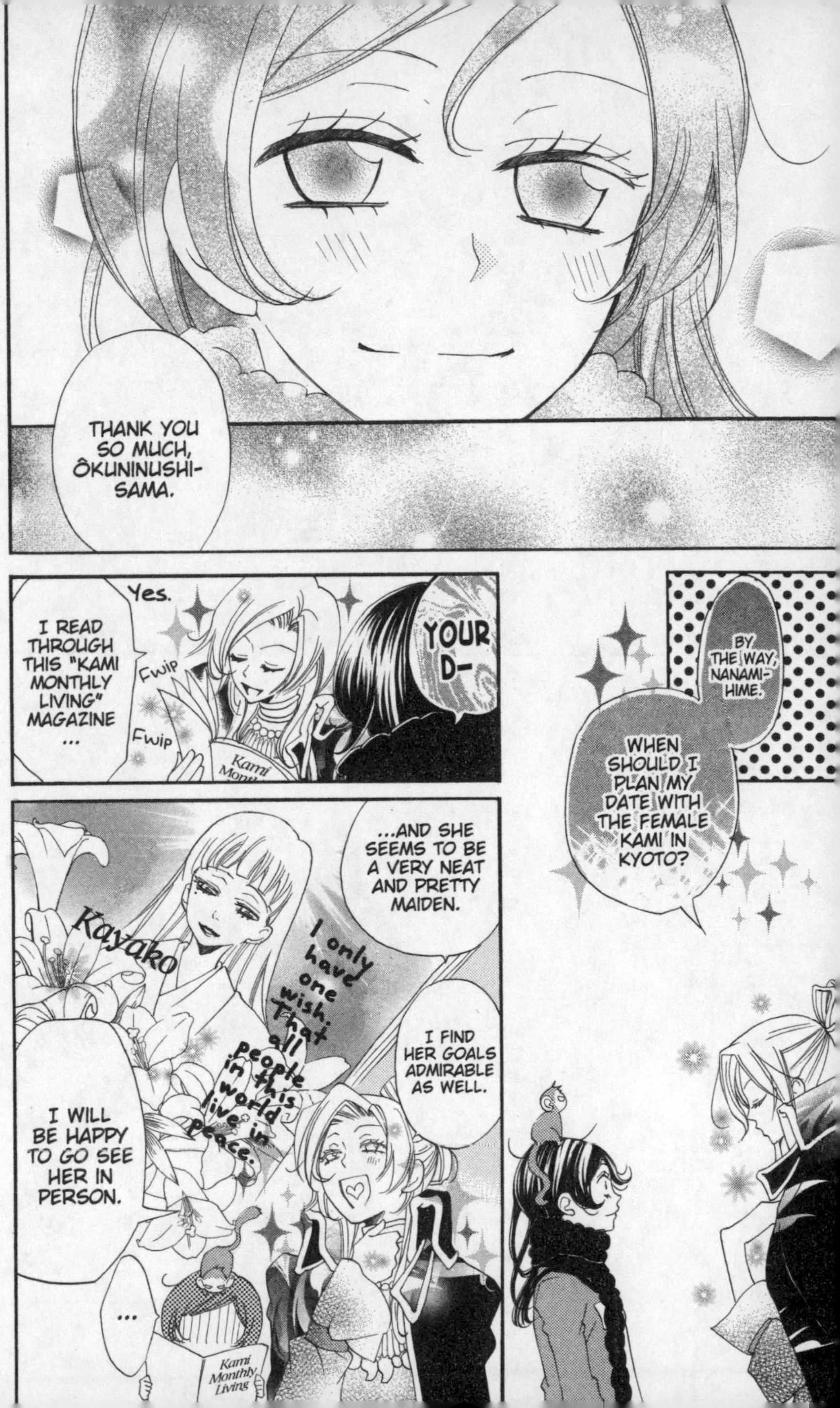
THANK YOU SO MUCH, ÔKUNINUSHI-SAMA.
BY THE WAY, NANAMI-HIME.
WHEN SHOULD I PLAN MY DATE WITH THE FEMALE KAMI IN KYOTO?
YOUR D-
Yes.
I READ THROUGH THIS "KAMI MONTHLY LIVING" MAGAZINE ...
Fwip
Fwip
Kami Month
...AND SHE SEEMS TO BE A VERY NEAT AND PRETTY MAIDEN.
Kayako
I only have one wish. That all people in this world live in peace.
I FIND HER GOALS ADMIRABLE AS WELL.
I WILL BE HAPPY TO GO SEE HER IN PERSON.
...
Kami Monthly Living

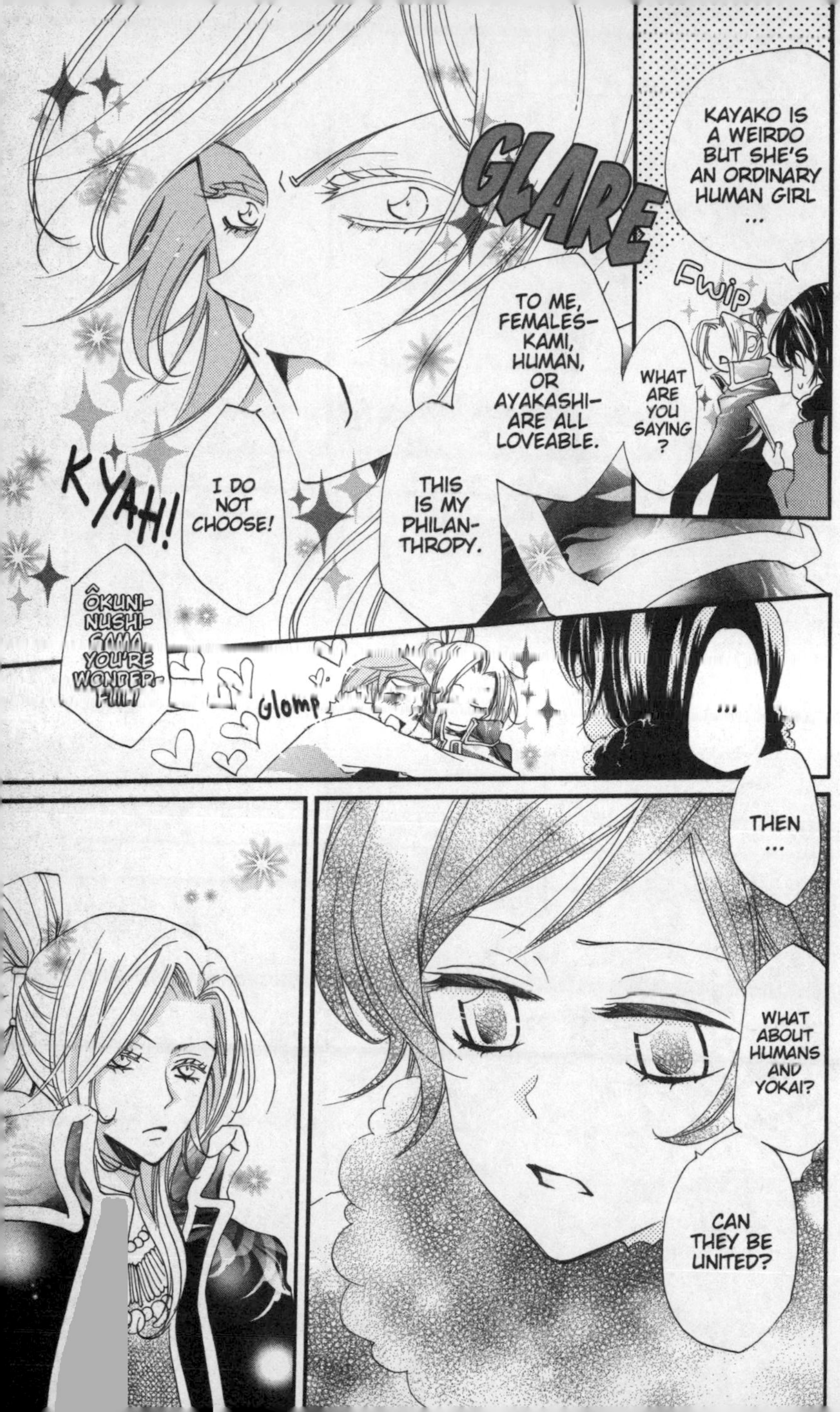
KAYAKO IS A WEIRDO BUT SHE'S AN ORDINARY HUMAN GIRL ...
Fwip
WHAT ARE YOU SAYING?
GLARE
TO ME, FEMALES-KAMI, HUMAN, OR AYAKASHI-ARE ALL LOVEABLE.
THIS IS MY PHILANTHROPY.
I DO NOT CHOOSE!
KYAH!
ÔKUNI-NUSHI-SAMA YOU'RE WONDER-FUL!
...
Glomp
THEN ...
WHAT ABOUT HUMANS AND YOKAI?
CAN THEY BE UNITED?

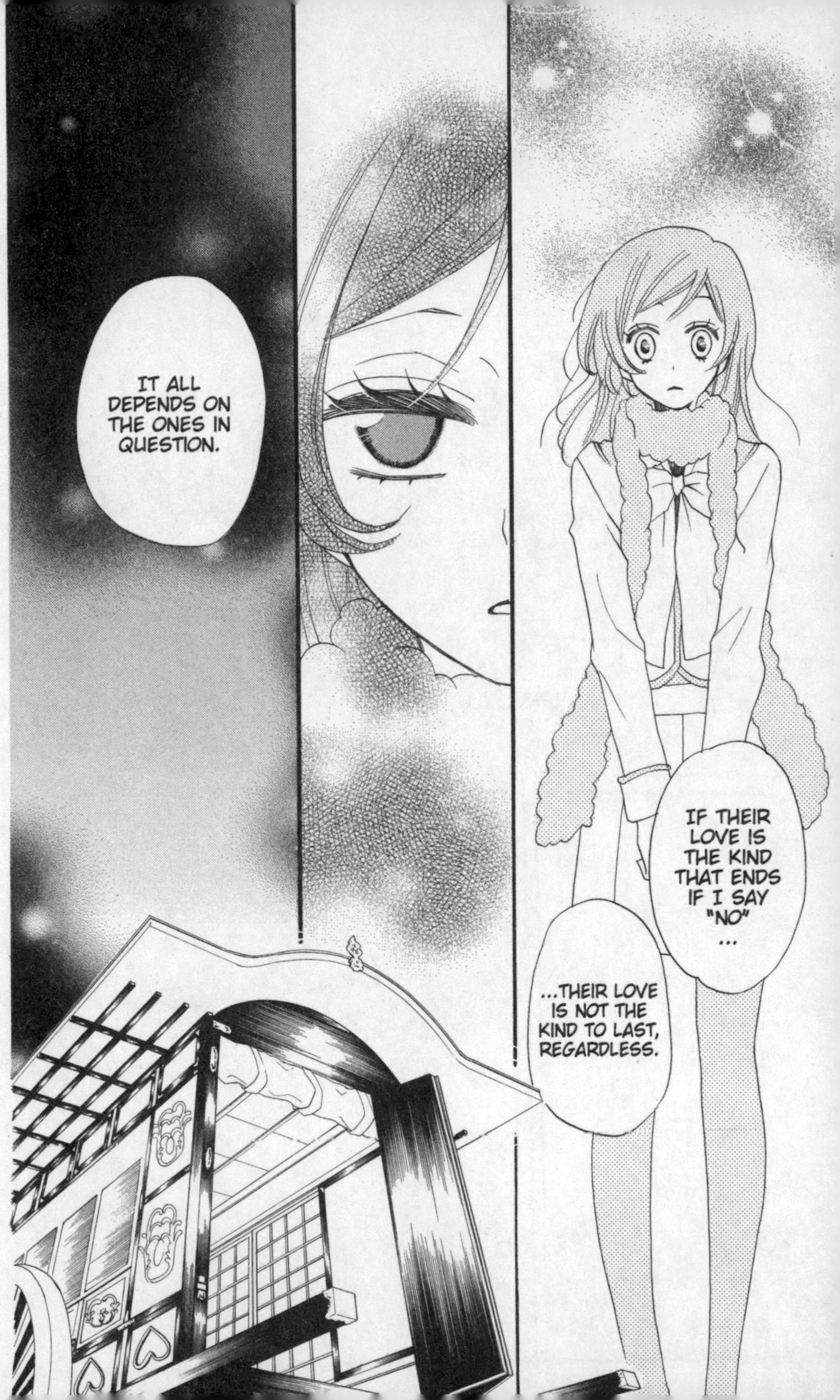
IF THEIR LOVE IS THE KIND THAT ENDS IF I SAY "NO" ...
...THEIR LOVE IS NOT THE KIND TO LAST, REGARDLESS.
IT ALL DEPENDS ON THE ONES IN QUESTION.

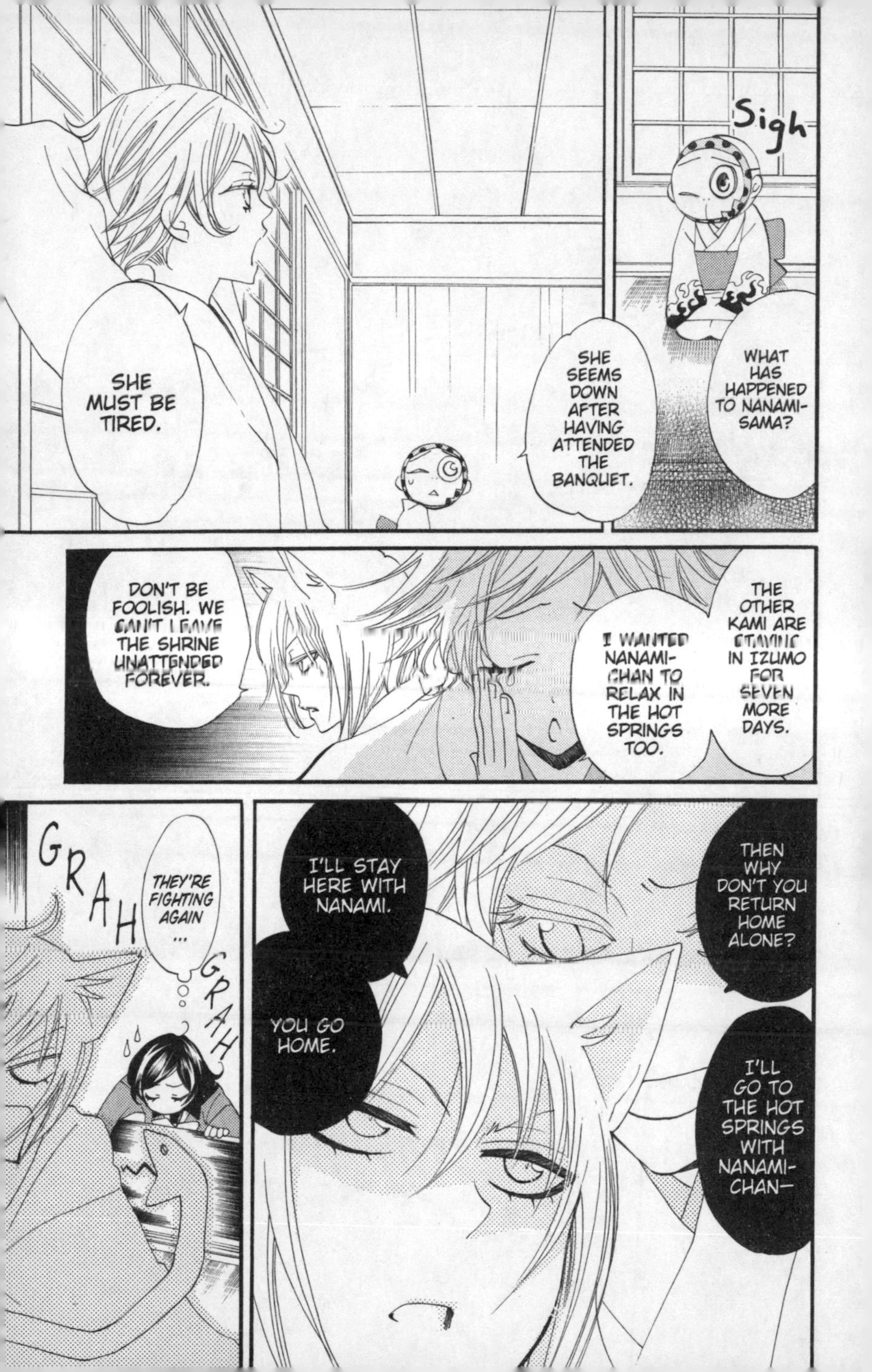
Sigh
WHAT HAS HAPPENED TO NANAMI-SAMA?
SHE SEEMS DOWN AFTER HAVING ATTENDED THE BANQUET.
SHE MUST BE TIRED.
THE OTHER KAMI ARE STAYING IN IZUMO FOR SEVEN MORE DAYS.
I WANTED NANAMI-CHAN TO RELAX IN THE HOT SPRINGS TOO.
DON'T BE FOOLISH. WE CAN'T LEAVE THE SHRINE UNATTENDED FOREVER.
THEN WHY DON'T YOU RETURN HOME ALONE?
I'LL GO TO THE HOT SPRINGS WITH NANAMI-CHAN—
I'LL STAY HERE WITH NANAMI.
YOU GO HOME.
GRAH
THEY'RE FIGHTING AGAIN ...
GRAH

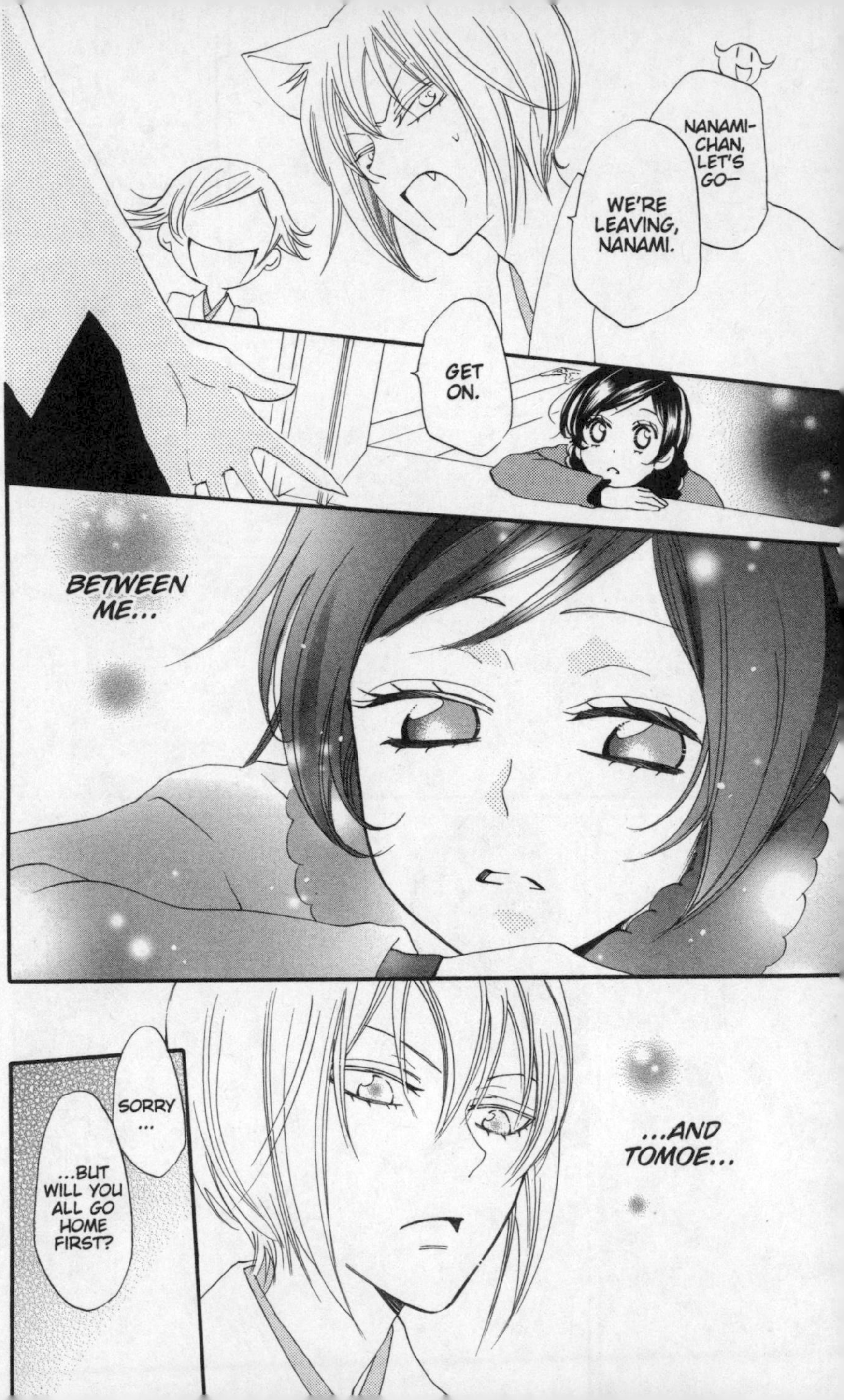
NANAMI-CHAN, LET'S GO—
WE'RE LEAVING, NANAMI.
GET ON.
BETWEEN ME...
...AND TOMOE...
SORRY...
...BUT WILL YOU ALL GO HOME FIRST?

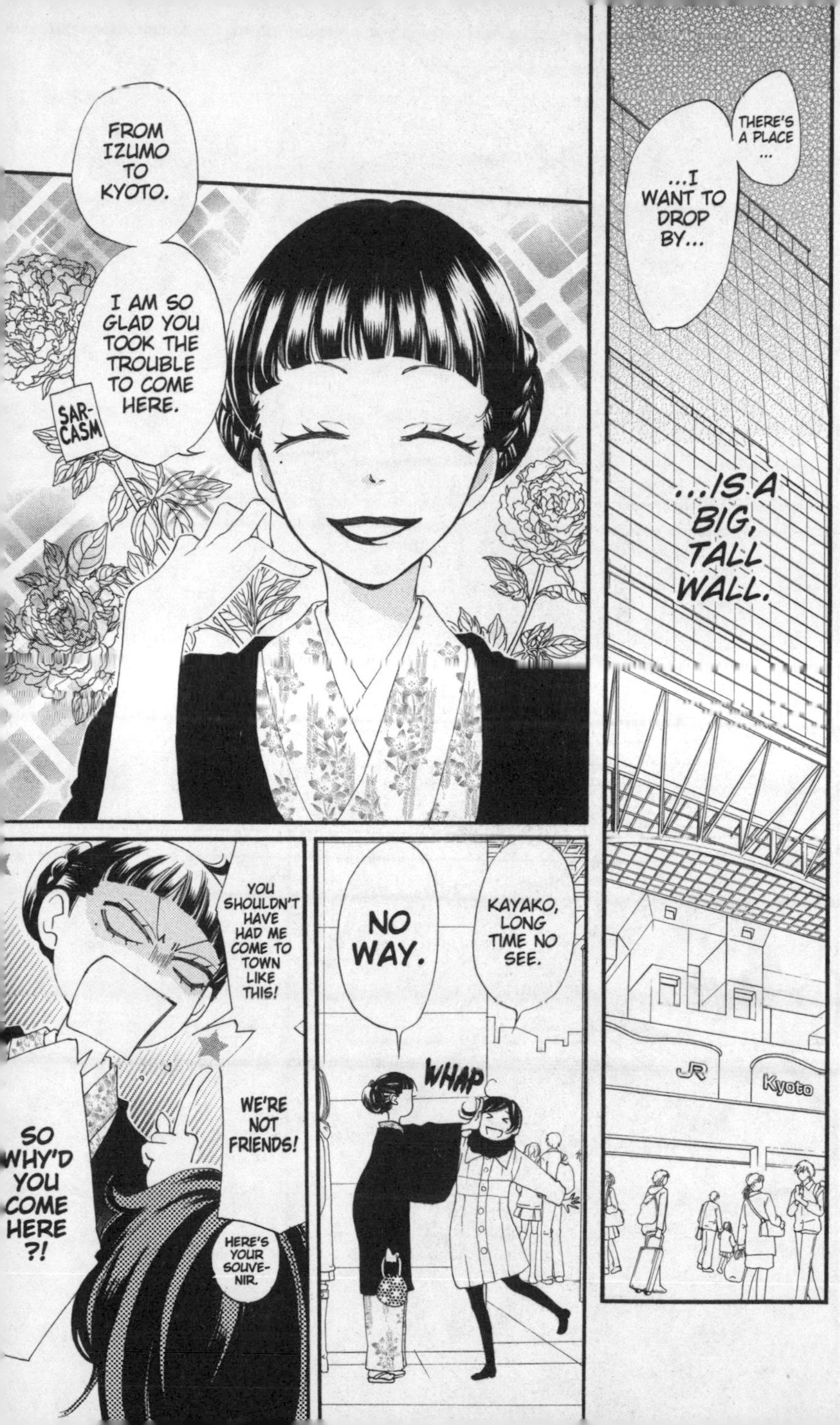
THERE'S A PLACE ...
...I WANT TO DROP BY...
...IS A BIG, TALL WALL.
JR
Kyoto
FROM IZUMO TO KYOTO.
I AM SO GLAD YOU TOOK THE TROUBLE TO COME HERE.
SAR-CASM
KAYAKO, LONG TIME NO SEE.
NO WAY.
WHAP
YOU SHOULDN'T HAVE HAD ME COME TO TOWN LIKE THIS!
WE'RE NOT FRIENDS!
SO WHY'D YOU COME HERE?!
HERE'S YOUR SOUVE-NIR.

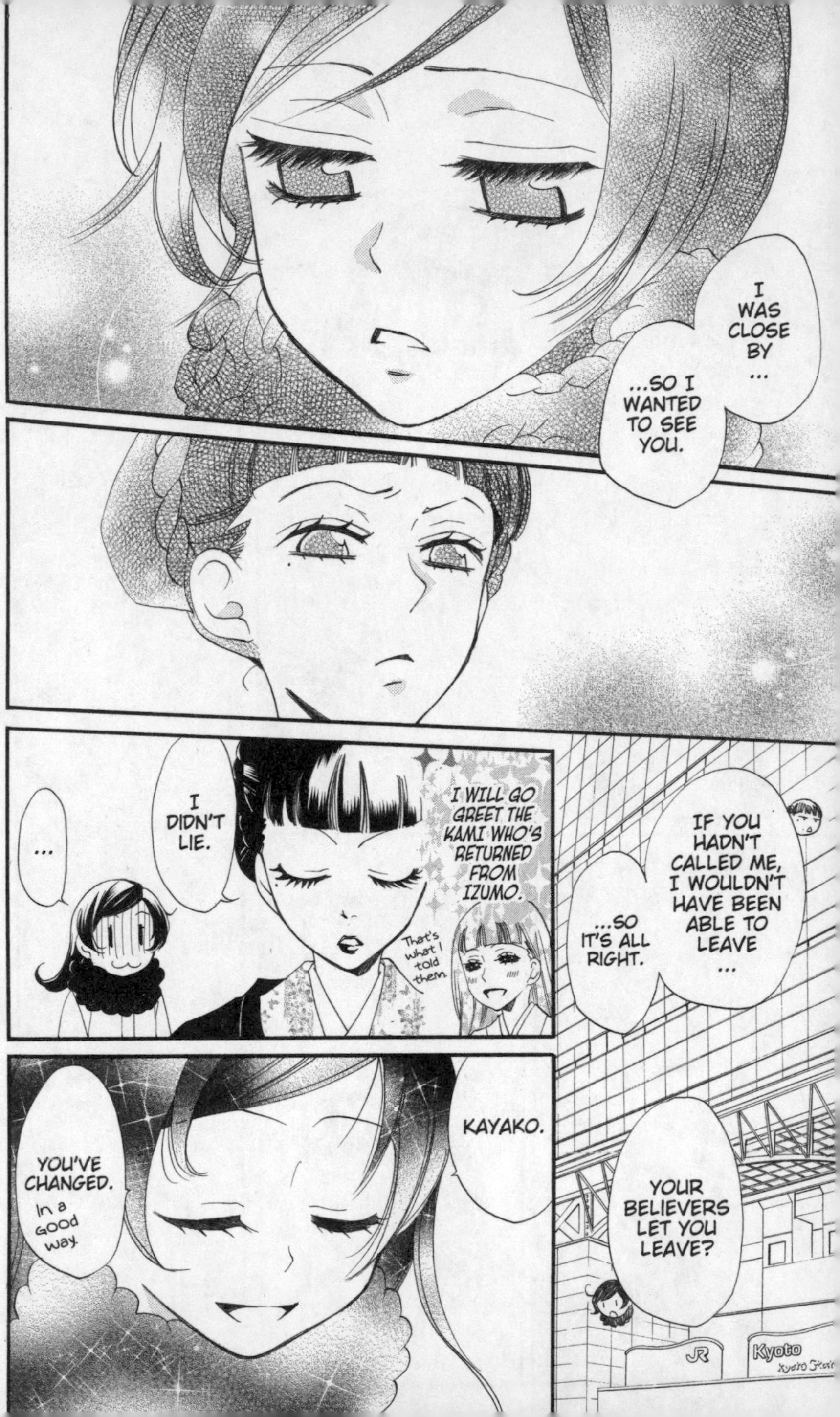
I WAS CLOSE BY ...
...SO I WANTED TO SEE YOU.
IF YOU HADN'T CALLED ME, I WOULDN'T HAVE BEEN ABLE TO LEAVE ...
...SO IT'S ALL RIGHT.
YOUR BELIEVERS LET YOU LEAVE?
JR
Kyoto
I WILL GO GREET THE KAMI WHO'S RETURNED FROM IZUMO.
I DIDN'T LIE.
That's what I told them.
...
KAYAKO.
YOU'VE CHANGED.
In a good way.

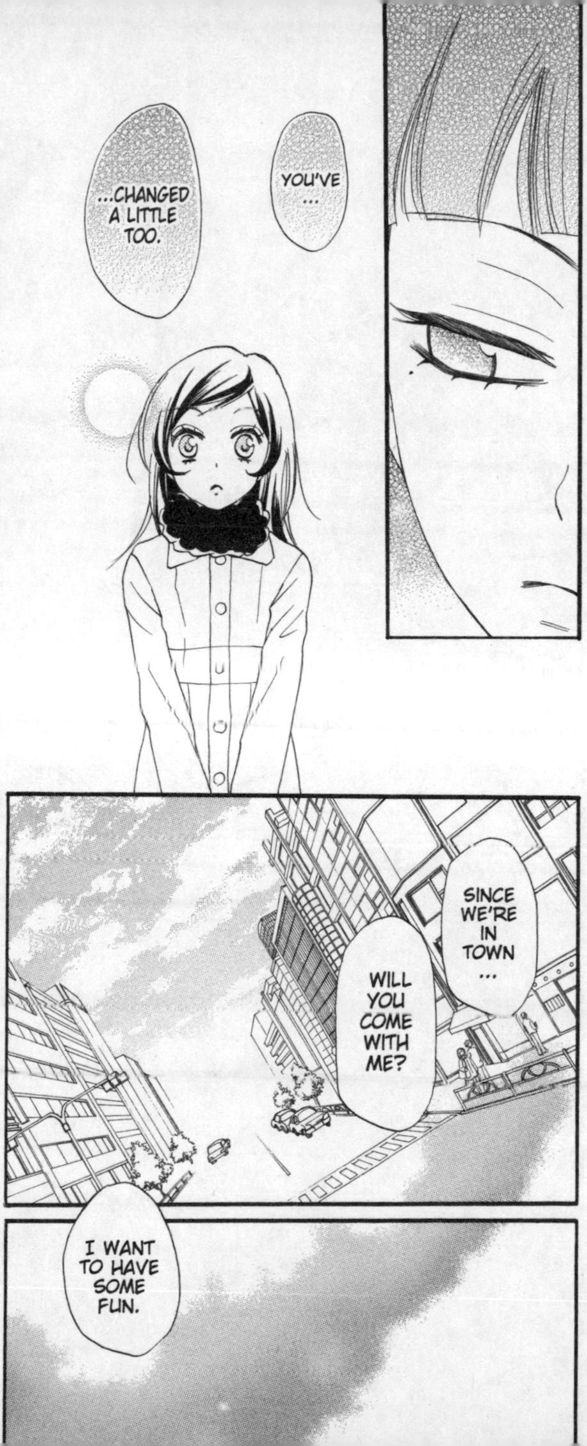
YOU'VE ...
...CHANGED A LITTLE TOO.
SINCE WE'RE IN TOWN ...
WILL YOU COME WITH ME?
I WANT TO HAVE SOME FUN.

1

Thank you for picking up volume 9 of Kamisama Kiss! I hope you enjoy reading it.

Kamisama Kiss is running in Hana to Yume (on sale in Japan the 5th and 20th of every month).

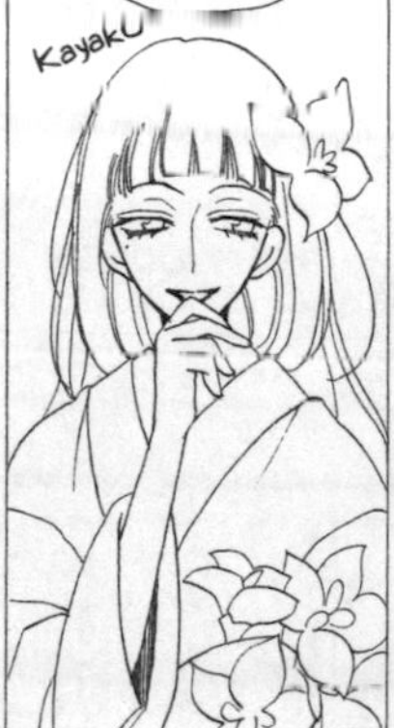
Kayako

I write a BLOG, and I post on twitter.

http://suzuju.jugem.jp/

My twitter account is @hiyokosweet

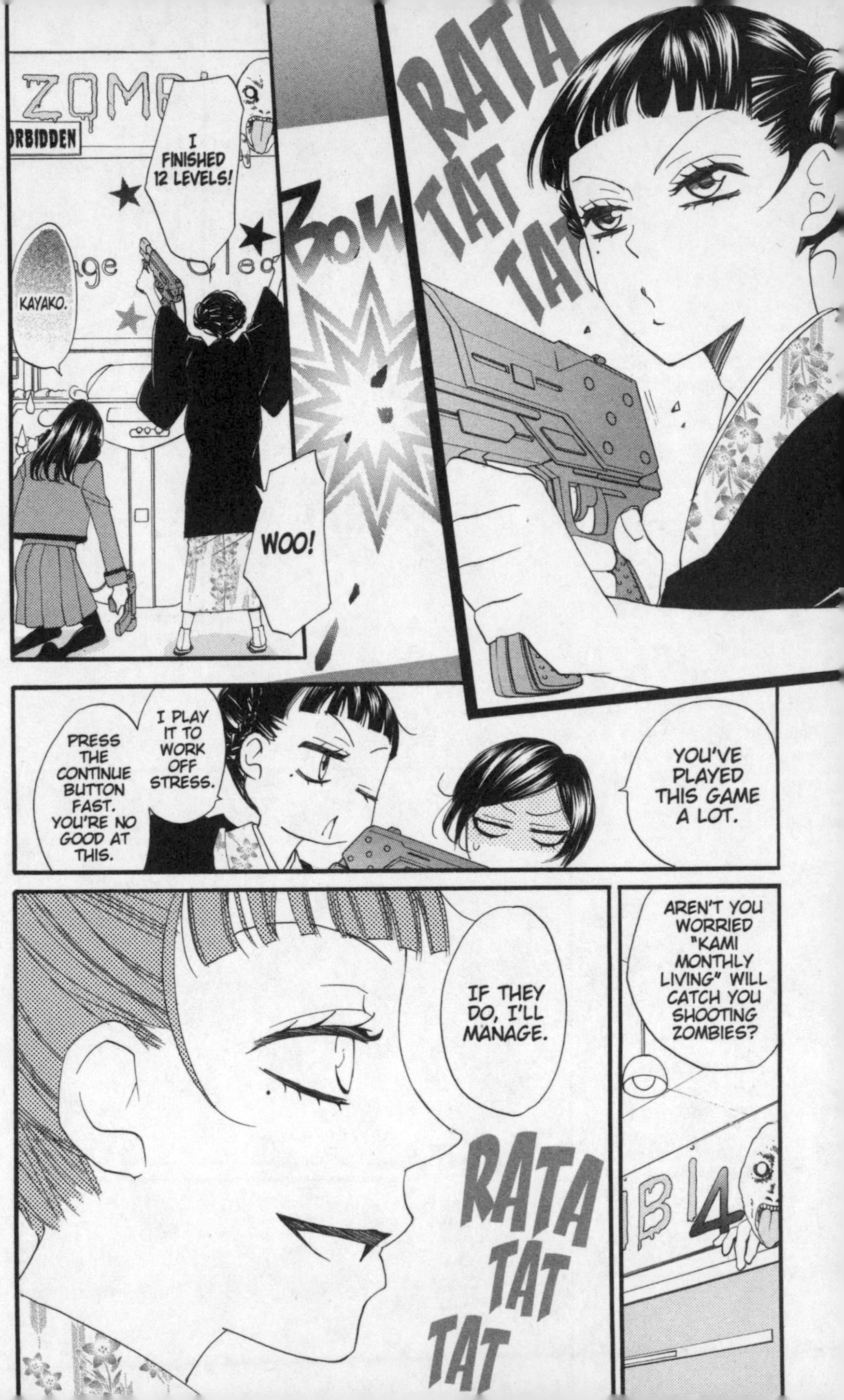

RATA TAT TAT
WOO!
I FINISHED 12 LEVELS!
KAYAKO.
YOU'VE PLAYED THIS GAME A LOT.
I PLAY IT TO WORK OFF STRESS.
PRESS THE CONTINUE BUTTON FAST. YOU'RE NO GOOD AT THIS.
AREN'T YOU WORRIED "KAMI MONTHLY LIVING" WILL CATCH YOU SHOOTING ZOMBIES?
IF THEY DO, I'LL MANAGE.
RATA TAT TAT

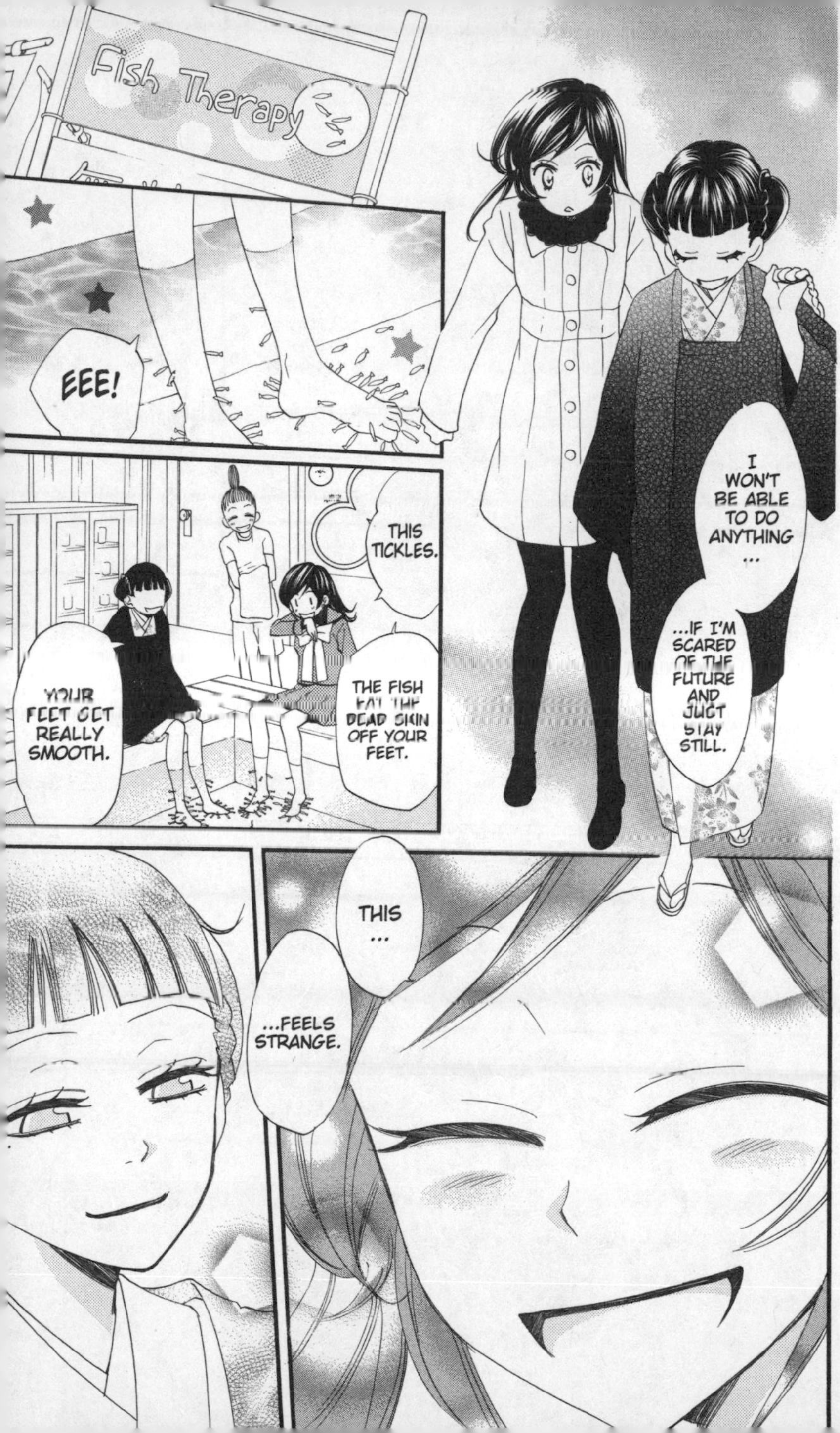
I WON'T BE ABLE TO DO ANYTHING...
...IF I'M SCARED OF THE FUTURE AND JUST STAY STILL.
Fish Therapy
EEE!
THIS TICKLES.
THE FISH EAT THE DEAD SKIN OFF YOUR FEET.
YOUR FEET GET REALLY SMOOTH.
THIS...
...FEELS STRANGE.

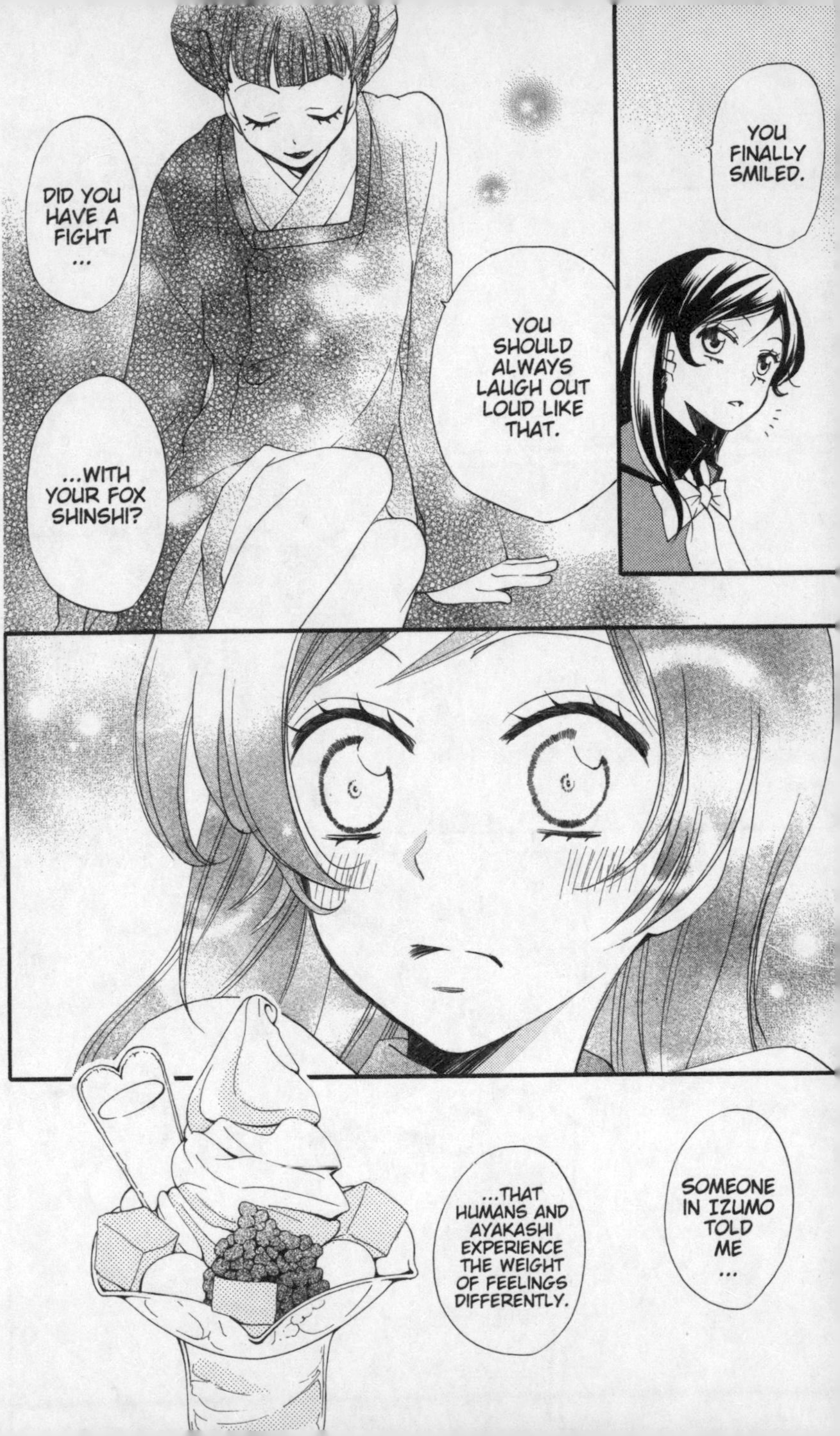
YOU FINALLY SMILED.
YOU SHOULD ALWAYS LAUGH OUT LOUD LIKE THAT.
DID YOU HAVE A FIGHT ...
...WITH YOUR FOX SHINSHI?
SOMEONE IN IZUMO TOLD ME ...
...THAT HUMANS AND AYAKASHI EXPERIENCE THE WEIGHT OF FEELINGS DIFFERENTLY.

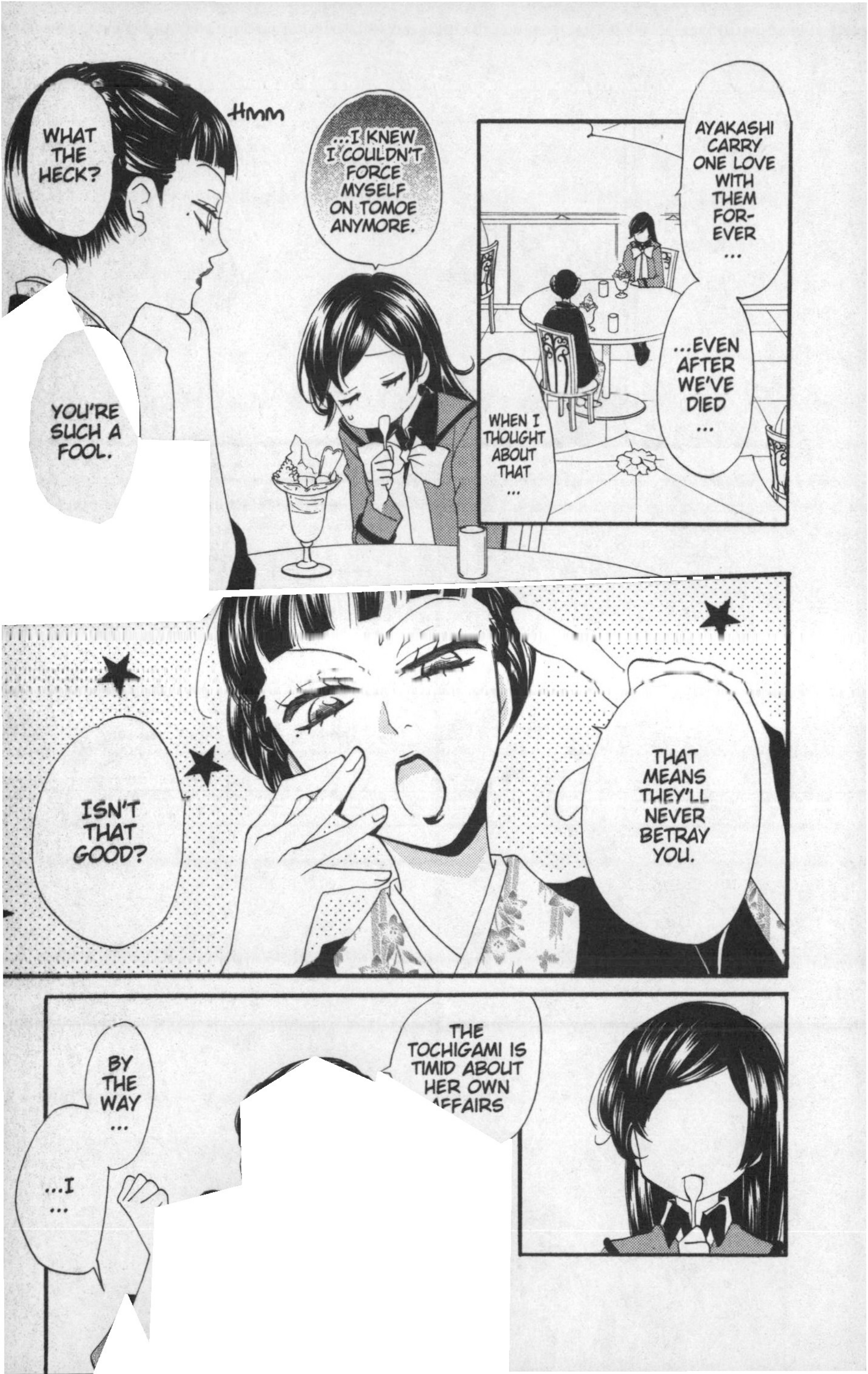
AYAKASHI CARRY ONE LOVE WITH THEM FOR-EVER...
...EVEN AFTER WE'VE DIED...
WHEN I THOUGHT ABOUT THAT...
...I KNEW I COULDN'T FORCE MYSELF ON TOMOE ANYMORE.
Hmm
WHAT THE HECK?
YOU'RE SUCH A FOOL.
THAT MEANS THEY'LL NEVER BETRAY YOU.
ISN'T THAT GOOD?
THE TOCHIGAMI IS TIMID ABOUT HER OWN AFFAIRS
BY THE WAY...
...I...

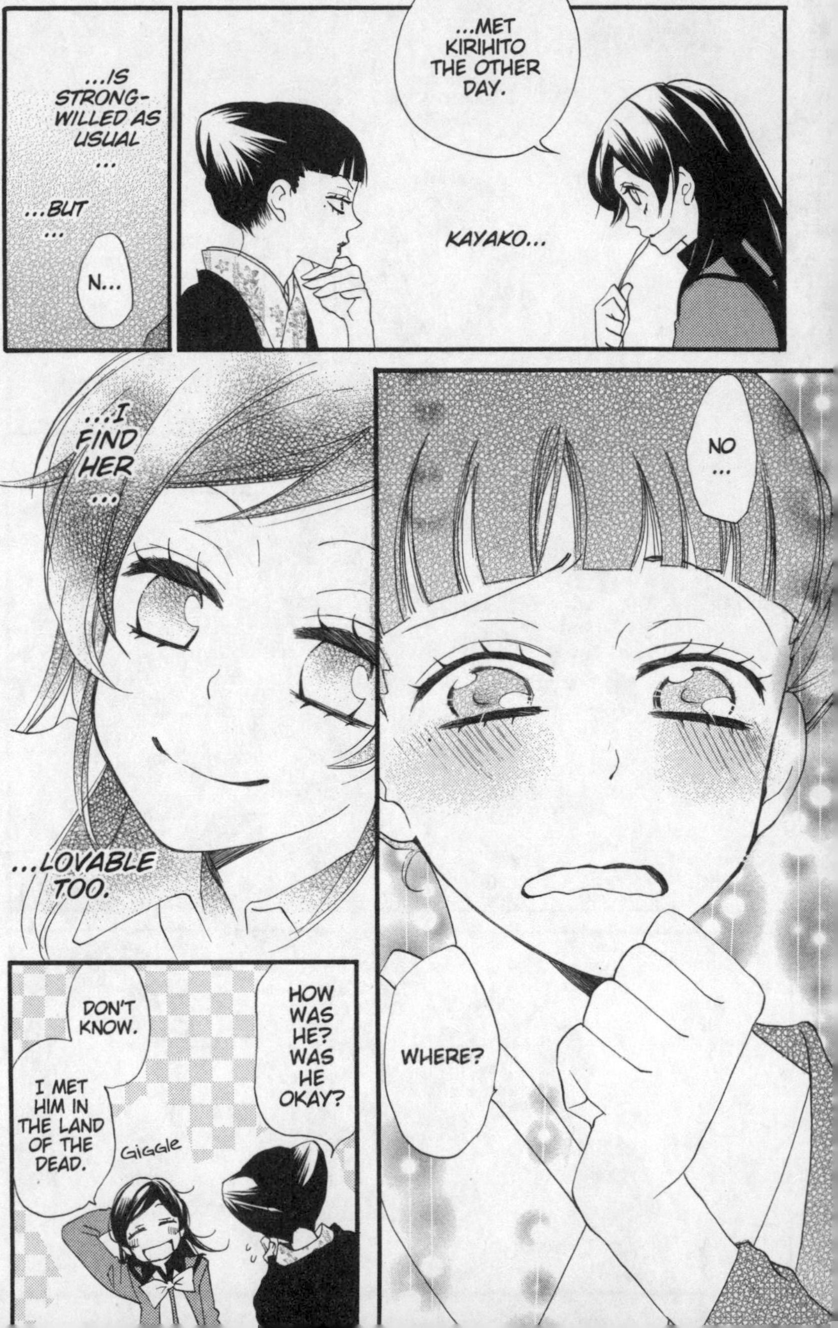
...MET KIRIHITO THE OTHER DAY.
KAYAKO...
...IS STRONG-WILLED AS USUAL ...
...BUT ...
N...
NO ...
WHERE?
...I FIND HER ...
...LOVABLE TOO.
HOW WAS HE? WAS HE OKAY?
DON'T KNOW.
I MET HIM IN THE LAND OF THE DEAD.
Giggle

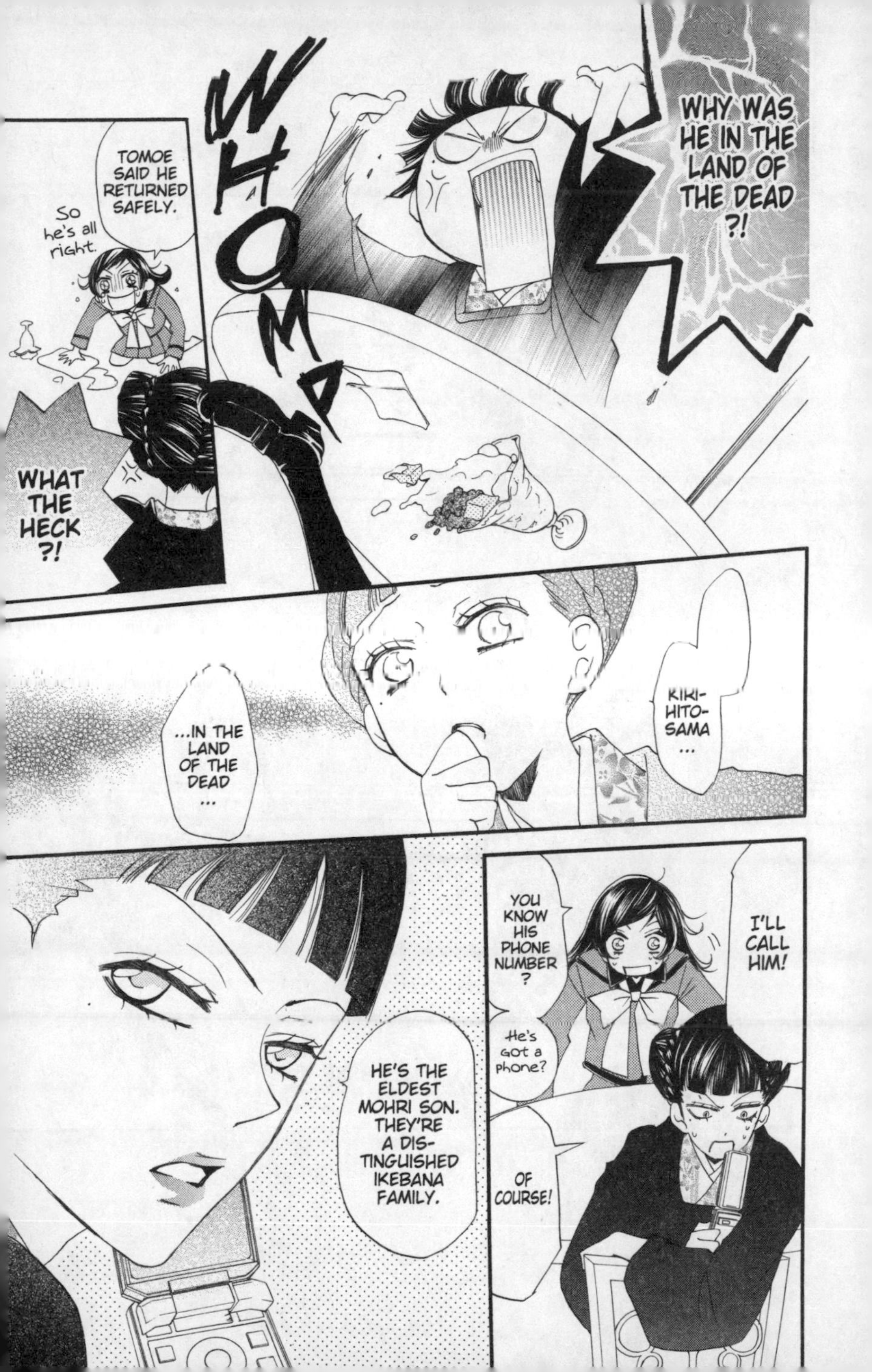
WHY WAS HE IN THE LAND OF THE DEAD ?!
WHOMP
TOMOE SAID HE RETURNED SAFELY.
So he's all right.
WHAT THE HECK ?!
KIKI-HITO-SAMA ...
...IN THE LAND OF THE DEAD ...
I'LL CALL HIM!
YOU KNOW HIS PHONE NUMBER ?
He's got a phone?
OF COURSE!
HE'S THE ELDEST MOHRI SON. THEY'RE A DIS-TINGUISHED IKEBANA FAMILY.

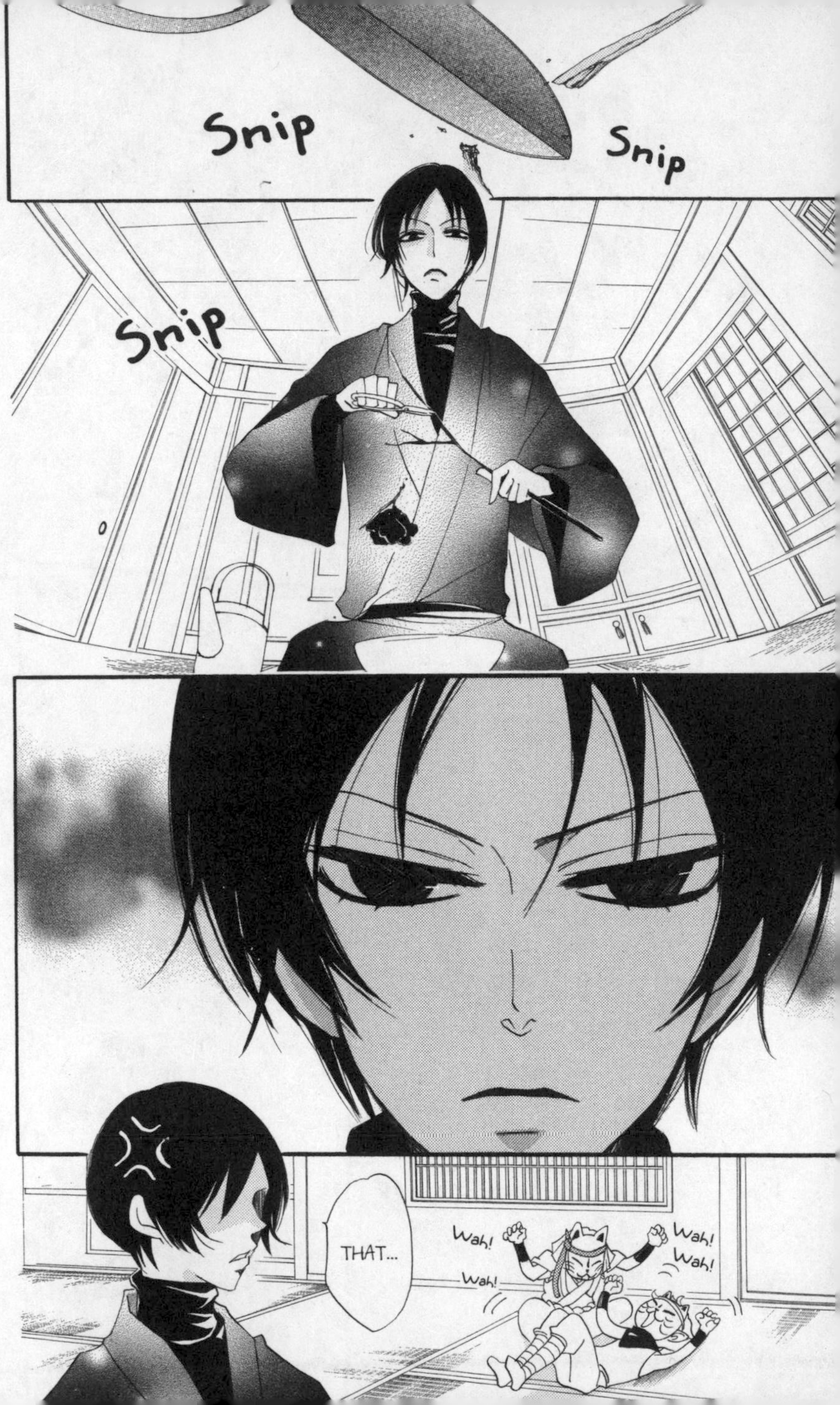
Snip
Snip
Snip
Wah!
Wah!
Wah!
Wah!
THAT...

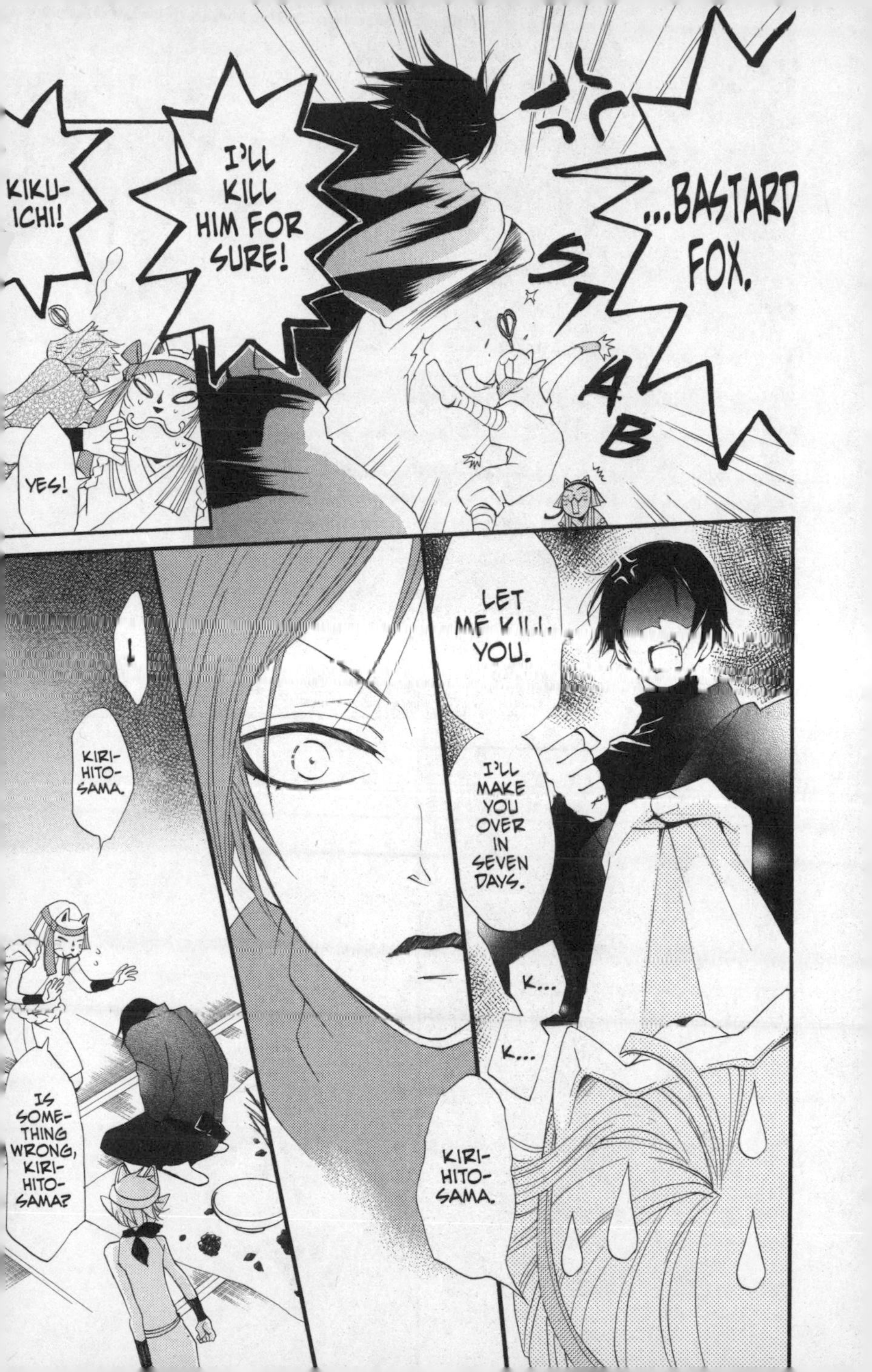
...BASTARD FOX.
STAB
I'LL KILL HIM FOR SURE!
KIKU-ICHI!
YES!
LET ME KILL YOU.
I'LL MAKE YOU OVER IN SEVEN DAYS.
K...
K...
KIRI-HITO-SAMA.
I
KIRI-HITO-SAMA.
IS SOMETHING WRONG, KIRI-HITO-SAMA?

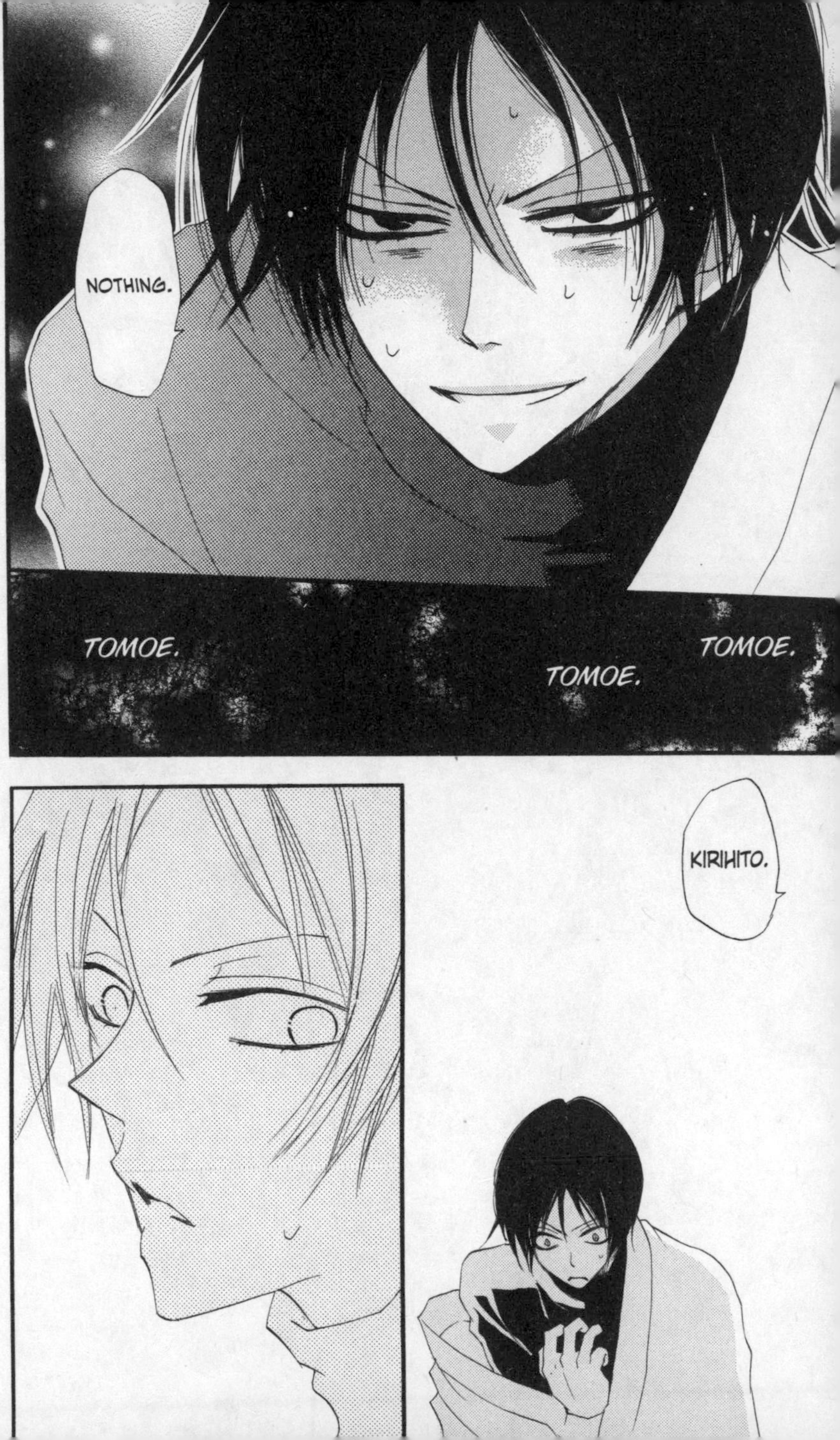
NOTHING.
TOMOE.
TOMOE.
TOMOE.
KIRIHITO.

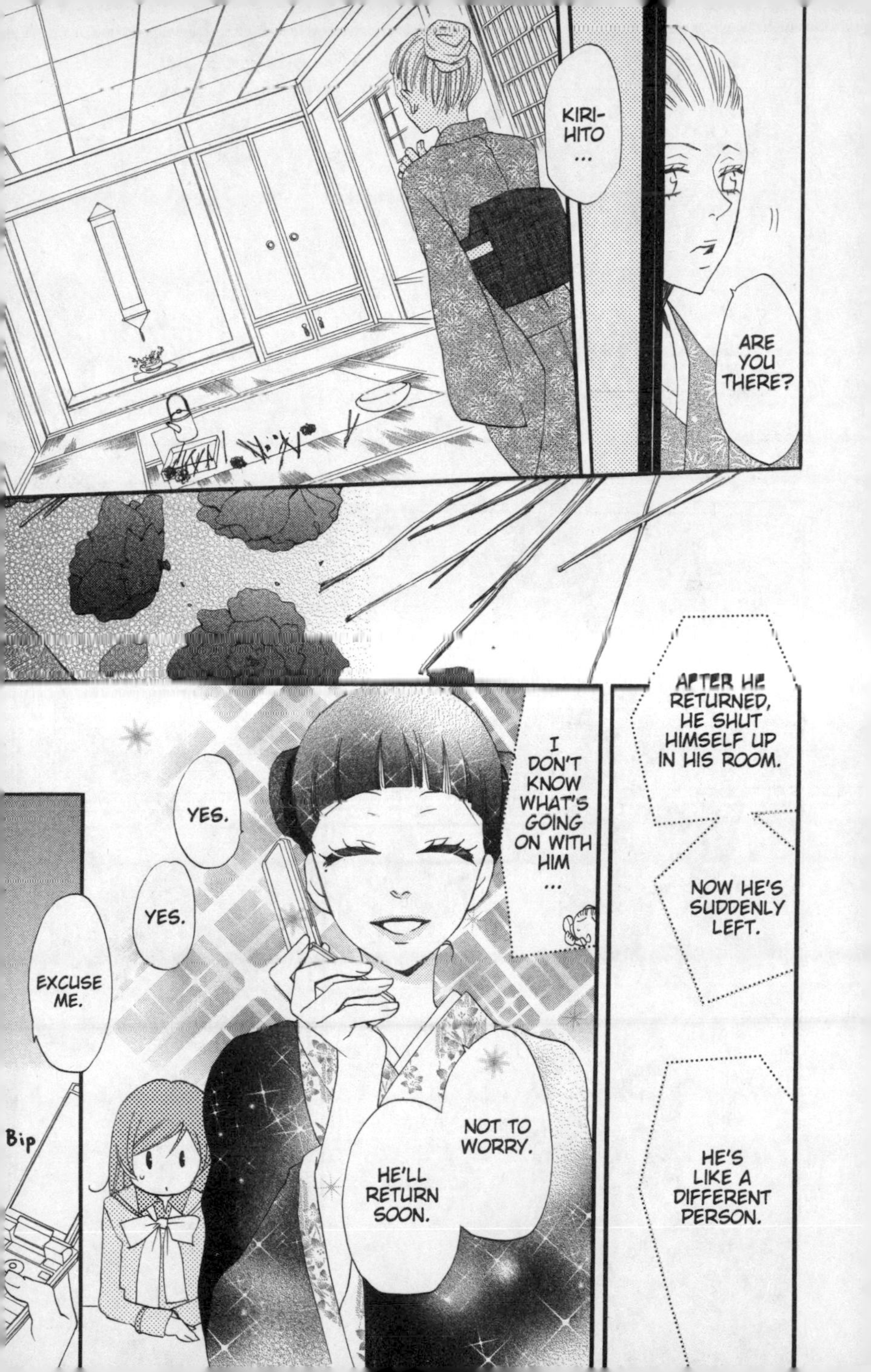
ARE YOU THERE?
KIRI-HITO ...
AFTER HE RETURNED, HE SHUT HIMSELF UP IN HIS ROOM.
NOW HE'S SUDDENLY LEFT.
HE'S LIKE A DIFFERENT PERSON.
I DON'T KNOW WHAT'S GOING ON WITH HIM ...
YES.
YES.
EXCUSE ME.
NOT TO WORRY.
HE'LL RETURN SOON.
Bip

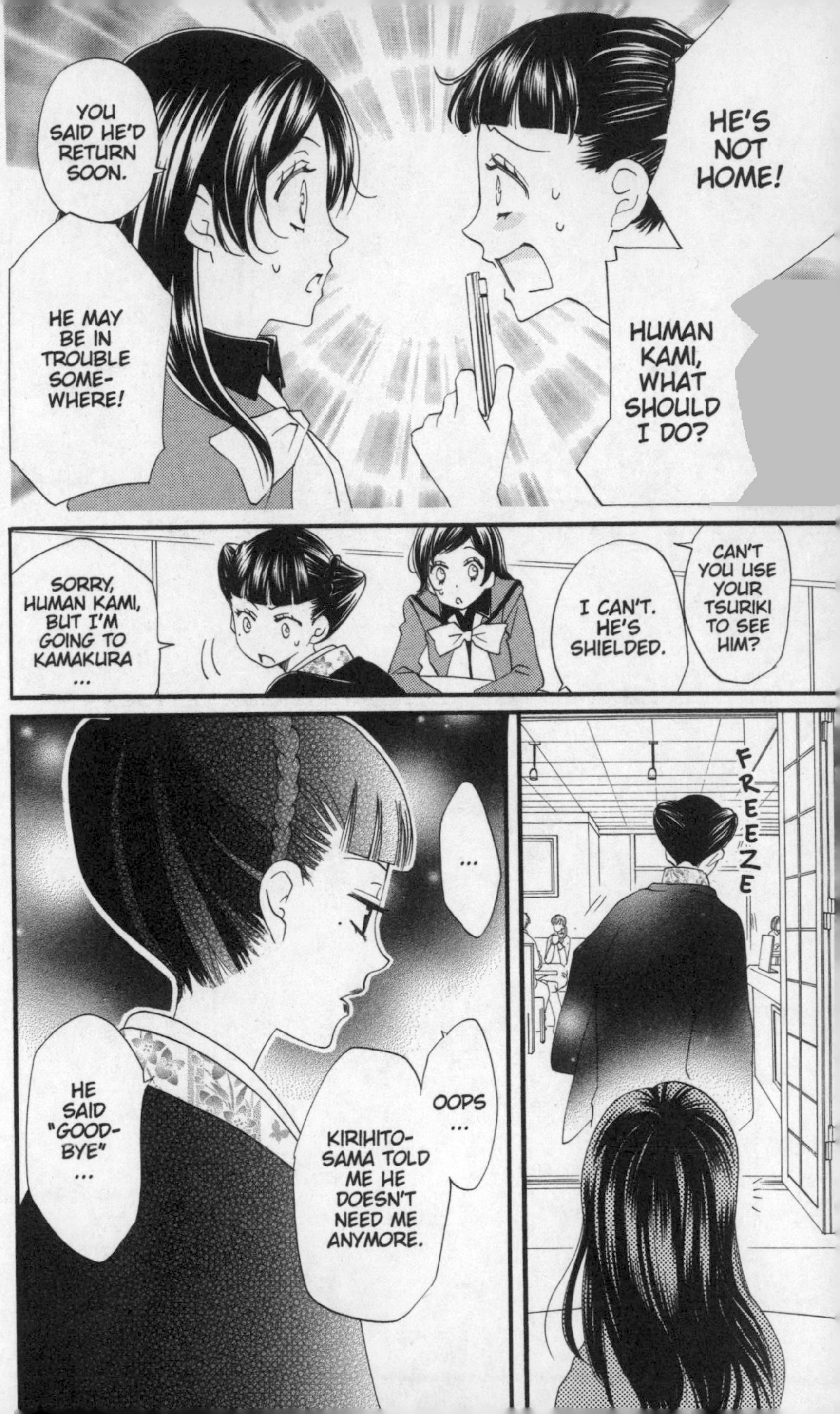
HE'S NOT HOME!
HUMAN KAMI, WHAT SHOULD I DO?
YOU SAID HE'D RETURN SOON.
HE MAY BE IN TROUBLE SOME-WHERE!
CAN'T YOU USE YOUR TSURIKI TO SEE HIM?
I CAN'T. HE'S SHIELDED.
SORRY, HUMAN KAMI, BUT I'M GOING TO KAMAKURA ...
FREEZE
...
OOPS ...
KIRIHITO-SAMA TOLD ME HE DOESN'T NEED ME ANYMORE.
HE SAID "GOOD-BYE" ...

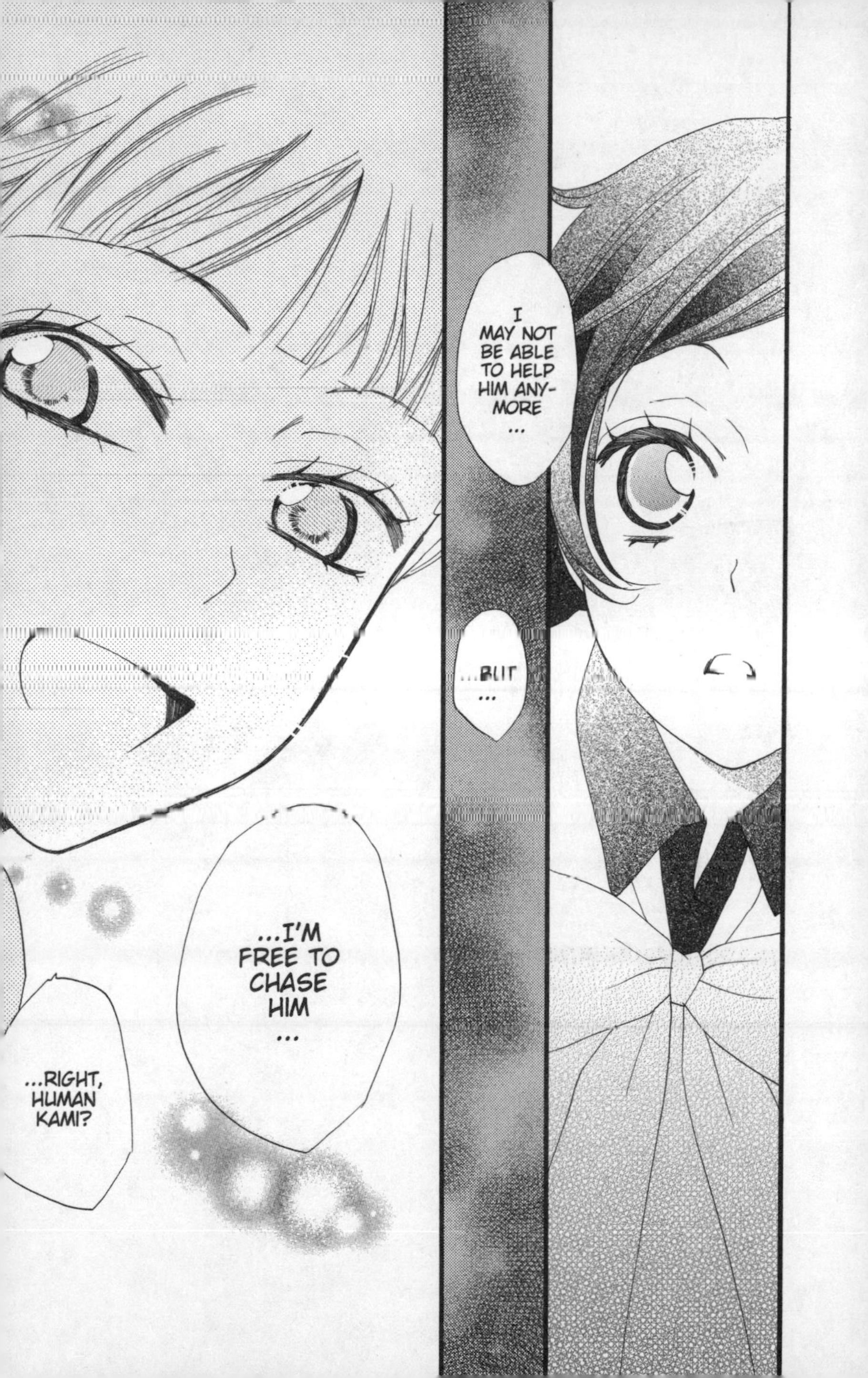
I MAY NOT BE ABLE TO HELP HIM ANY-MORE ...
...BUT ...
...I'M FREE TO CHASE HIM ...
...RIGHT, HUMAN KAMI?

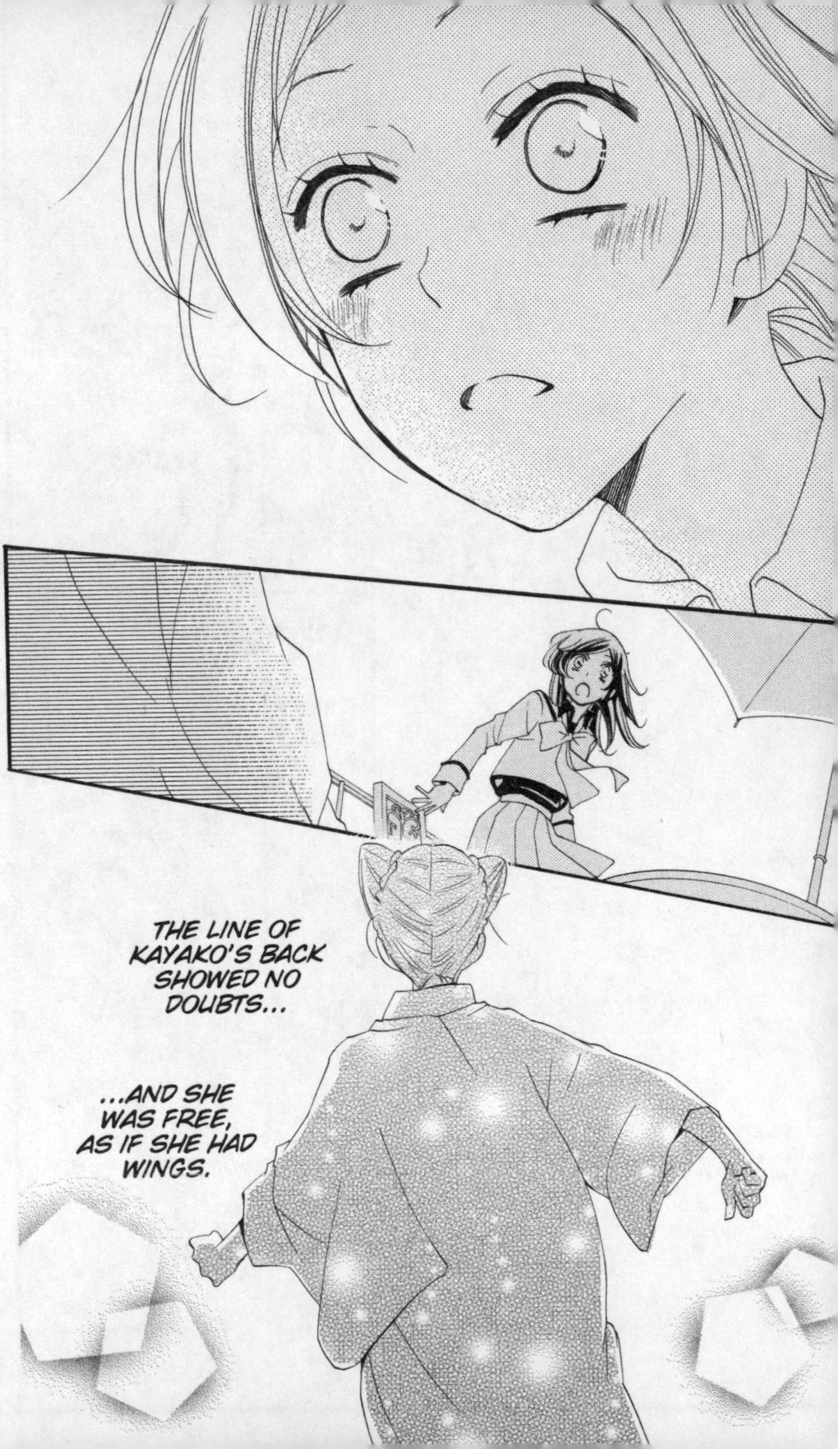
THE LINE OF KAYAKO'S BACK SHOWED NO DOUBTS...
...AND SHE WAS FREE, AS IF SHE HAD WINGS.

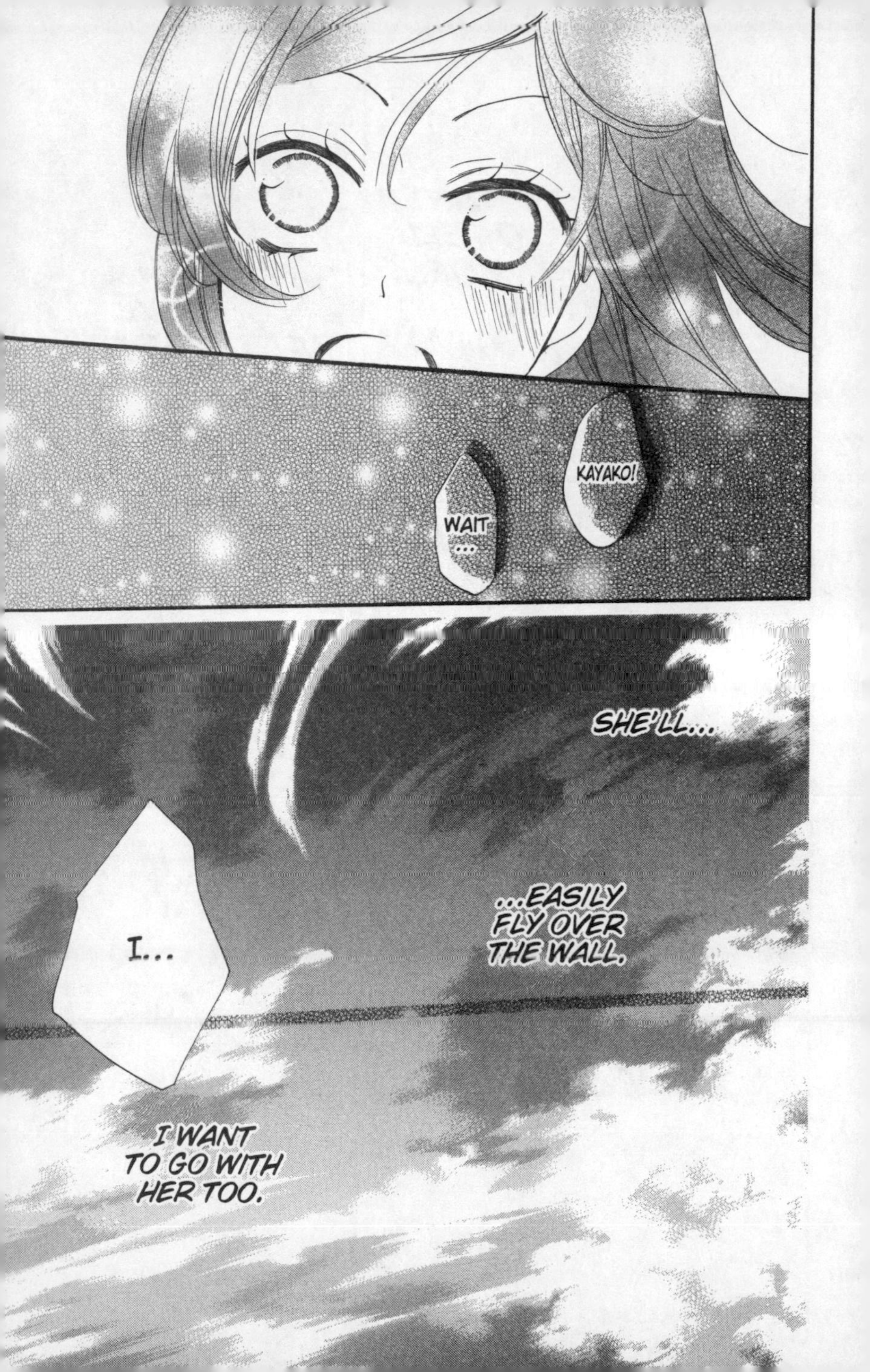
KAYAKO!
WAIT...
SHE'LL...
...EASILY FLY OVER THE WALL.
I...
I WANT TO GO WITH HER TOO.

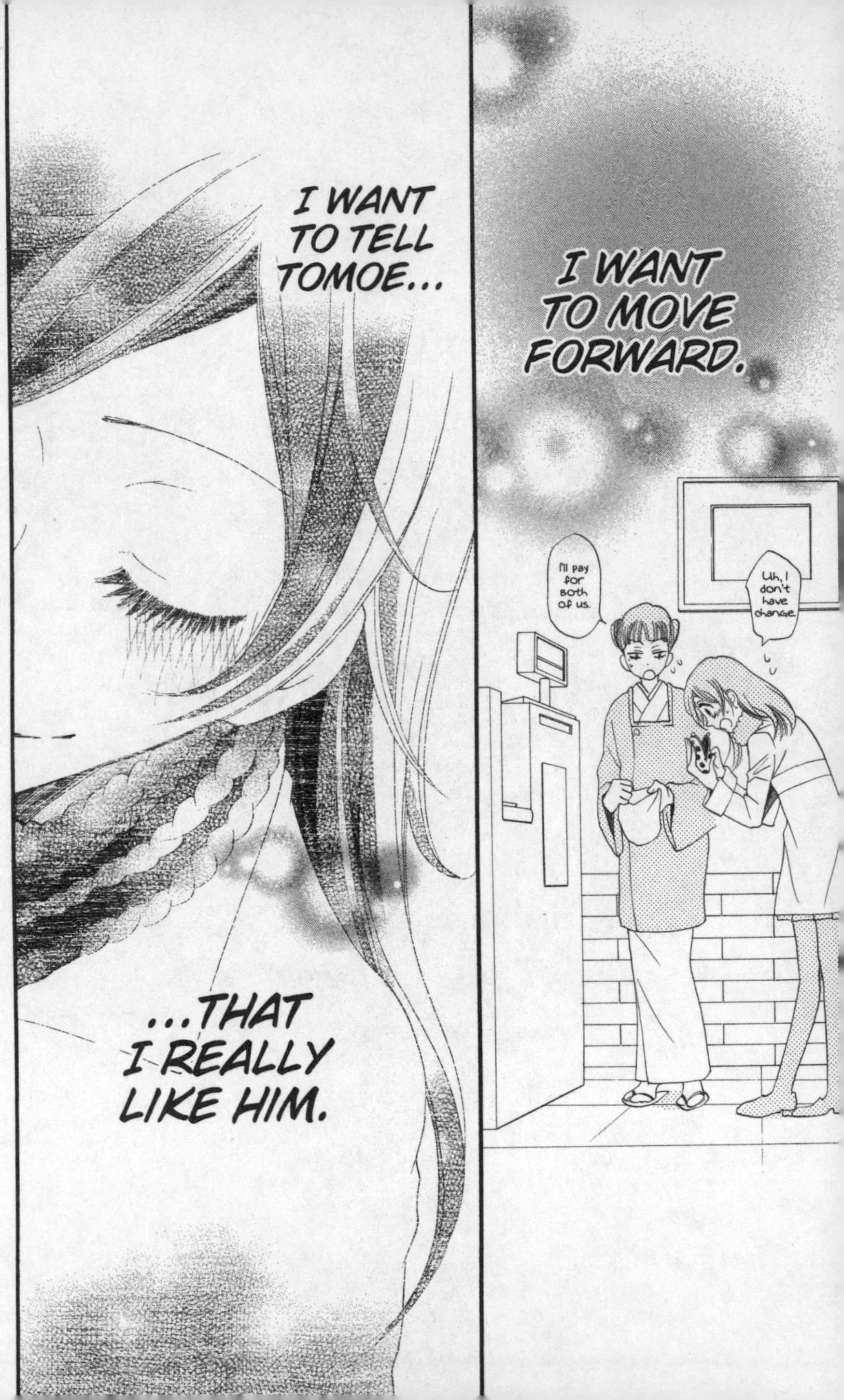
I WANT TO MOVE FORWARD.
Uh, I don't have change.
I'll pay for both of us.
I WANT TO TELL TOMOE...
...THAT I REALLY LIKE HIM.

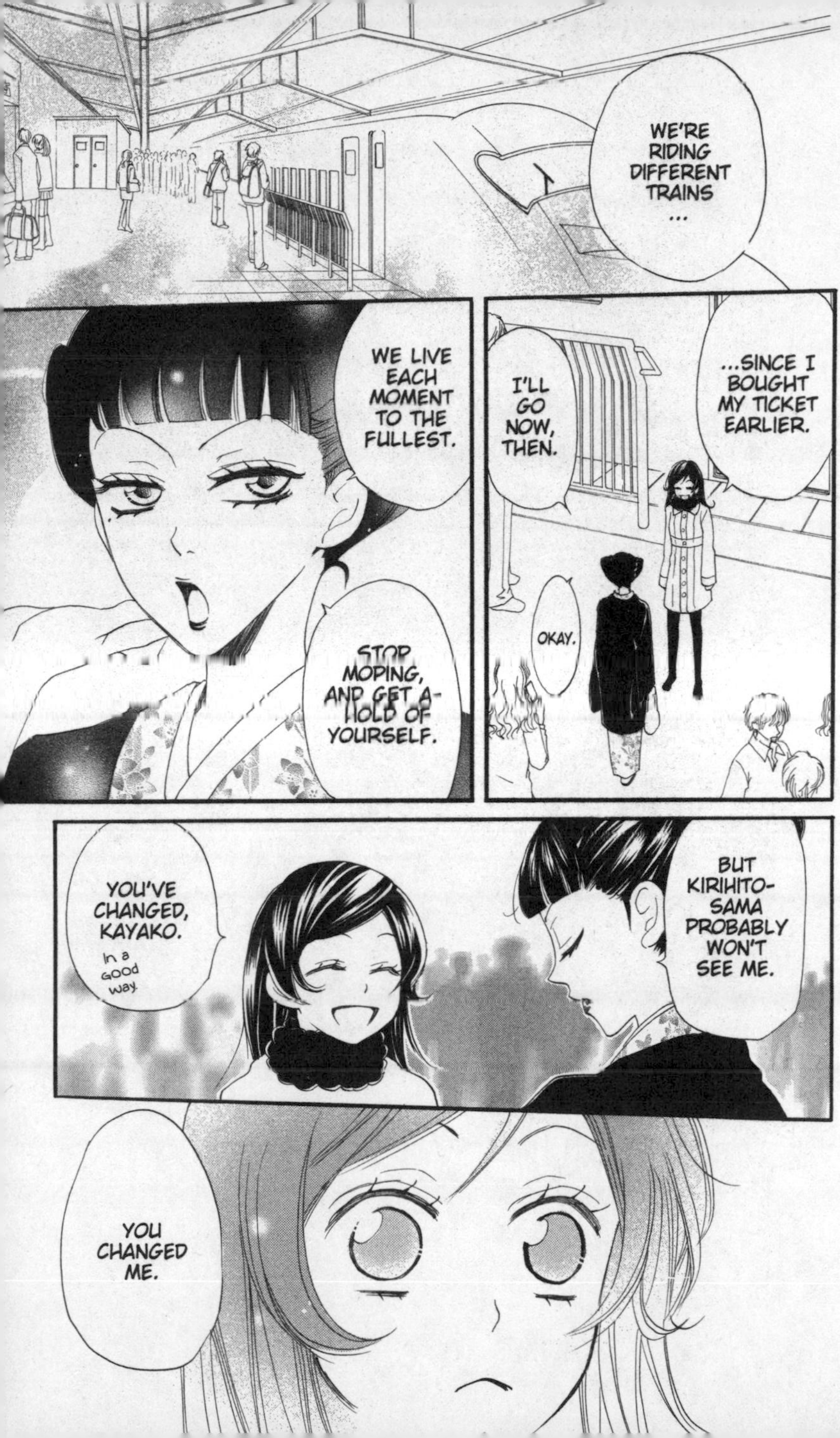
WE'RE RIDING DIFFERENT TRAINS ...
...SINCE I BOUGHT MY TICKET EARLIER.
I'LL GO NOW, THEN.
OKAY.
WE LIVE EACH MOMENT TO THE FULLEST.
STOP MOPING, AND GET A-HOLD OF YOURSELF.
BUT KIRIHITO-SAMA PROBABLY WON'T SEE ME.
YOU'VE CHANGED, KAYAKO.
In a good way.
YOU CHANGED ME.

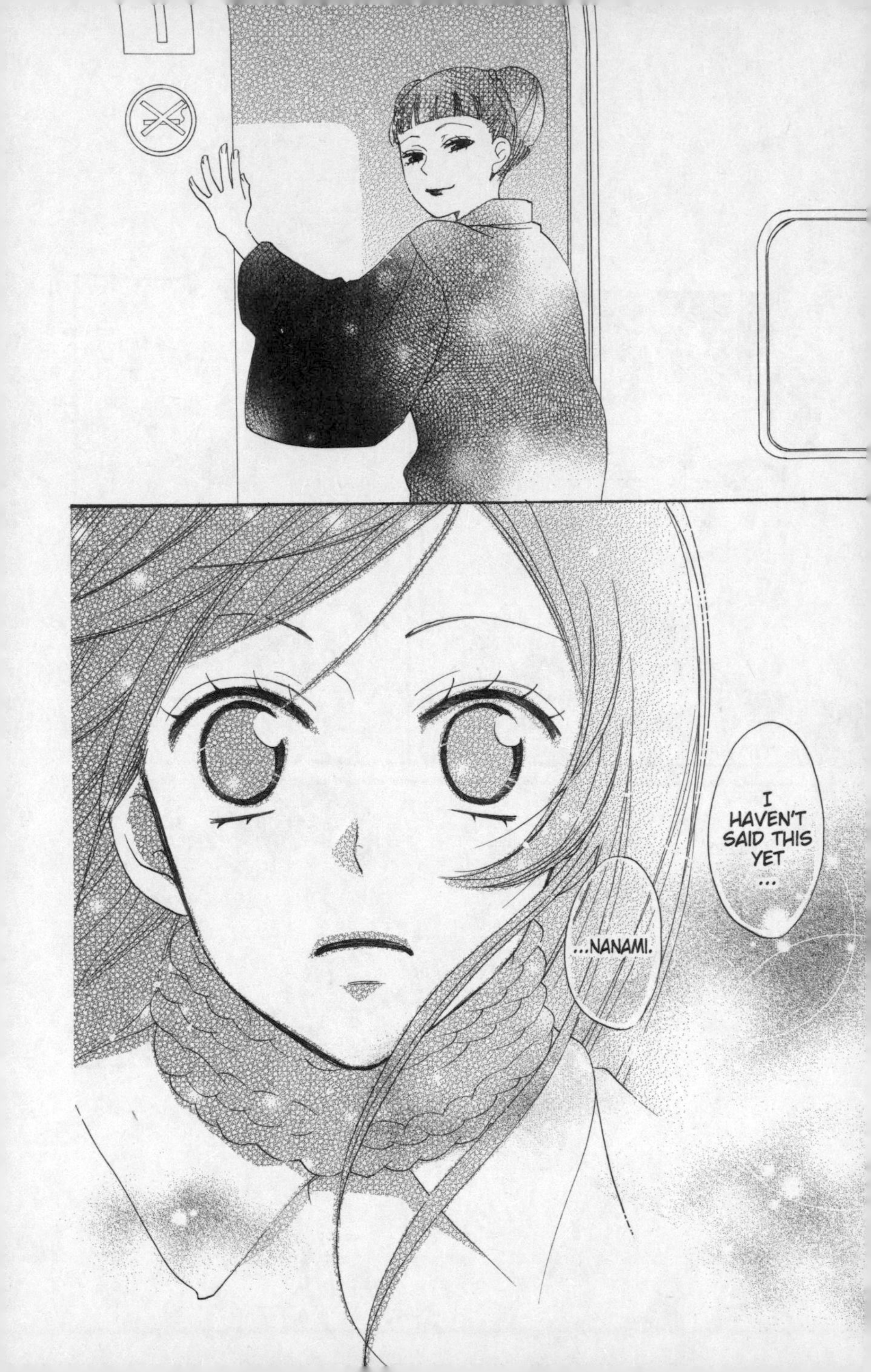
I HAVEN'T SAID THIS YET ...
...NANAMI.

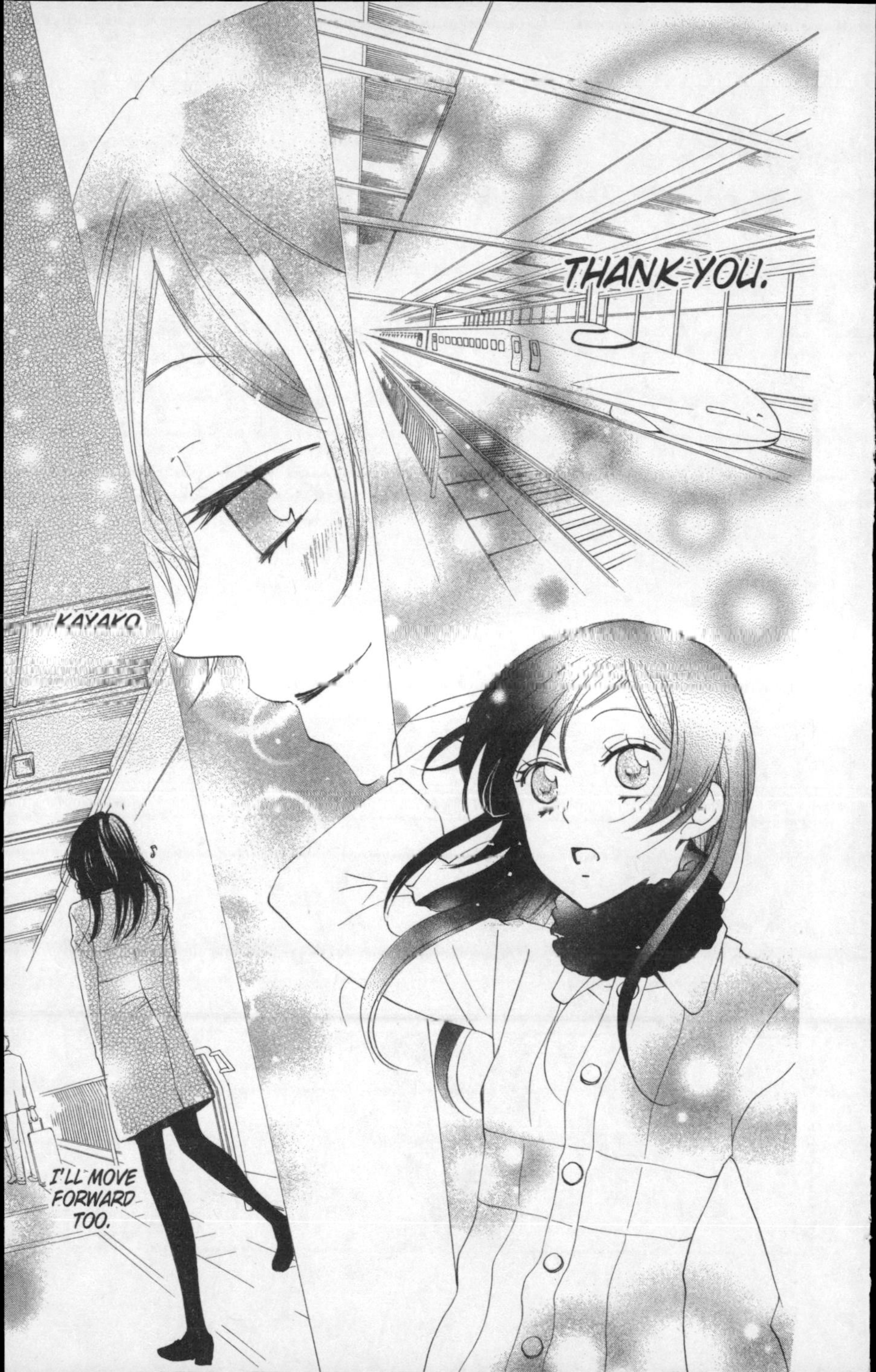
THANK YOU.
KAYAKO.
I'LL MOVE FORWARD TOO.

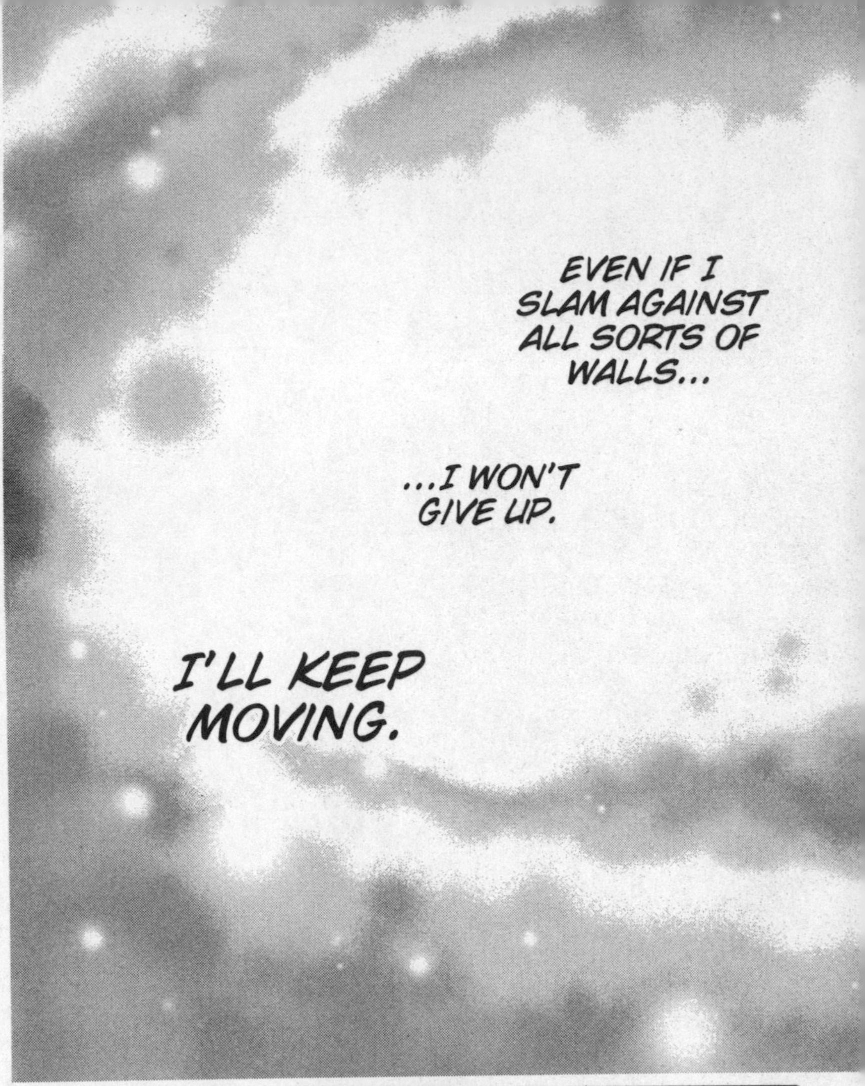
EVEN IF I SLAM AGAINST ALL SORTS OF WALLS...
...I WON'T GIVE UP.
I'LL KEEP MOVING.

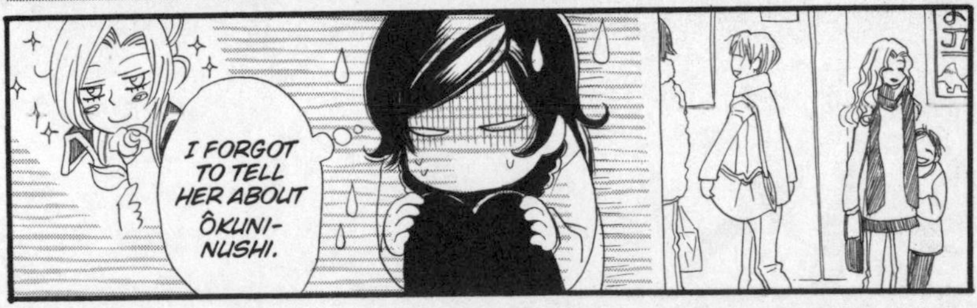
I FORGOT TO TELL HER ABOUT ÔKUNI-NUSHI.

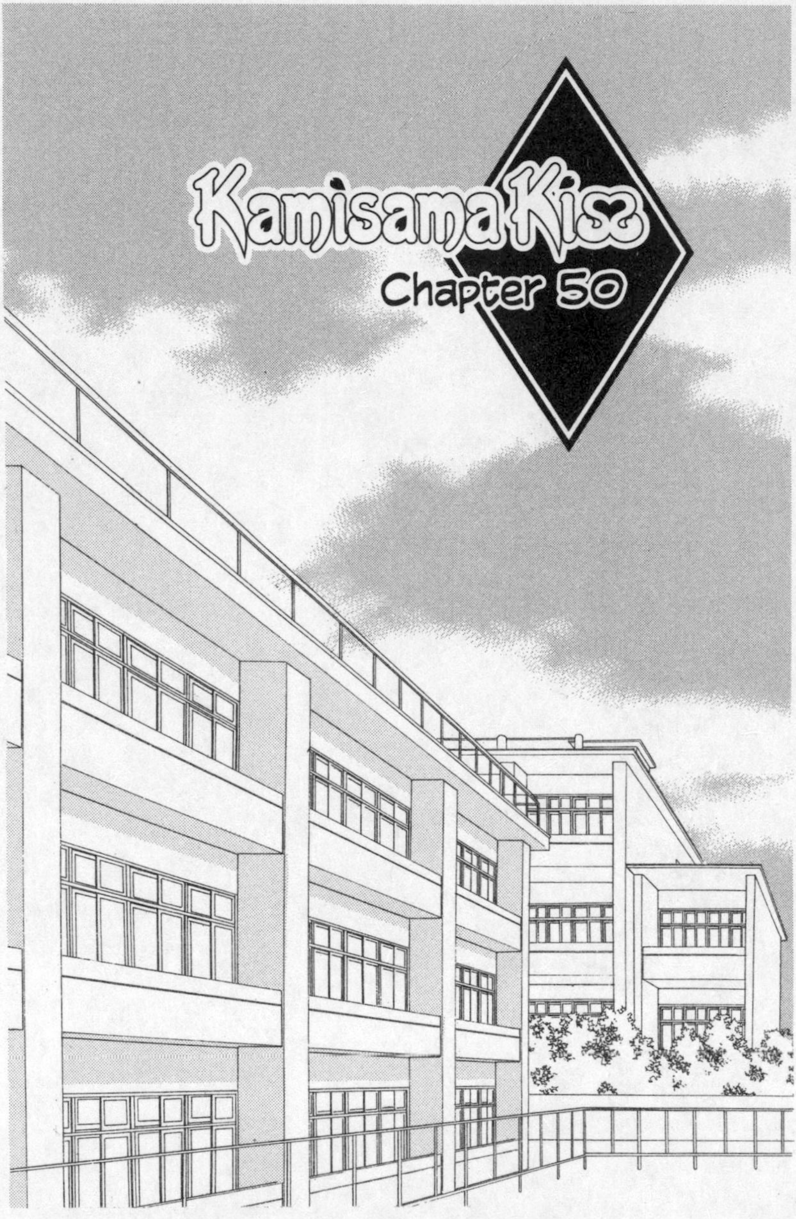
Kamisama Kiss
Chapter 50

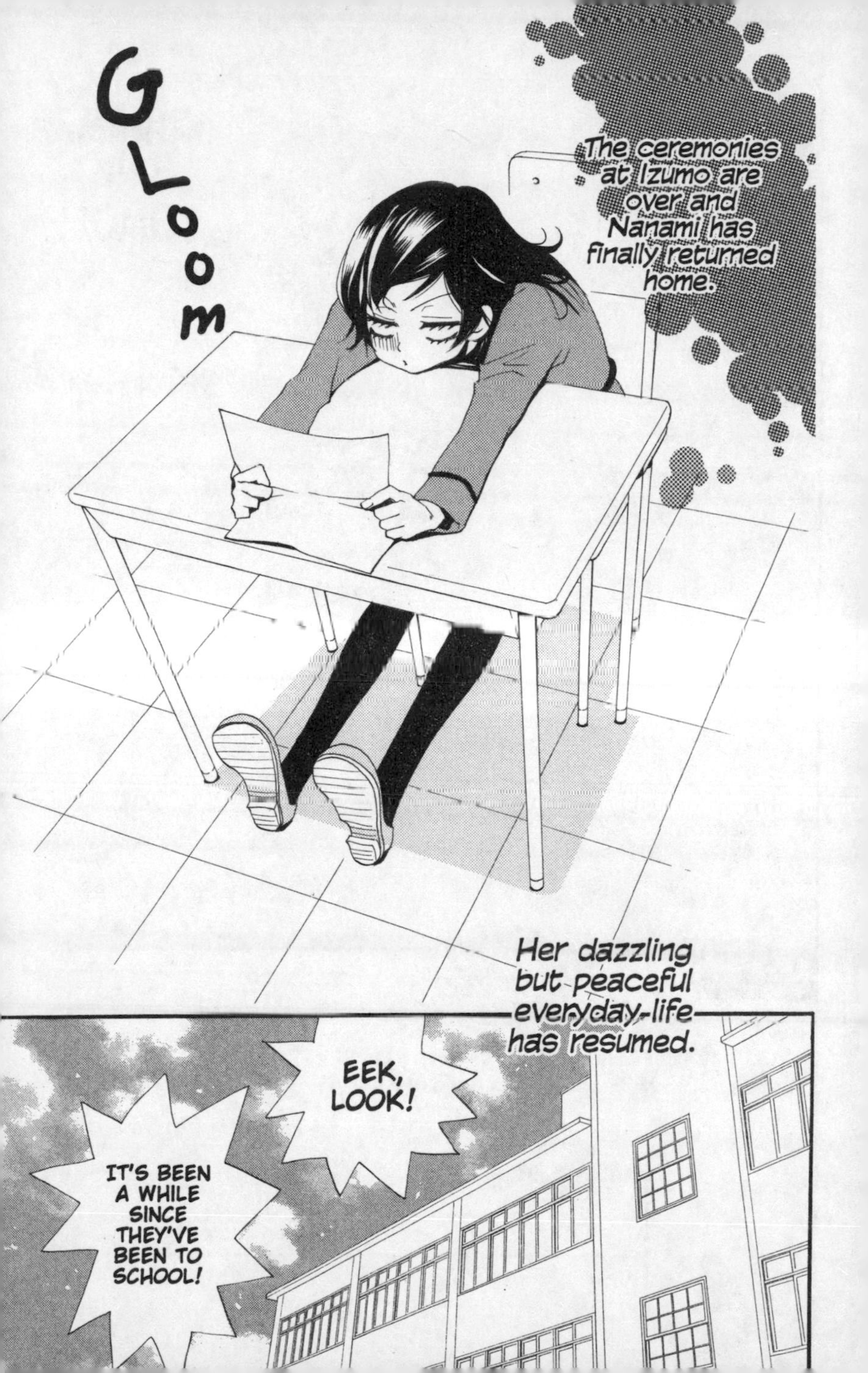
The ceremonies at Izumo are over and Nanami has finally returned home.
GLOOM
Her dazzling but peaceful everyday-life has resumed.
EEK, LOOK!
IT'S BEEN A WHILE SINCE THEY'VE BEEN TO SCHOOL!

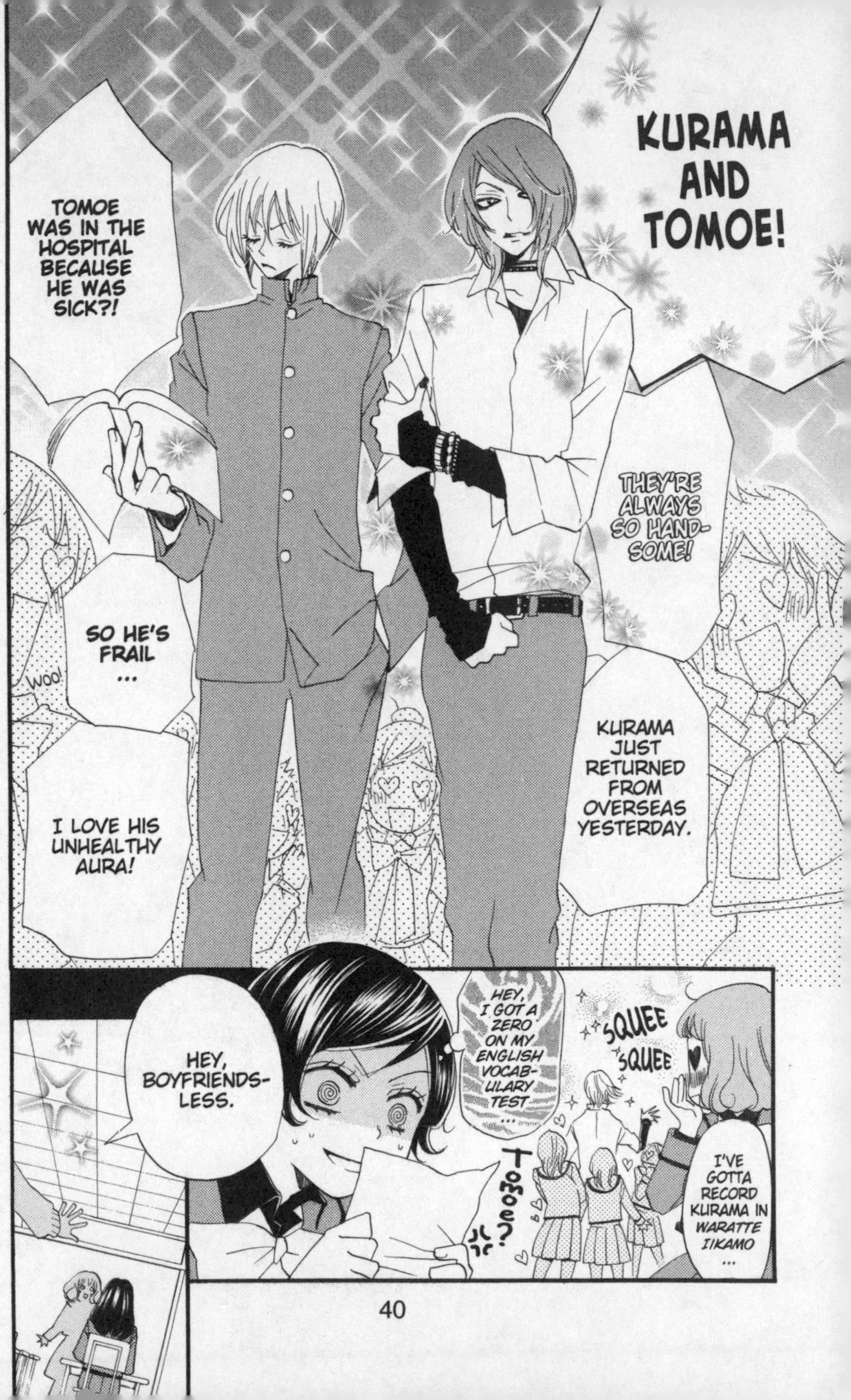
KURAMA AND TOMOE!
TOMOE WAS IN THE HOSPITAL BECAUSE HE WAS SICK?!
THEY'RE ALWAYS SO HAND-SOME!
KURAMA JUST RETURNED FROM OVERSEAS YESTERDAY.
SO HE'S FRAIL ...
WOO!
I LOVE HIS UNHEALTHY AURA!
SQUEE
SQUEE
I'VE GOTTA RECORD KURAMA IN *WARATTE IKAMO* ...
HEY, I GOT A ZERO ON MY ENGLISH VOCAB-ULARY TEST ...
Tomoe?
HEY, BOYFRIENDS-LESS.

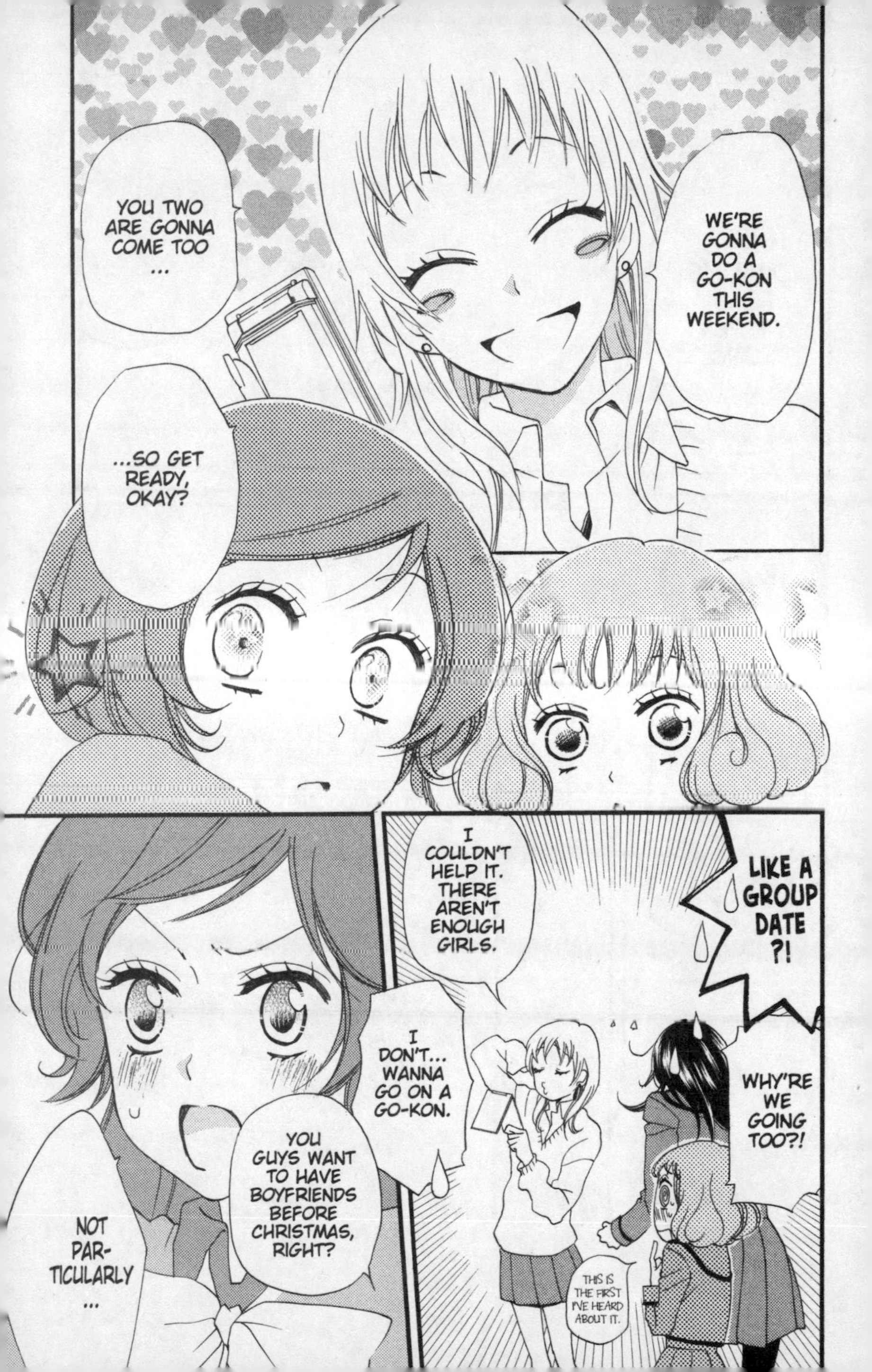
WE'RE GONNA DO A GO-KON THIS WEEKEND.
YOU TWO ARE GONNA COME TOO ...
...SO GET READY, OKAY?
LIKE A GROUP DATE ?!
I COULDN'T HELP IT. THERE AREN'T ENOUGH GIRLS.
WHY'RE WE GOING TOO?!
THIS IS THE FIRST I'VE HEARD ABOUT IT.
I DON'T... WANNA GO ON A GO-KON.
YOU GUYS WANT TO HAVE BOYFRIENDS BEFORE CHRISTMAS, RIGHT?
NOT PAR-TICULARLY ...

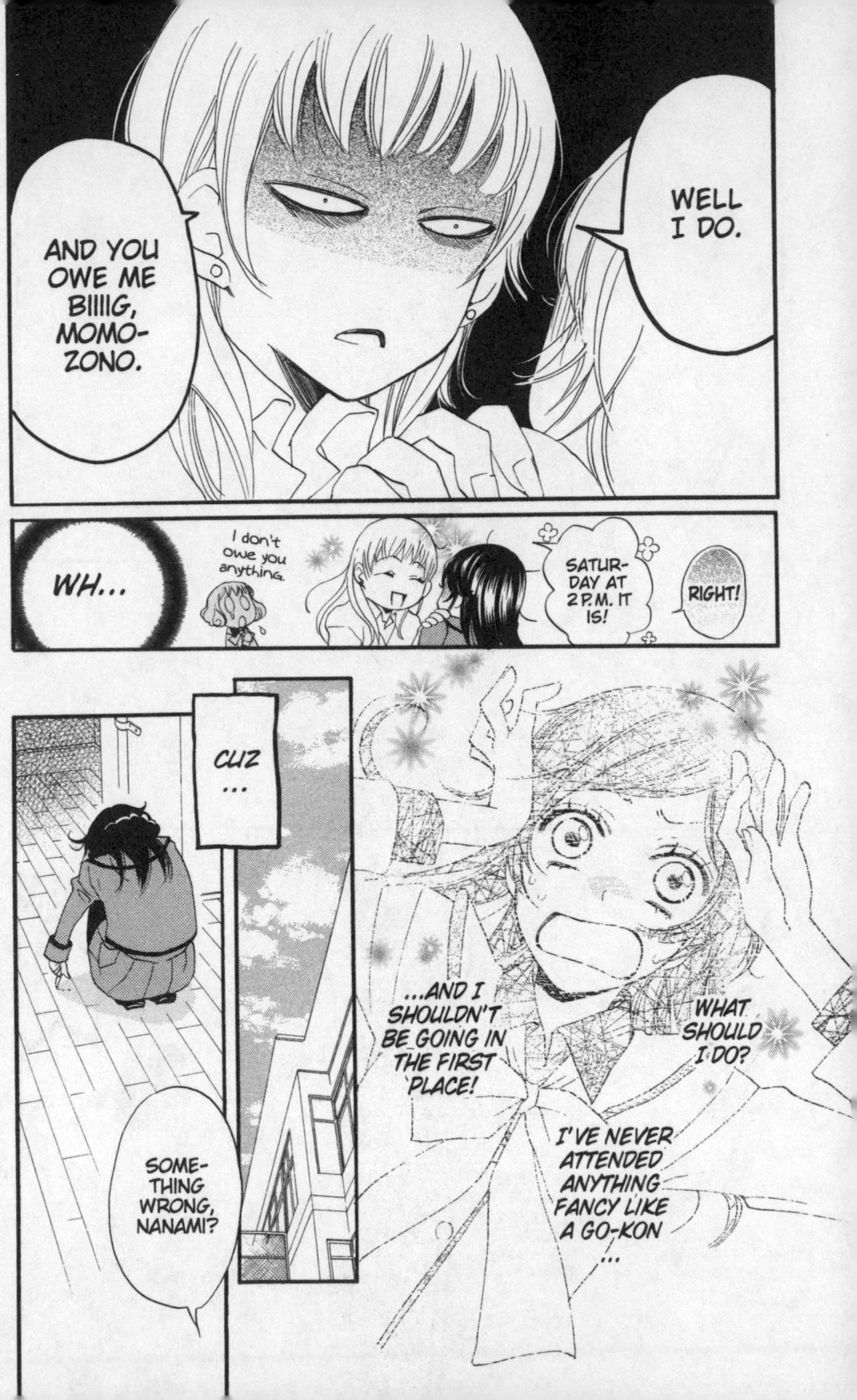
WELL I DO.
AND YOU OWE ME BIIIIG, MOMO-ZONO.
RIGHT!
SATUR-DAY AT 2 P.M. IT IS!
I don't owe you anything.
WH...
WHAT SHOULD I DO?
I'VE NEVER ATTENDED ANYTHING FANCY LIKE A GO-KON ...
...AND I SHOULDN'T BE GOING IN THE FIRST PLACE!
CUZ ...
SOME-THING WRONG, NANAMI?

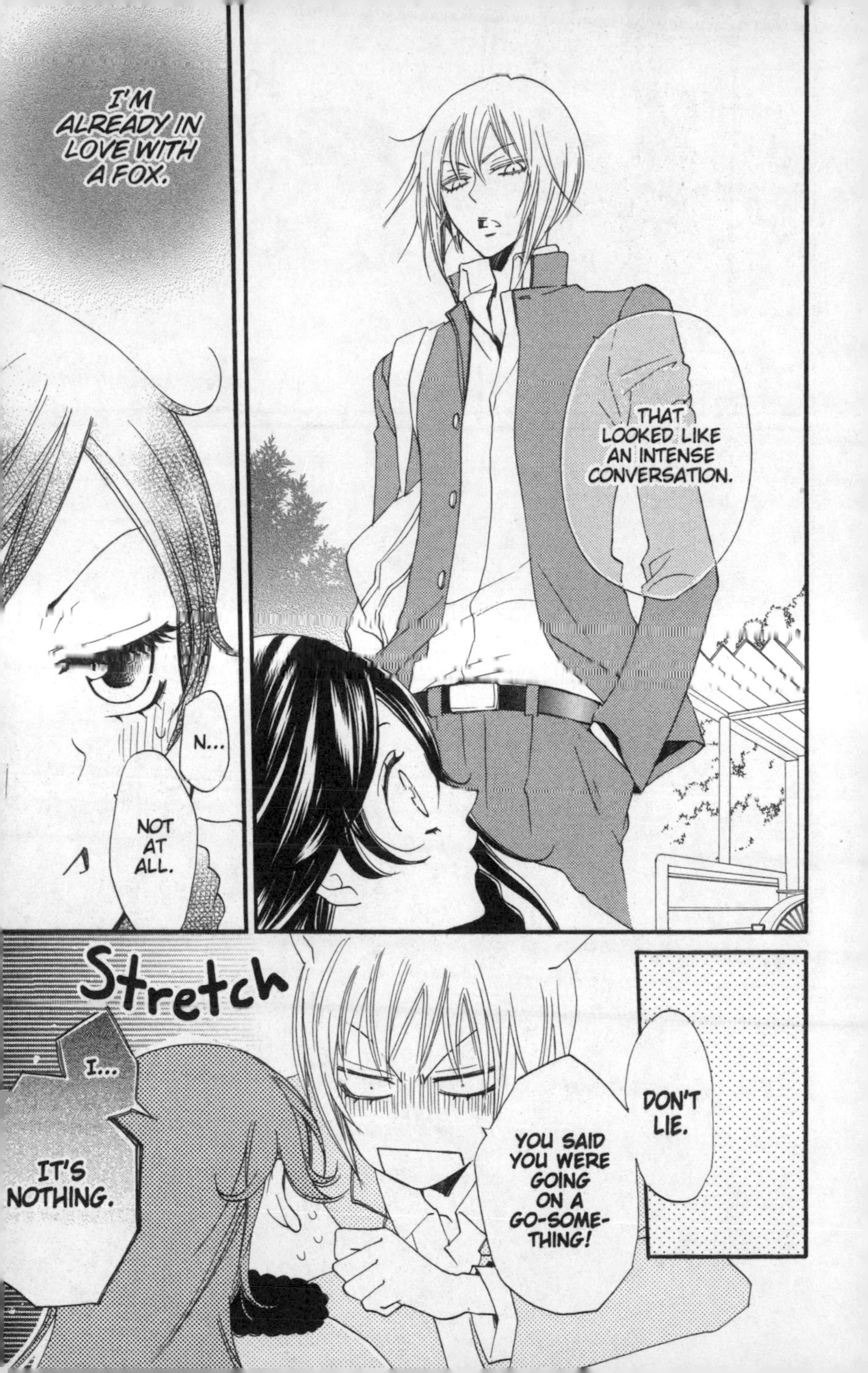
THAT LOOKED LIKE AN INTENSE CONVERSATION.
I'M ALREADY IN LOVE WITH A FOX.
N...
NOT AT ALL.
Stretch
DON'T LIE.
YOU SAID YOU WERE GOING ON A GO-SOME-THING!
I...
IT'S NOTHING.

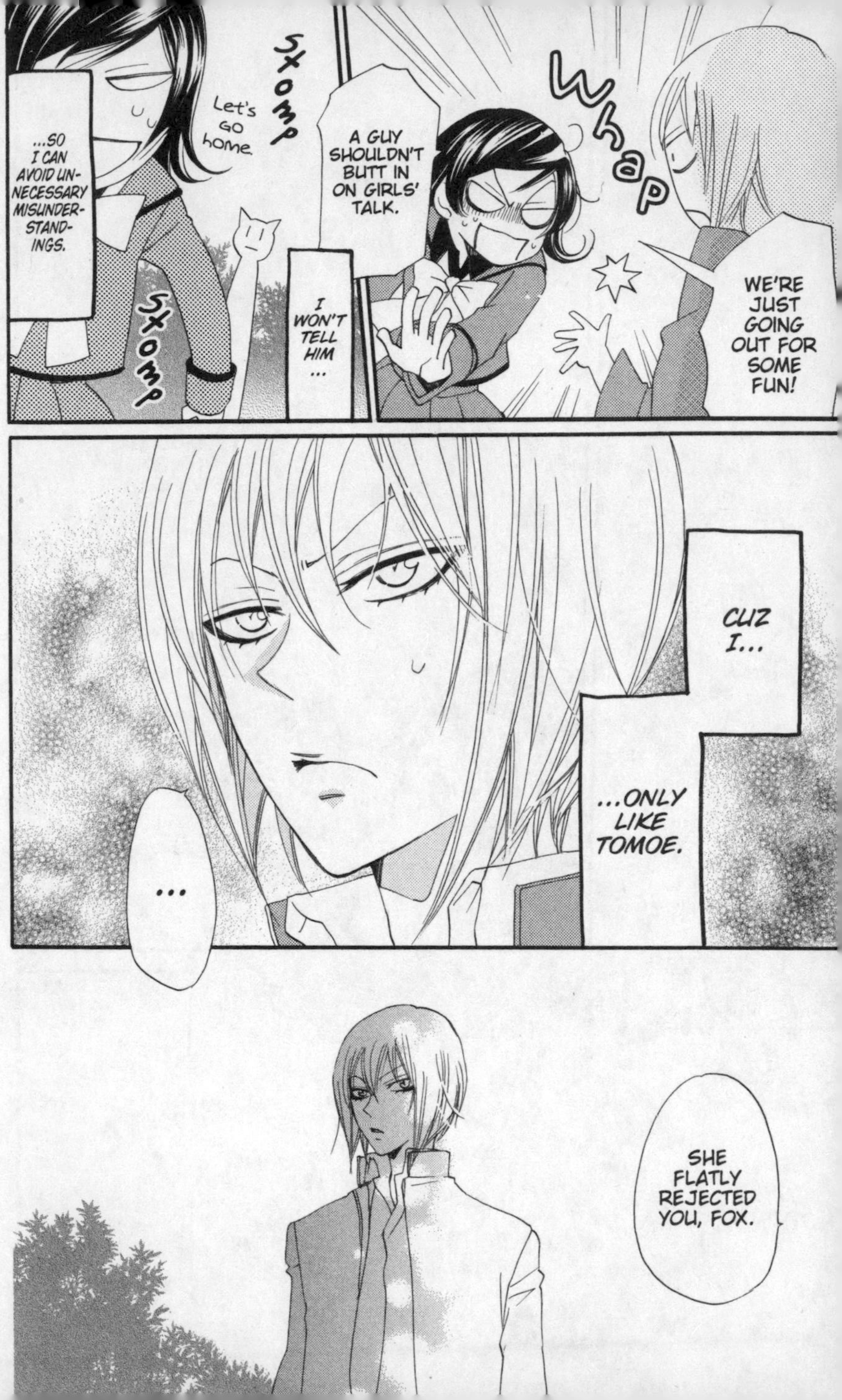
Whap
WE'RE JUST GOING OUT FOR SOME FUN!
A GUY SHOULDN'T BUTT IN ON GIRLS' TALK.
I WON'T TELL HIM...
Stomp
Let's go home.
...SO I CAN AVOID UN-NECESSARY MISUNDER-STAND-INGS.
Stomp
CUZ I...
...ONLY LIKE TOMOE.
...
SHE FLATLY REJECTED YOU, FOX.

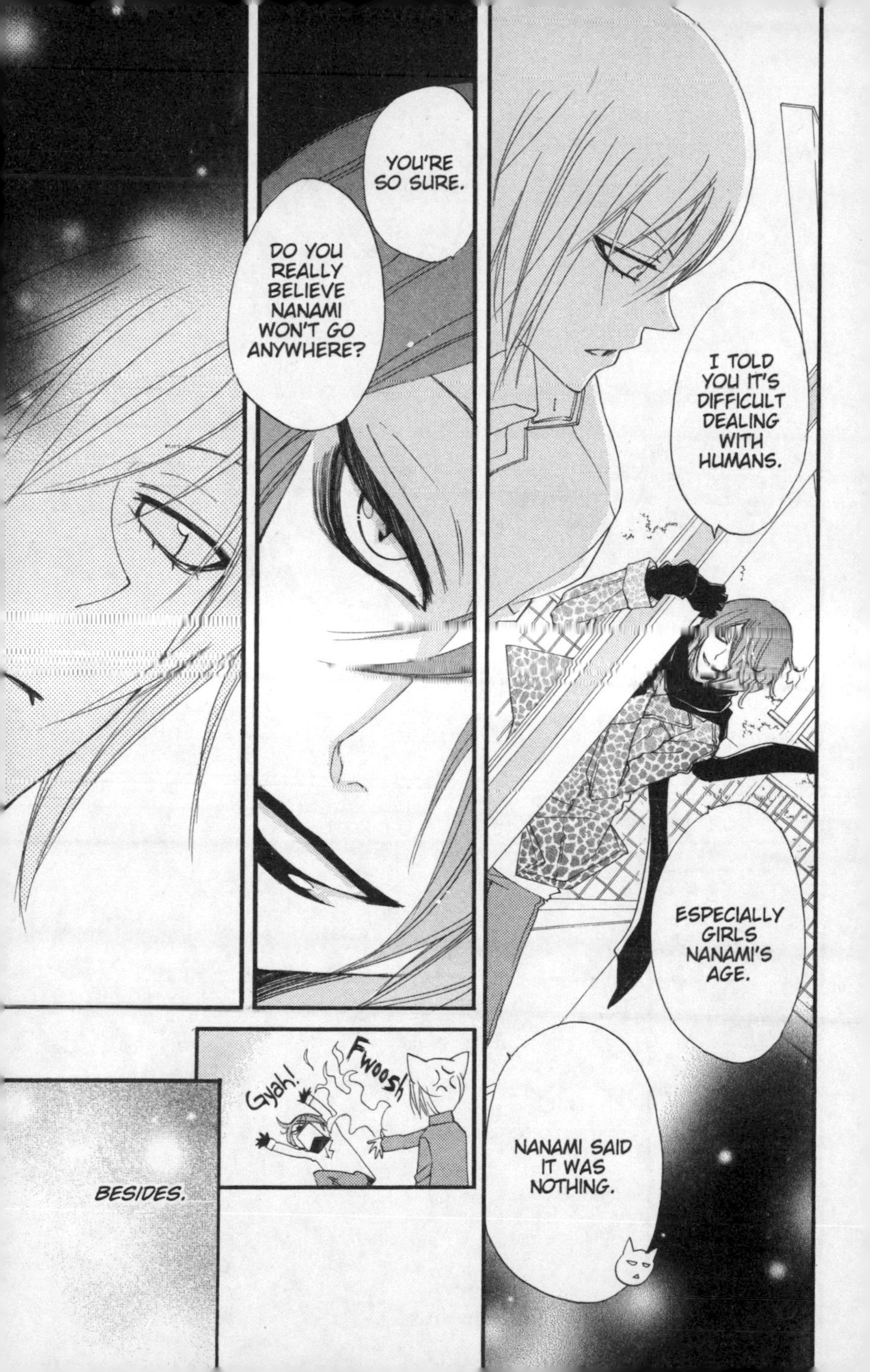
I TOLD YOU IT'S DIFFICULT DEALING WITH HUMANS.
ESPECIALLY GIRLS NANAMI'S AGE.
NANAMI SAID IT WAS NOTHING.
YOU'RE SO SURE.
DO YOU REALLY BELIEVE NANAMI WON'T GO ANYWHERE?
Fwoosh
Gyah!
BESIDES.

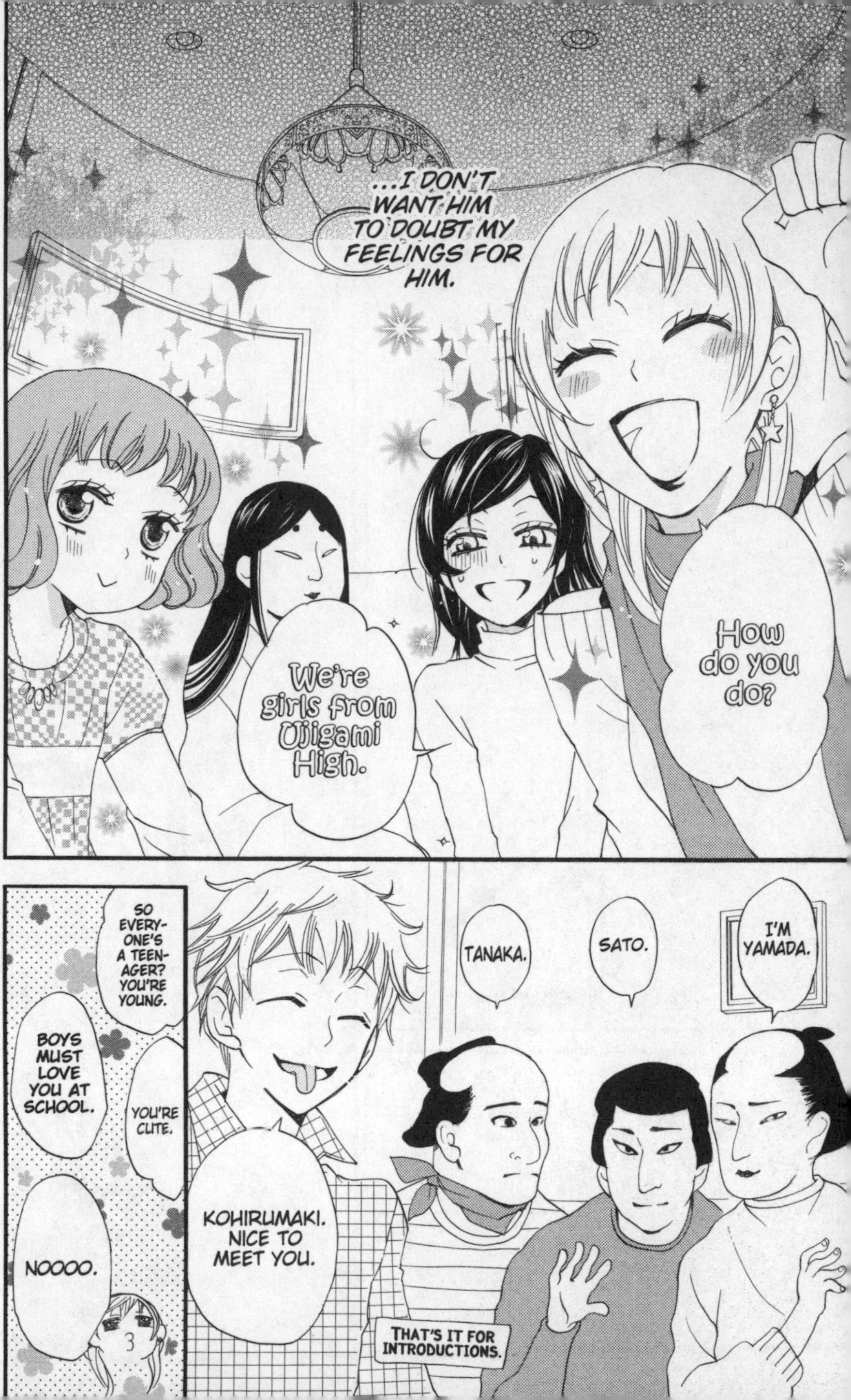
...I DON'T WANT HIM TO DOUBT MY FEELINGS FOR HIM.
How do you do?
We're girls from Ujigami High.
I'M YAMADA.
SATO.
TANAKA.
KOHIRUMAKI. NICE TO MEET YOU.
THAT'S IT FOR INTRODUCTIONS.
SO EVERYONE'S A TEENAGER? YOU'RE YOUNG.
YOU'RE CUTE.
BOYS MUST LOVE YOU AT SCHOOL.
NOOOO.

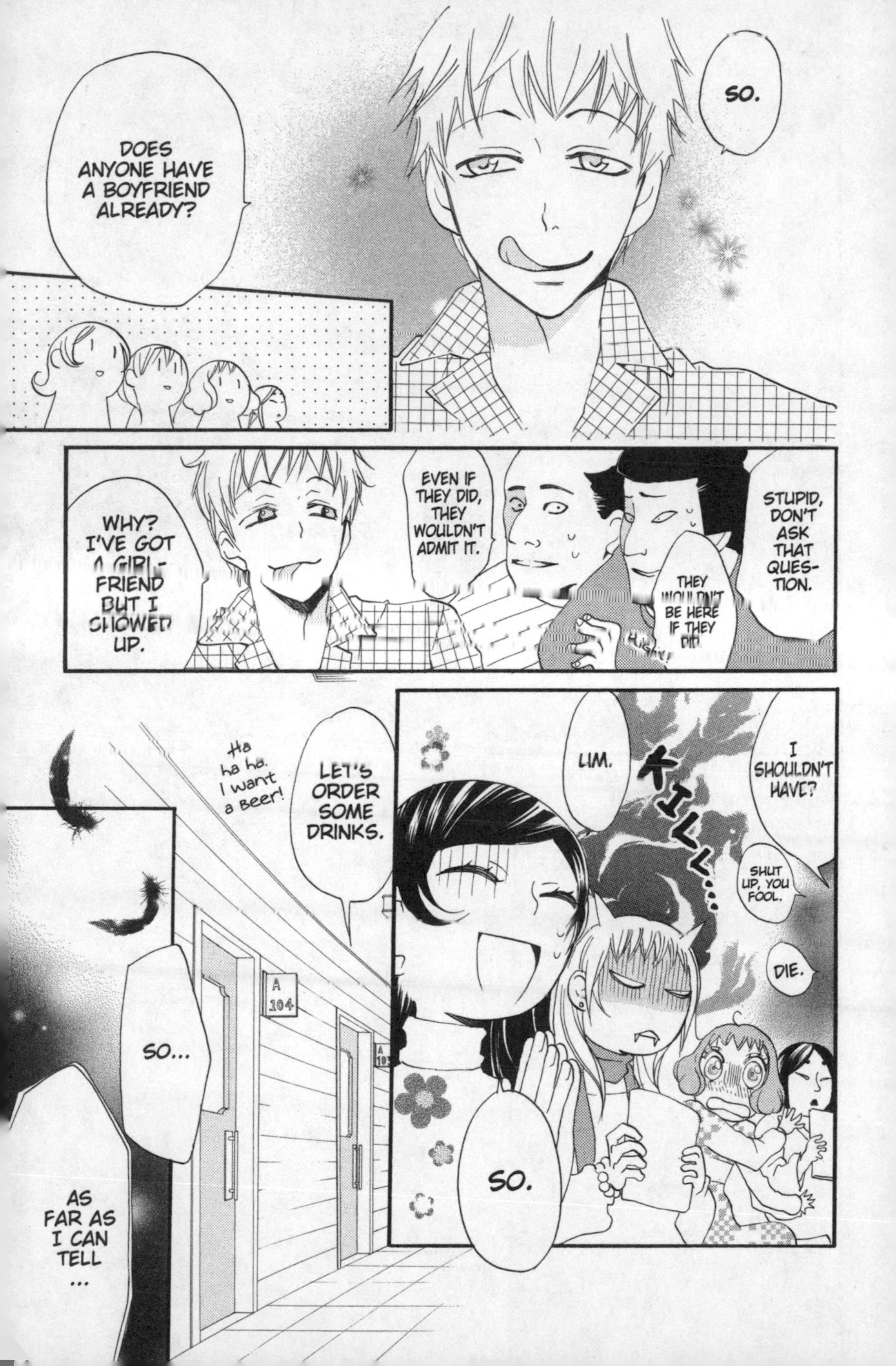
SO.
DOES ANYONE HAVE A BOYFRIEND ALREADY?
STUPID, DON'T ASK THAT QUESTION.
THEY WOULDN'T BE HERE IF THEY DID.
EVEN IF THEY DID, THEY WOULDN'T ADMIT IT.
WHY? I'VE GOT A GIRLFRIEND BUT I SHOWED UP.
I SHOULDN'T HAVE?
UM.
KILL...
SHUT UP, YOU FOOL.
DIE.
LET'S ORDER SOME DRINKS.
Ha ha ha. I want a beer!
SO.
A 104
SO...
AS FAR AS I CAN TELL...

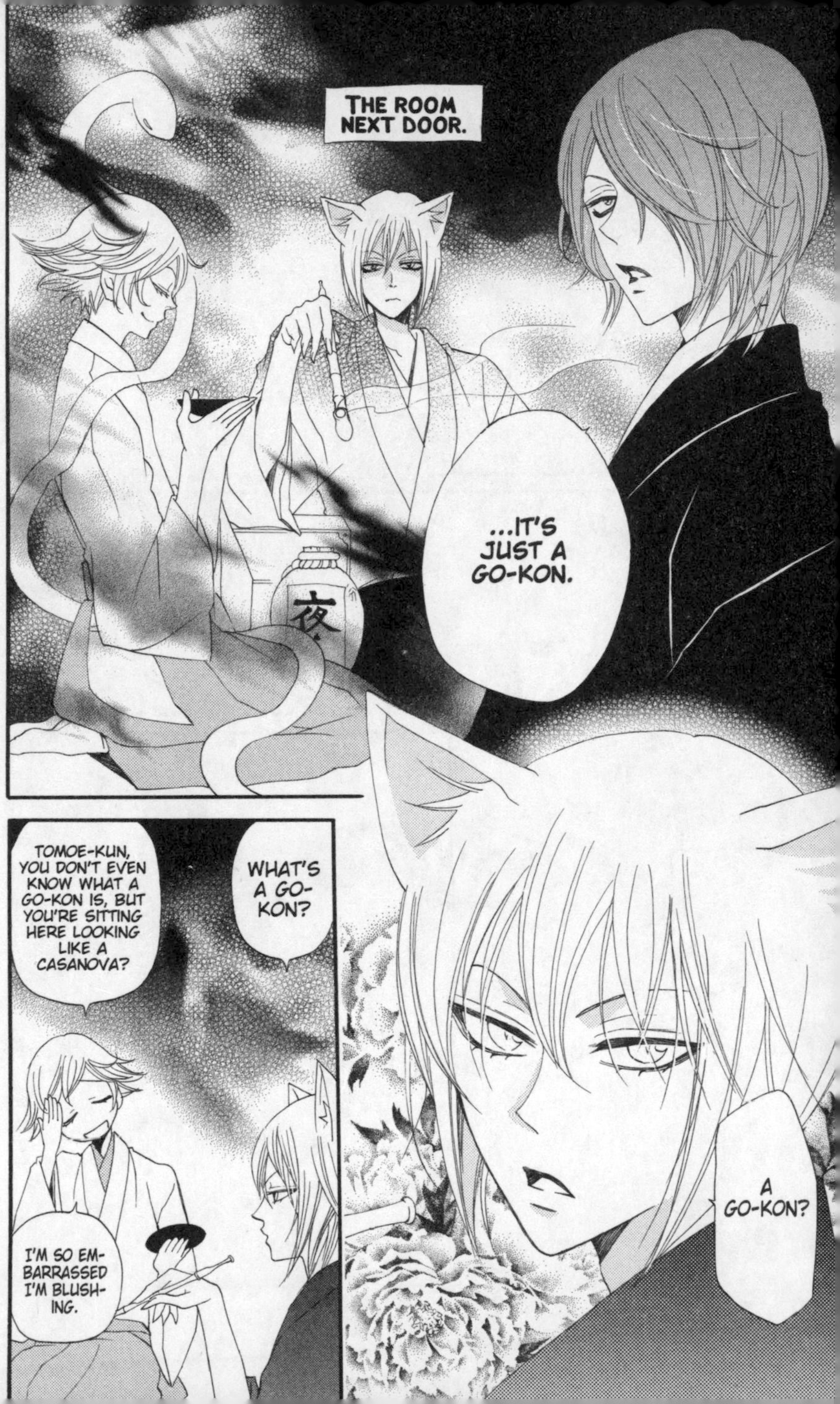
THE ROOM NEXT DOOR.
...IT'S JUST A GO-KON.
A GO-KON?
WHAT'S A GO-KON?
TOMOE-KUN, YOU DON'T EVEN KNOW WHAT A GO-KON IS, BUT YOU'RE SITTING HERE LOOKING LIKE A CASANOVA?
I'M SO EM-BARRASSED I'M BLUSH-ING.

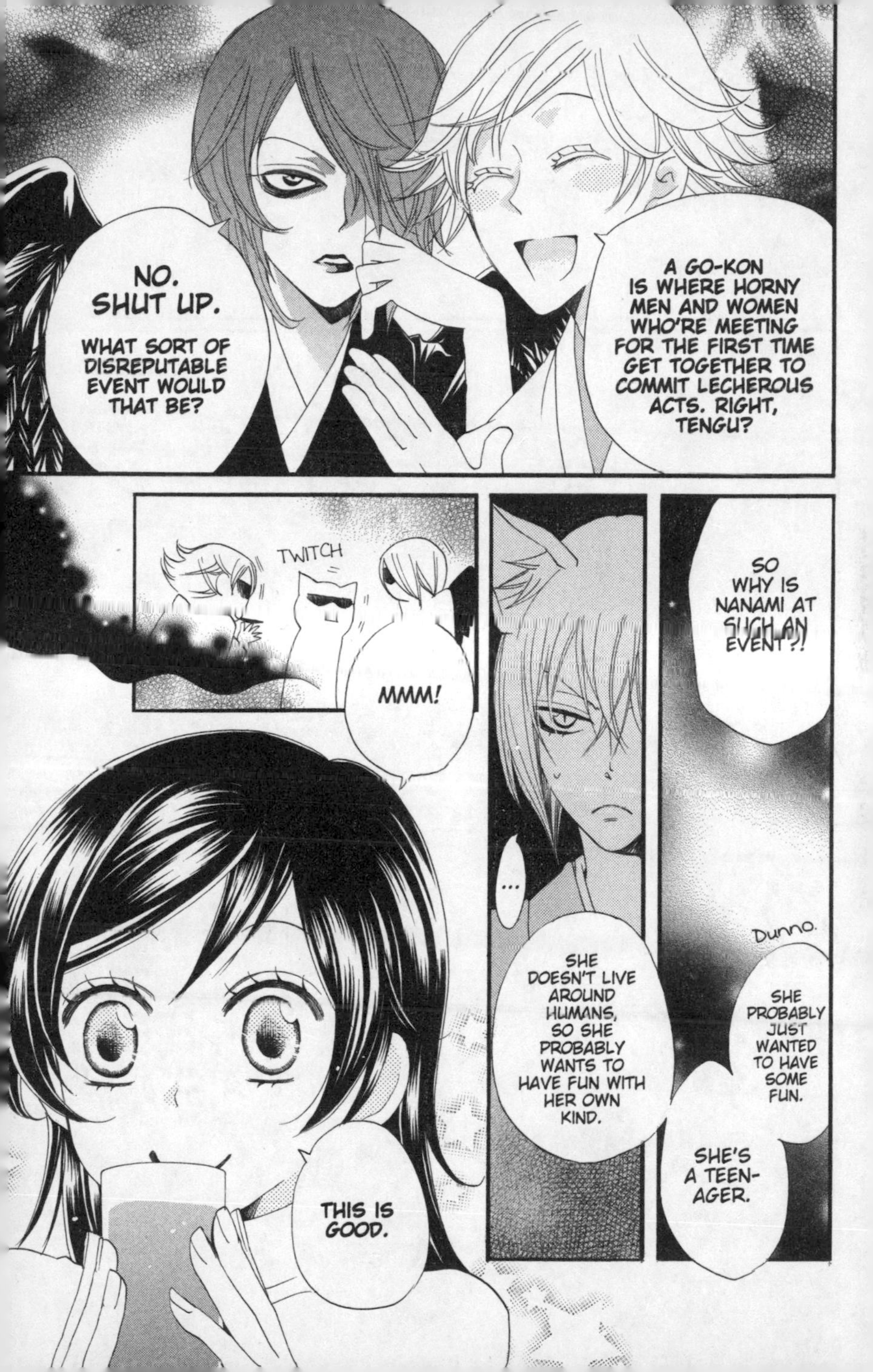
A GO-KON IS WHERE HORNY MEN AND WOMEN WHO'RE MEETING FOR THE FIRST TIME GET TOGETHER TO COMMIT LECHEROUS ACTS. RIGHT, TENGU?
NO. SHUT UP.
WHAT SORT OF DISREPUTABLE EVENT WOULD THAT BE?
SO WHY IS NANAMI AT SUCH AN EVENT?!
Dunno.
SHE PROBABLY JUST WANTED TO HAVE SOME FUN.
SHE'S A TEEN-AGER.
...
SHE DOESN'T LIVE AROUND HUMANS, SO SHE PROBABLY WANTS TO HAVE FUN WITH HER OWN KIND.
TWITCH
MMM!
THIS IS GOOD.

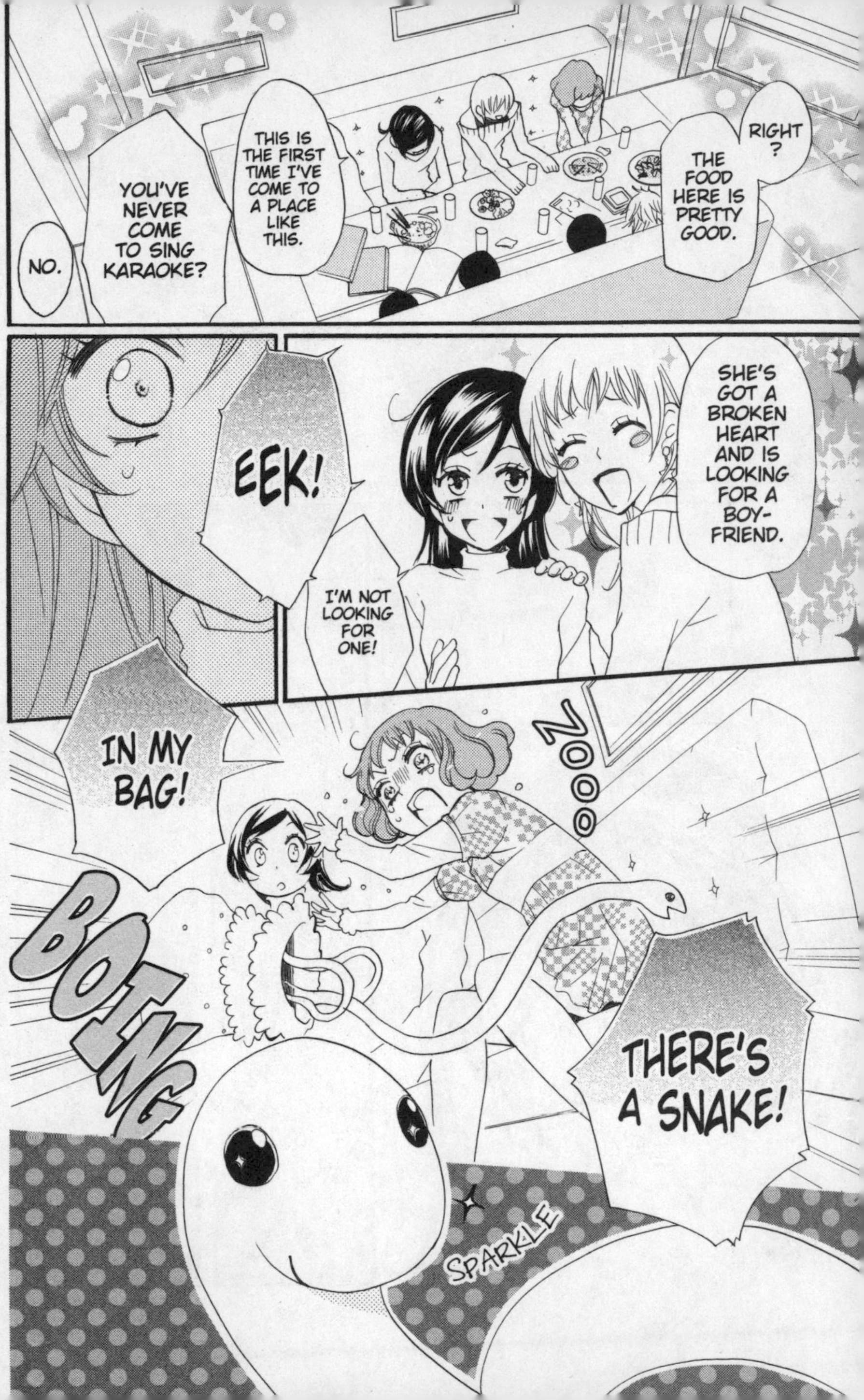
RIGHT?
THE FOOD HERE IS PRETTY GOOD.
THIS IS THE FIRST TIME I'VE COME TO A PLACE LIKE THIS.
YOU'VE NEVER COME TO SING KARAOKE?
NO.
SHE'S GOT A BROKEN HEART AND IS LOOKING FOR A BOY-FRIEND.
I'M NOT LOOKING FOR ONE!
EEK!
ZOOOO
THERE'S A SNAKE!
IN MY BAG!
BOING
SPARKLE

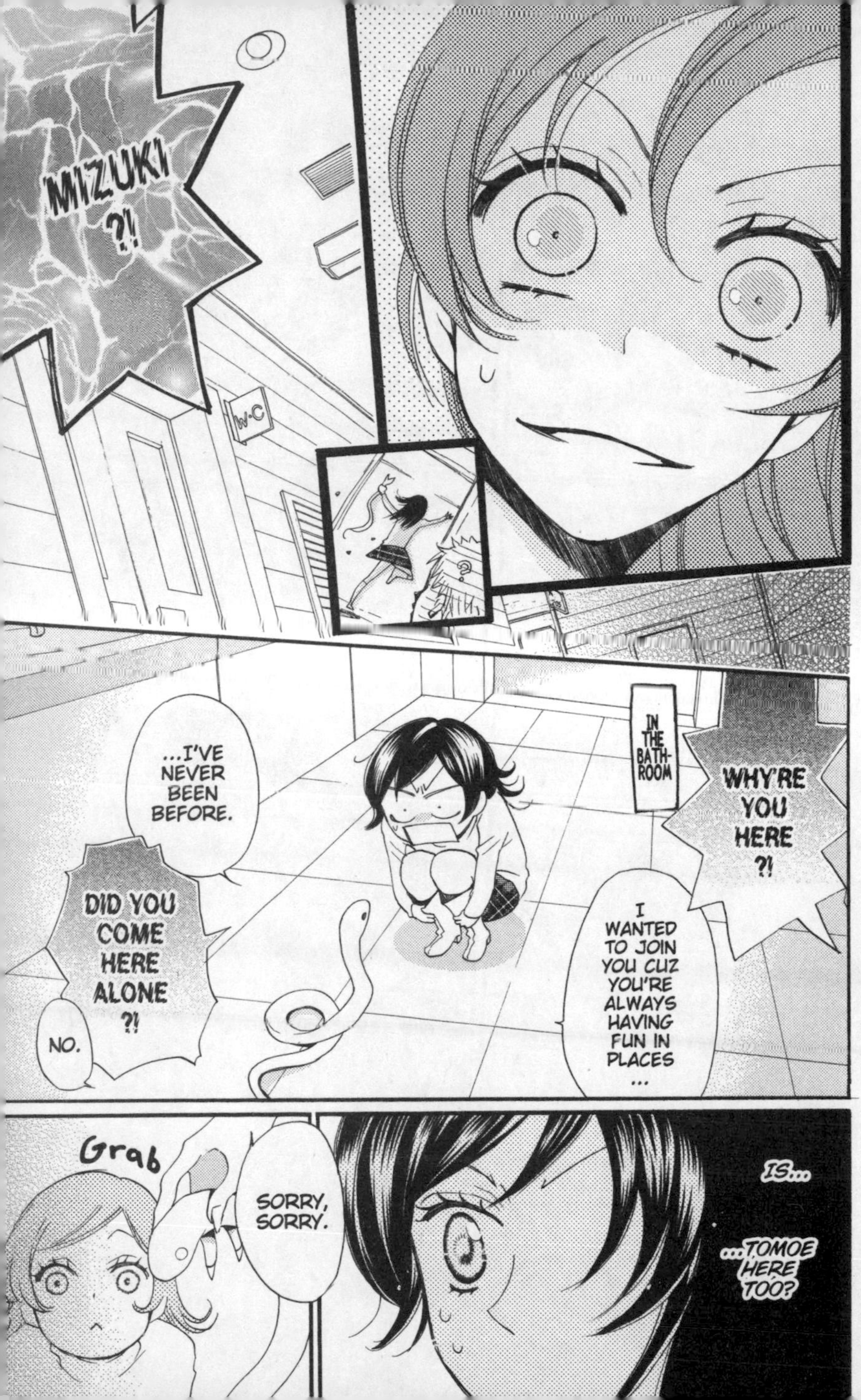
MIZUKI ?!
IN THE BATH-ROOM
WHY'RE YOU HERE ?!
I WANTED TO JOIN YOU CUZ YOU'RE ALWAYS HAVING FUN IN PLACES ...
...I'VE NEVER BEEN BEFORE.
DID YOU COME HERE ALONE ?!
NO.
IS...
...TOMOE HERE TOO?
SORRY, SORRY.
Grab

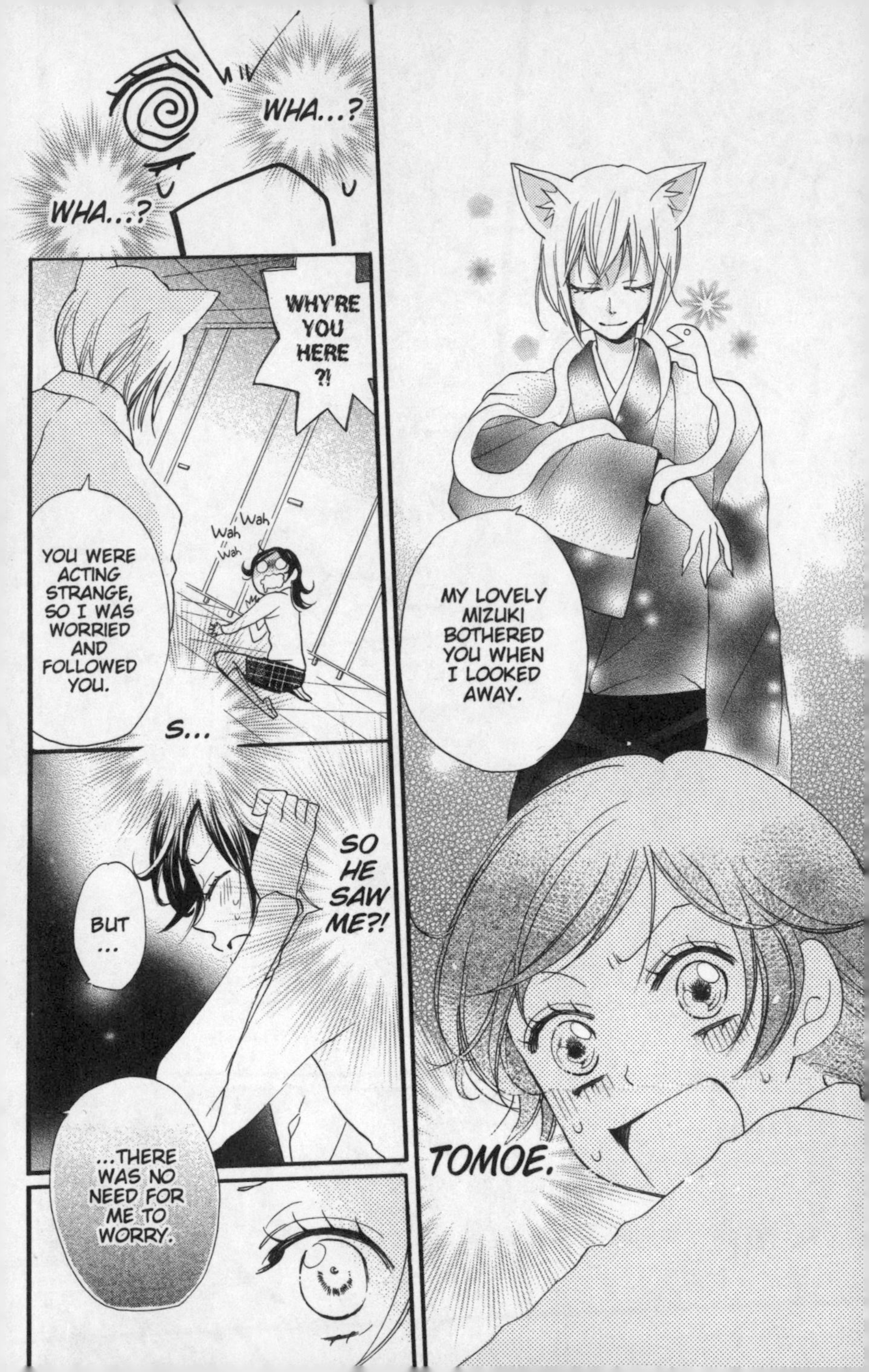
MY LOVELY MIZUKI BOTHERED YOU WHEN I LOOKED AWAY.
TOMOE.
WHA...?
WHA...?
WHY'RE YOU HERE ?!
Wah
Wah
Wah
YOU WERE ACTING STRANGE, SO I WAS WORRIED AND FOLLOWED YOU.
S...
SO HE SAW ME?!
BUT ...
...THERE WAS NO NEED FOR ME TO WORRY.

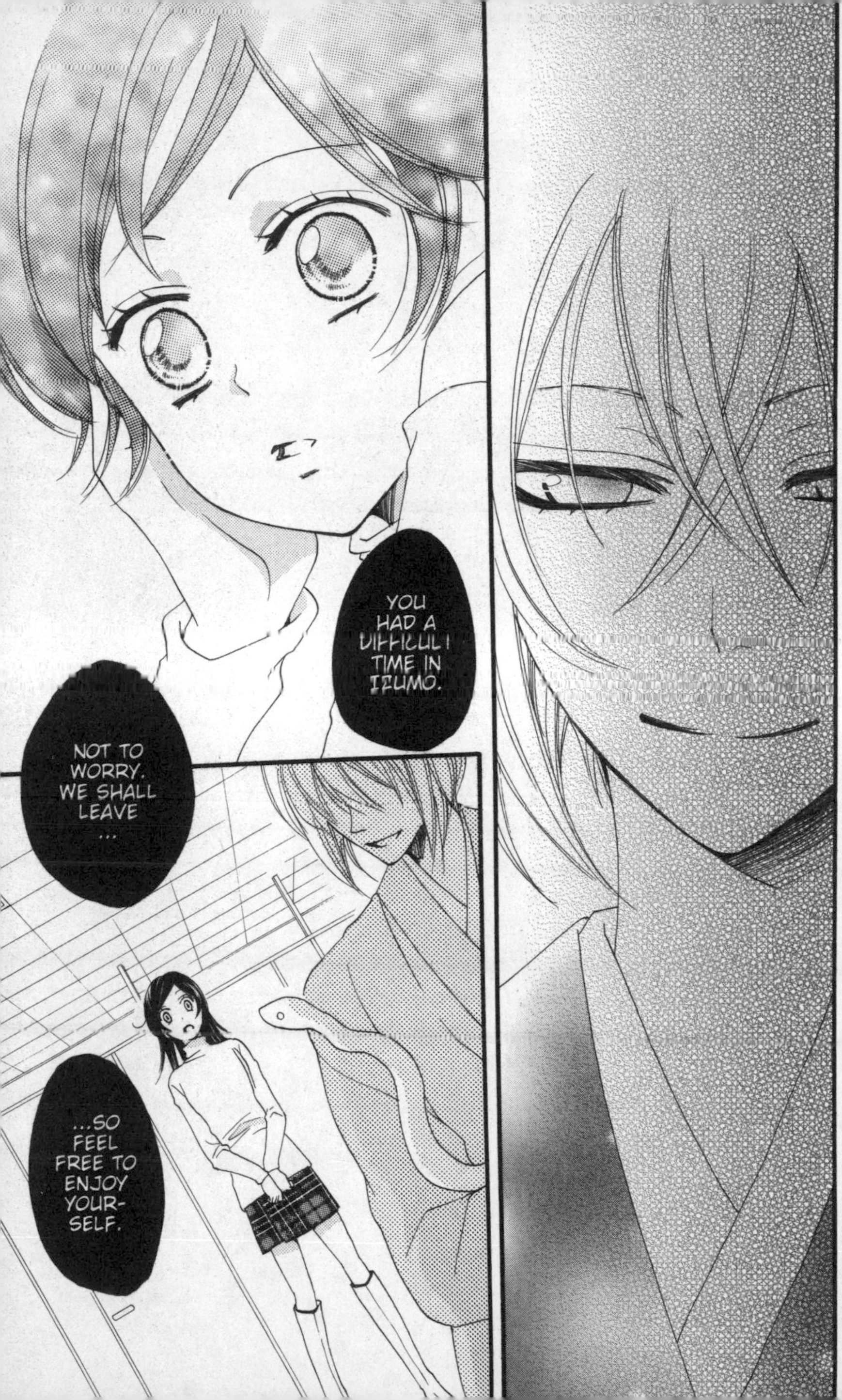
YOU HAD A DIFFICULT TIME IN IZUMO.
NOT TO WORRY. WE SHALL LEAVE ...
...SO FEEL FREE TO ENJOY YOUR-SELF.

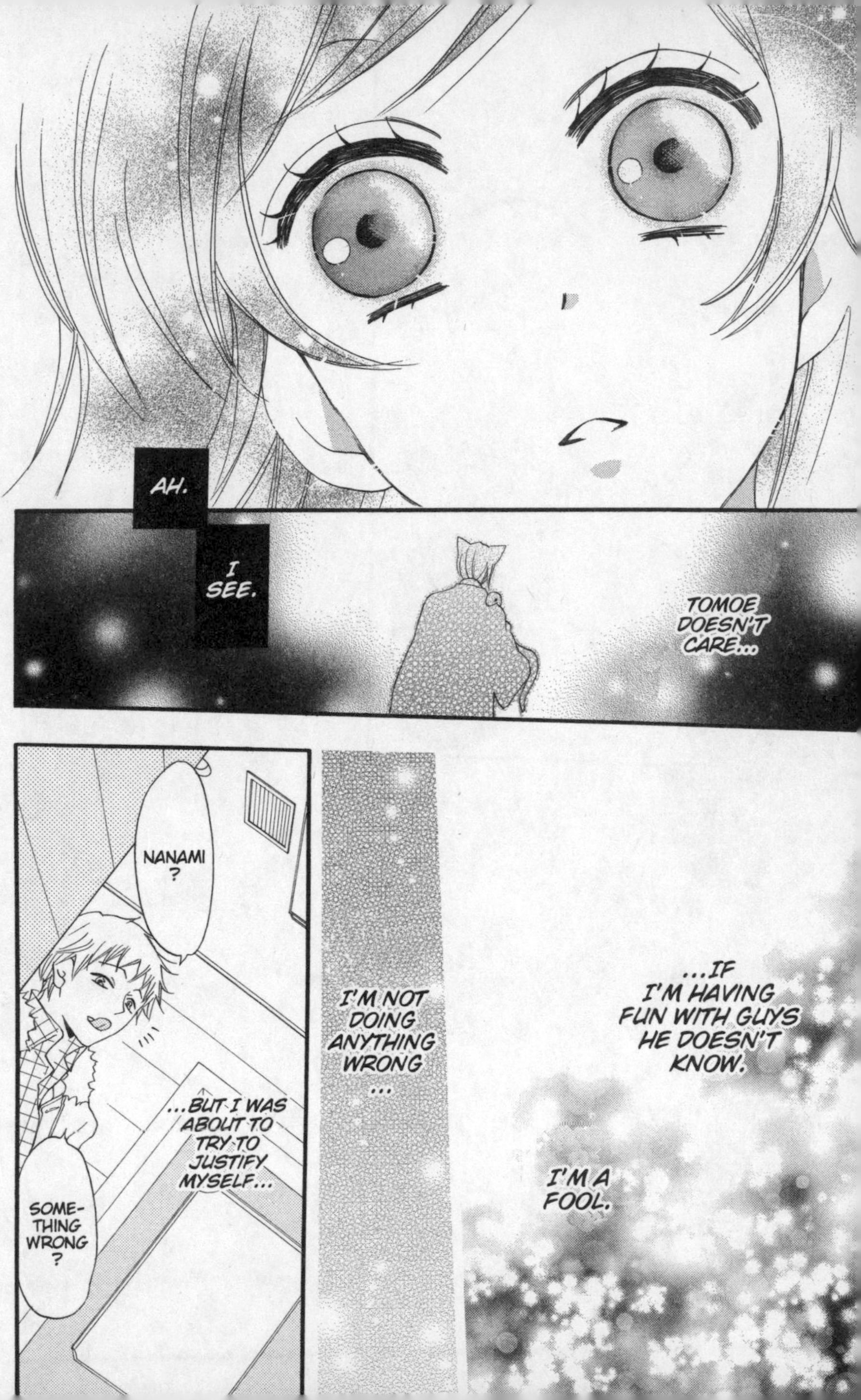
AH.
I SEE.
TOMOE DOESN'T CARE...
...IF I'M HAVING FUN WITH GUYS HE DOESN'T KNOW.
I'M A FOOL.
I'M NOT DOING ANYTHING WRONG...
...BUT I WAS ABOUT TO TRY TO JUSTIFY MYSELF...
NANAMI?
SOME-THING WRONG?

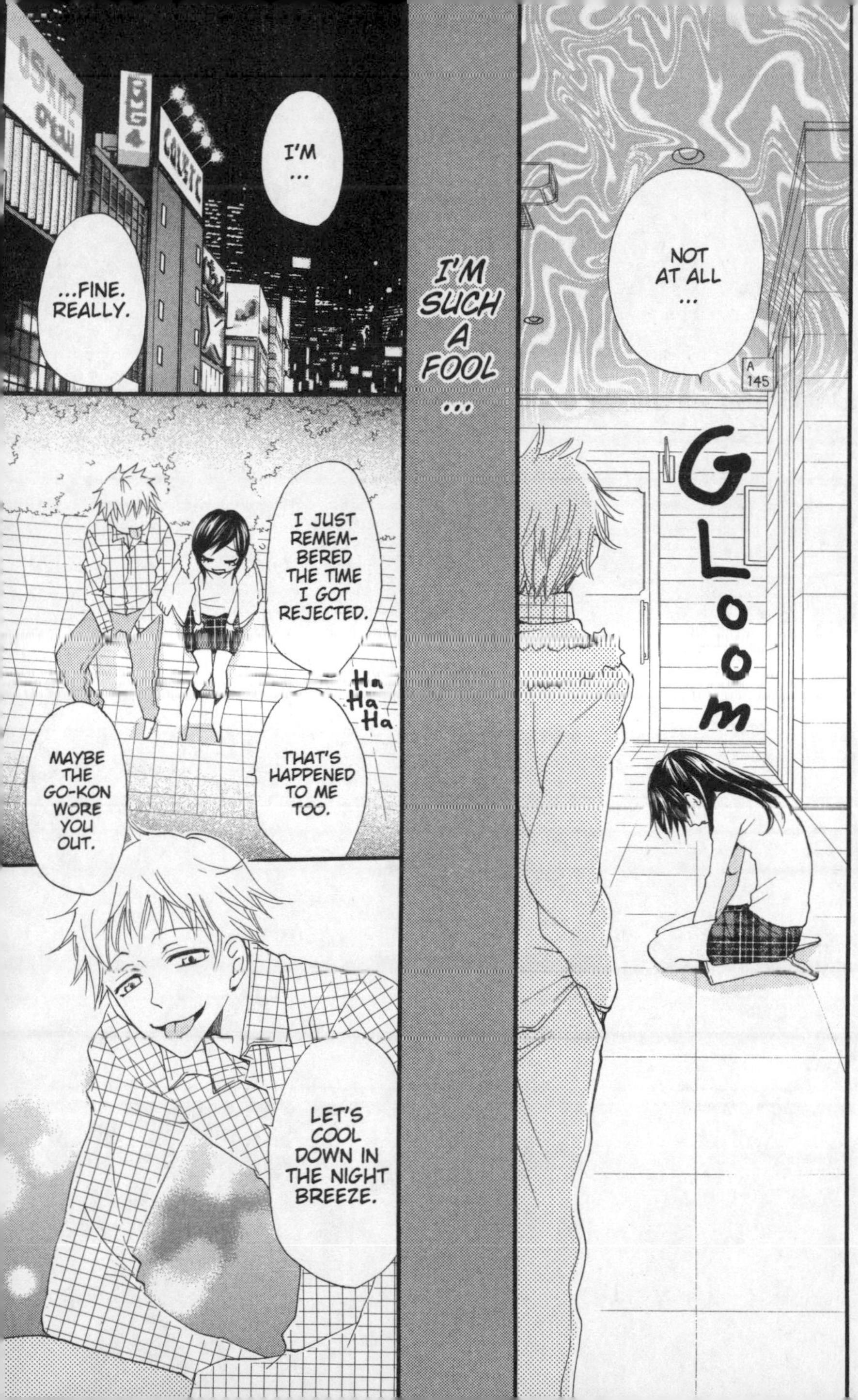
NOT AT ALL ...
A 145
GLOOM
I'M SUCH A FOOL ...
I'M ...
...FINE. REALLY.
I JUST REMEMBERED THE TIME I GOT REJECTED.
HA HA HA
THAT'S HAPPENED TO ME TOO.
MAYBE THE GO-KON WORE YOU OUT.
LET'S COOL DOWN IN THE NIGHT BREEZE.

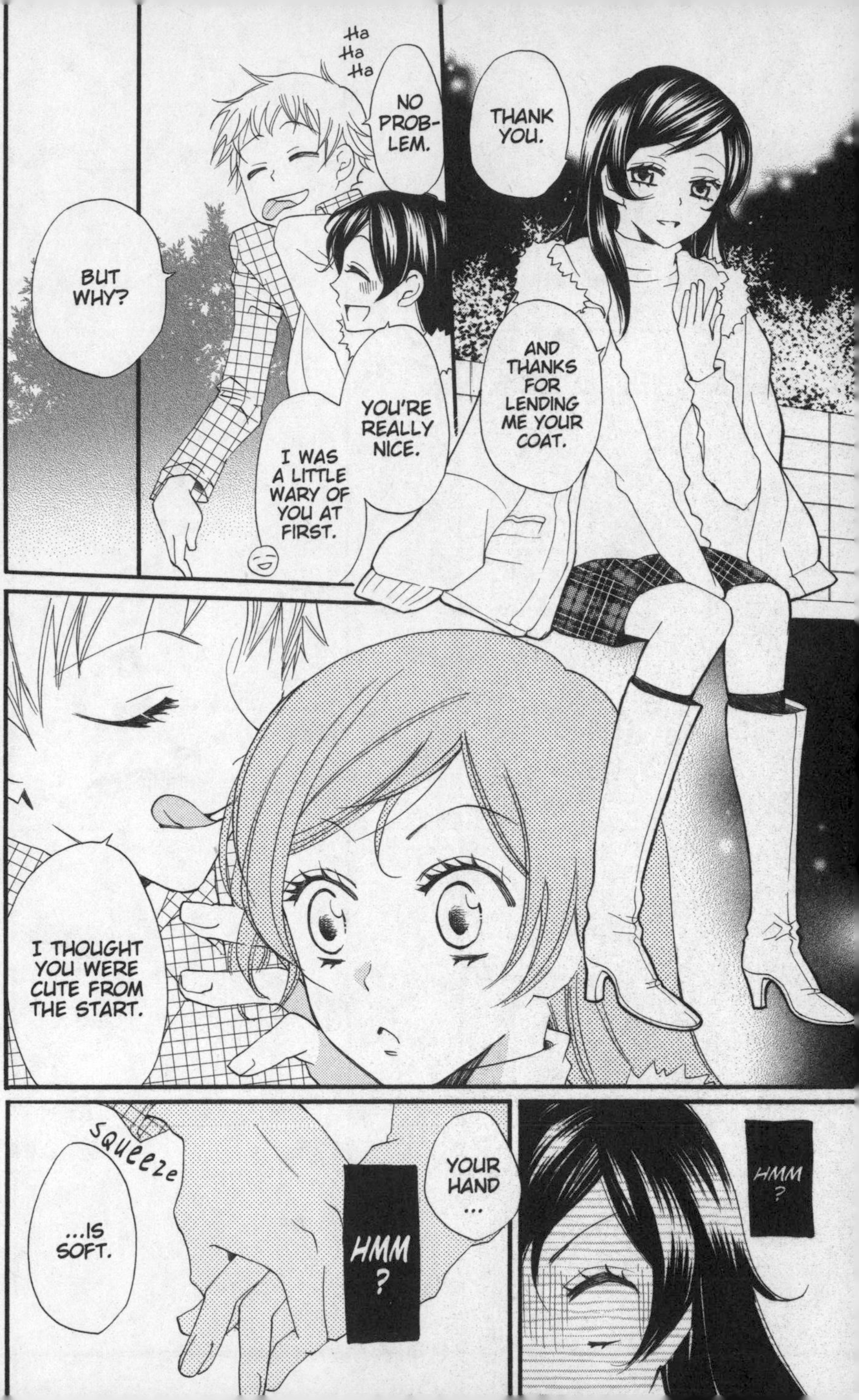
THANK YOU.
AND THANKS FOR LENDING ME YOUR COAT.
Ha Ha Ha
NO PROB-LEM.
YOU'RE REALLY NICE.
I WAS A LITTLE WARY OF YOU AT FIRST.
BUT WHY?
I THOUGHT YOU WERE CUTE FROM THE START.
HMM ?
YOUR HAND ...
HMM ?
squeeze
...IS SOFT.

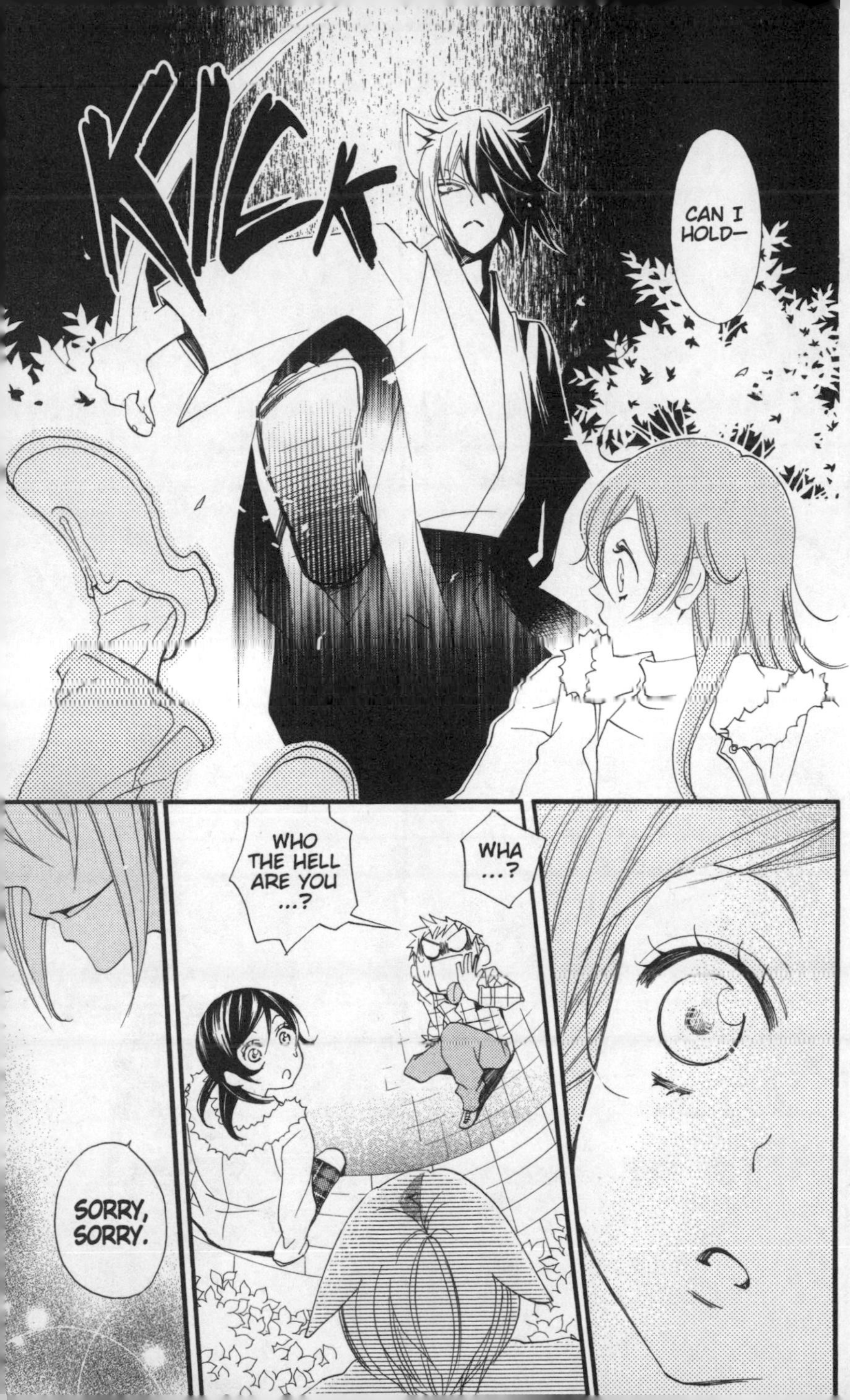
CAN I HOLD—
KICK
WHA ...?
WHO THE HELL ARE YOU ...?
SORRY, SORRY.

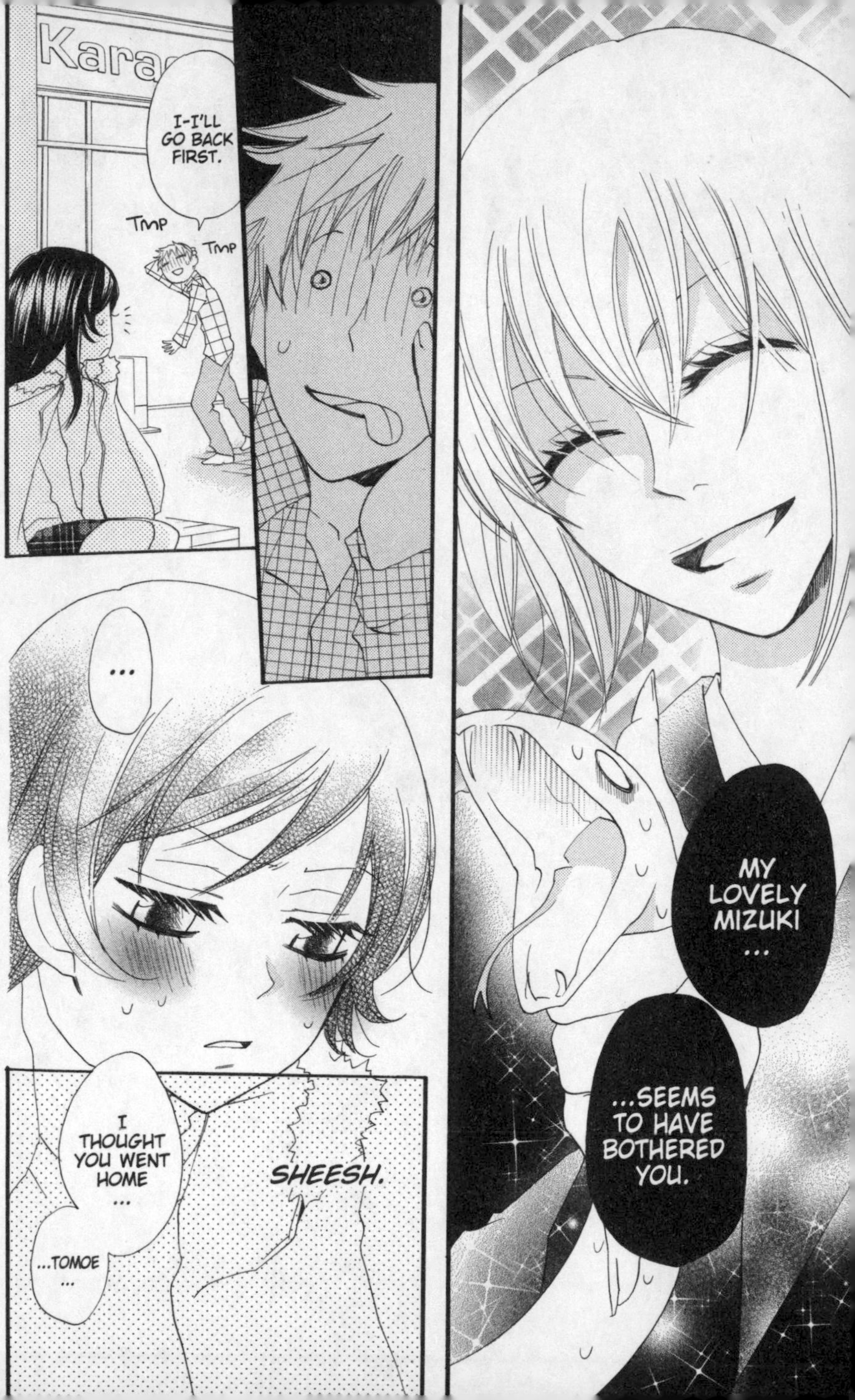
MY LOVELY MIZUKI ...
...SEEMS TO HAVE BOTHERED YOU.
I-I'LL GO BACK FIRST.
TMP
TMP
...
I THOUGHT YOU WENT HOME ...
...TOMOE ...
SHEESH.

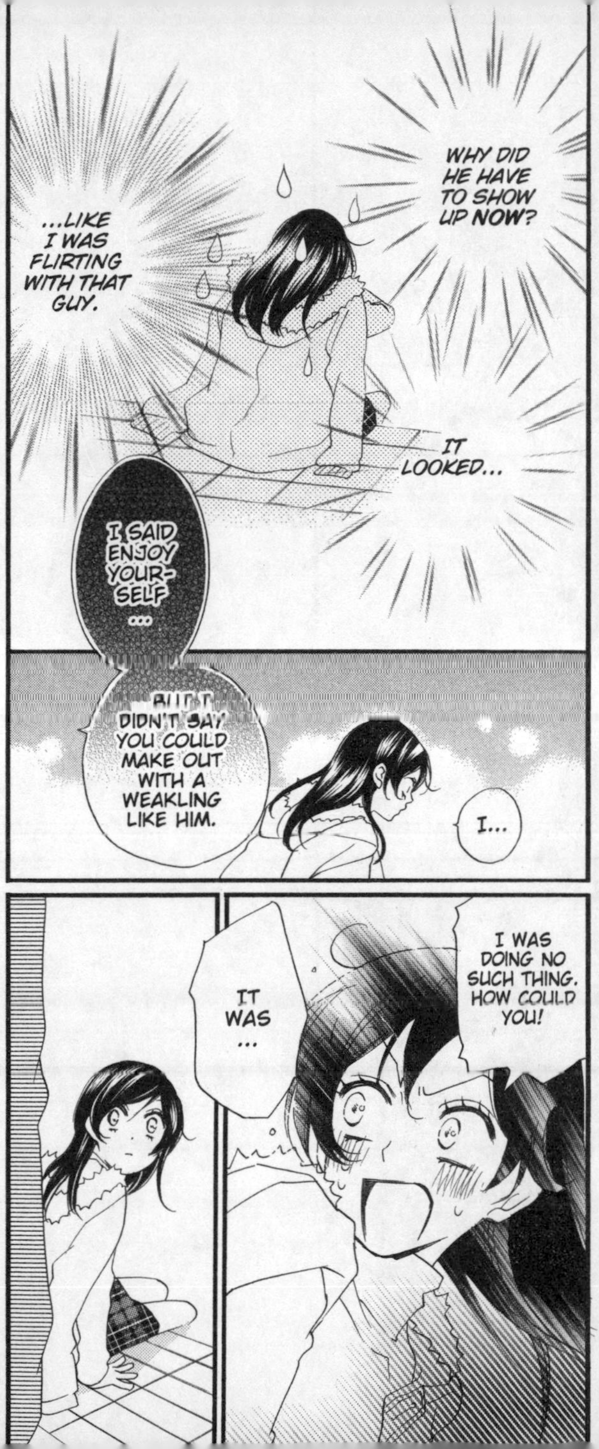
WHY DID HE HAVE TO SHOW UP NOW?
IT LOOKED...
...LIKE I WAS FLIRTING WITH THAT GUY.
I SAID ENJOY YOURSELF...
I...
BUT I DIDN'T SAY YOU COULD MAKE OUT WITH A WEAKLING LIKE HIM.
I WAS DOING NO SUCH THING. HOW COULD YOU!
IT WAS...

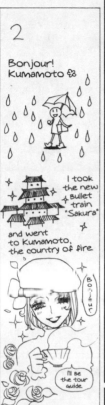

2

Bonjour! Kumamoto ✿

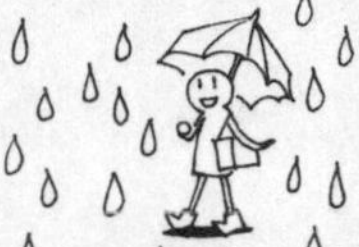

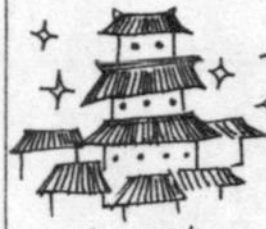

I took the new Bullet train "Sakura" and went to Kumamoto, the country of fire.

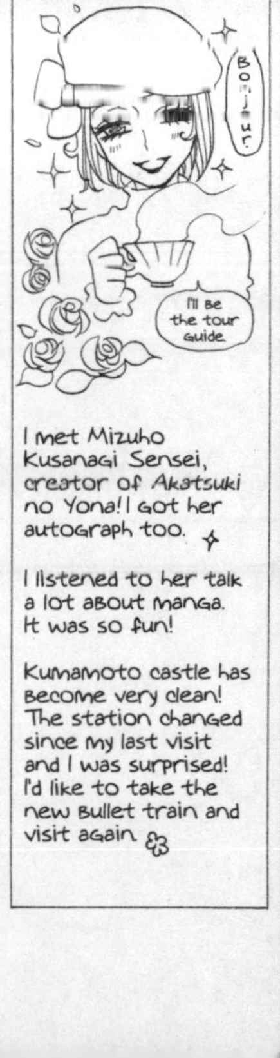
Bonjour.
I'll be the tour guide.

I met Mizuho Kusanagi Sensei, creator of Akatsuki no Yona! I got her autograph too.

I listened to her talk a lot about manga. It was so fun!

Kumamoto castle has become very clean! The station changed since my last visit and I was surprised! I'd like to take the new bullet train and visit again. ✿

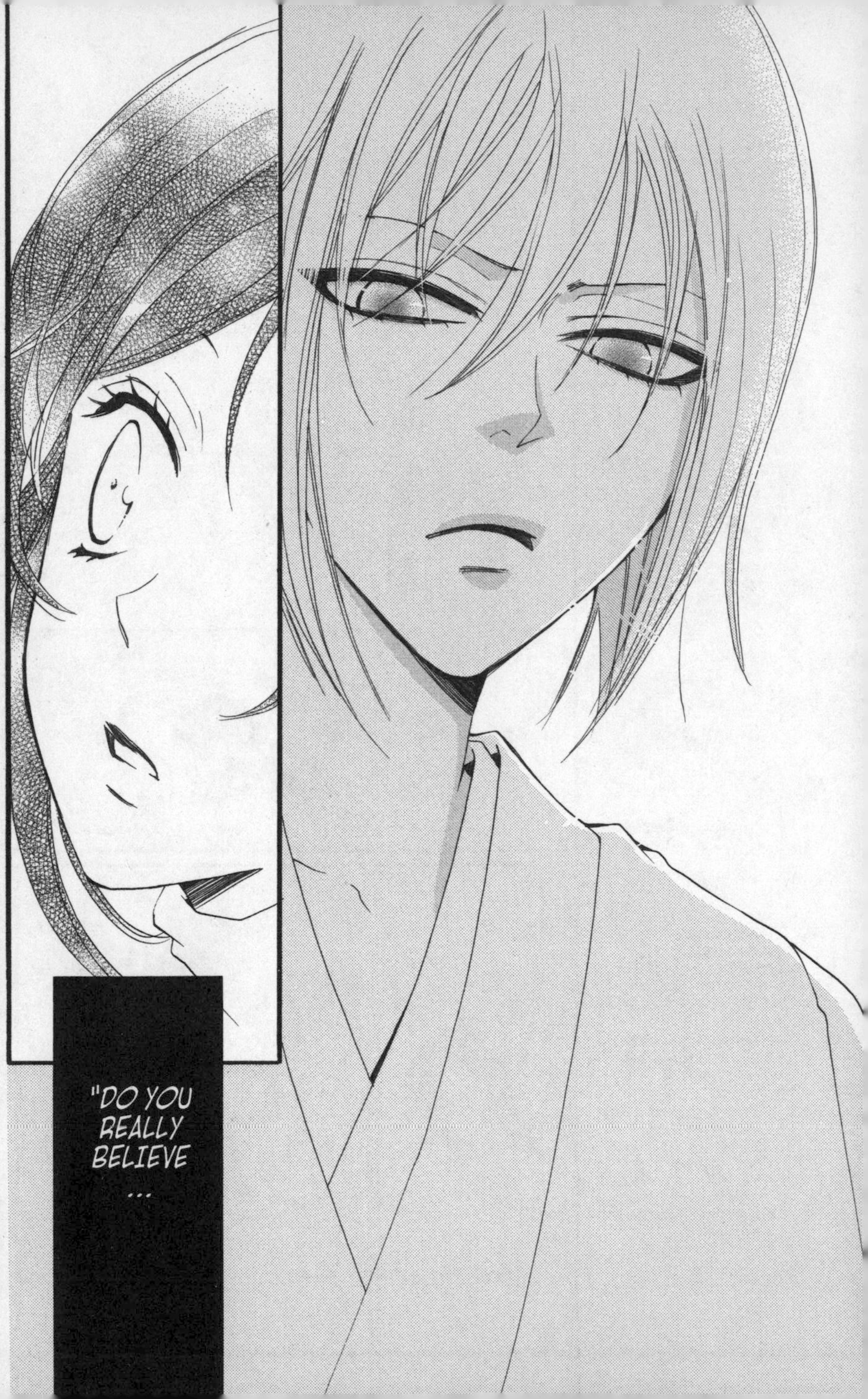
"DO YOU REALLY BELIEVE ...

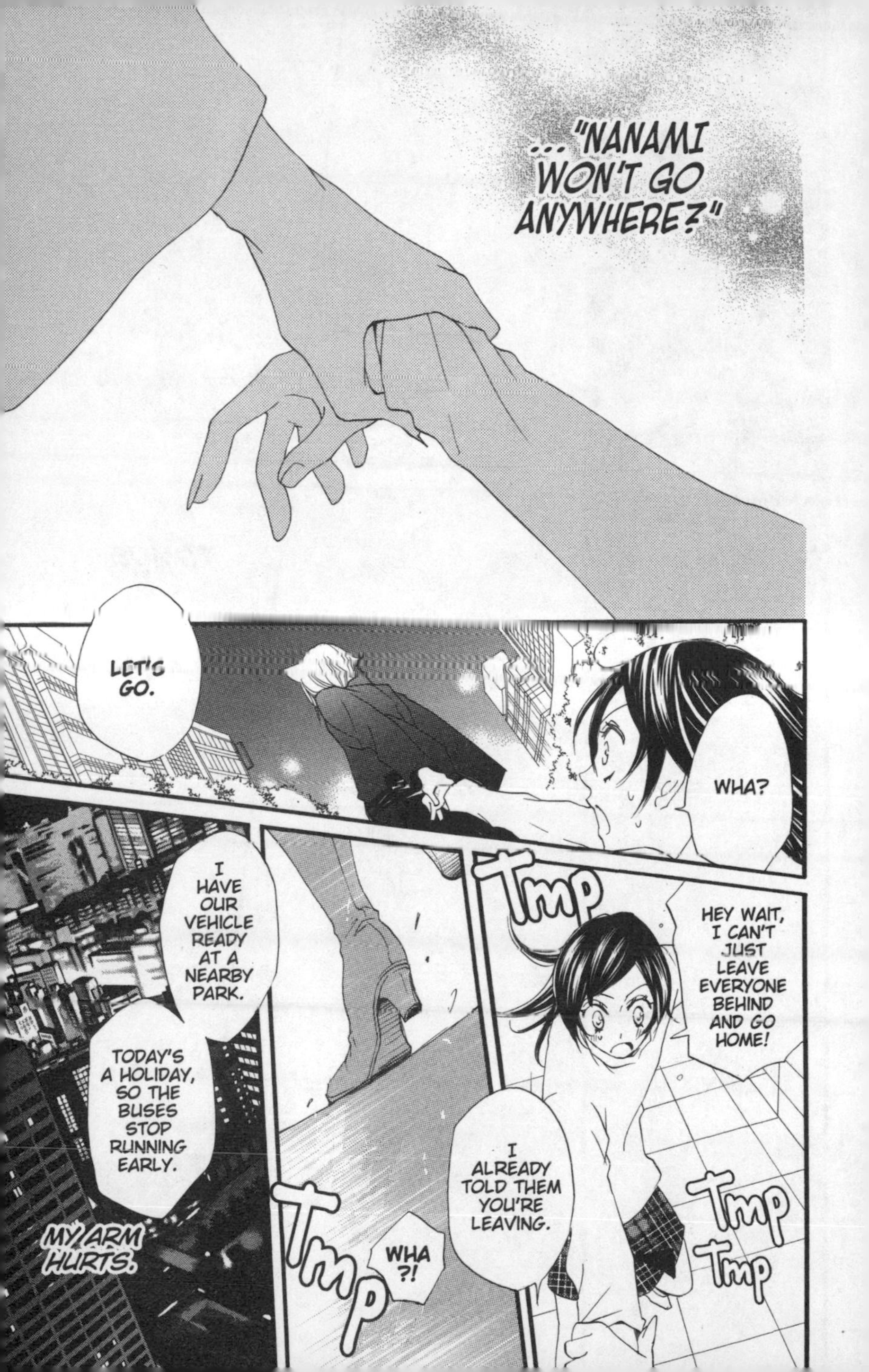
..."NANAMI WON'T GO ANYWHERE?"
LET'S GO.
WHA?
Tmp
HEY WAIT, I CAN'T JUST LEAVE EVERYONE BEHIND AND GO HOME!
I ALREADY TOLD THEM YOU'RE LEAVING.
Tmp
Tmp
WHA ?!
Tmp
I HAVE OUR VEHICLE READY AT A NEARBY PARK.
TODAY'S A HOLIDAY, SO THE BUSES STOP RUNNING EARLY.
MY ARM HURTS.

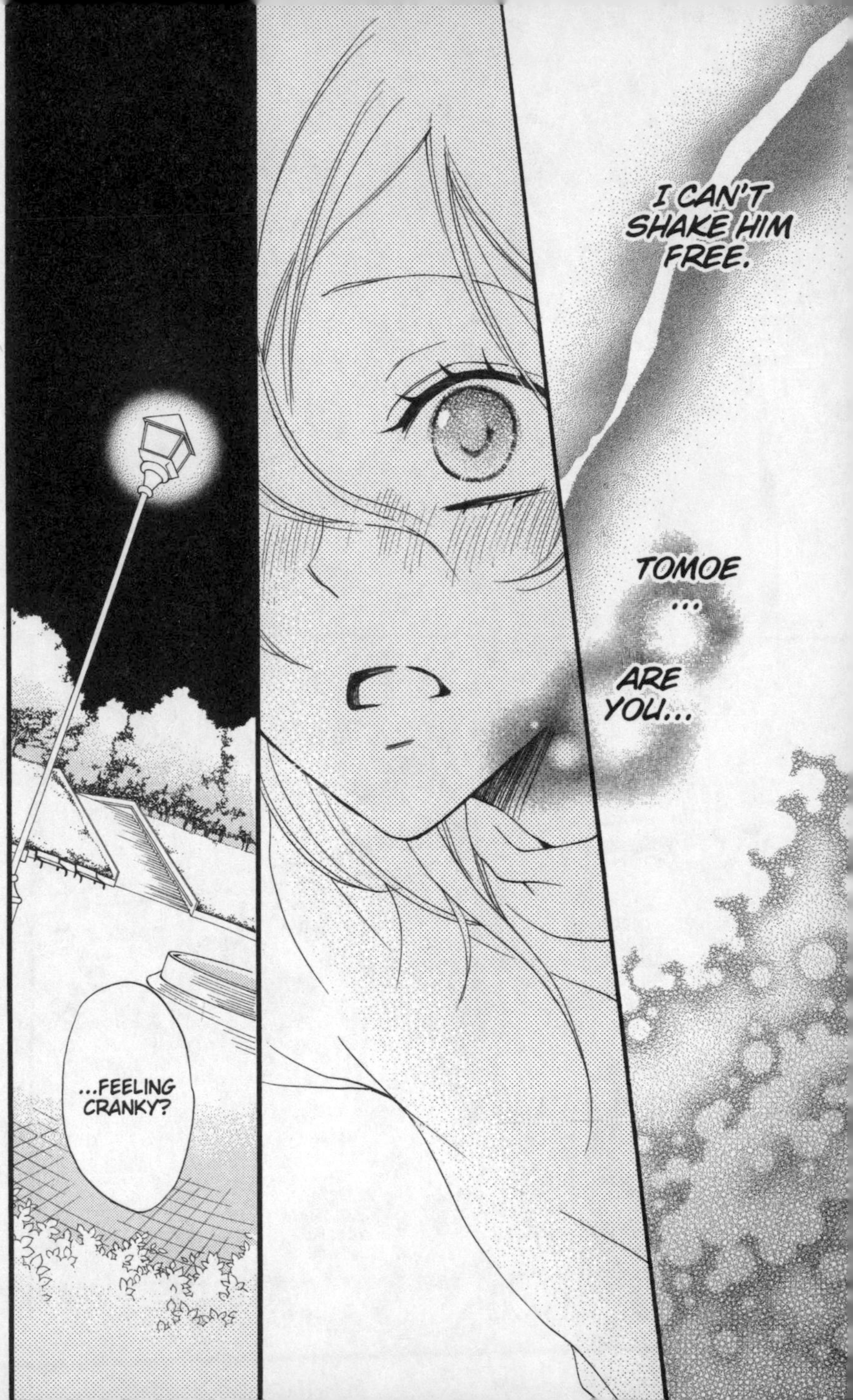
I CAN'T SHAKE HIM FREE.
TOMOE ...
ARE YOU...
...FEELING CRANKY?

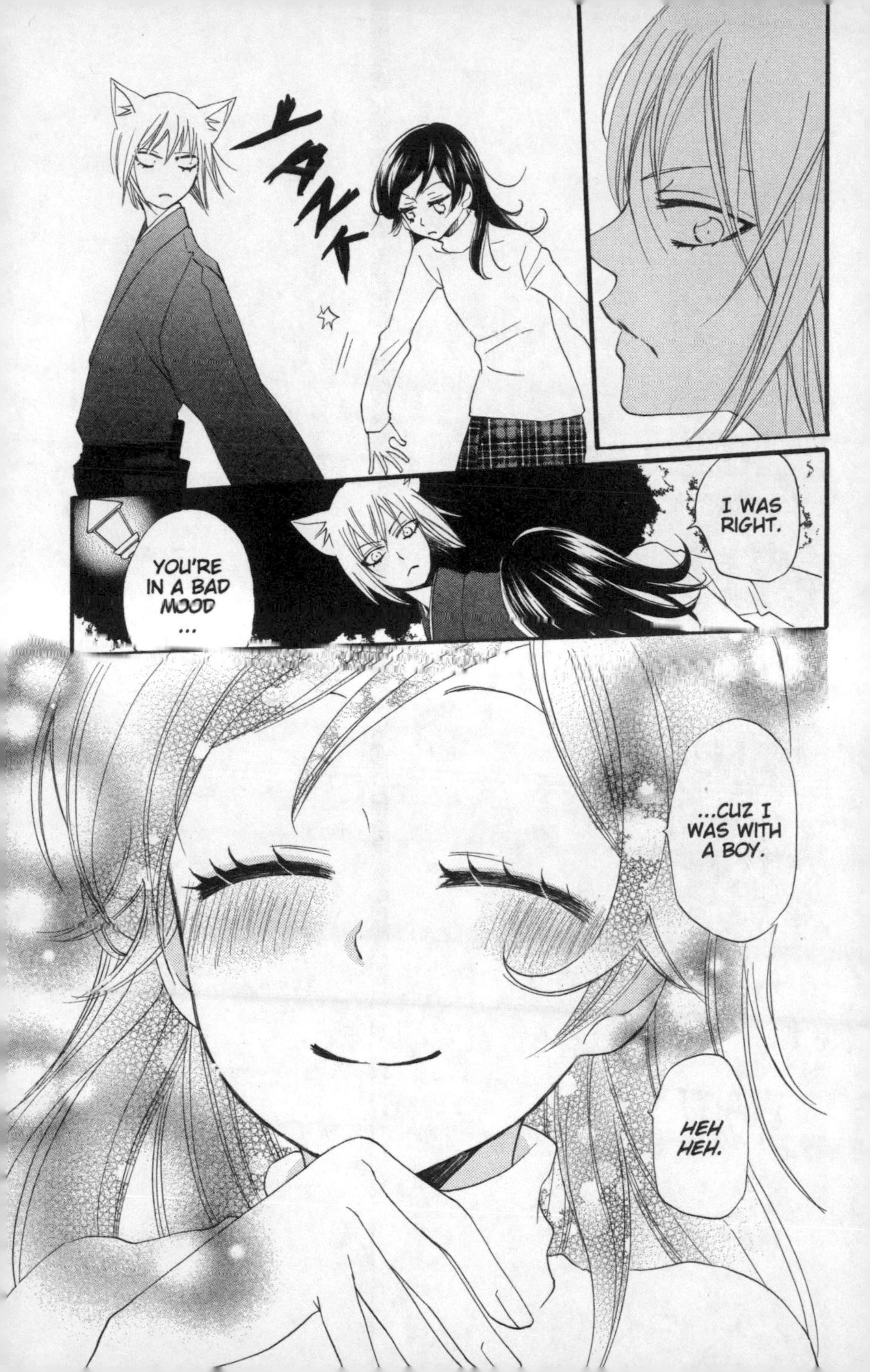
YANK
I WAS RIGHT.
YOU'RE IN A BAD MOOD ...
...CUZ I WAS WITH A BOY.
HEH HEH.

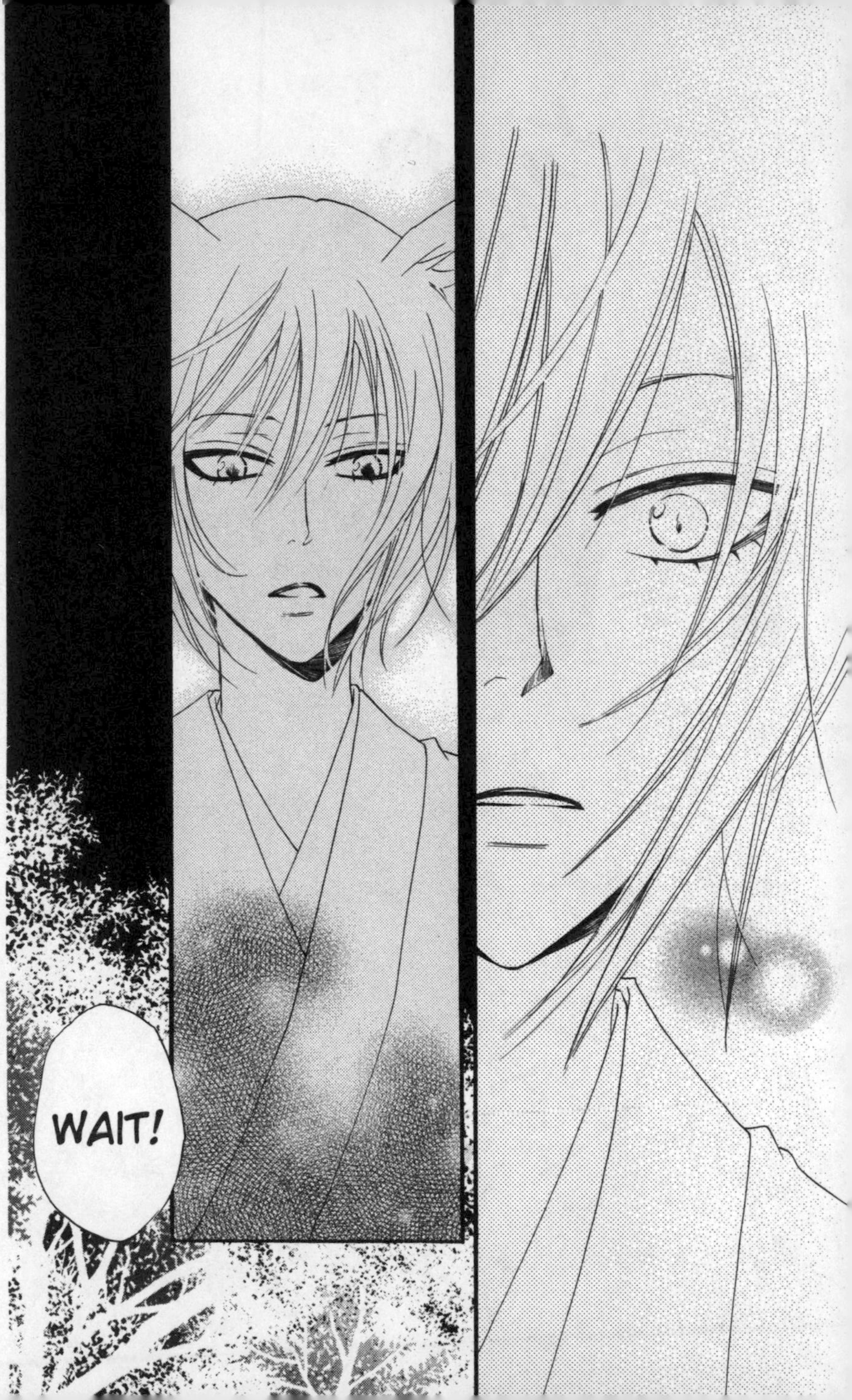
WAIT!

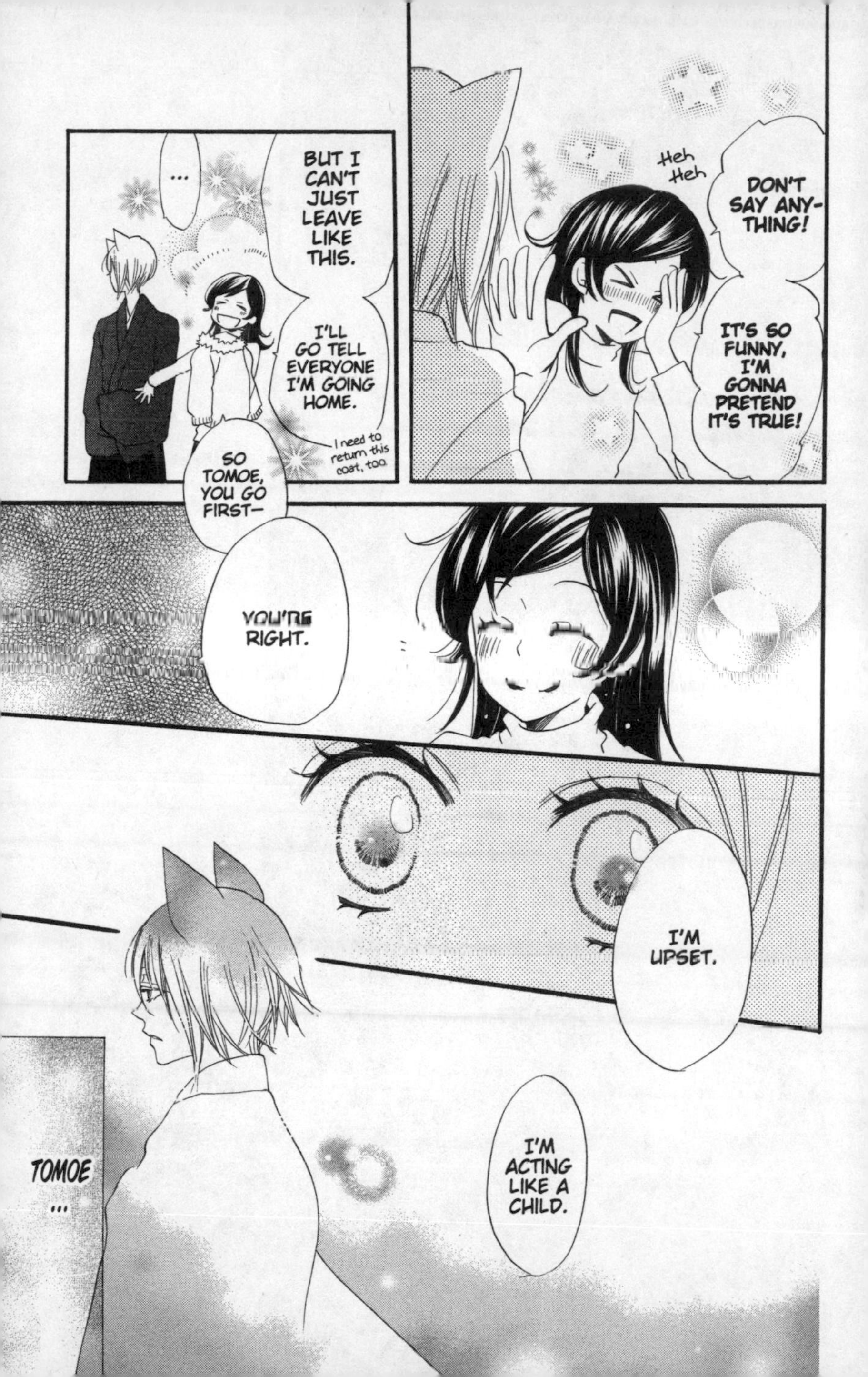
Heh Heh
DON'T SAY ANY-THING!
IT'S SO FUNNY, I'M GONNA PRETEND IT'S TRUE!
...
BUT I CAN'T JUST LEAVE LIKE THIS.
I'LL GO TELL EVERYONE I'M GOING HOME.
I need to return this coat, too.
SO TOMOE, YOU GO FIRST—
YOU'RE RIGHT.
I'M UPSET.
I'M ACTING LIKE A CHILD.
TOMOE ...

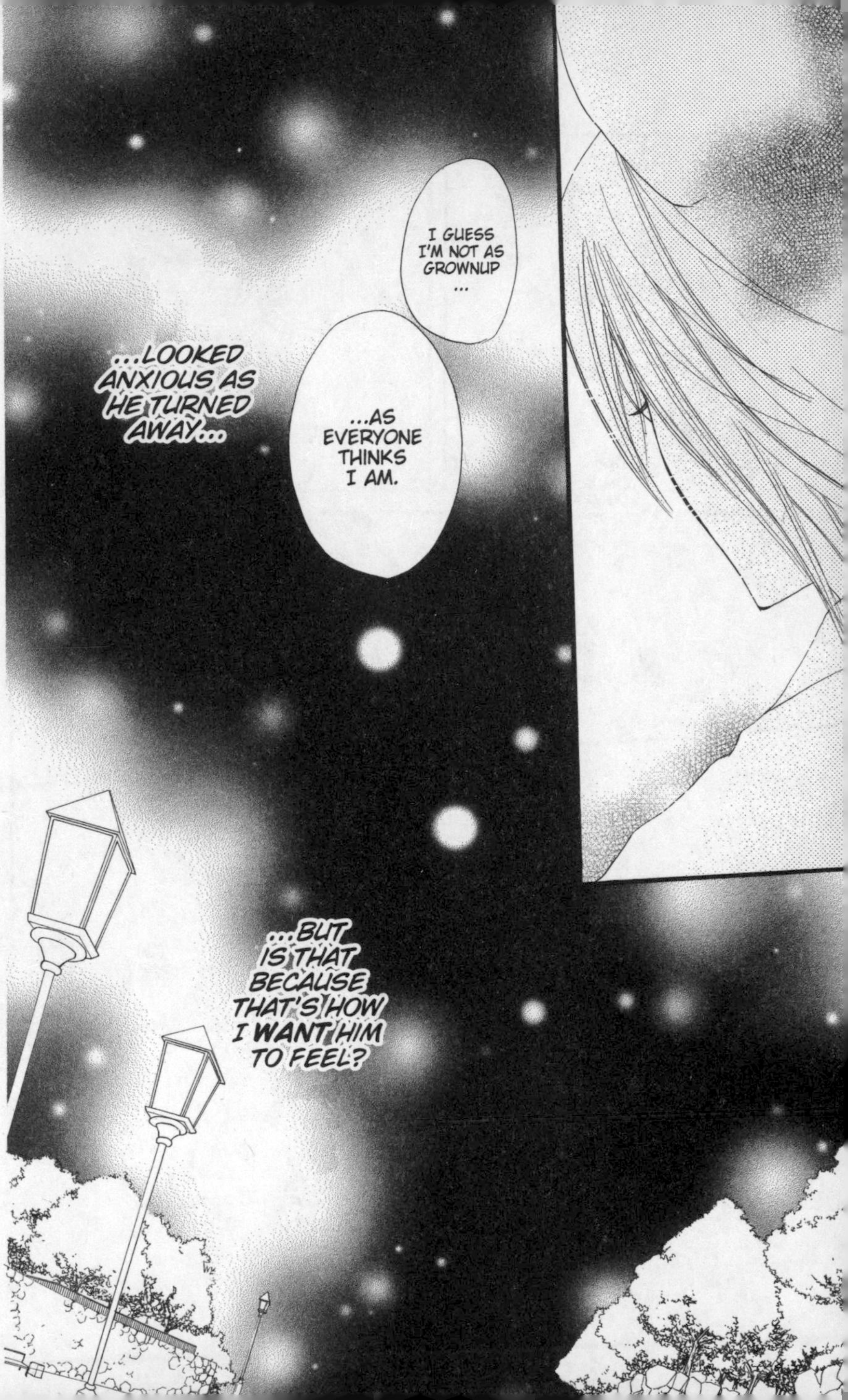
I GUESS I'M NOT AS GROWNUP ...
...AS EVERYONE THINKS I AM.
...LOOKED ANXIOUS AS HE TURNED AWAY...
...BUT IS THAT BECAUSE THAT'S HOW I WANT HIM TO FEEL?

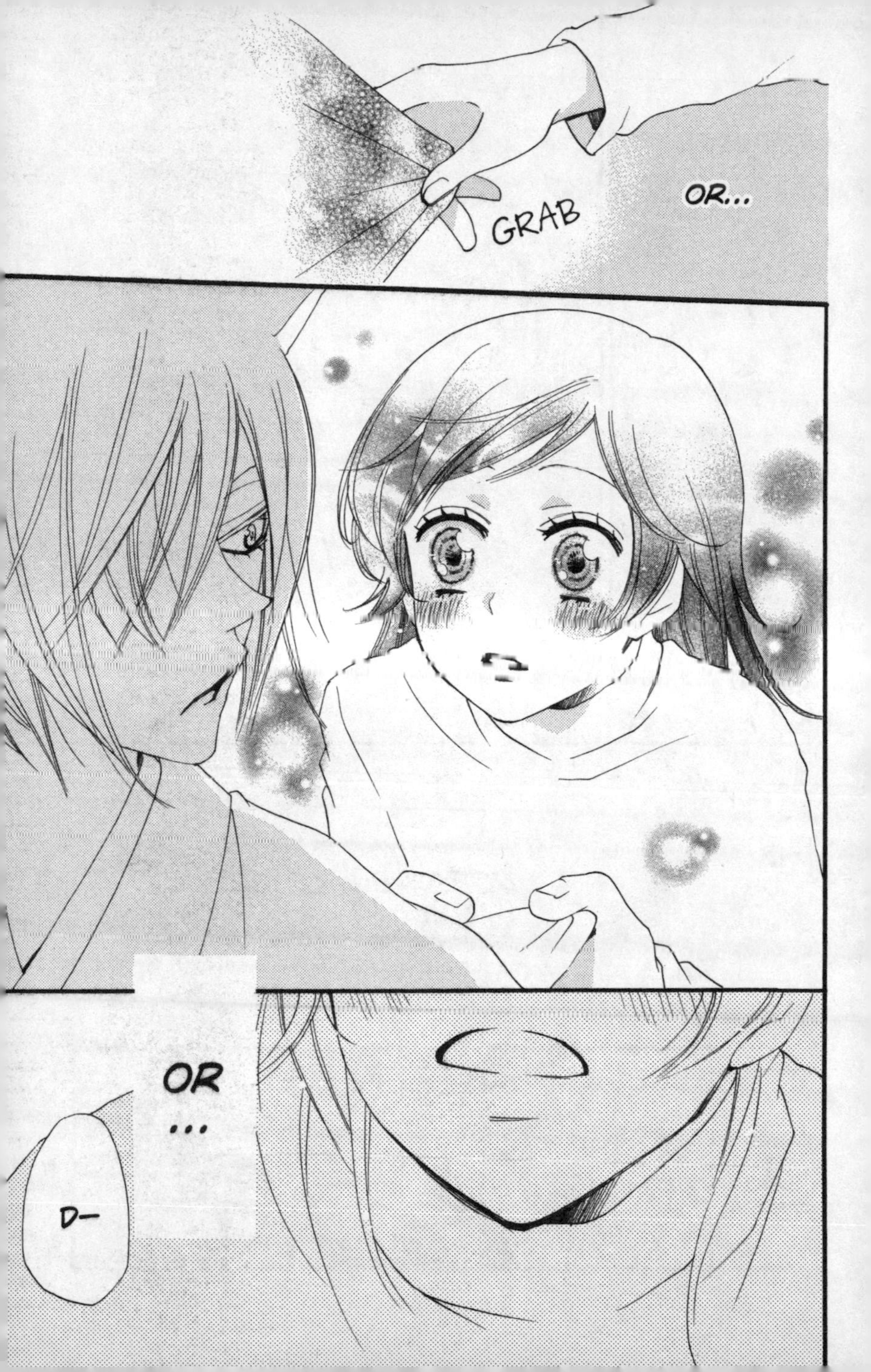
OR...
GRAB
OR
...
D–

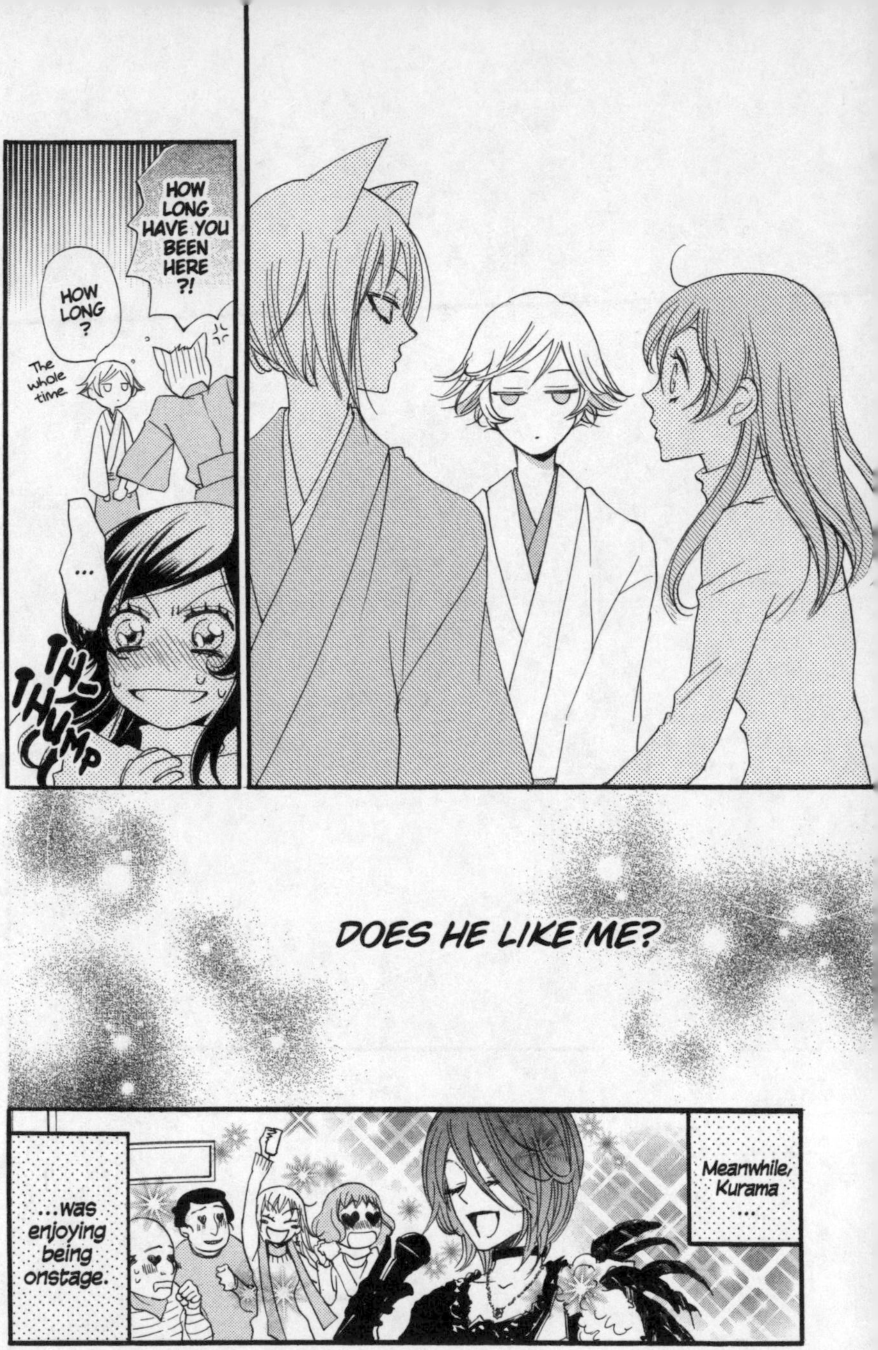
HOW LONG HAVE YOU BEEN HERE ?!
HOW LONG ?
The whole time
...
TH-THUMP
DOES HE LIKE ME?
Meanwhile, Kurama ...
...was enjoying being onstage.

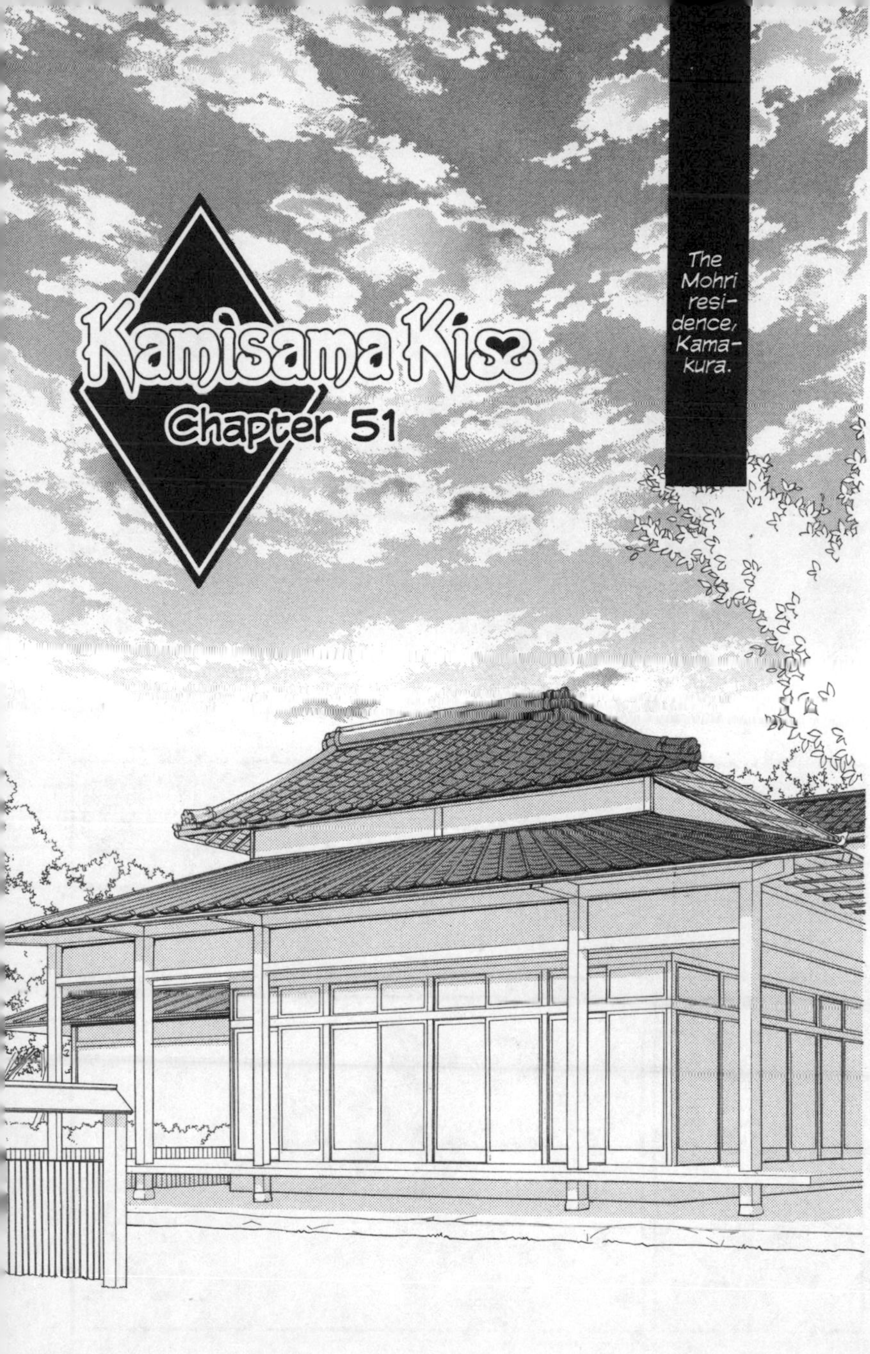
The Mohri residence, Kamakura.
Kamisama Kiss
Chapter 51

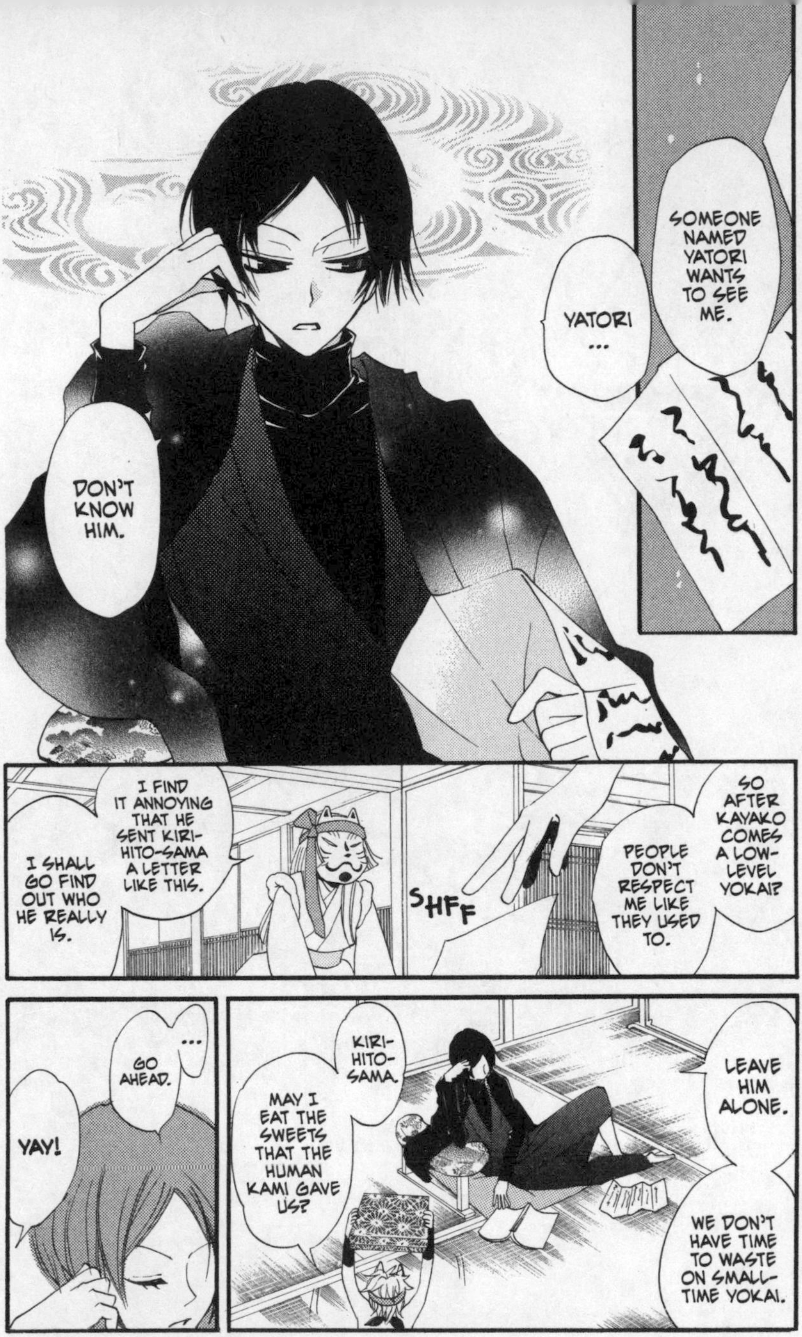
SOMEONE NAMED YATORI WANTS TO SEE ME.
YATORI ...
DON'T KNOW HIM.
SO AFTER KAYAKO COMES A LOW-LEVEL YOKAI?
PEOPLE DON'T RESPECT ME LIKE THEY USED TO.
SHFF
I FIND IT ANNOYING THAT HE SENT KIRI-HITO-SAMA A LETTER LIKE THIS.
I SHALL GO FIND OUT WHO HE REALLY IS.
LEAVE HIM ALONE.
WE DON'T HAVE TIME TO WASTE ON SMALL-TIME YOKAI.
KIRI-HITO-SAMA.
MAY I EAT THE SWEETS THAT THE HUMAN KAMI GAVE US?
...
GO AHEAD.
YAY!

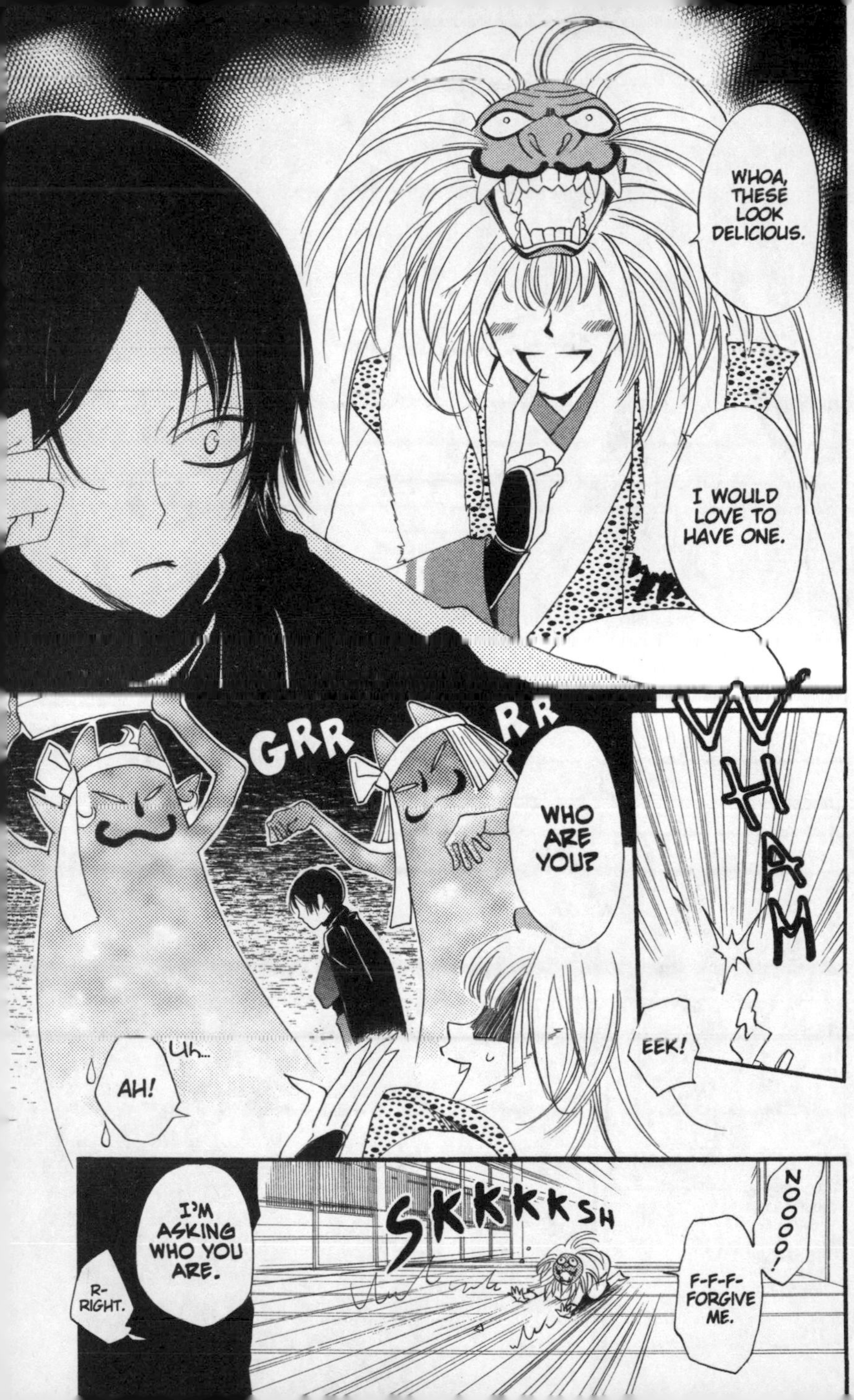
WHOA, THESE LOOK DELICIOUS.
I WOULD LOVE TO HAVE ONE.
WHAM
EEK!
GRR RR
WHO ARE YOU?
Uh...
AH!
NOOOOO!
F-F-F-FORGIVE ME.
SKKKKSH
I'M ASKING WHO YOU ARE.
R-RIGHT.

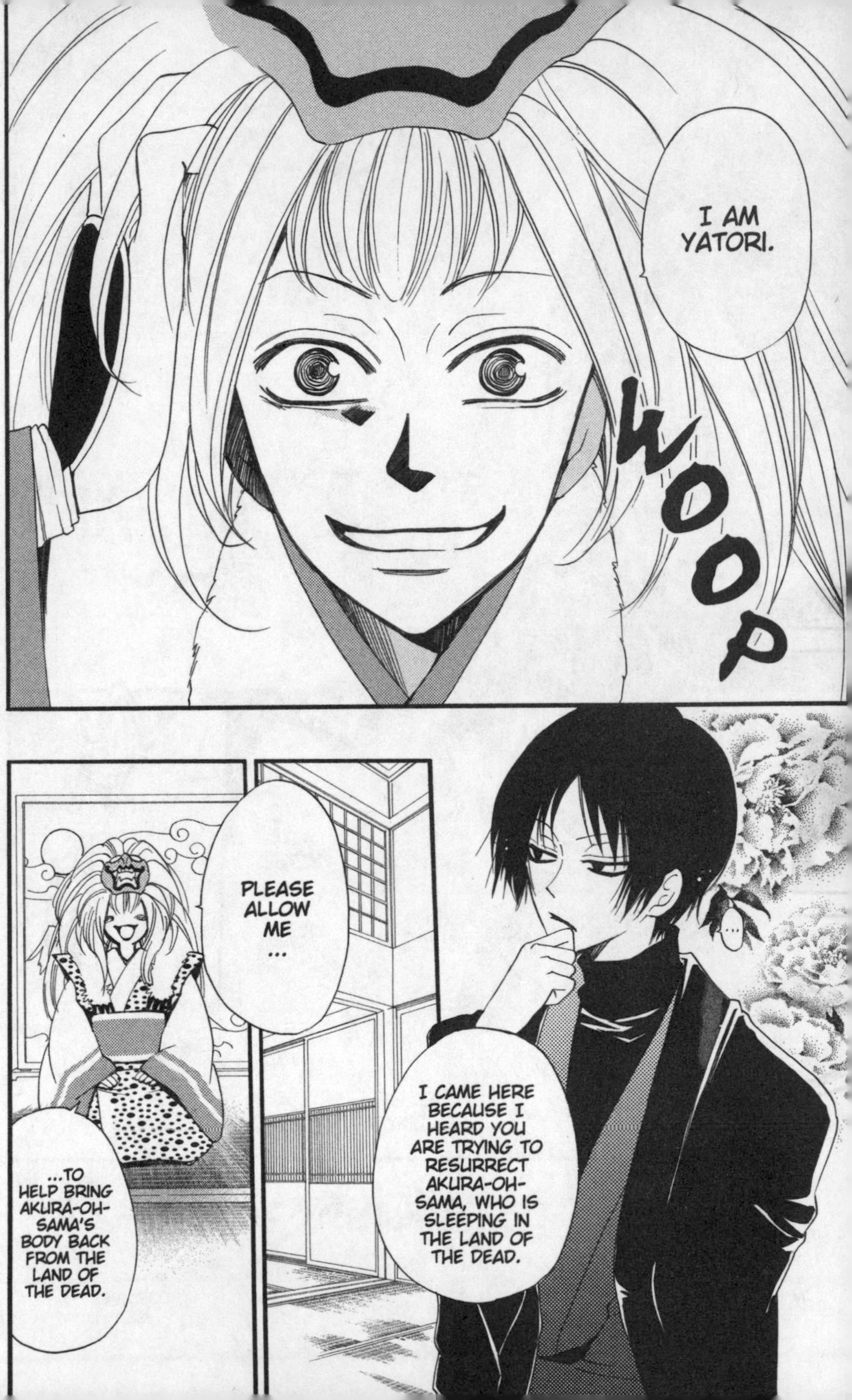
I AM YATORI.
WOOP
...
I CAME HERE BECAUSE I HEARD YOU ARE TRYING TO RESURRECT AKURA-OH-SAMA, WHO IS SLEEPING IN THE LAND OF THE DEAD.
PLEASE ALLOW ME ...
...TO HELP BRING AKURA-OH-SAMA'S BODY BACK FROM THE LAND OF THE DEAD.

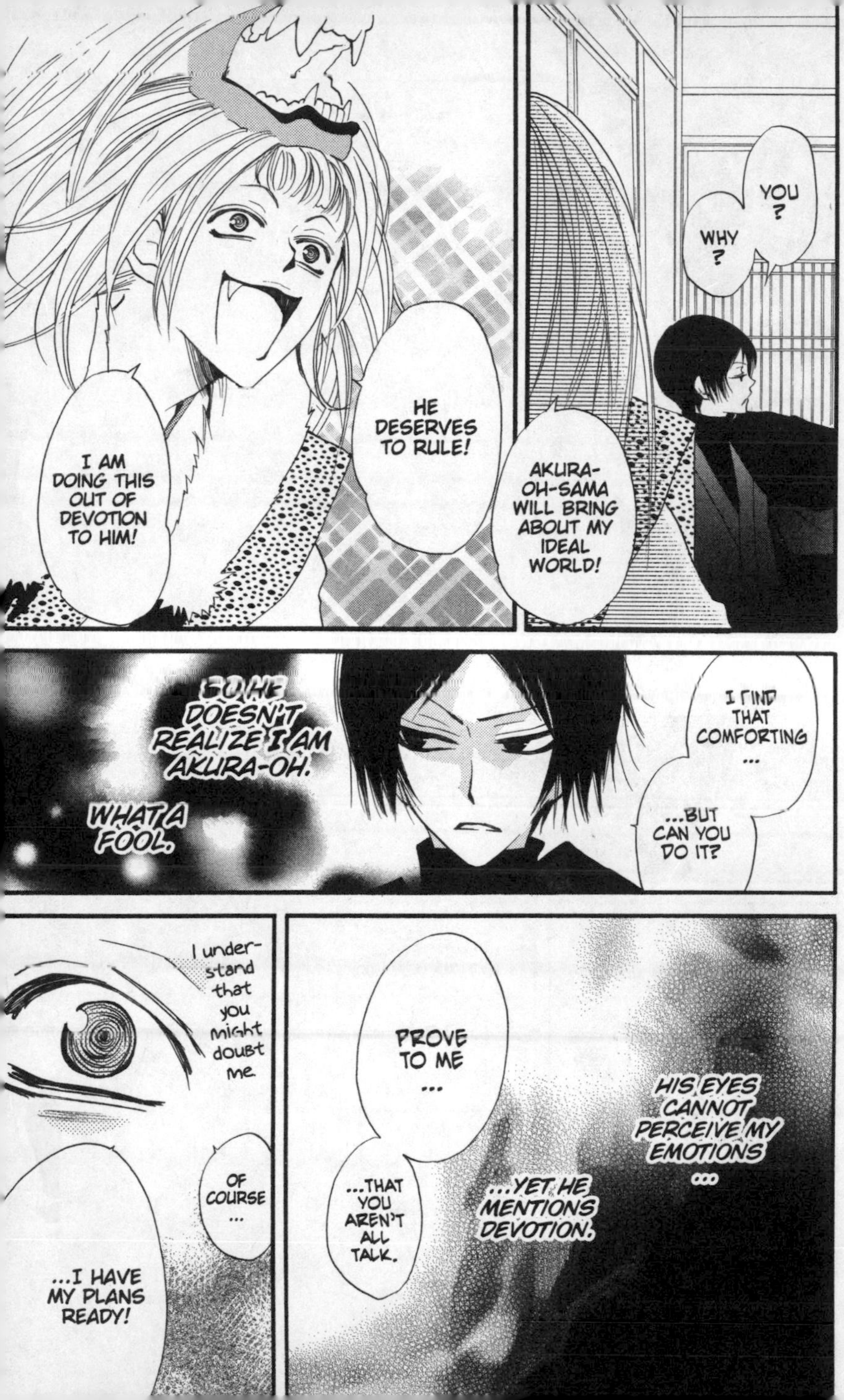
YOU?
WHY?
AKURA-OH-SAMA WILL BRING ABOUT MY IDEAL WORLD!
HE DESERVES TO RULE!
I AM DOING THIS OUT OF DEVOTION TO HIM!
I FIND THAT COMFORTING...
...BUT CAN YOU DO IT?
SO HE DOESN'T REALIZE I AM AKURA-OH.
WHAT A FOOL.
HIS EYES CANNOT PERCEIVE MY EMOTIONS...
PROVE TO ME...
...YET HE MENTIONS DEVOTION.
...THAT YOU AREN'T ALL TALK.
I understand that you might doubt me.
OF COURSE...
...I HAVE MY PLANS READY!

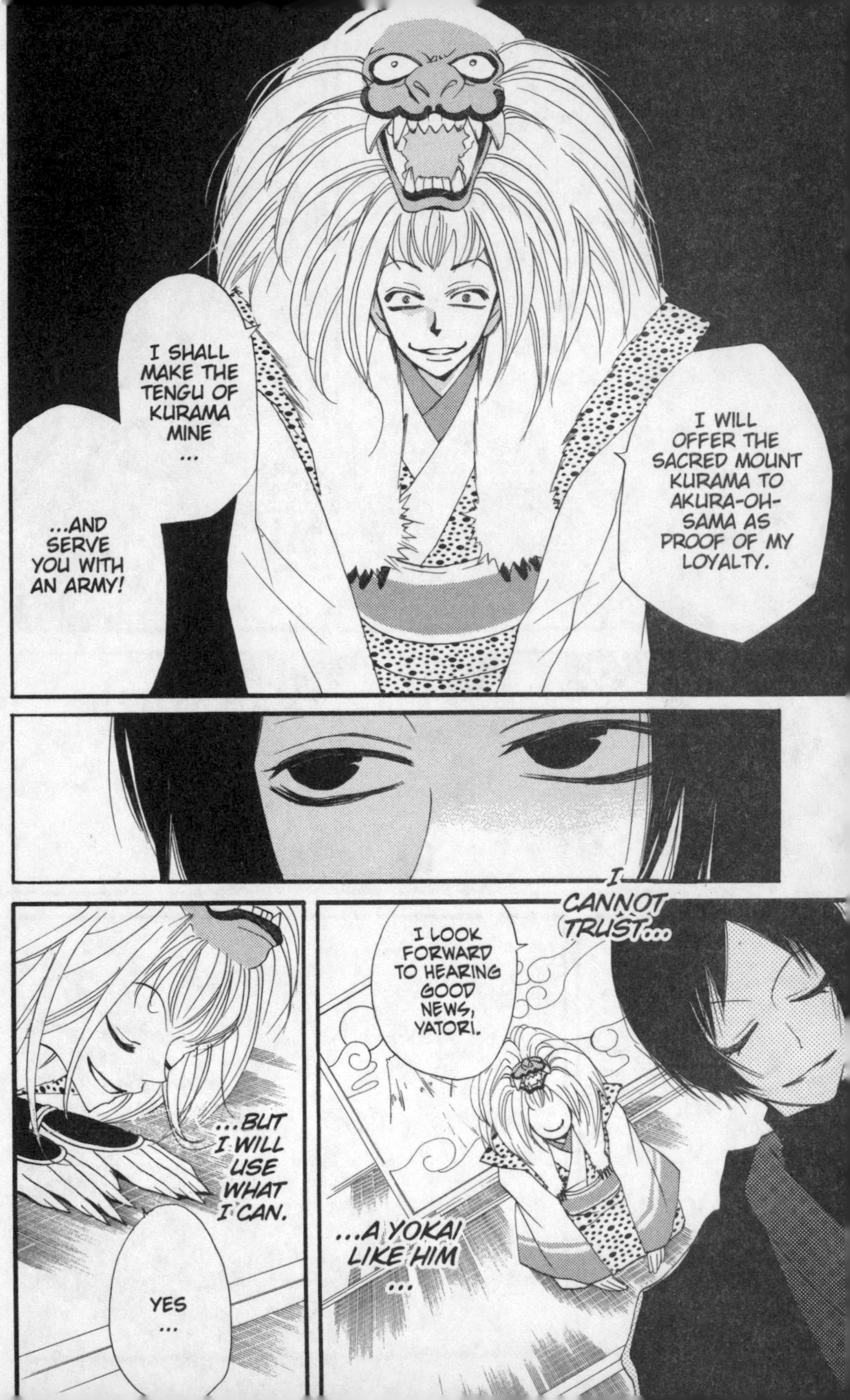
I WILL OFFER THE SACRED MOUNT KURAMA TO AKURA-OH-SAMA AS PROOF OF MY LOYALTY.
I SHALL MAKE THE TENGU OF KURAMA MINE ...
...AND SERVE YOU WITH AN ARMY!
I CANNOT TRUST...
I LOOK FORWARD TO HEARING GOOD NEWS, YATORI.
...A YOKAI LIKE HIM ...
...BUT I WILL USE WHAT I CAN.
YES ...

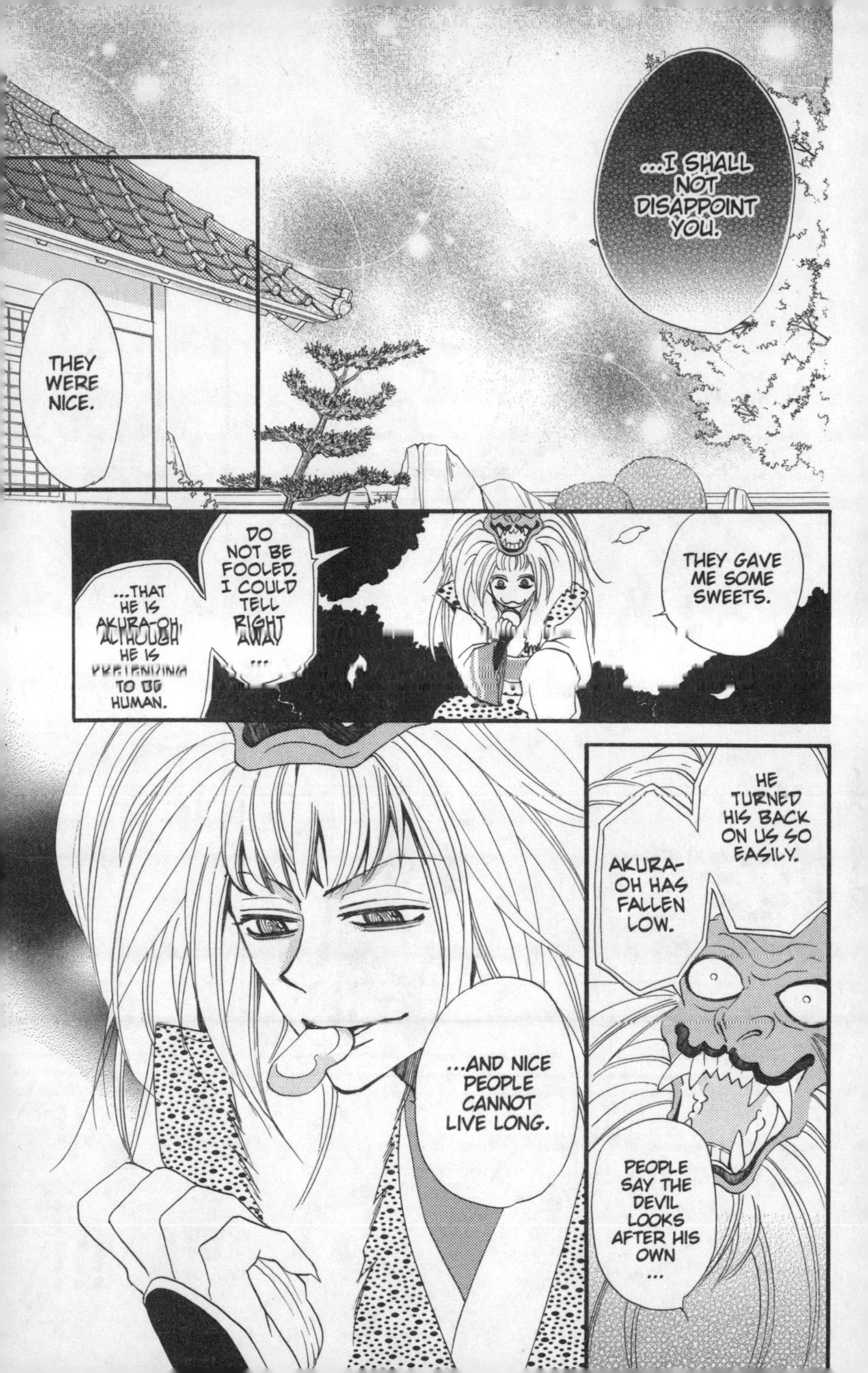
...I SHALL NOT DISAPPOINT YOU.
THEY WERE NICE.
THEY GAVE ME SOME SWEETS.
DO NOT BE FOOLED. I COULD TELL RIGHT AWAY...
...THAT HE IS AKURA-OH, ALTHOUGH HE IS PRETENDING TO BE HUMAN.
HE TURNED HIS BACK ON US SO EASILY.
AKURA-OH HAS FALLEN LOW.
PEOPLE SAY THE DEVIL LOOKS AFTER HIS OWN...
...AND NICE PEOPLE CANNOT LIVE LONG.

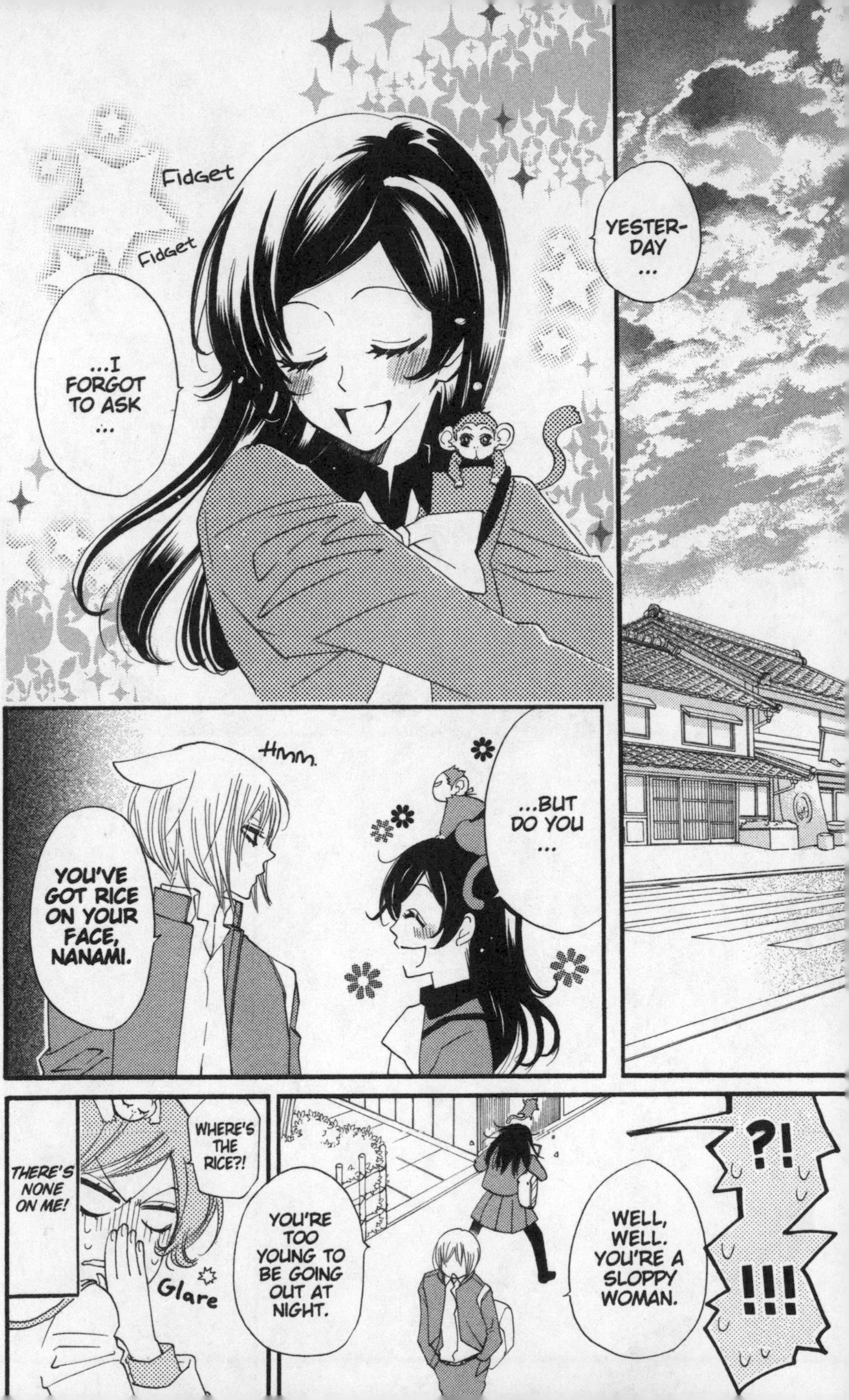
YESTER-DAY ...
Fidget
Fidget
...I FORGOT TO ASK ...
...BUT DO YOU ...
Hmm.
YOU'VE GOT RICE ON YOUR FACE, NANAMI.
?!
!!!
WELL, WELL. YOU'RE A SLOPPY WOMAN.
YOU'RE TOO YOUNG TO BE GOING OUT AT NIGHT.
WHERE'S THE RICE?!
THERE'S NONE ON ME!
Glare

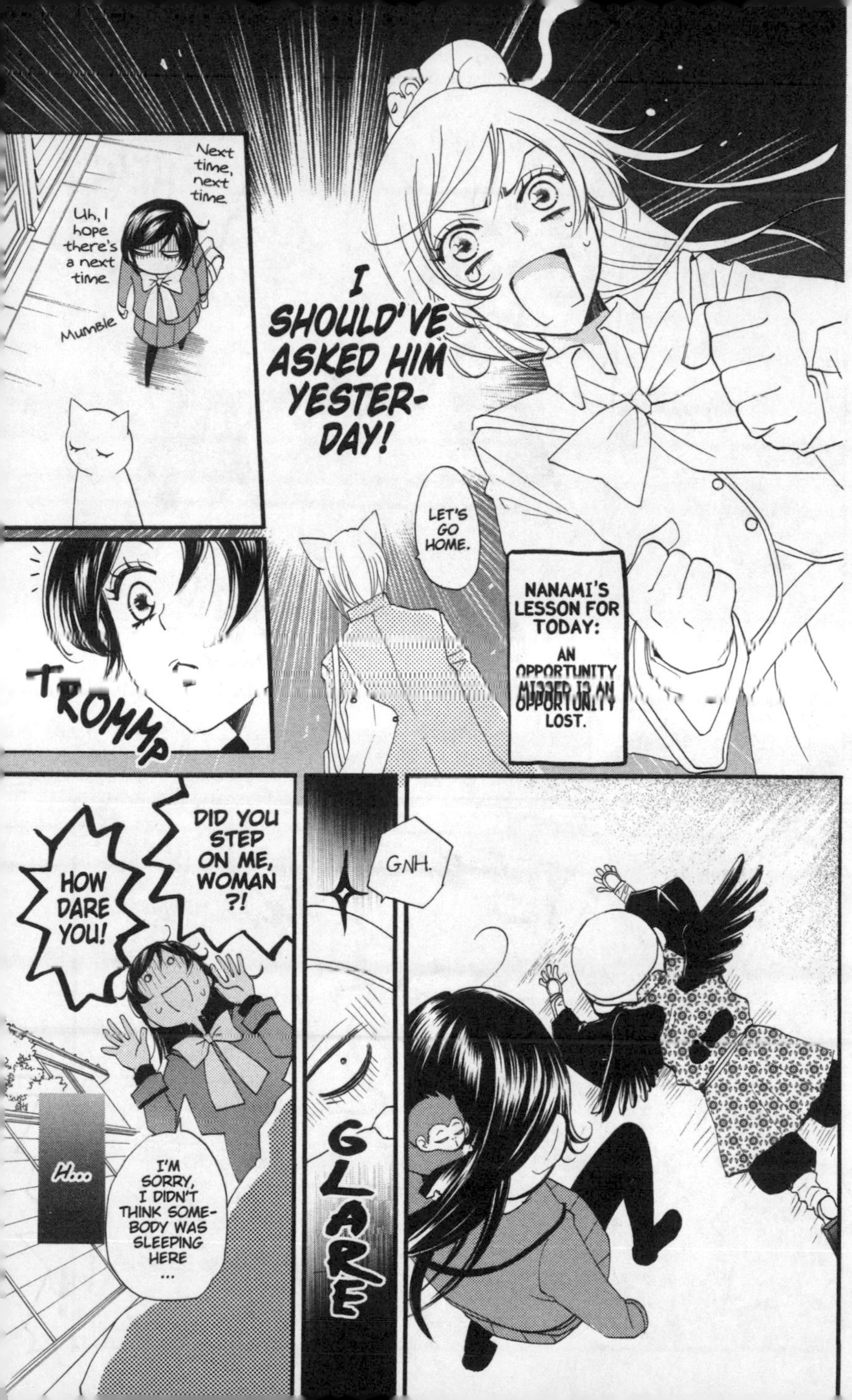
I SHOULD'VE ASKED HIM YESTER-DAY!
LET'S GO HOME.
NANAMI'S LESSON FOR TODAY: AN OPPORTUNITY MISSED IS AN OPPORTUNITY LOST.
Next time, next time.
Uh, I hope there's a next time.
Mumble
TROMMP
GNH.
GLARE
DID YOU STEP ON ME, WOMAN?!
HOW DARE YOU!
I'M SORRY, I DIDN'T THINK SOME-BODY WAS SLEEPING HERE...
H...

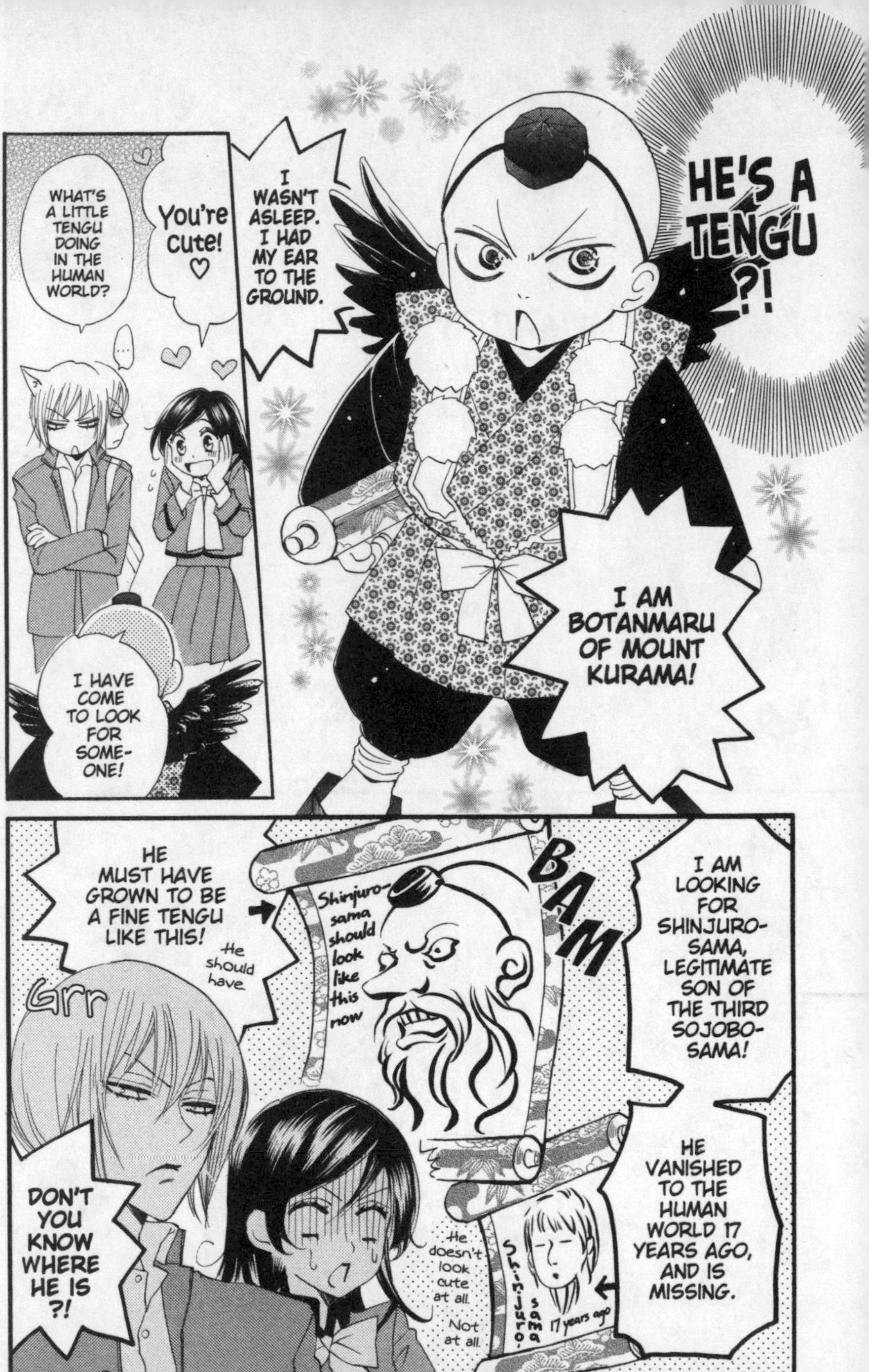
HE'S A TENGU ?!
I AM BOTANMARU OF MOUNT KURAMA!
I WASN'T ASLEEP. I HAD MY EAR TO THE GROUND.
You're cute! ♡
WHAT'S A LITTLE TENGU DOING IN THE HUMAN WORLD?
...
I HAVE COME TO LOOK FOR SOME-ONE!
I AM LOOKING FOR SHINJURO-SAMA, LEGITIMATE SON OF THE THIRD SOJOBO-SAMA!
BAM
Shinjuro-sama should look like this now
HE MUST HAVE GROWN TO BE A FINE TENGU LIKE THIS!
He should have.
Grr
HE VANISHED TO THE HUMAN WORLD 17 YEARS AGO, AND IS MISSING.
17 years ago
Shinjuro-sama
He doesn't look cute at all.
Not at all.
DON'T YOU KNOW WHERE HE IS ?!

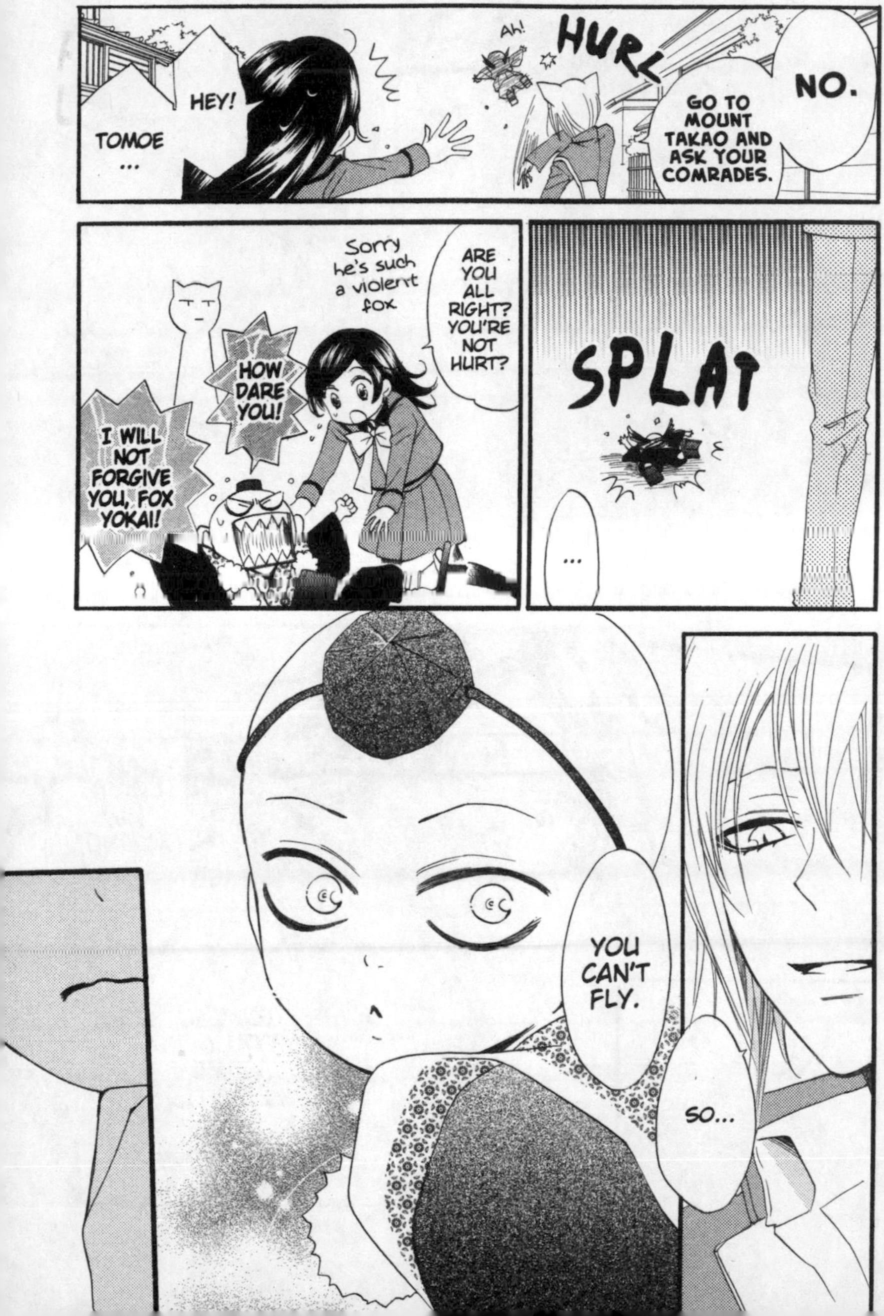
NO.
GO TO MOUNT TAKAO AND ASK YOUR COMRADES.
HURL
Ah!
HEY!
TOMOE ...
SPLAT
...
ARE YOU ALL RIGHT? YOU'RE NOT HURT?
Sorry he's such a violent fox
HOW DARE YOU!
I WILL NOT FORGIVE YOU, FOX YOKAI!
YOU CAN'T FLY.
SO...

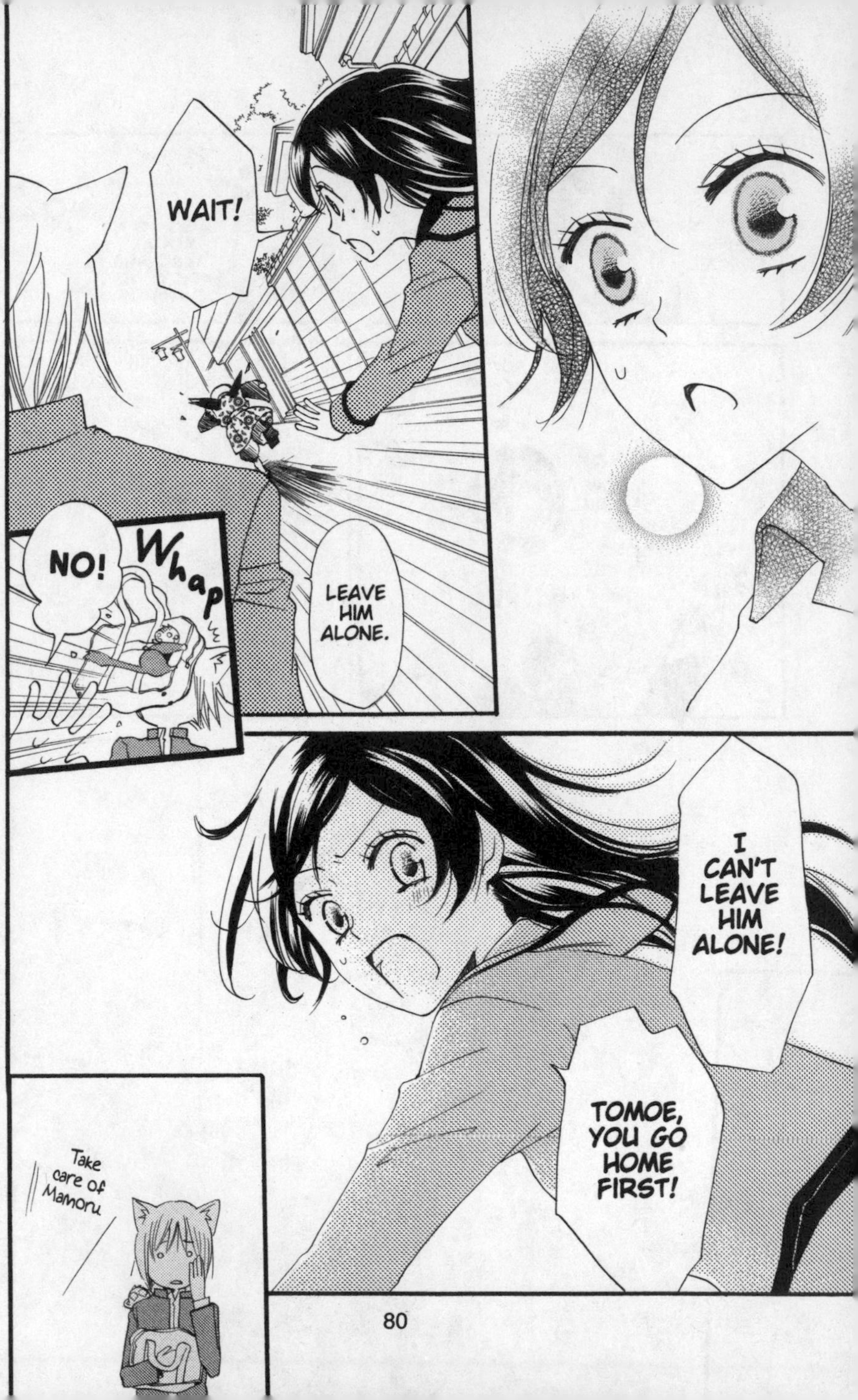
WAIT!
LEAVE HIM ALONE.
NO!
Whap
I CAN'T LEAVE HIM ALONE!
TOMOE, YOU GO HOME FIRST!
Take care of Mamoru.

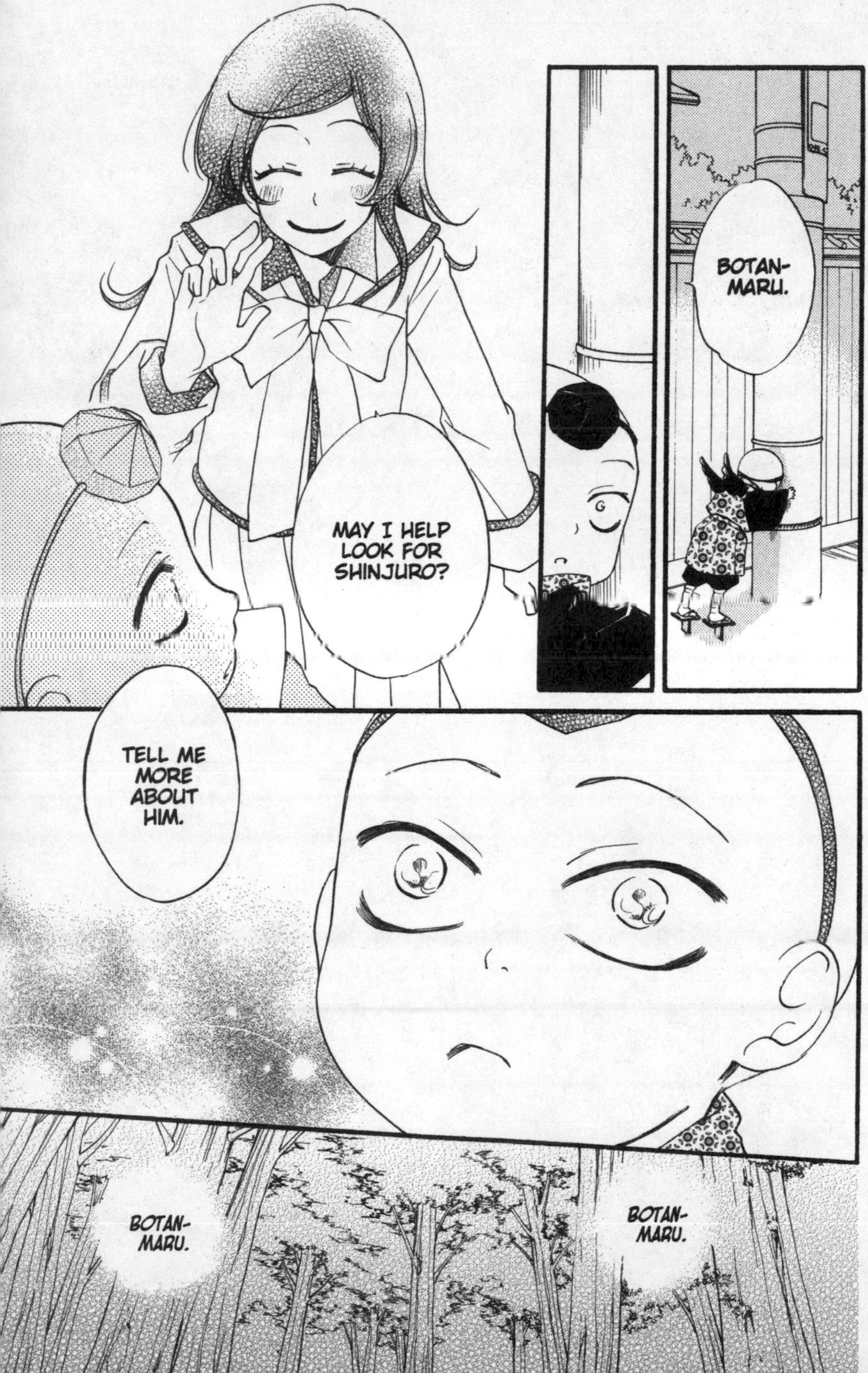
BOTAN-MARU.
MAY I HELP LOOK FOR SHINJURO?
TELL ME MORE ABOUT HIM.
BOTAN-MARU.
BOTAN-MARU.

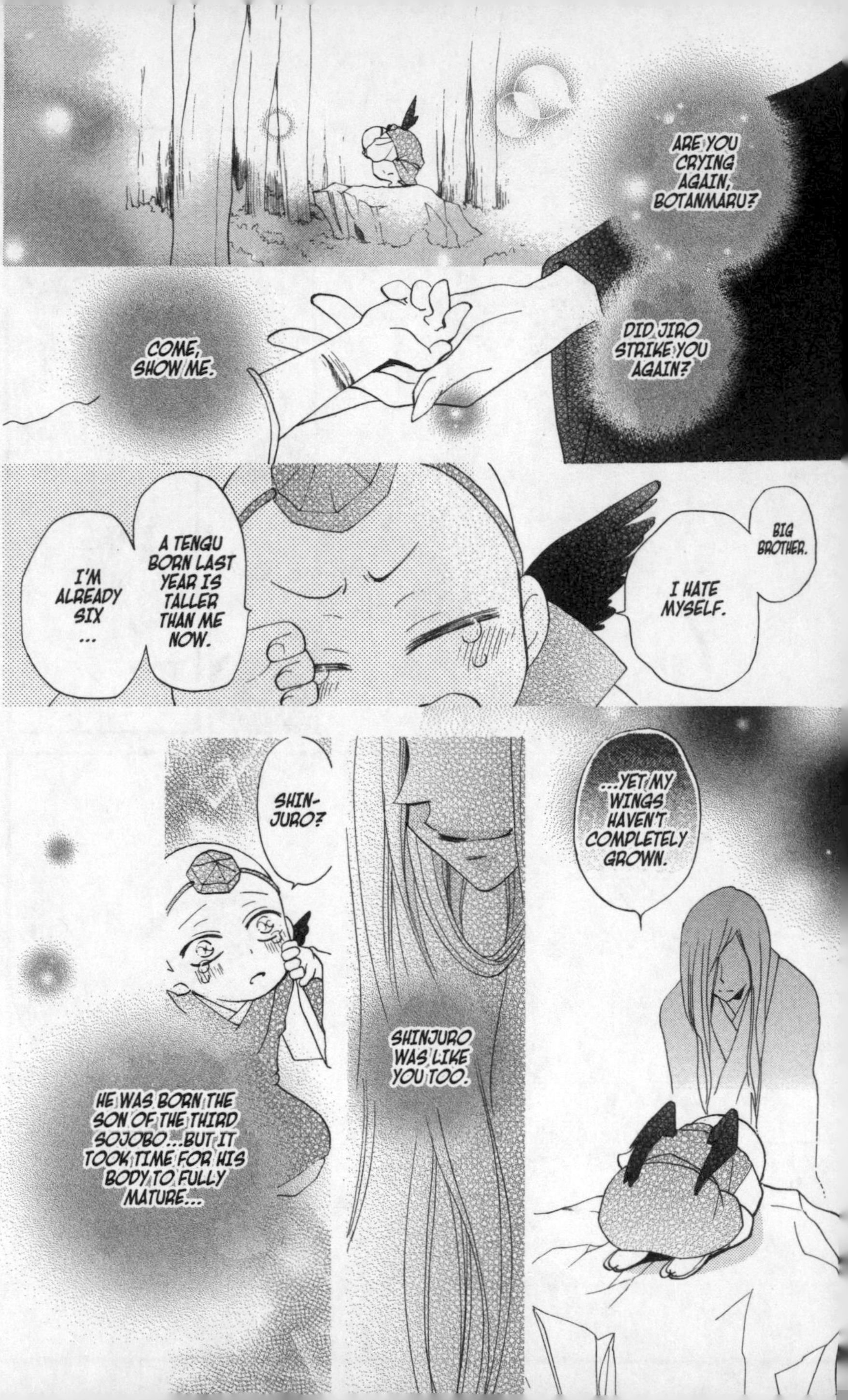
ARE YOU CRYING AGAIN, BOTANMARU?
DID JIRO STRIKE YOU AGAIN?
COME, SHOW ME.
BIG BROTHER.
I HATE MYSELF.
A TENGU BORN LAST YEAR IS TALLER THAN ME NOW.
I'M ALREADY SIX...
...YET MY WINGS HAVEN'T COMPLETELY GROWN.
SHINJURO WAS LIKE YOU TOO.
SHIN-JURO?
HE WAS BORN THE SON OF THE THIRD SOJOBO...BUT IT TOOK TIME FOR HIS BODY TO FULLY MATURE...

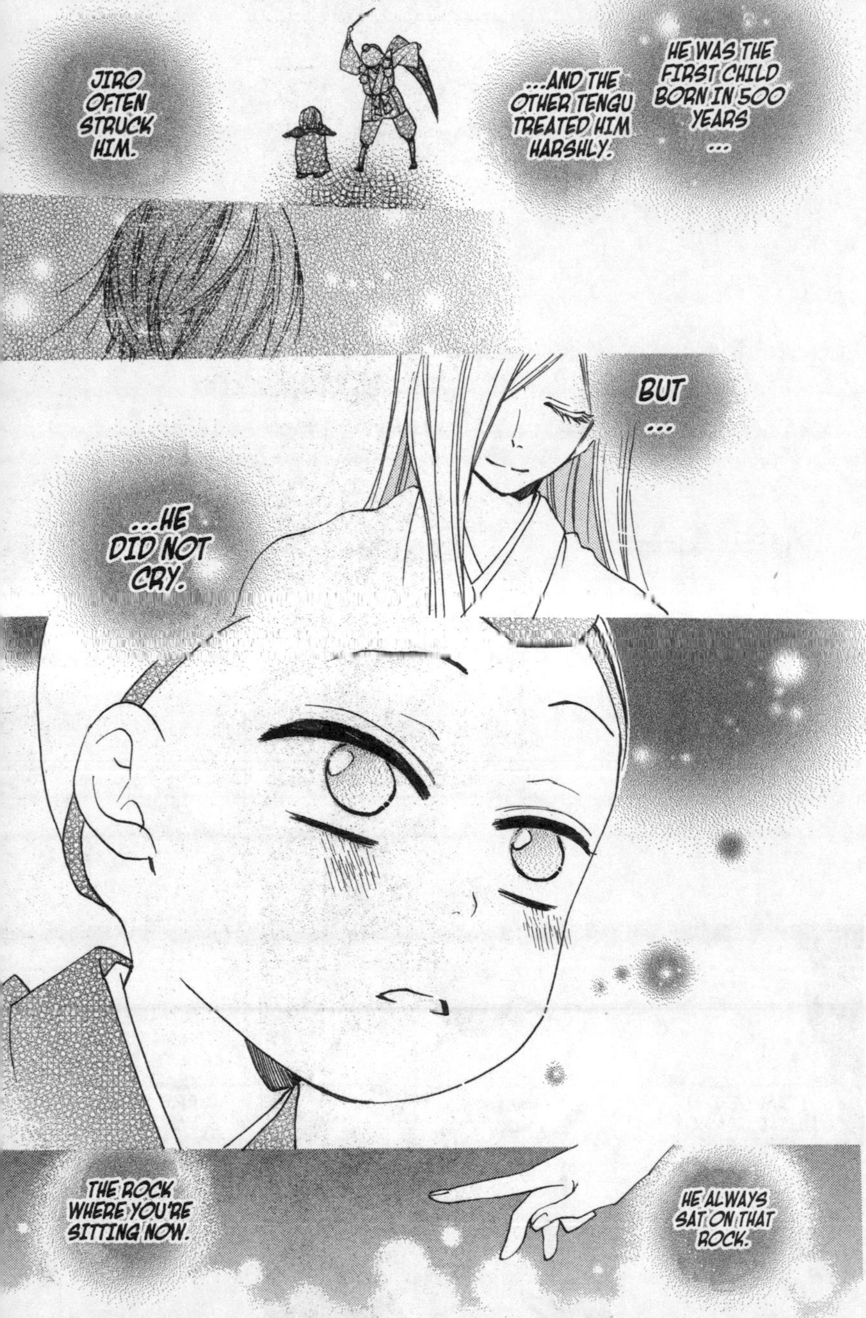
HE WAS THE FIRST CHILD BORN IN 500 YEARS ...
...AND THE OTHER TENGU TREATED HIM HARSHLY.
JIRO OFTEN STRUCK HIM.
BUT ...
...HE DID NOT CRY.
HE ALWAYS SAT ON THAT ROCK.
THE ROCK WHERE YOU'RE SITTING NOW.

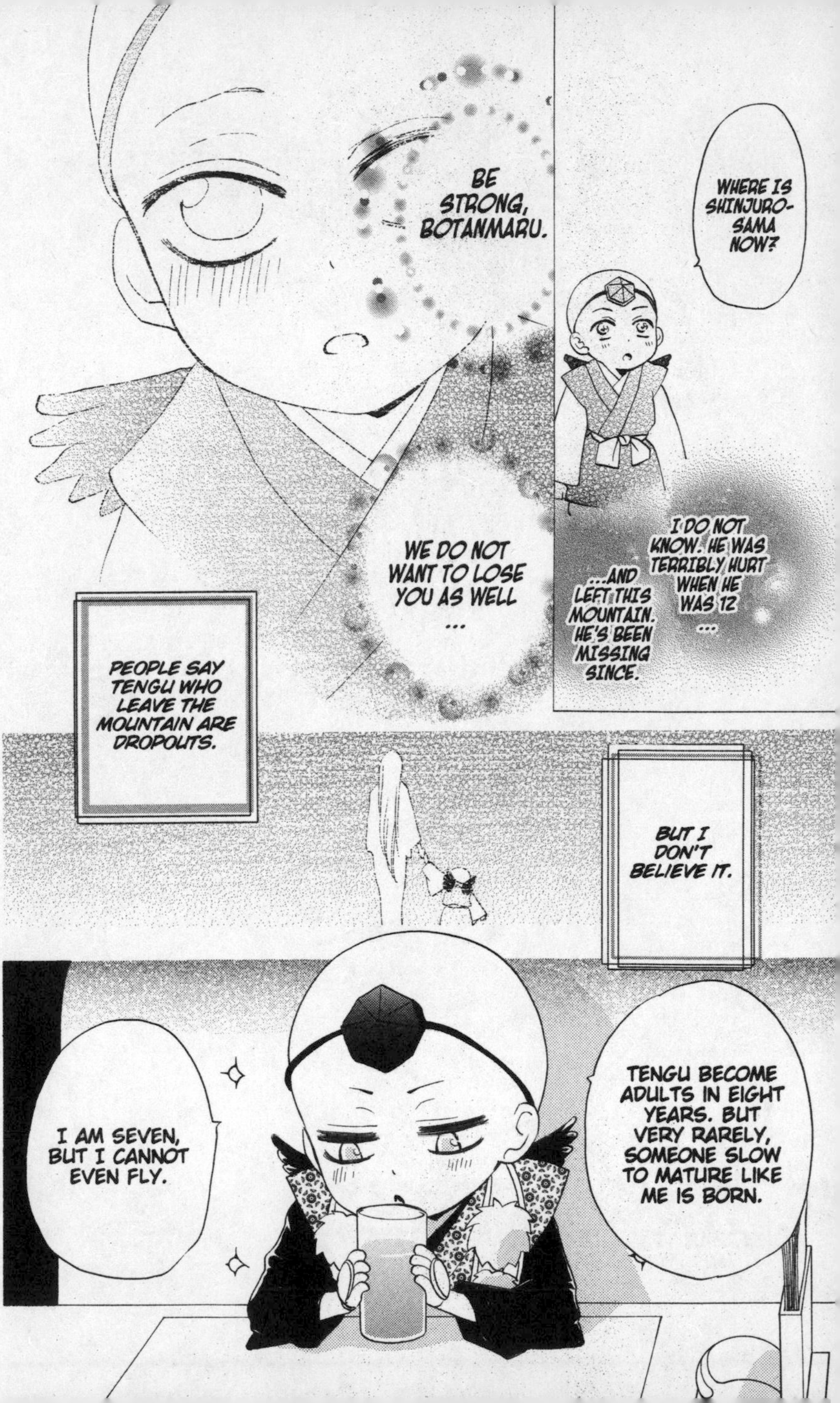

WHERE IS SHINJURO-SAMA NOW?
I DO NOT KNOW. HE WAS TERRIBLY HURT WHEN HE WAS 12 ...
...AND LEFT THIS MOUNTAIN. HE'S BEEN MISSING SINCE.
BE STRONG, BOTANMARU.
WE DO NOT WANT TO LOSE YOU AS WELL ...
PEOPLE SAY TENGU WHO LEAVE THE MOUNTAIN ARE DROPOUTS.
BUT I DON'T BELIEVE IT.
TENGU BECOME ADULTS IN EIGHT YEARS. BUT VERY RARELY, SOMEONE SLOW TO MATURE LIKE ME IS BORN.
I AM SEVEN, BUT I CANNOT EVEN FLY.

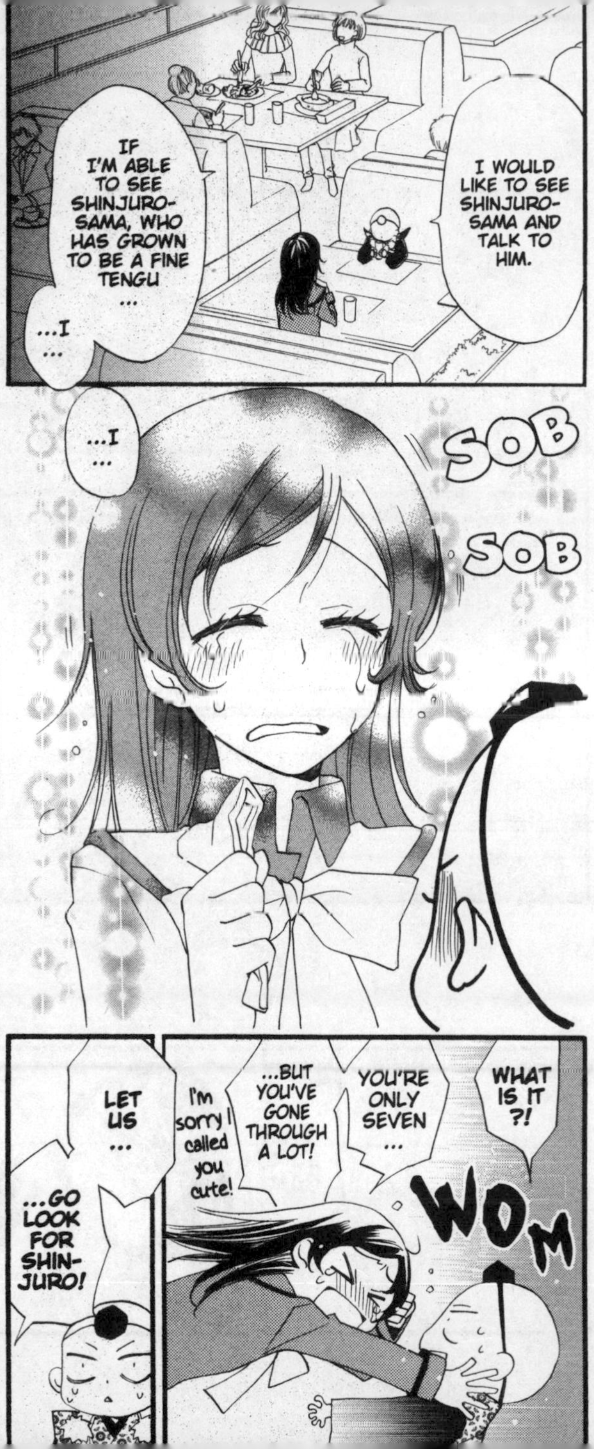
I WOULD LIKE TO SEE SHINJURO-SAMA AND TALK TO HIM.
IF I'M ABLE TO SEE SHINJURO-SAMA, WHO HAS GROWN TO BE A FINE TENGU ...
...I ...
...I ...
SOB
SOB
WHAT IS IT ?!
YOU'RE ONLY SEVEN ...
...BUT YOU'VE GONE THROUGH A LOT!
I'm sorry I called you cute!
WOM
LET US ...
...GO LOOK FOR SHINJURO!

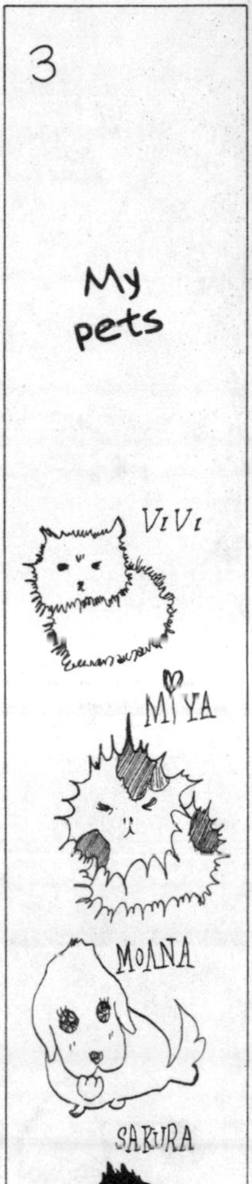
3
My pets
VIVI
MIYA
MOANA
SAKURA
CIRO

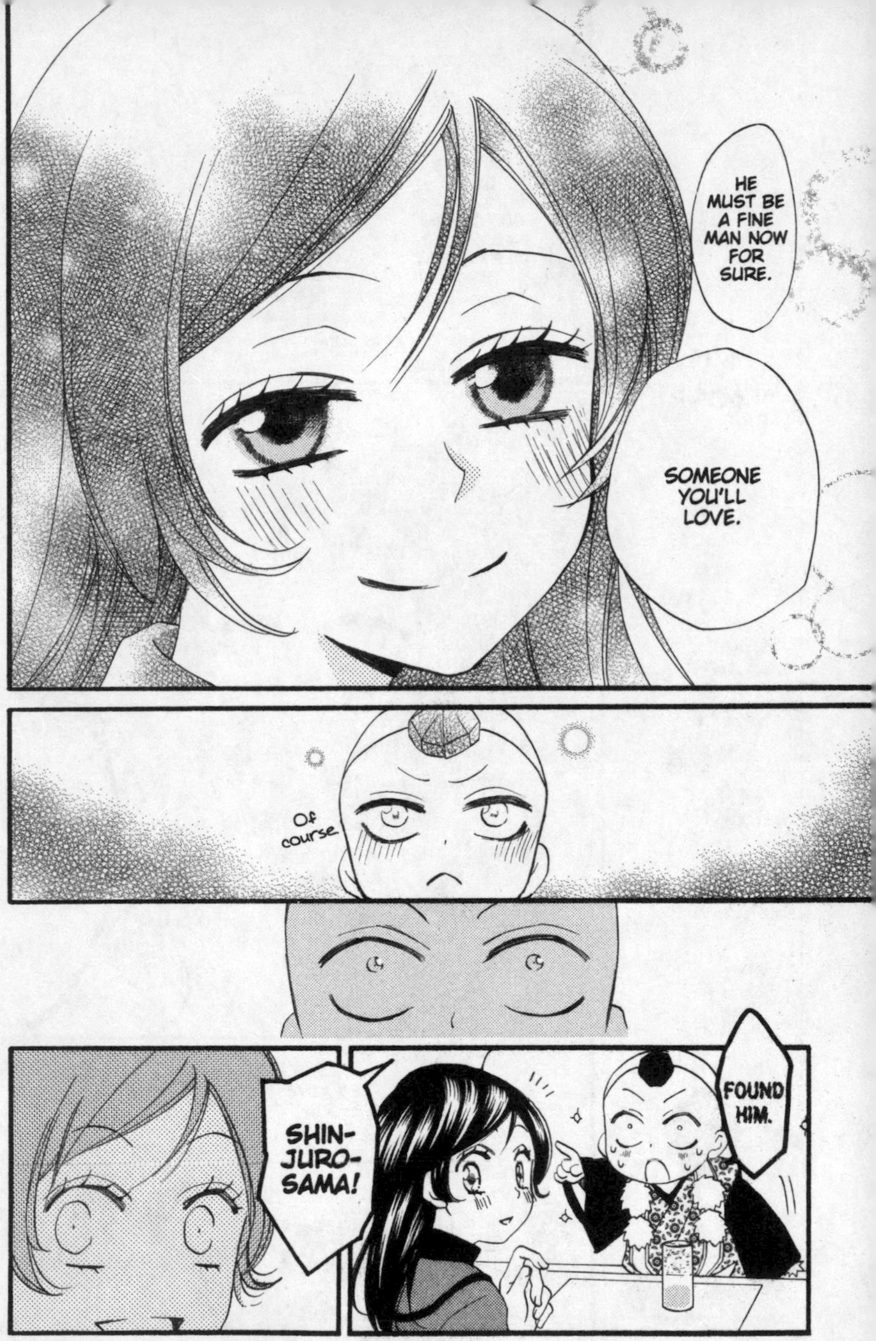
HE MUST BE A FINE MAN NOW FOR SURE.
SOMEONE YOU'LL LOVE.
Of course
FOUND HIM.
SHIN-JURO-SAMA!

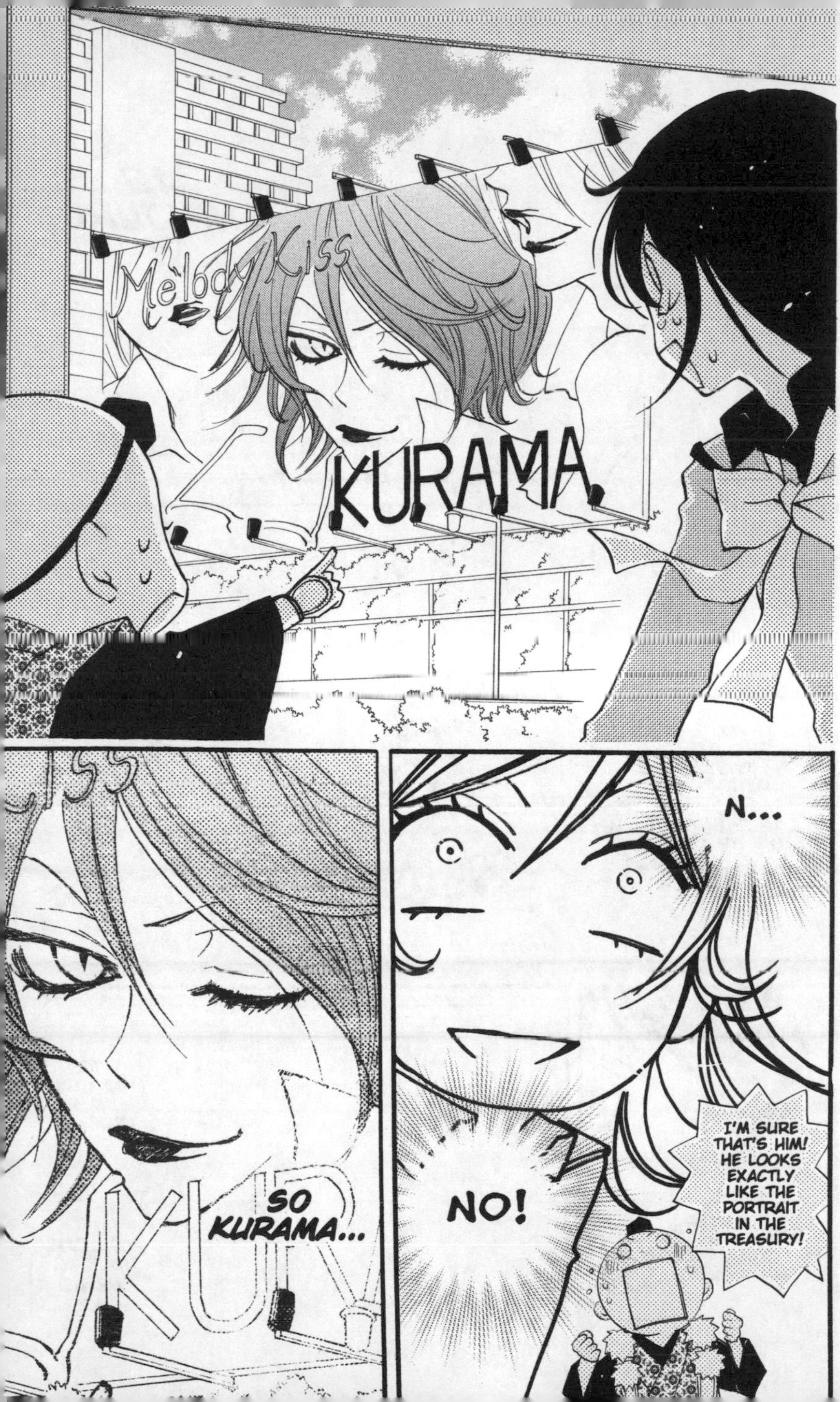
Melody Kiss
KURAMA
N...
NO!
I'M SURE THAT'S HIM! HE LOOKS EXACTLY LIKE THE PORTRAIT IN THE TREASURY!
SO KURAMA...

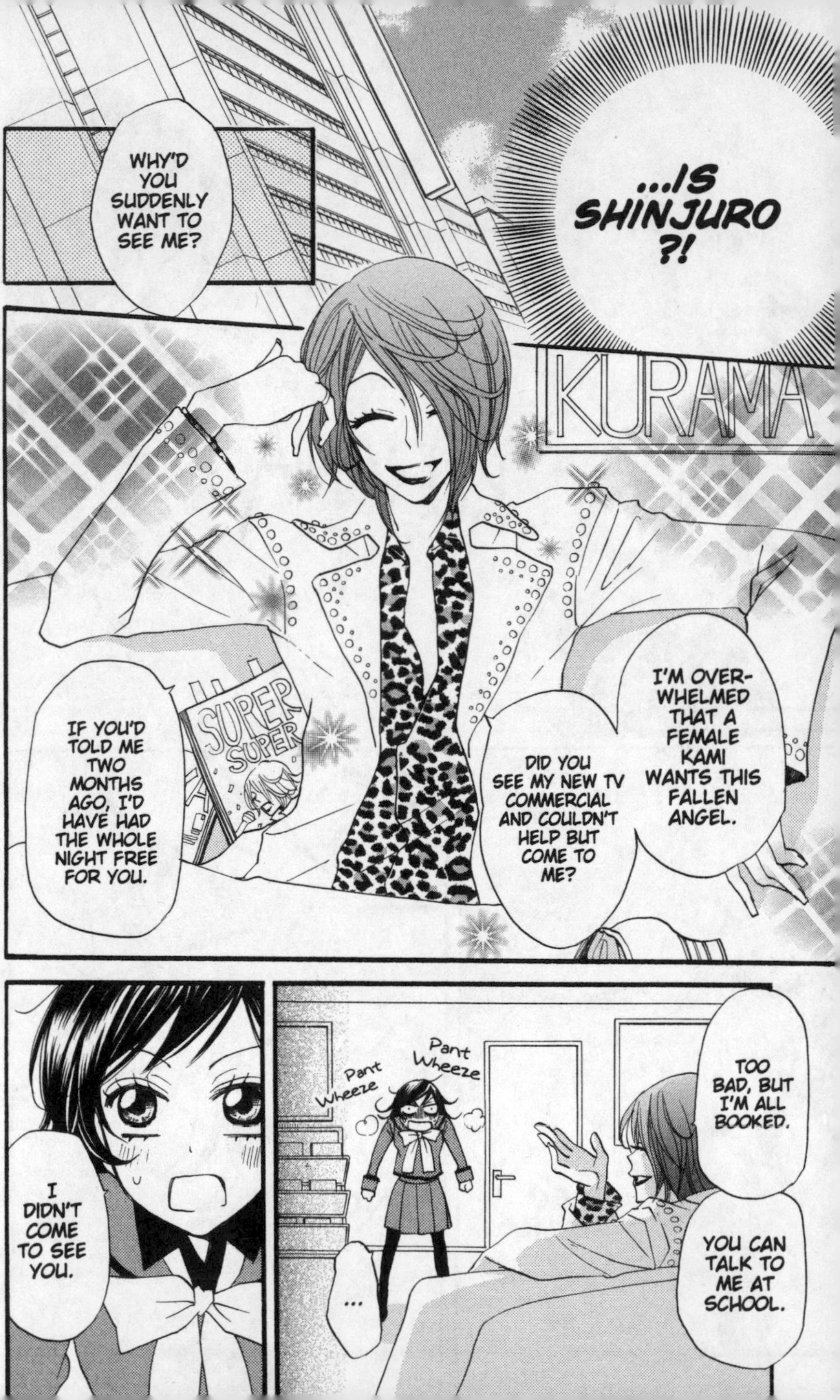
...IS SHINJURO ?!
WHY'D YOU SUDDENLY WANT TO SEE ME?
KURAMA
I'M OVER-WHELMED THAT A FEMALE KAMI WANTS THIS FALLEN ANGEL.
DID YOU SEE MY NEW TV COMMERCIAL AND COULDN'T HELP BUT COME TO ME?
SUPER SUPER
IF YOU'D TOLD ME TWO MONTHS AGO, I'D HAVE HAD THE WHOLE NIGHT FREE FOR YOU.
TOO BAD, BUT I'M ALL BOOKED.
YOU CAN TALK TO ME AT SCHOOL.
Pant Wheeze
Pant Wheeze
...
I DIDN'T COME TO SEE YOU.

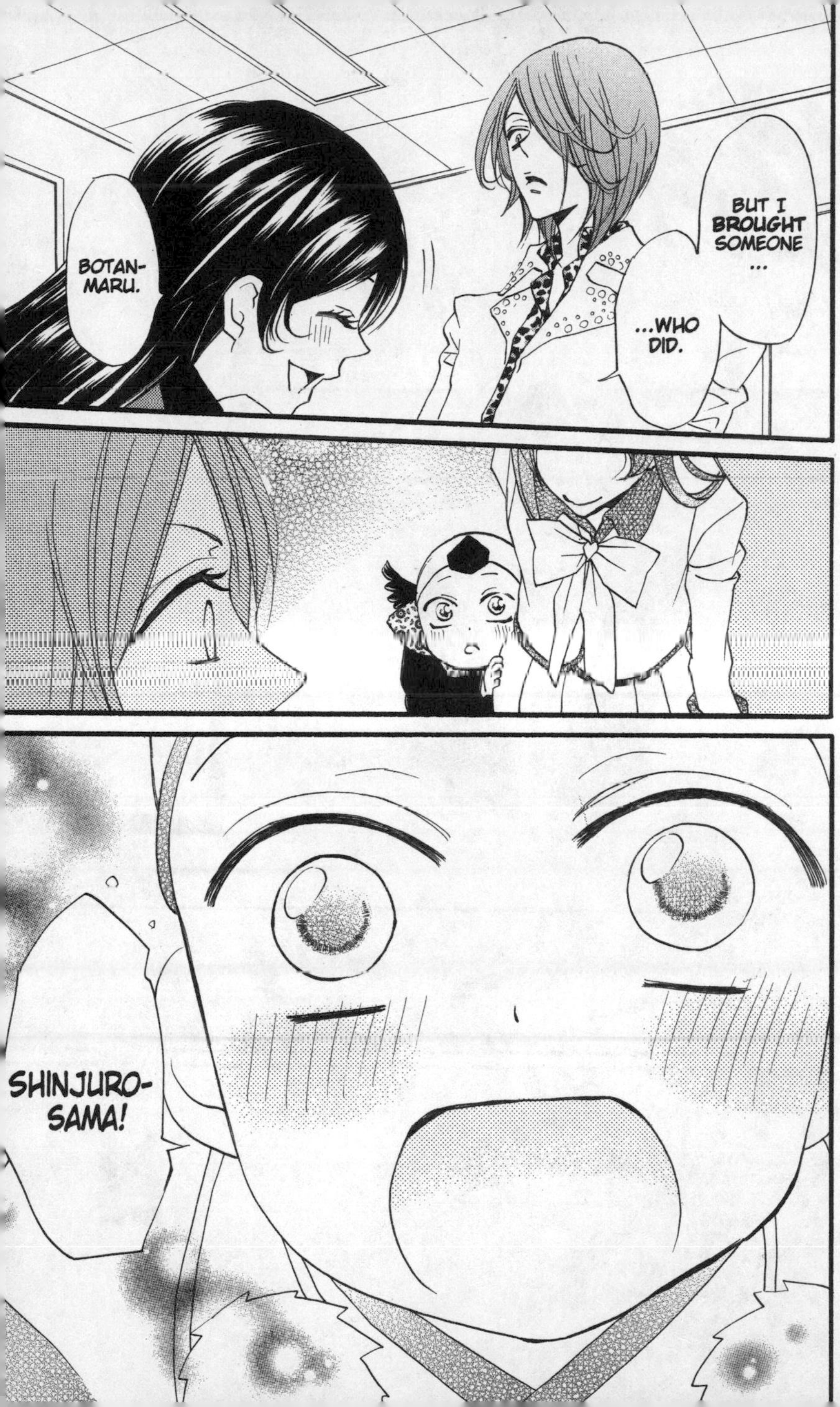
BUT I BROUGHT SOMEONE ...
...WHO DID.
BOTAN-MARU.
SHINJURO-SAMA!

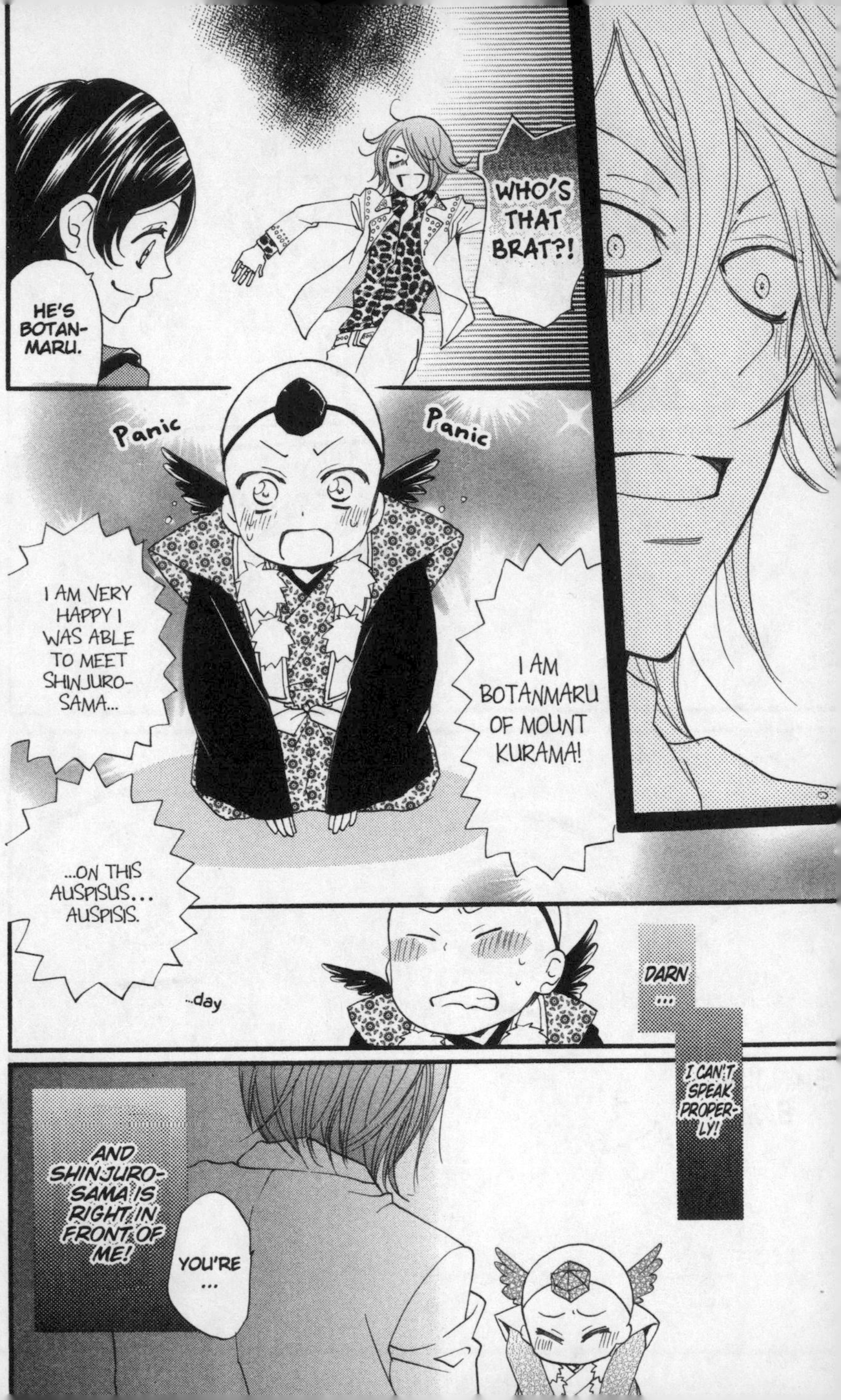
WHO'S THAT BRAT?!
HE'S BOTAN-MARU.
Panic
Panic
I AM BOTANMARU OF MOUNT KURAMA!
I AM VERY HAPPY I WAS ABLE TO MEET SHINJURO-SAMA...
...ON THIS AUSPISUS... AUSPISIS.
...day
DARN...
I CAN'T SPEAK PROPER-LY!
AND SHINJURO-SAMA IS RIGHT IN FRONT OF ME!
YOU'RE ...

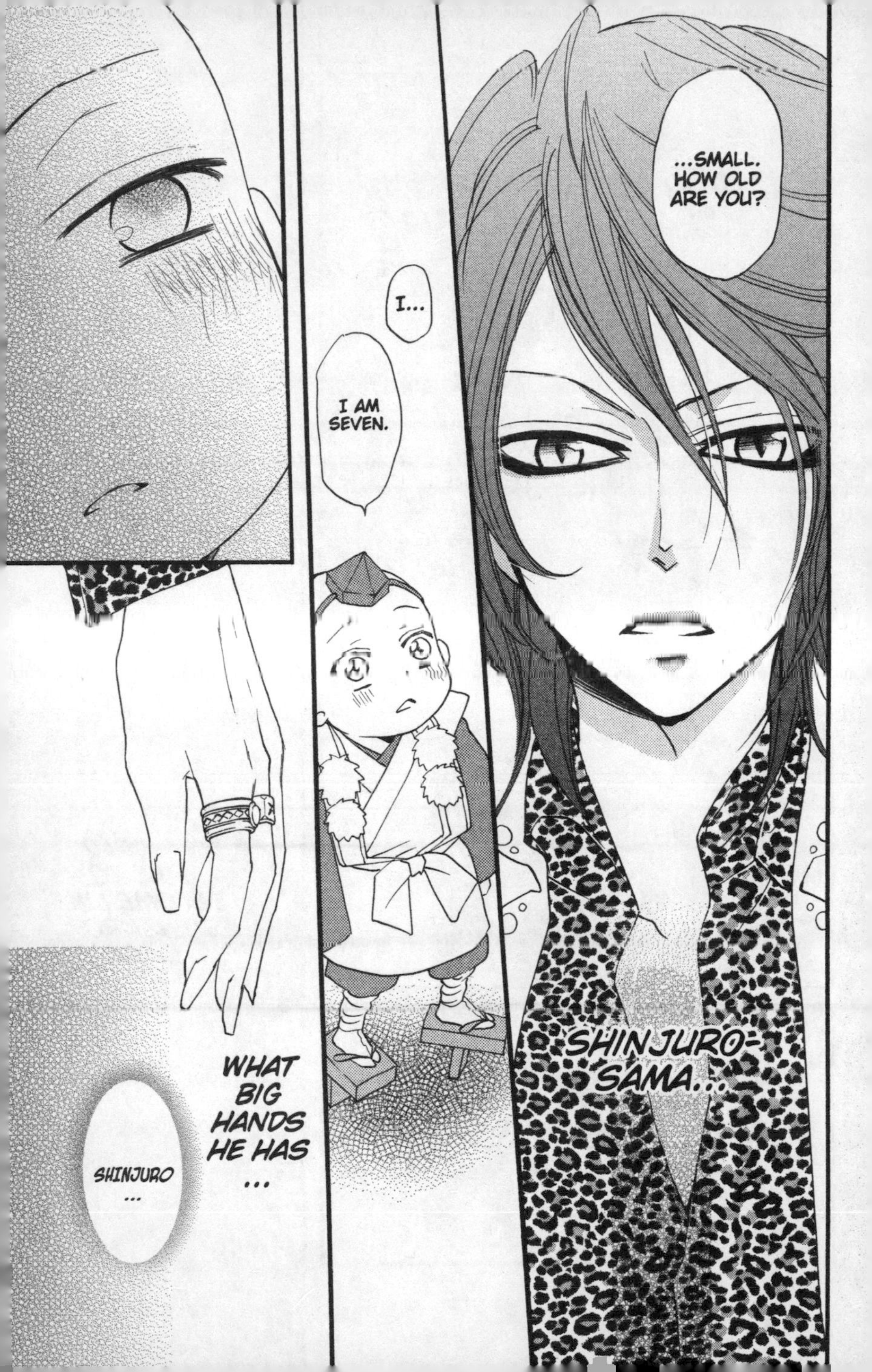
...SMALL. HOW OLD ARE YOU?
SHINJURO-SAMA...
I...
I AM SEVEN.
WHAT BIG HANDS HE HAS ...
SHINJURO ...

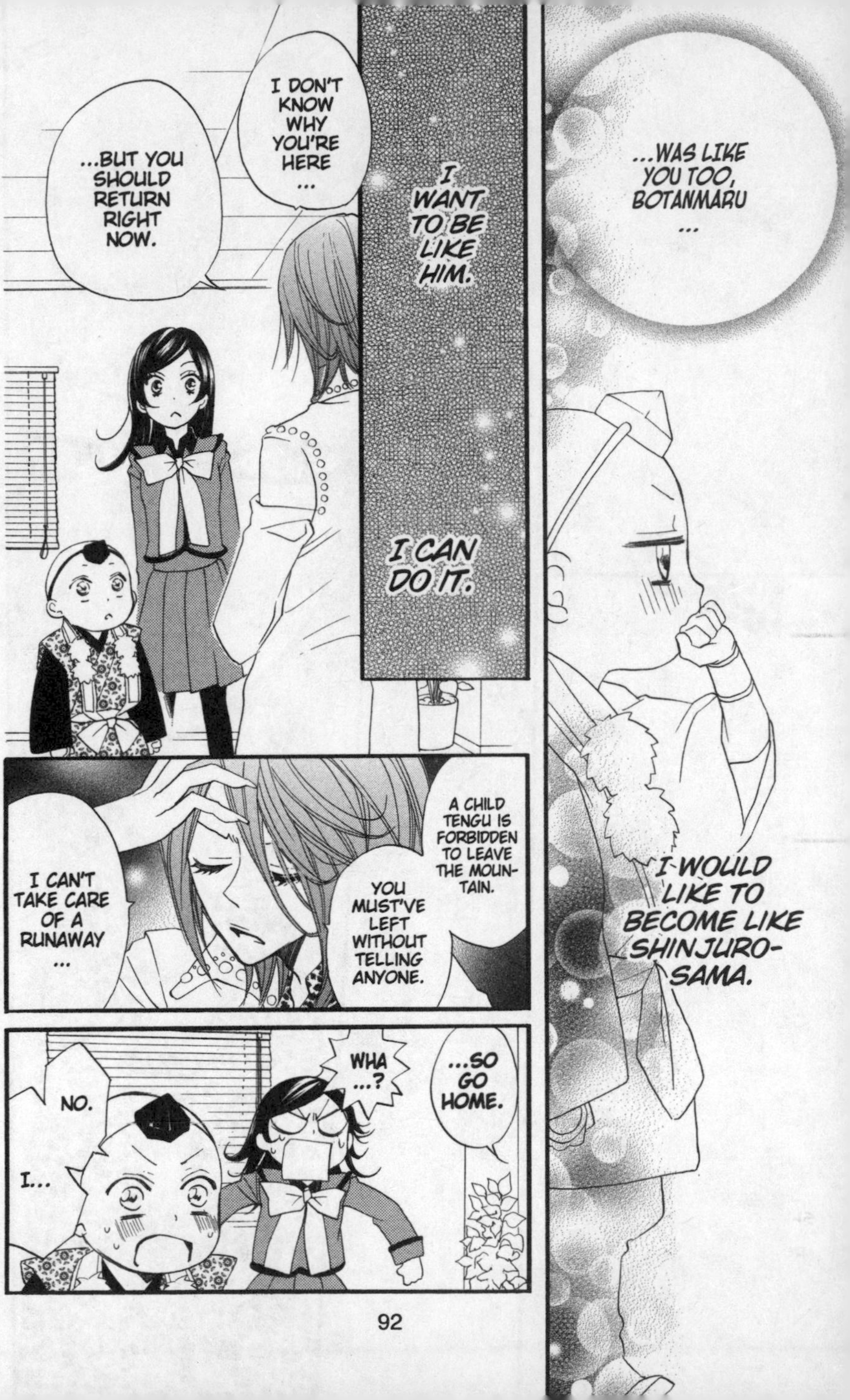

...WAS LIKE YOU TOO, BOTANMARU ...
I WOULD LIKE TO BECOME LIKE SHINJURO-SAMA.
I WANT TO BE LIKE HIM.
I CAN DO IT.
I DON'T KNOW WHY YOU'RE HERE ...
...BUT YOU SHOULD RETURN RIGHT NOW.
A CHILD TENGU IS FORBIDDEN TO LEAVE THE MOUN-TAIN.
YOU MUST'VE LEFT WITHOUT TELLING ANYONE.
I CAN'T TAKE CARE OF A RUNAWAY ...
...SO GO HOME.
WHA ...?
NO.
I...

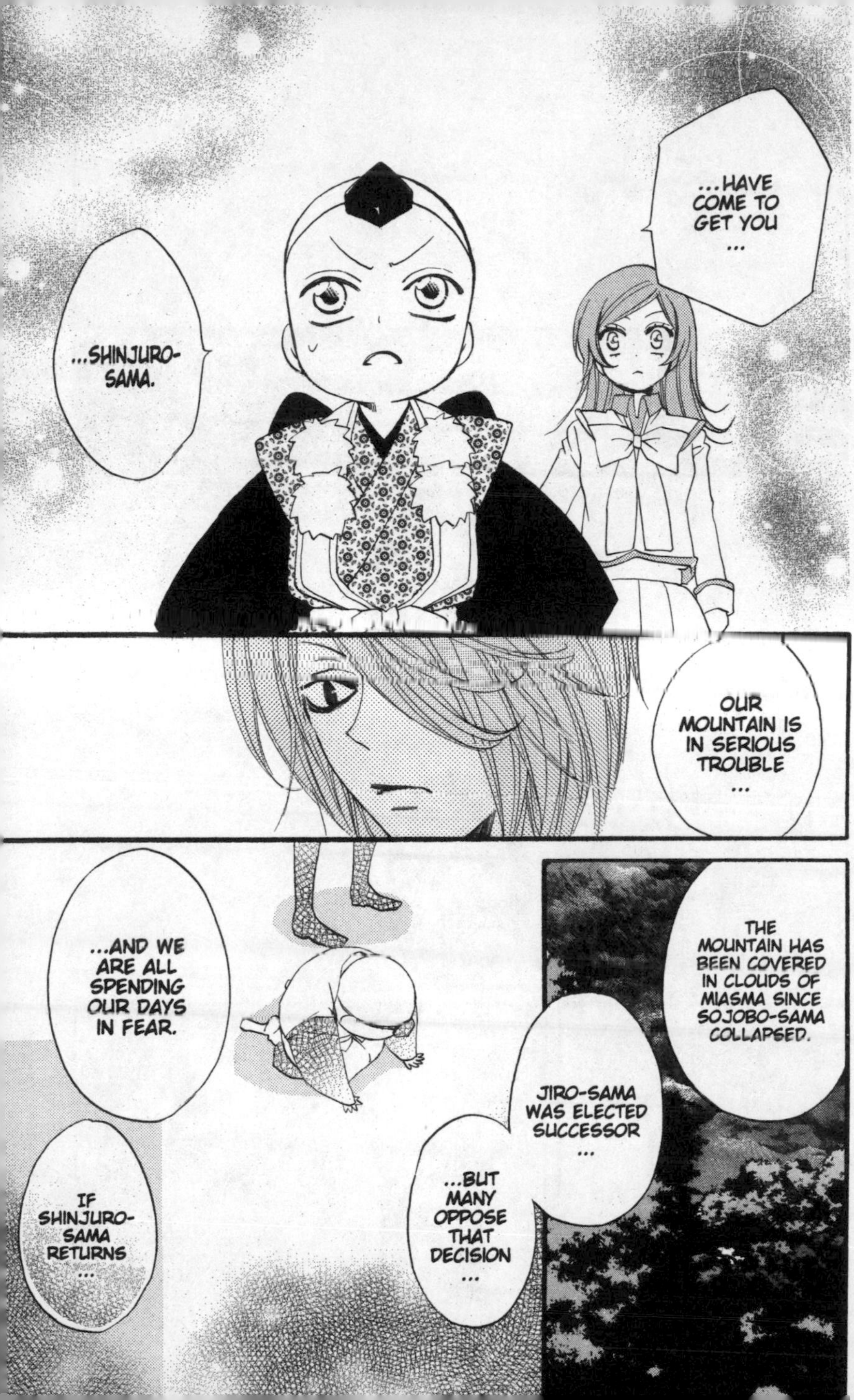
...HAVE COME TO GET YOU ...
...SHINJURO-SAMA.
OUR MOUNTAIN IS IN SERIOUS TROUBLE ...
THE MOUNTAIN HAS BEEN COVERED IN CLOUDS OF MIASMA SINCE SOJOBO-SAMA COLLAPSED.
JIRO-SAMA WAS ELECTED SUCCESSOR ...
...BUT MANY OPPOSE THAT DECISION ...
...AND WE ARE ALL SPENDING OUR DAYS IN FEAR.
IF SHINJURO-SAMA RETURNS ...

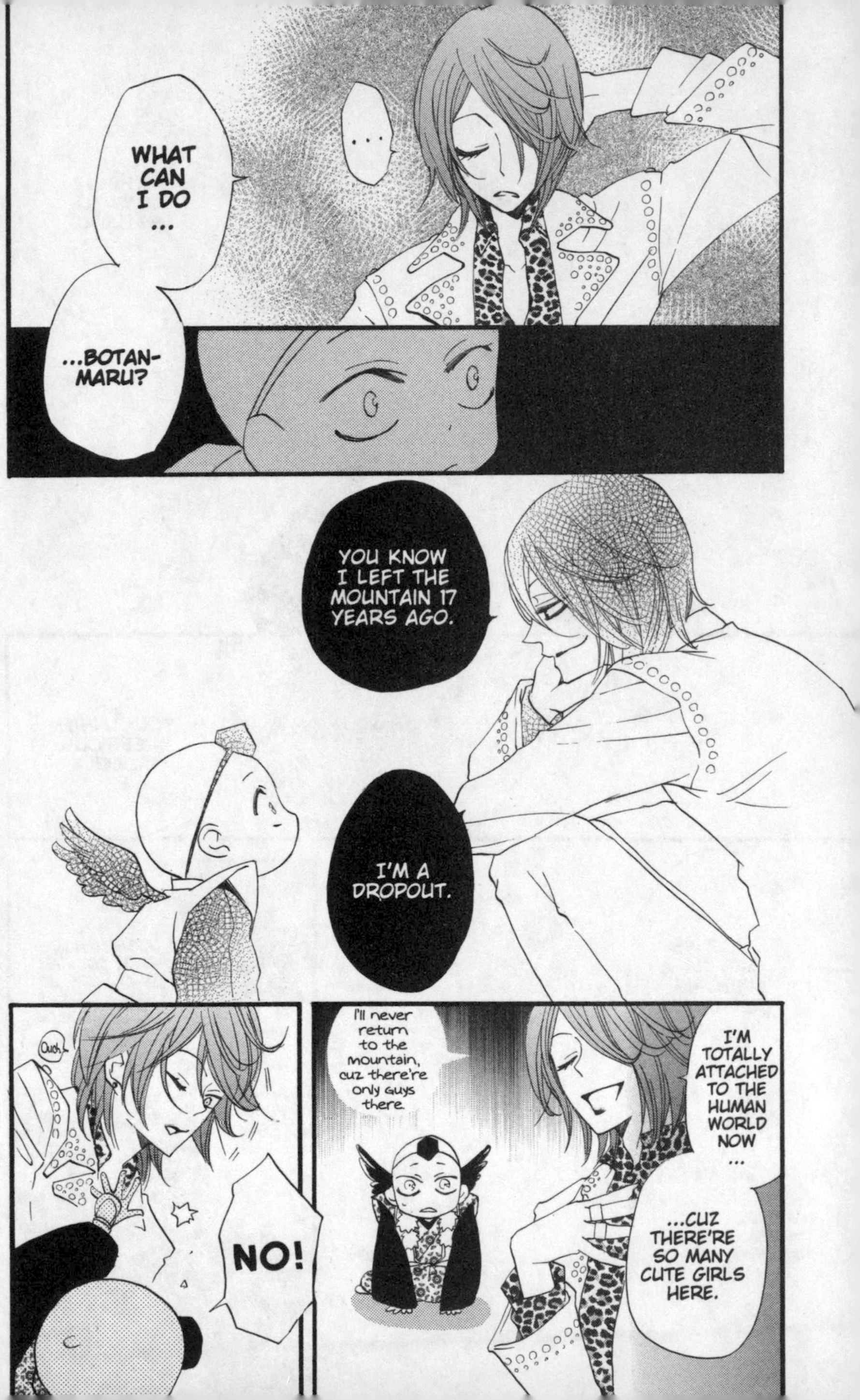
...
WHAT CAN I DO ...
...BOTAN-MARU?
YOU KNOW I LEFT THE MOUNTAIN 17 YEARS AGO.
I'M A DROPOUT.
I'M TOTALLY ATTACHED TO THE HUMAN WORLD NOW ...
...CUZ THERE'RE SO MANY CUTE GIRLS HERE.
I'll never return to the mountain, cuz there're only guys there.
NO!
Ouch.

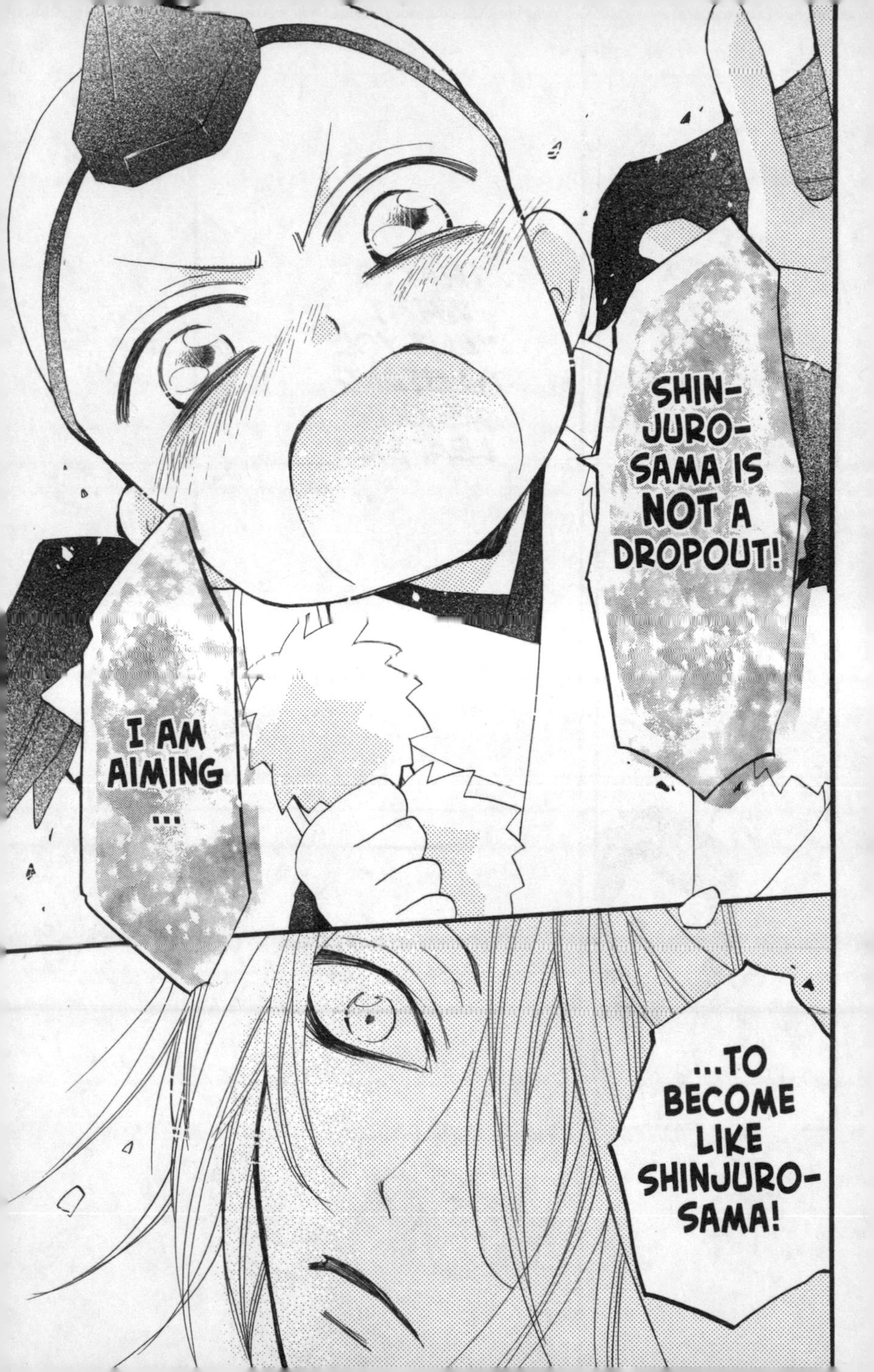
SHIN-JURO-SAMA IS NOT A DROPOUT!
I AM AIMING ...
...TO BECOME LIKE SHINJURO-SAMA!

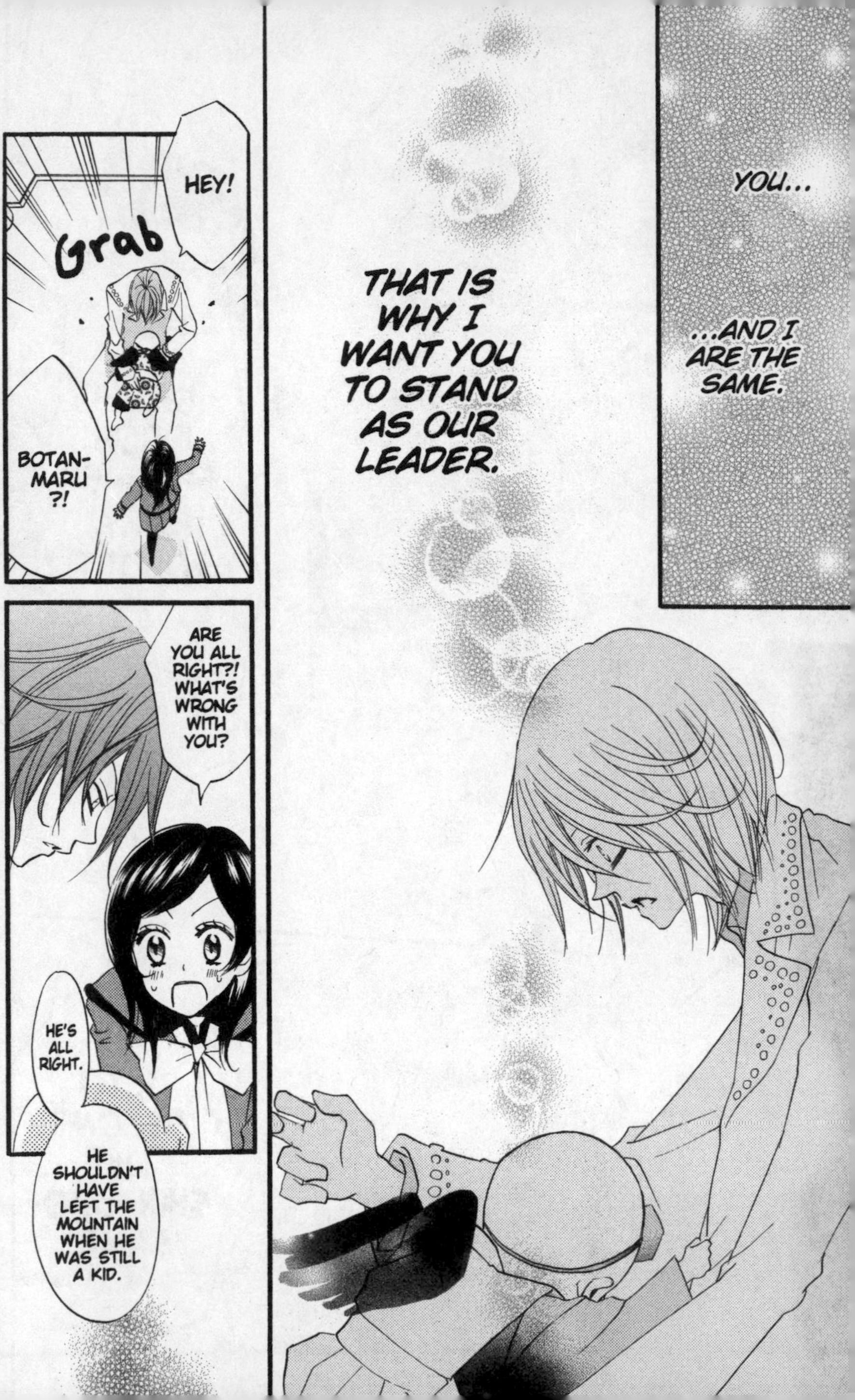
YOU...
...AND I ARE THE SAME.
THAT IS WHY I WANT YOU TO STAND AS OUR LEADER.
HEY!
Grab
BOTAN-MARU ?!
ARE YOU ALL RIGHT?! WHAT'S WRONG WITH YOU?
HE'S ALL RIGHT.
HE SHOULDN'T HAVE LEFT THE MOUNTAIN WHEN HE WAS STILL A KID.

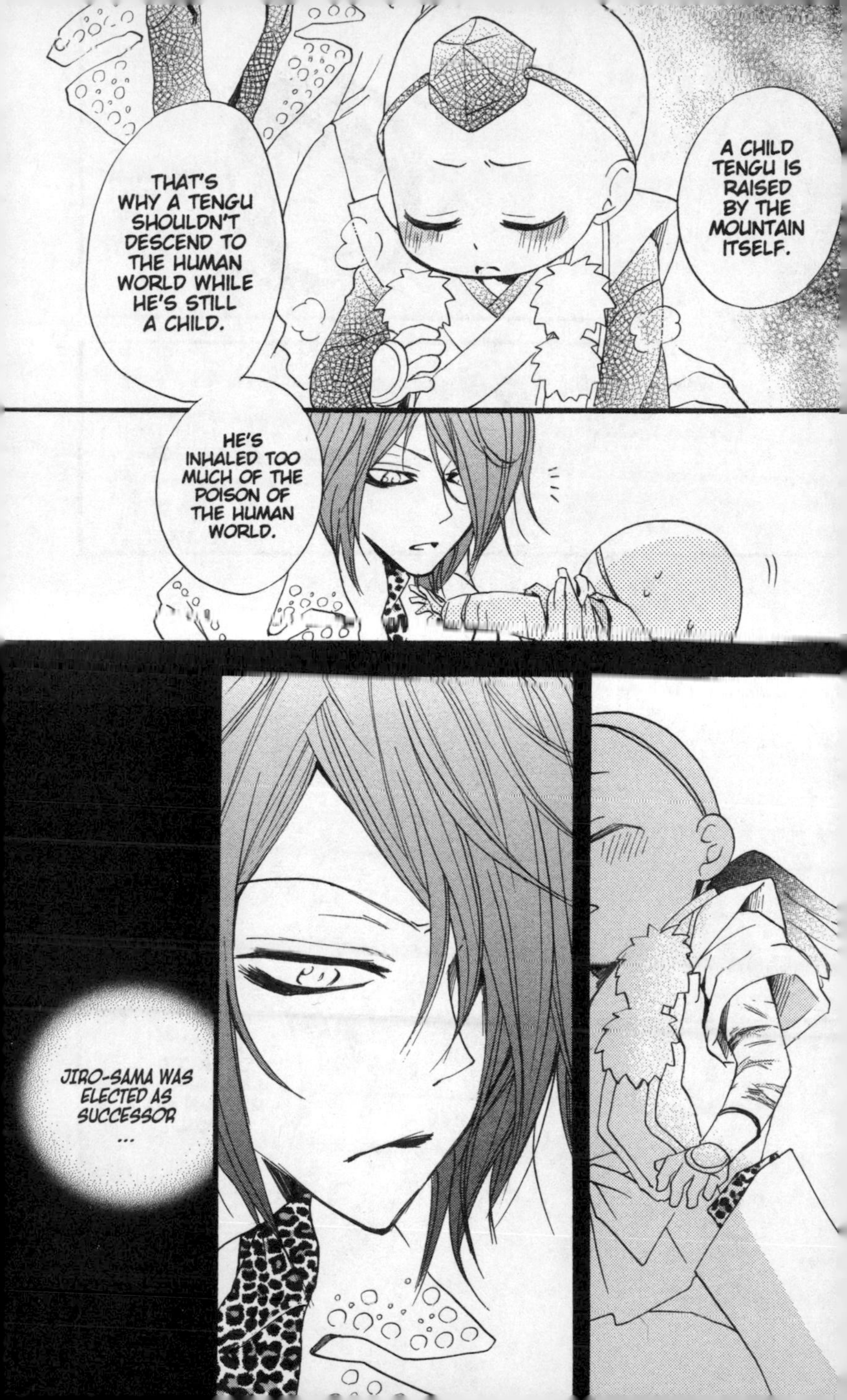
A CHILD TENGU IS RAISED BY THE MOUNTAIN ITSELF.
THAT'S WHY A TENGU SHOULDN'T DESCEND TO THE HUMAN WORLD WHILE HE'S STILL A CHILD.
HE'S INHALED TOO MUCH OF THE POISON OF THE HUMAN WORLD.
JIRO-SAMA WAS ELECTED AS SUCCESSOR ...

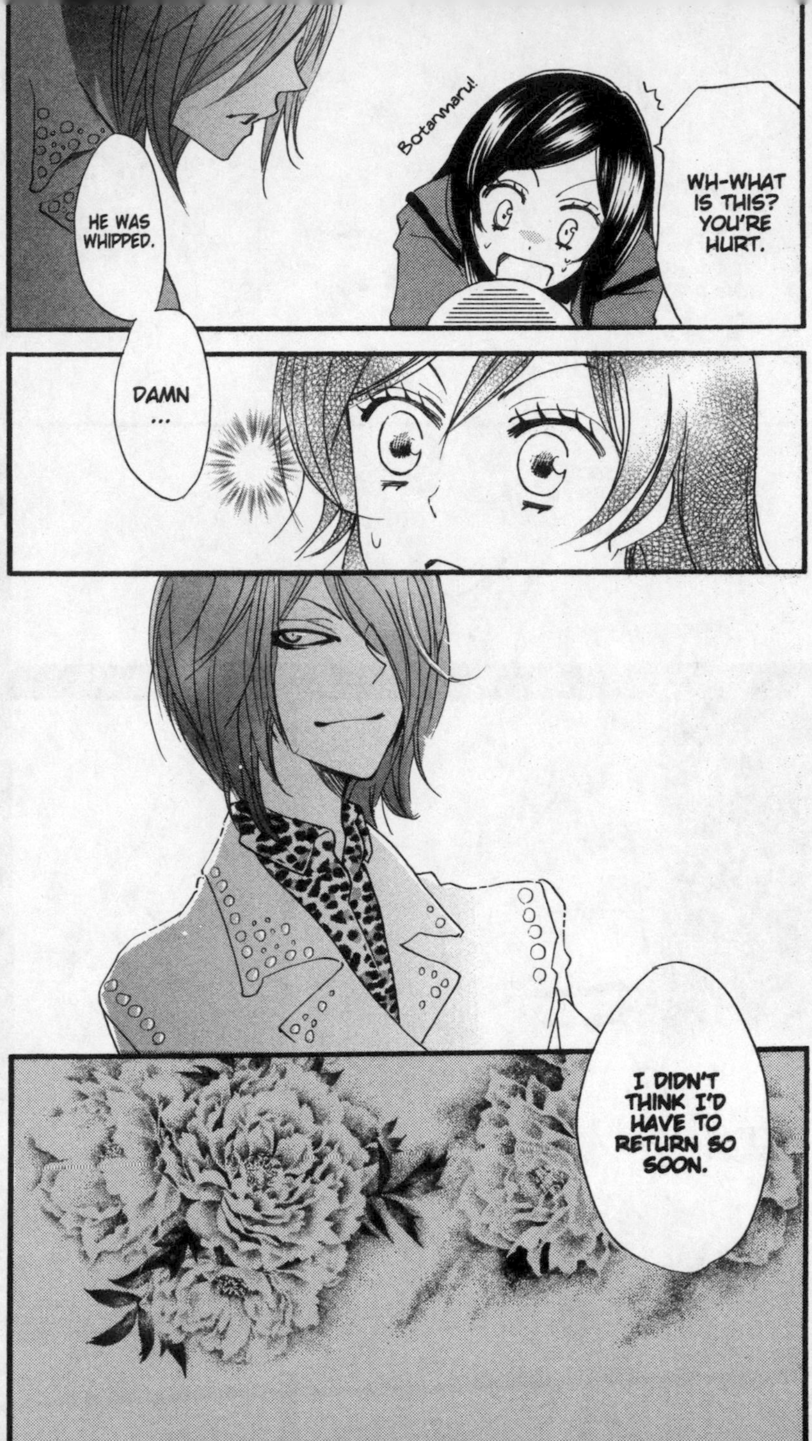
Botanmaru!
WH-WHAT IS THIS? YOU'RE HURT.
HE WAS WHIPPED.
DAMN...
I DIDN'T THINK I'D HAVE TO RETURN SO SOON.

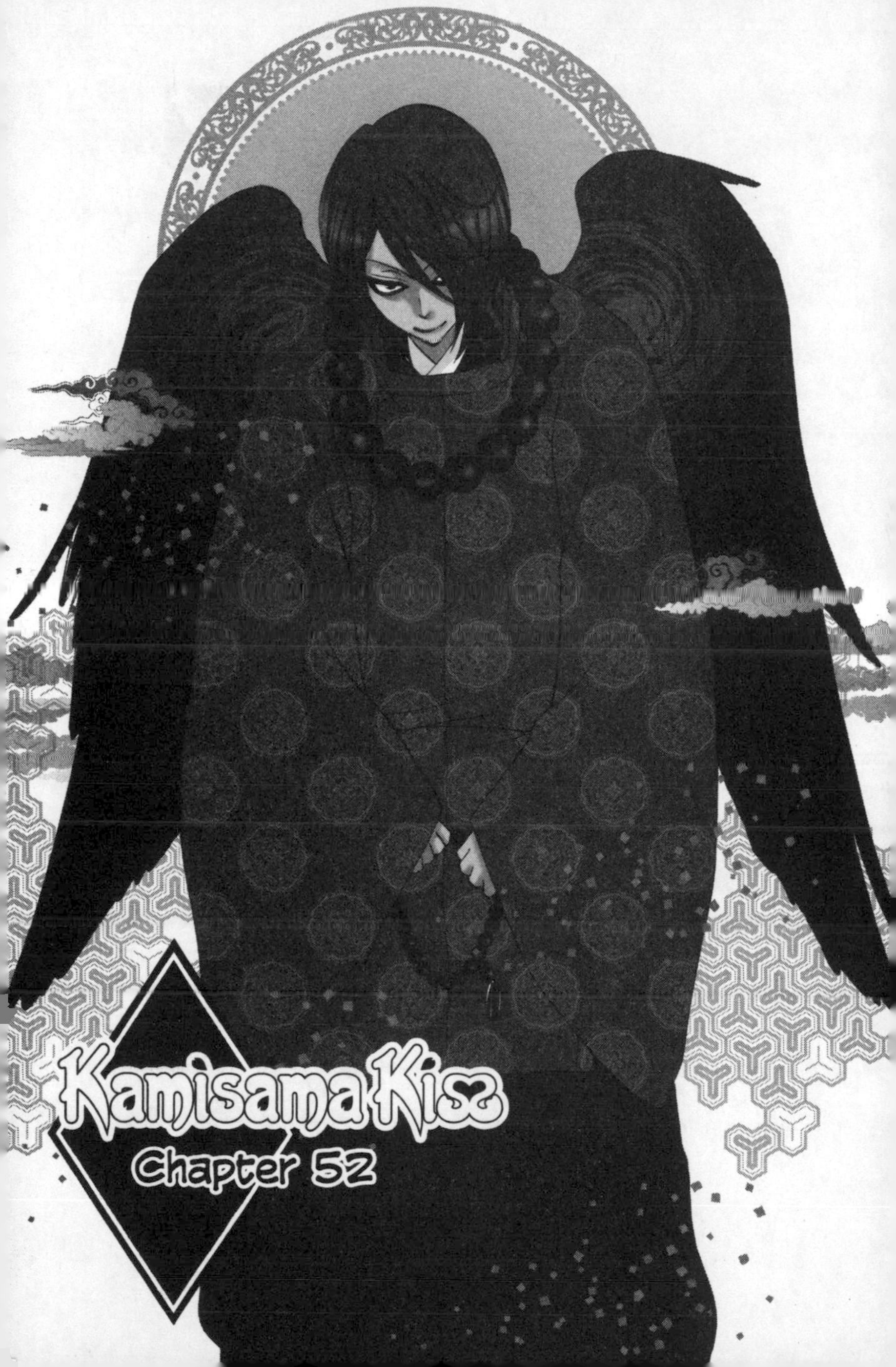
Kamisama Kiss
Chapter 52

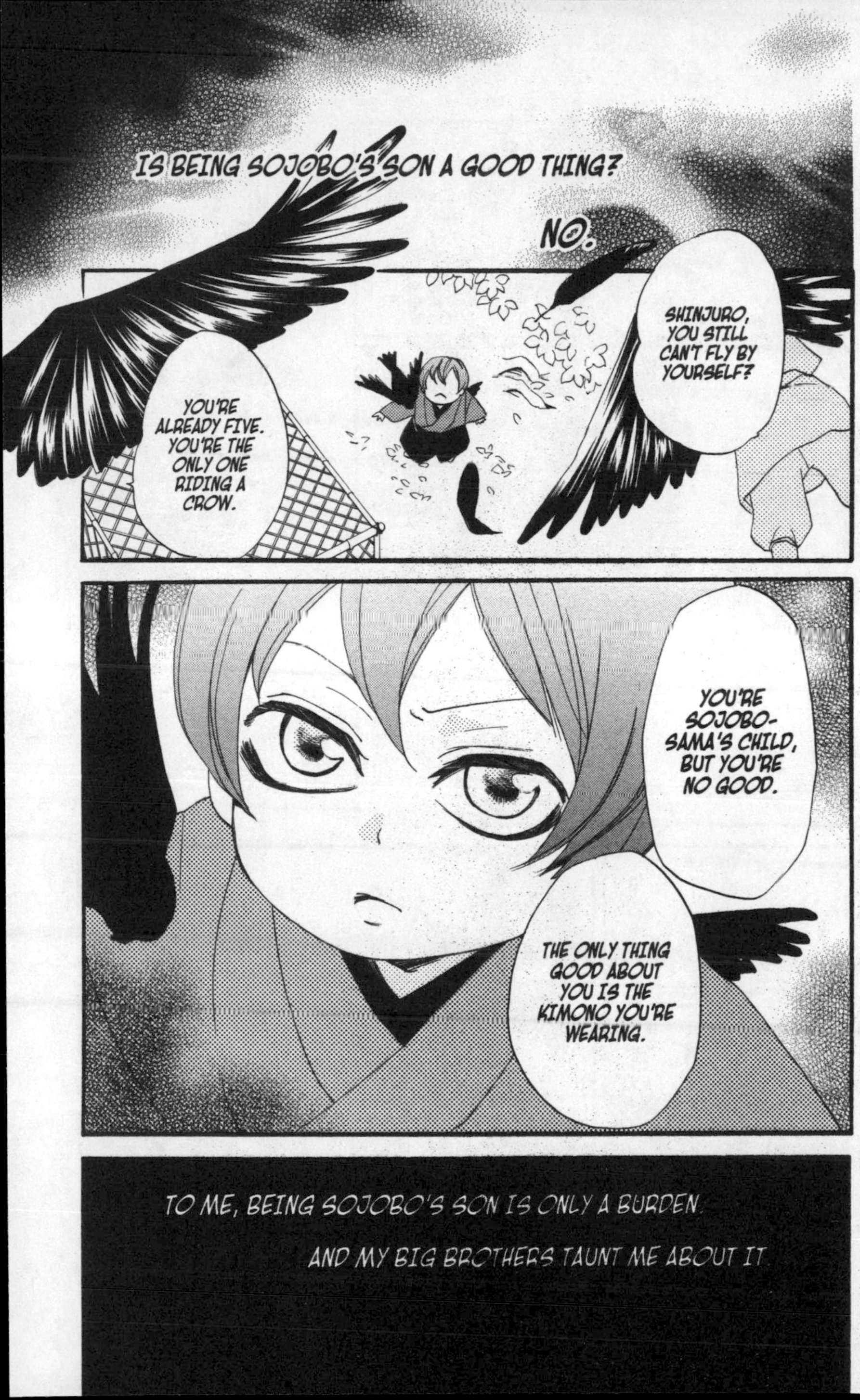
IS BEING SOJOBO'S SON A GOOD THING?
NO.
SHINJURO, YOU STILL CAN'T FLY BY YOURSELF?
YOU'RE ALREADY FIVE. YOU'RE THE ONLY ONE RIDING A CROW.
YOU'RE SOJOBO-SAMA'S CHILD, BUT YOU'RE NO GOOD.
THE ONLY THING GOOD ABOUT YOU IS THE KIMONO YOU'RE WEARING.
TO ME, BEING SOJOBO'S SON IS ONLY A BURDEN.
AND MY BIG BROTHERS TAUNT ME ABOUT IT.

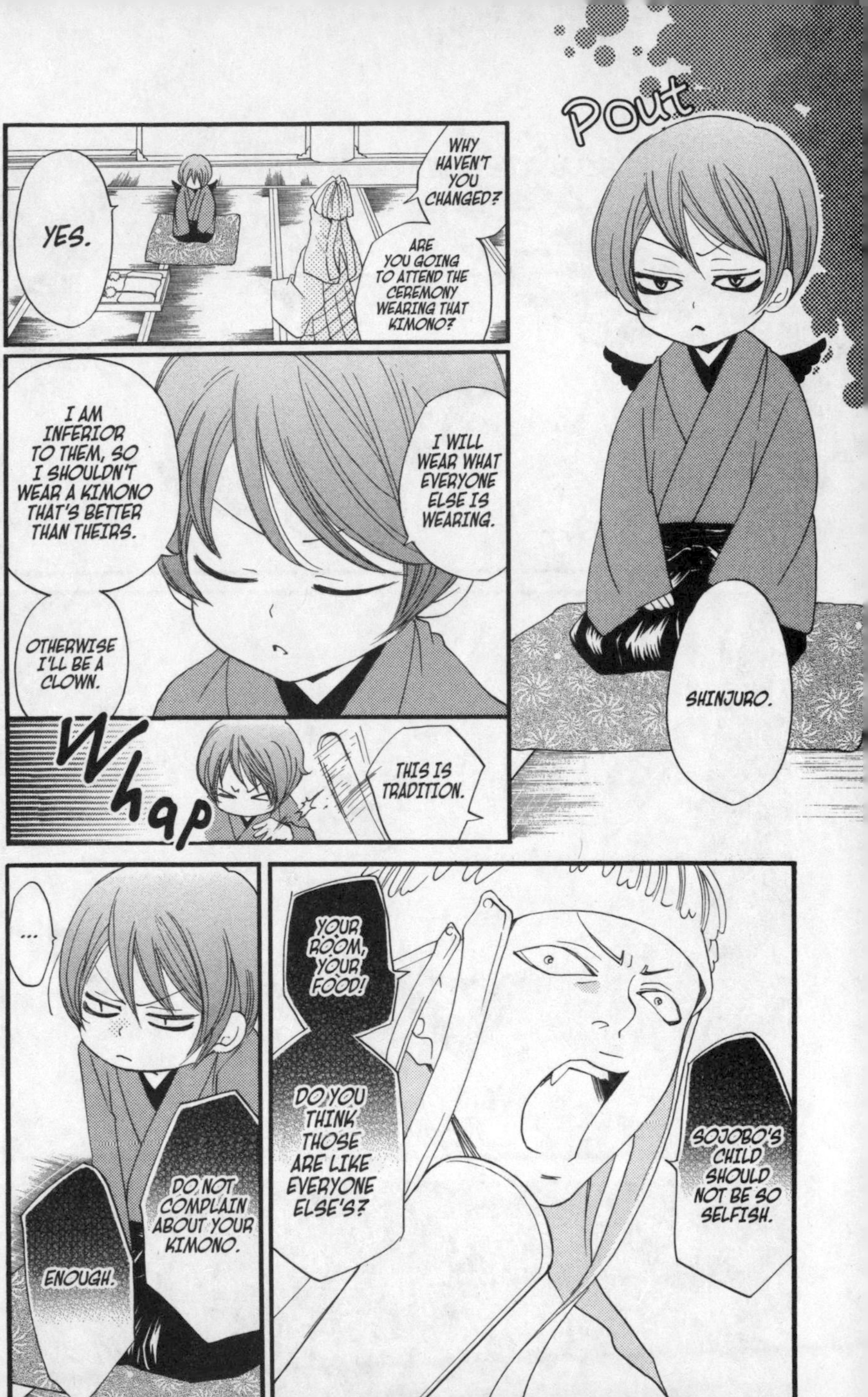
Pout
SHINJURO.
WHY HAVEN'T YOU CHANGED?
ARE YOU GOING TO ATTEND THE CEREMONY WEARING THAT KIMONO?
YES.
I WILL WEAR WHAT EVERYONE ELSE IS WEARING.
I AM INFERIOR TO THEM, SO I SHOULDN'T WEAR A KIMONO THAT'S BETTER THAN THEIRS.
OTHERWISE I'LL BE A CLOWN.
THIS IS TRADITION.
Whap
SOJOBO'S CHILD SHOULD NOT BE SO SELFISH.
YOUR ROOM, YOUR FOOD!
DO YOU THINK THOSE ARE LIKE EVERYONE ELSE'S?
...
DO NOT COMPLAIN ABOUT YOUR KIMONO.
ENOUGH.

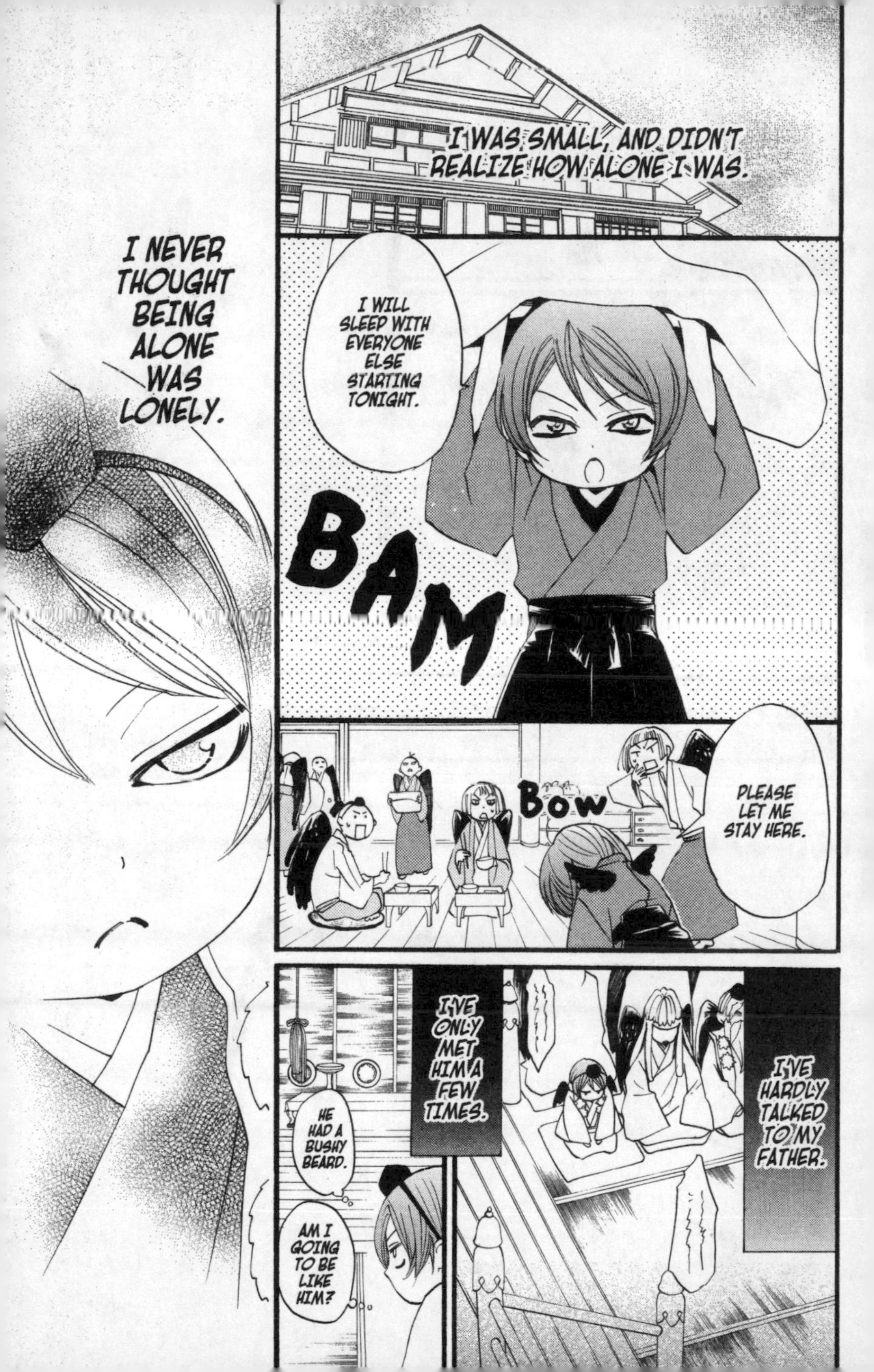
I WAS SMALL, AND DIDN'T REALIZE HOW ALONE I WAS.
I WILL SLEEP WITH EVERYONE ELSE STARTING TONIGHT.
BAM
PLEASE LET ME STAY HERE.
BOW
I'VE HARDLY TALKED TO MY FATHER.
I'VE ONLY MET HIM A FEW TIMES.
HE HAD A BUSHY BEARD.
AM I GOING TO BE LIKE HIM?
I NEVER THOUGHT BEING ALONE WAS LONELY.

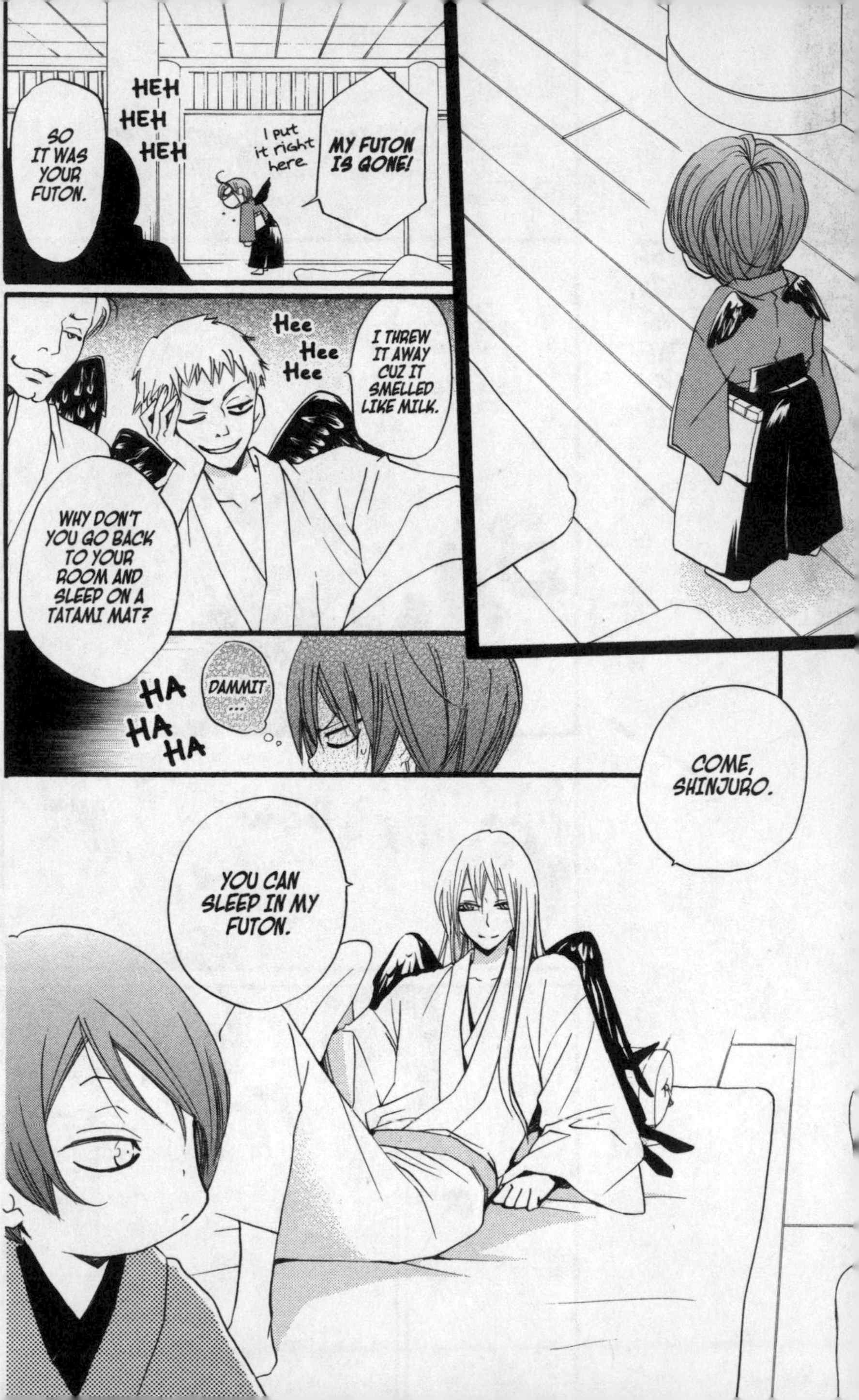
MY FUTON IS GONE!
I put it right here.
HEH HEH HEH
SO IT WAS YOUR FUTON.
I THREW IT AWAY CUZ IT SMELLED LIKE MILK.
Hee Hee Hee
WHY DON'T YOU GO BACK TO YOUR ROOM AND SLEEP ON A TATAMI MAT?
DAMMIT...
HA HA HA
COME, SHINJURO.
YOU CAN SLEEP IN MY FUTON.

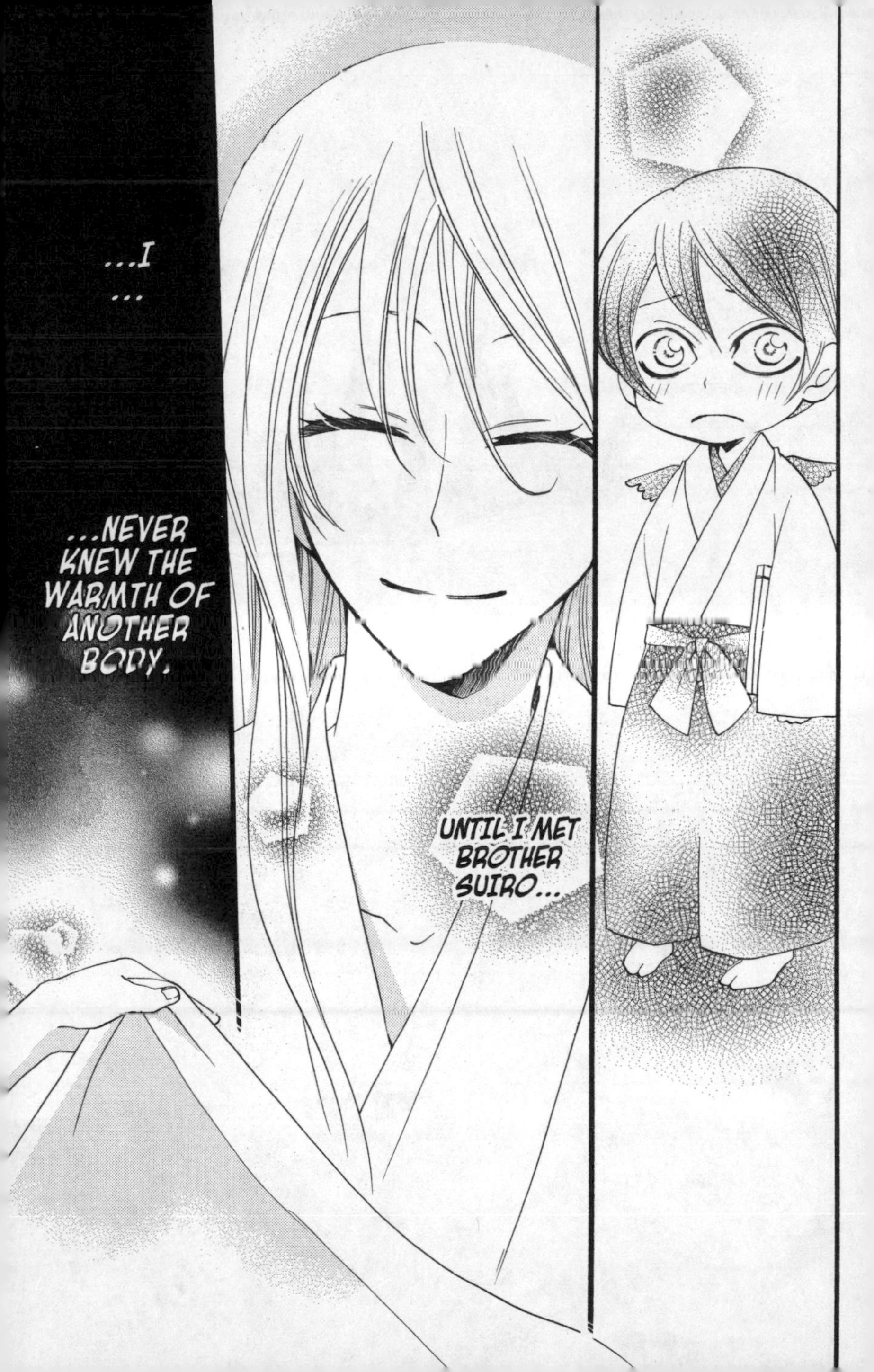
...I
...
...NEVER KNEW THE WARMTH OF ANOTHER BODY.
UNTIL I MET BROTHER SUIRO...

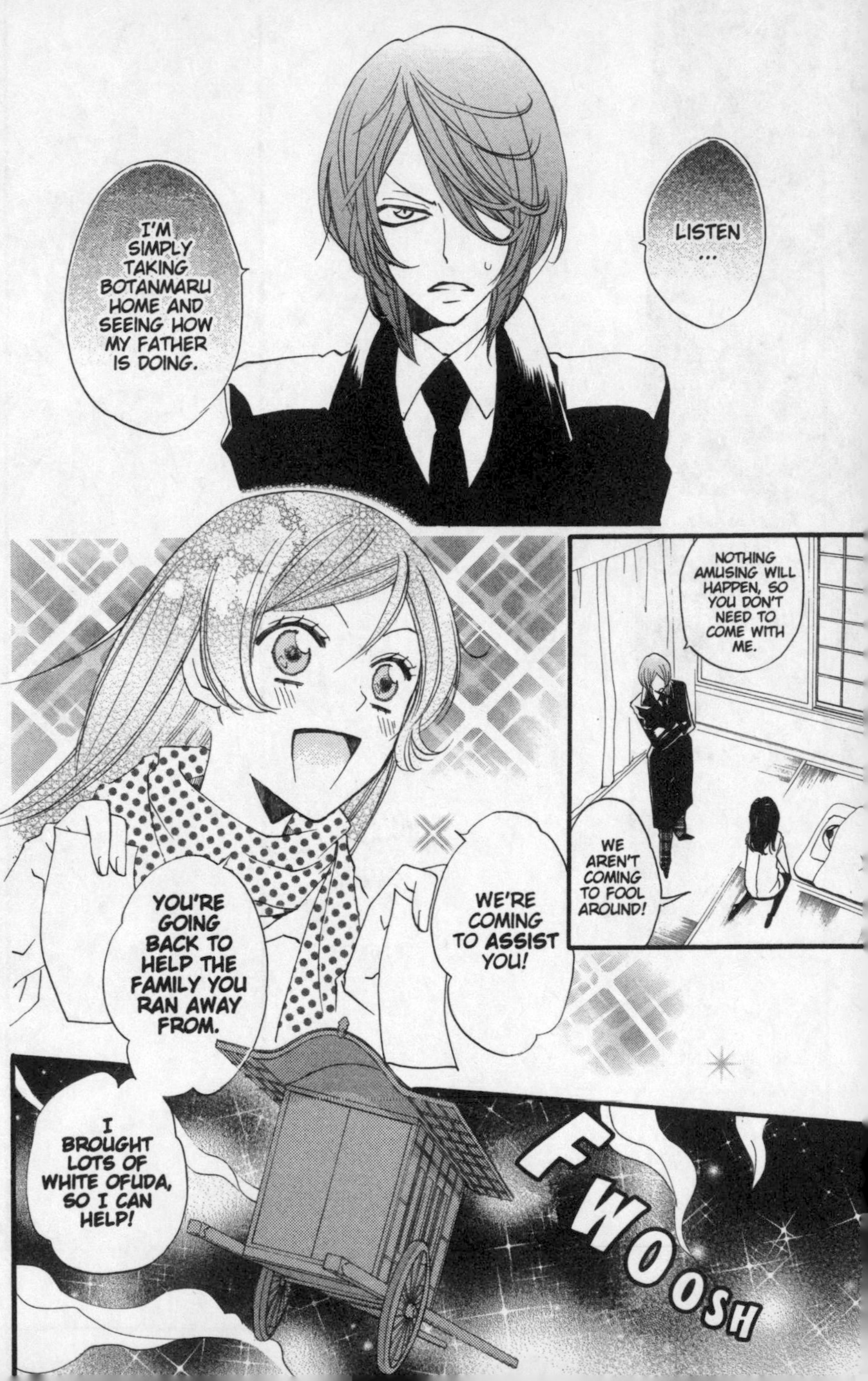
LISTEN ...
I'M SIMPLY TAKING BOTANMARU HOME AND SEEING HOW MY FATHER IS DOING.
NOTHING AMUSING WILL HAPPEN, SO YOU DON'T NEED TO COME WITH ME.
WE AREN'T COMING TO FOOL AROUND!
WE'RE COMING TO ASSIST YOU!
YOU'RE GOING BACK TO HELP THE FAMILY YOU RAN AWAY FROM.
I BROUGHT LOTS OF WHITE OFUDA, SO I CAN HELP!
FWOOSH

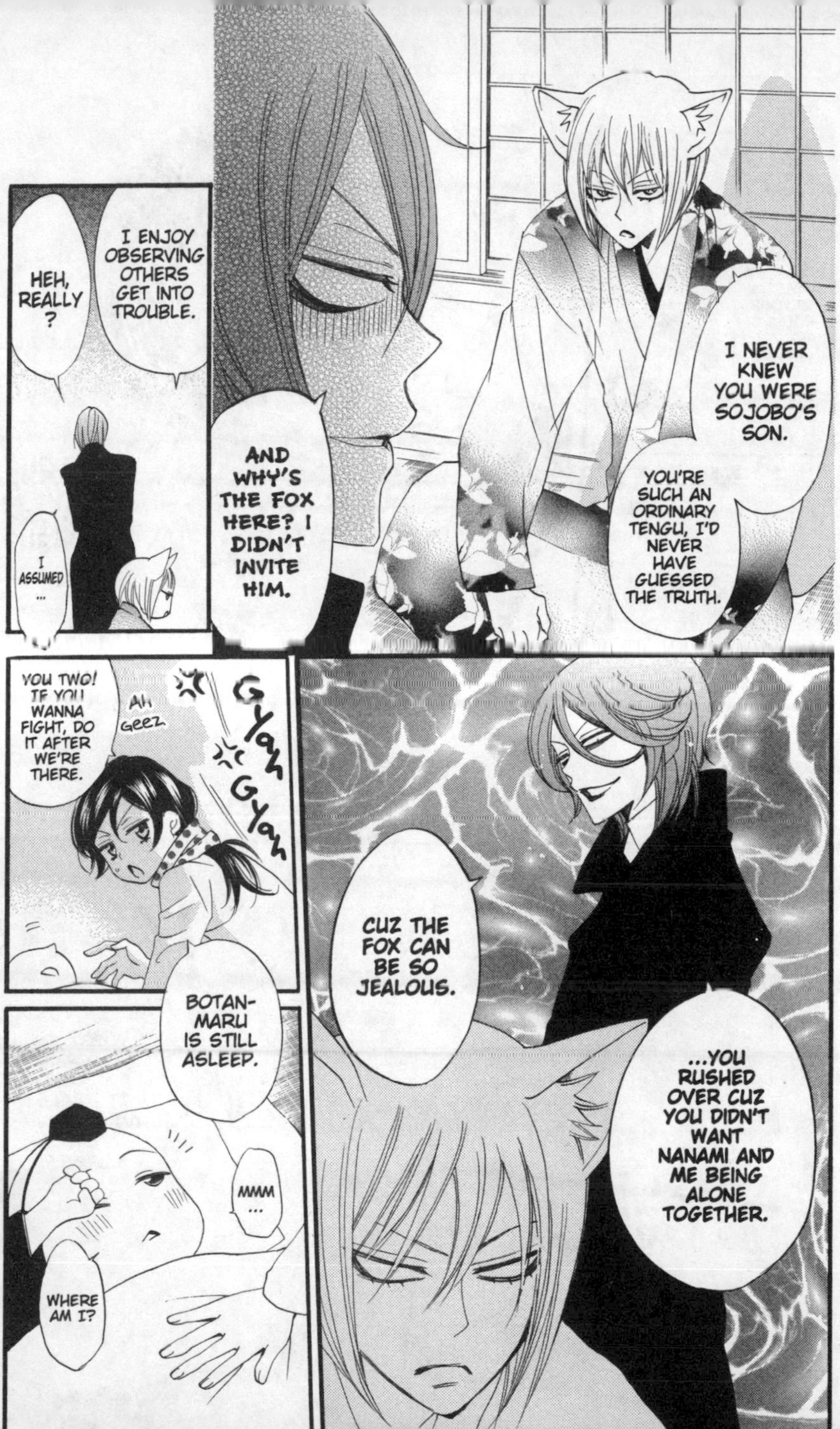
I NEVER KNEW YOU WERE SOJOBO'S SON.
YOU'RE SUCH AN ORDINARY TENGU, I'D NEVER HAVE GUESSED THE TRUTH.
AND WHY'S THE FOX HERE? I DIDN'T INVITE HIM.
I ENJOY OBSERVING OTHERS GET INTO TROUBLE.
HEH, REALLY?
I ASSUMED ...
CUZ THE FOX CAN BE SO JEALOUS.
...YOU RUSHED OVER CUZ YOU DIDN'T WANT NANAMI AND ME BEING ALONE TOGETHER.
Gyah Gyah
Ah Geez
YOU TWO! IF YOU WANNA FIGHT, DO IT AFTER WE'RE THERE.
BOTAN-MARU IS STILL ASLEEP.
MMM ...
WHERE AM I?

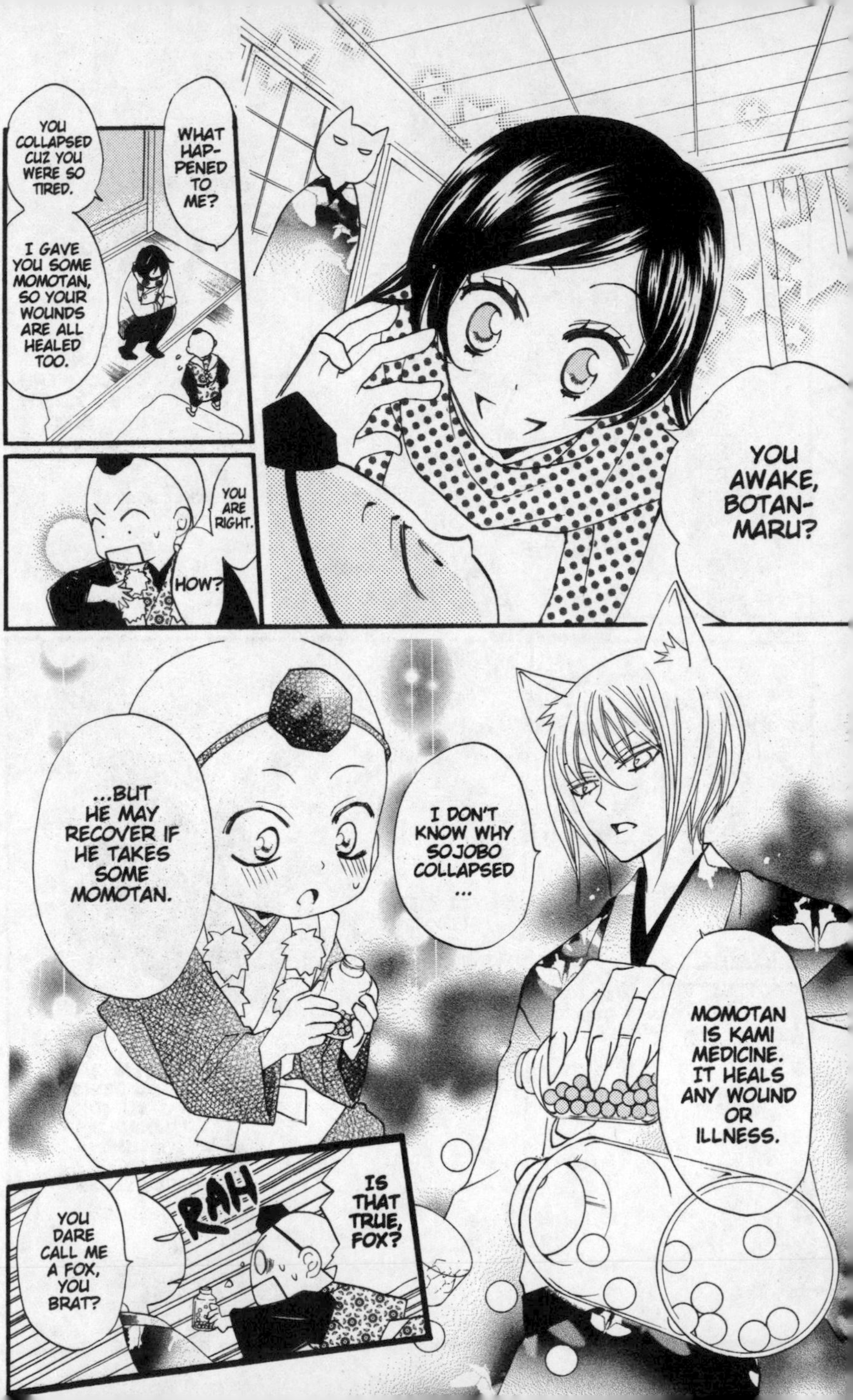
YOU AWAKE, BOTANMARU?
WHAT HAPPENED TO ME?
YOU COLLAPSED CUZ YOU WERE SO TIRED.
I GAVE YOU SOME MOMOTAN, SO YOUR WOUNDS ARE ALL HEALED TOO.
YOU ARE RIGHT.
HOW?
MOMOTAN IS KAMI MEDICINE. IT HEALS ANY WOUND OR ILLNESS.
I DON'T KNOW WHY SOJOBO COLLAPSED...
...BUT HE MAY RECOVER IF HE TAKES SOME MOMOTAN.
IS THAT TRUE, FOX?
RAH
YOU DARE CALL ME A FOX, YOU BRAT?

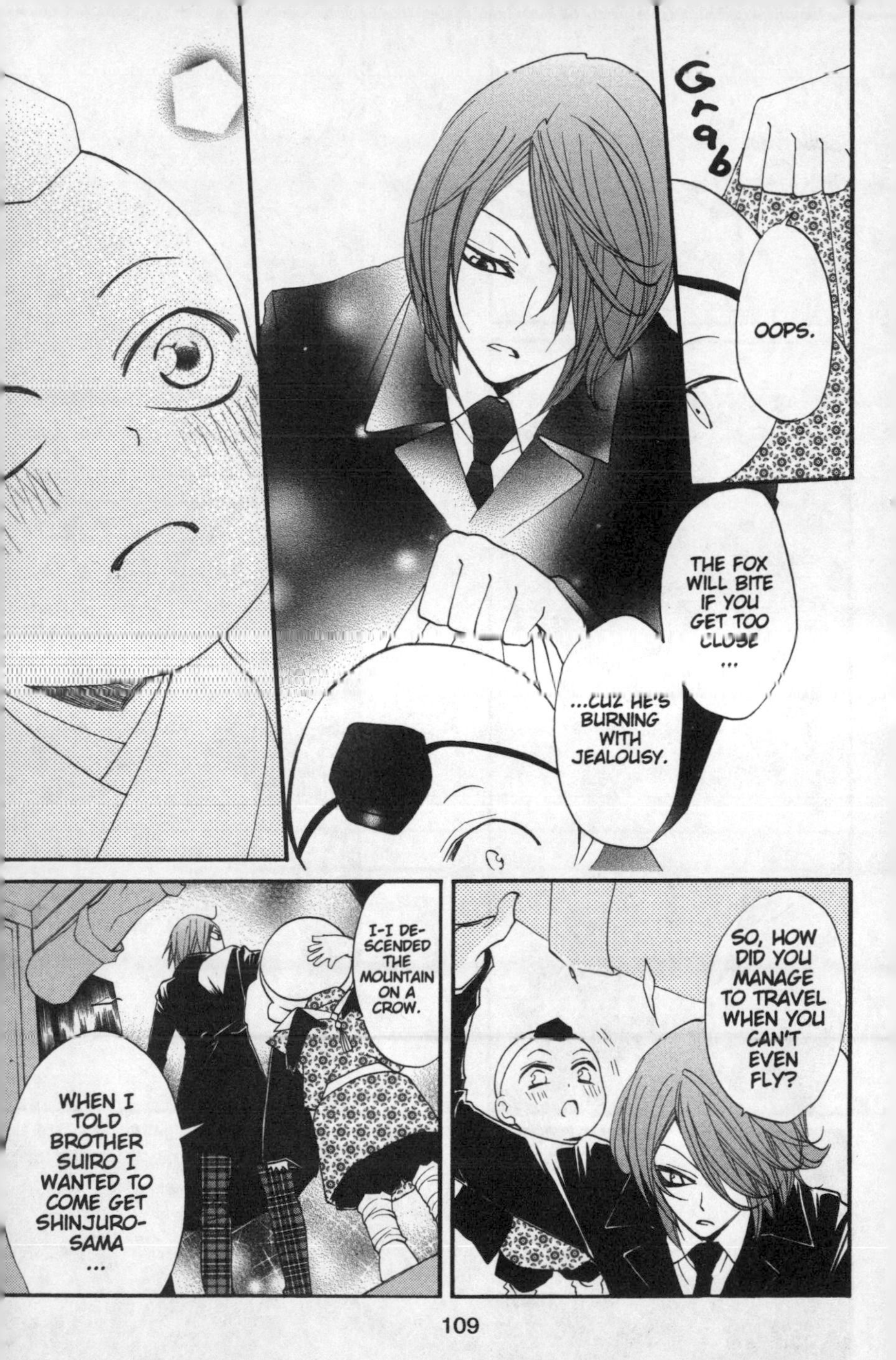
Grab
OOPS.
THE FOX WILL BITE IF YOU GET TOO CLOSE ...
...CUZ HE'S BURNING WITH JEALOUSY.
SO, HOW DID YOU MANAGE TO TRAVEL WHEN YOU CAN'T EVEN FLY?
I-I DESCENDED THE MOUNTAIN ON A CROW.
WHEN I TOLD BROTHER SUIRO I WANTED TO COME GET SHINJURO-SAMA ...

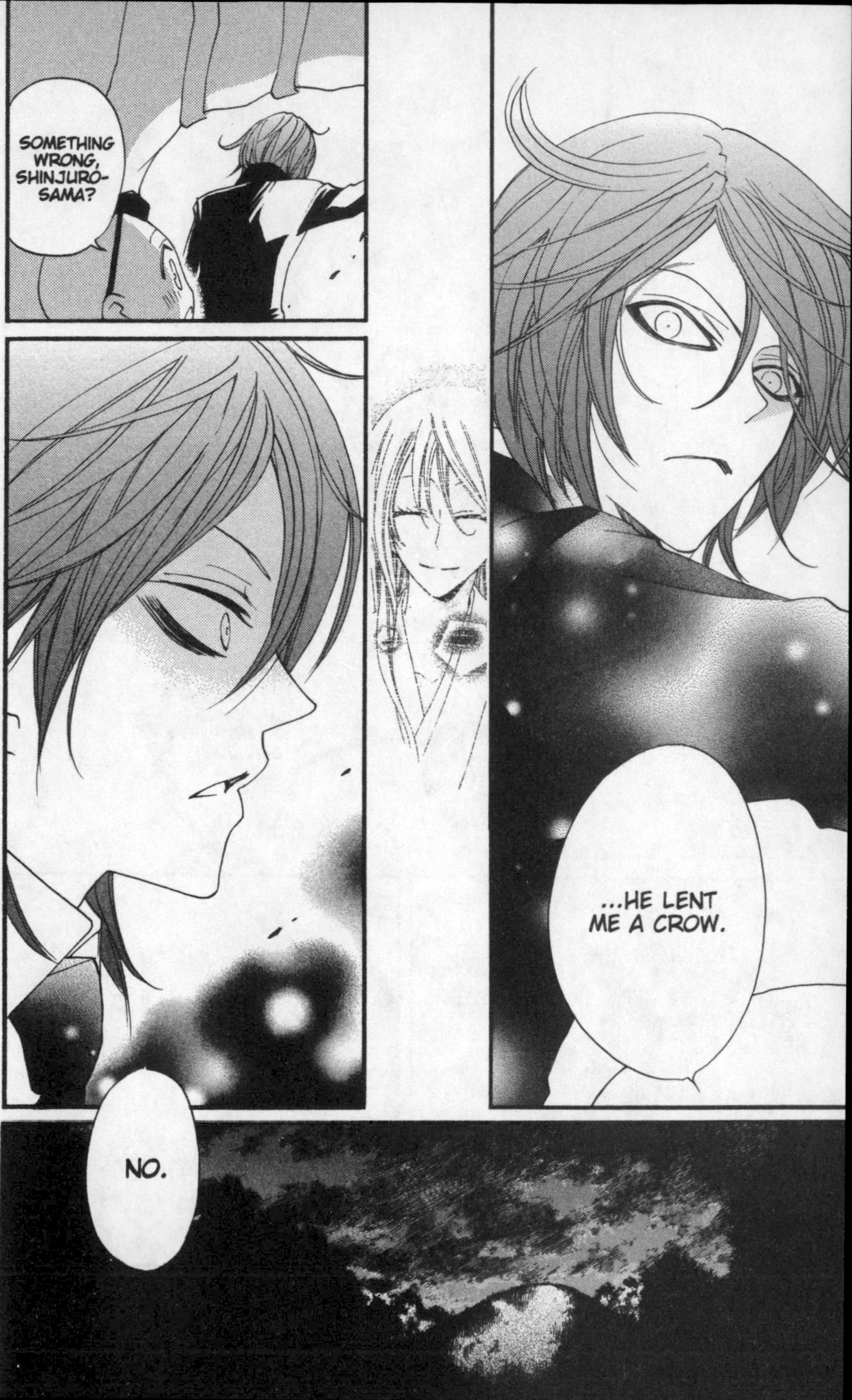
...HE LENT ME A CROW.
SOMETHING WRONG, SHINJURÓ-SAMA?
NO.

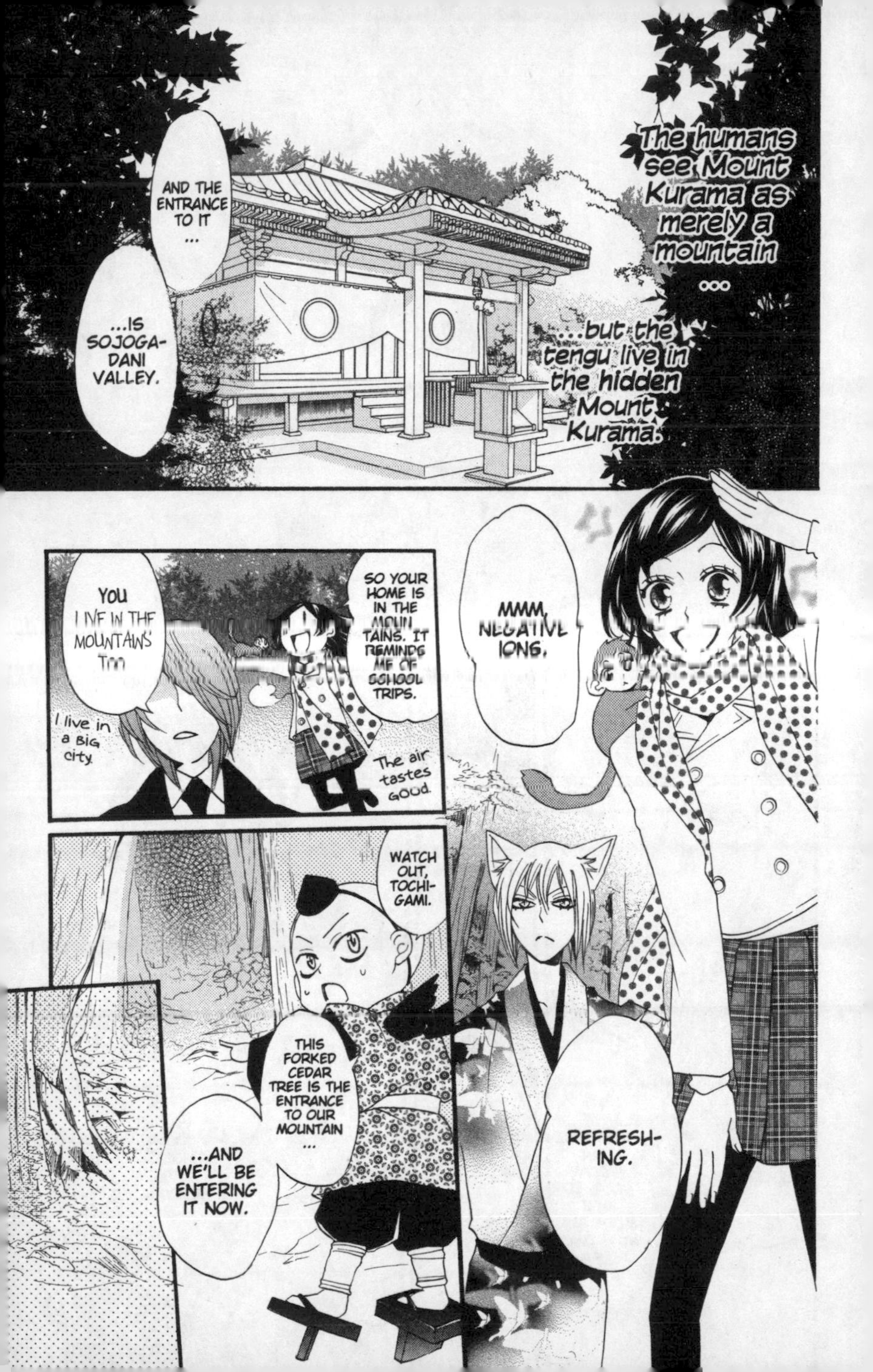
The humans see Mount Kurama as merely a mountain...
...but the tengu live in the hidden Mount Kurama.
AND THE ENTRANCE TO IT...
...IS SOJOGA-DANI VALLEY.
MMM, NEGATIVE IONS.
REFRESHING.
SO YOUR HOME IS IN THE MOUNTAINS. IT REMINDS ME OF SCHOOL TRIPS.
YOU LIVE IN THE MOUNTAINS TOO
The air tastes good.
I live in a BIG city.
WATCH OUT, TOCHIGAMI.
THIS FORKED CEDAR TREE IS THE ENTRANCE TO OUR MOUNTAIN...
...AND WE'LL BE ENTERING IT NOW.

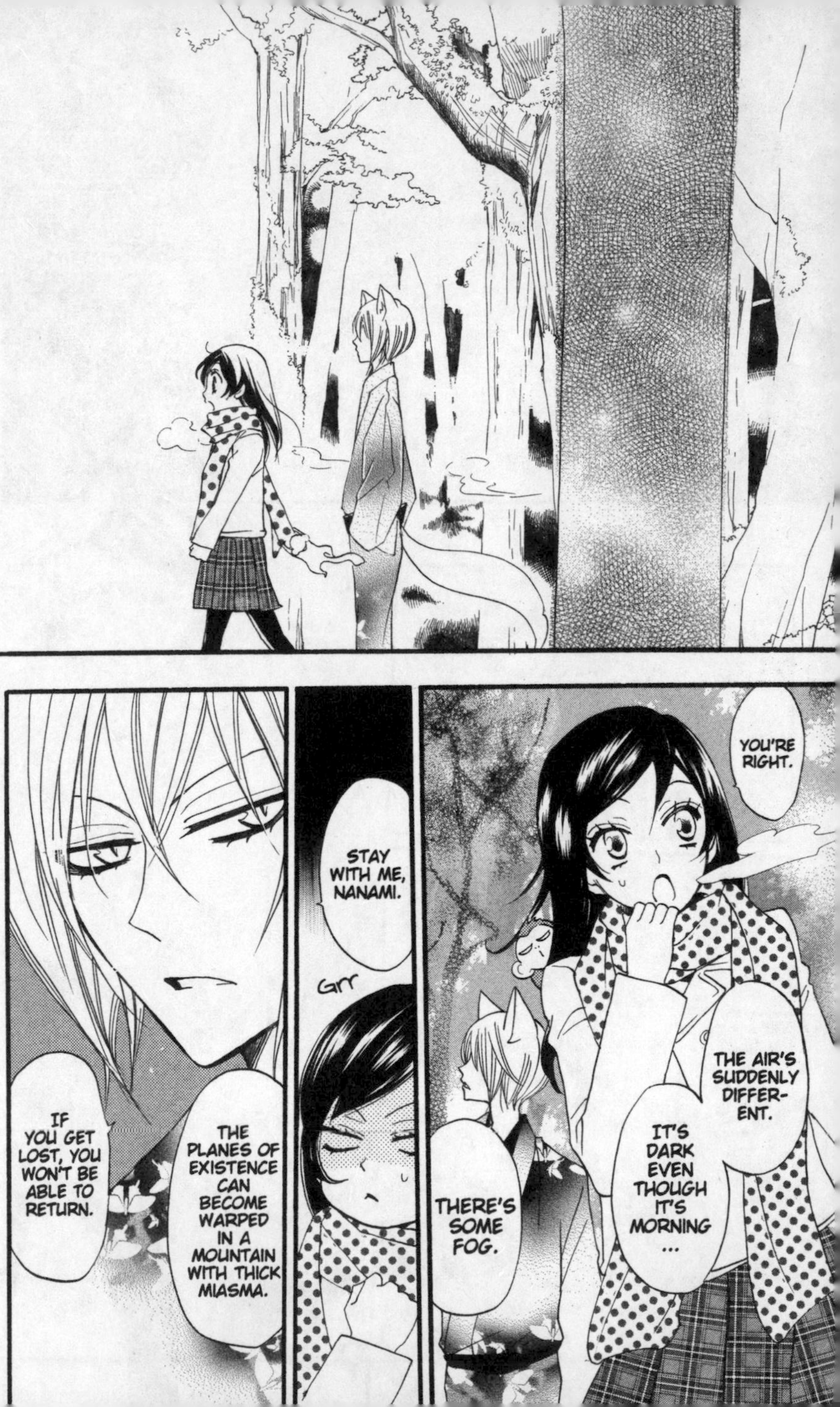
YOU'RE RIGHT.
THE AIR'S SUDDENLY DIFFER-ENT.
IT'S DARK EVEN THOUGH IT'S MORNING...
THERE'S SOME FOG.
STAY WITH ME, NANAMI.
Grr
THE PLANES OF EXISTENCE CAN BECOME WARPED IN A MOUNTAIN WITH THICK MIASMA.
IF YOU GET LOST, YOU WON'T BE ABLE TO RETURN.

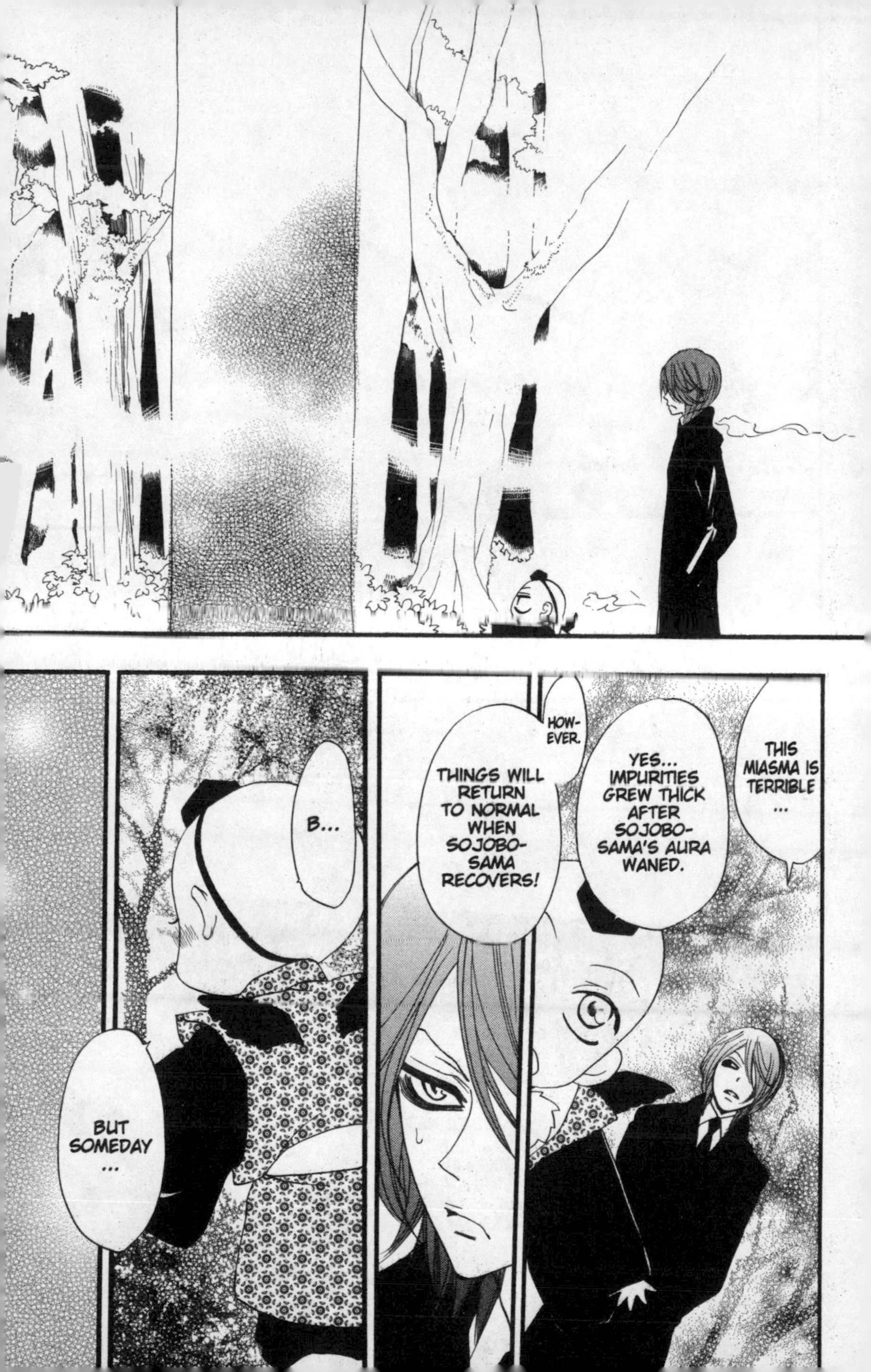
THIS MIASMA IS TERRIBLE ...
YES... IMPURITIES GREW THICK AFTER SOJOBO-SAMA'S AURA WANED.
HOW-EVER.
THINGS WILL RETURN TO NORMAL WHEN SOJOBO-SAMA RECOVERS!
B...
BUT SOMEDAY ...

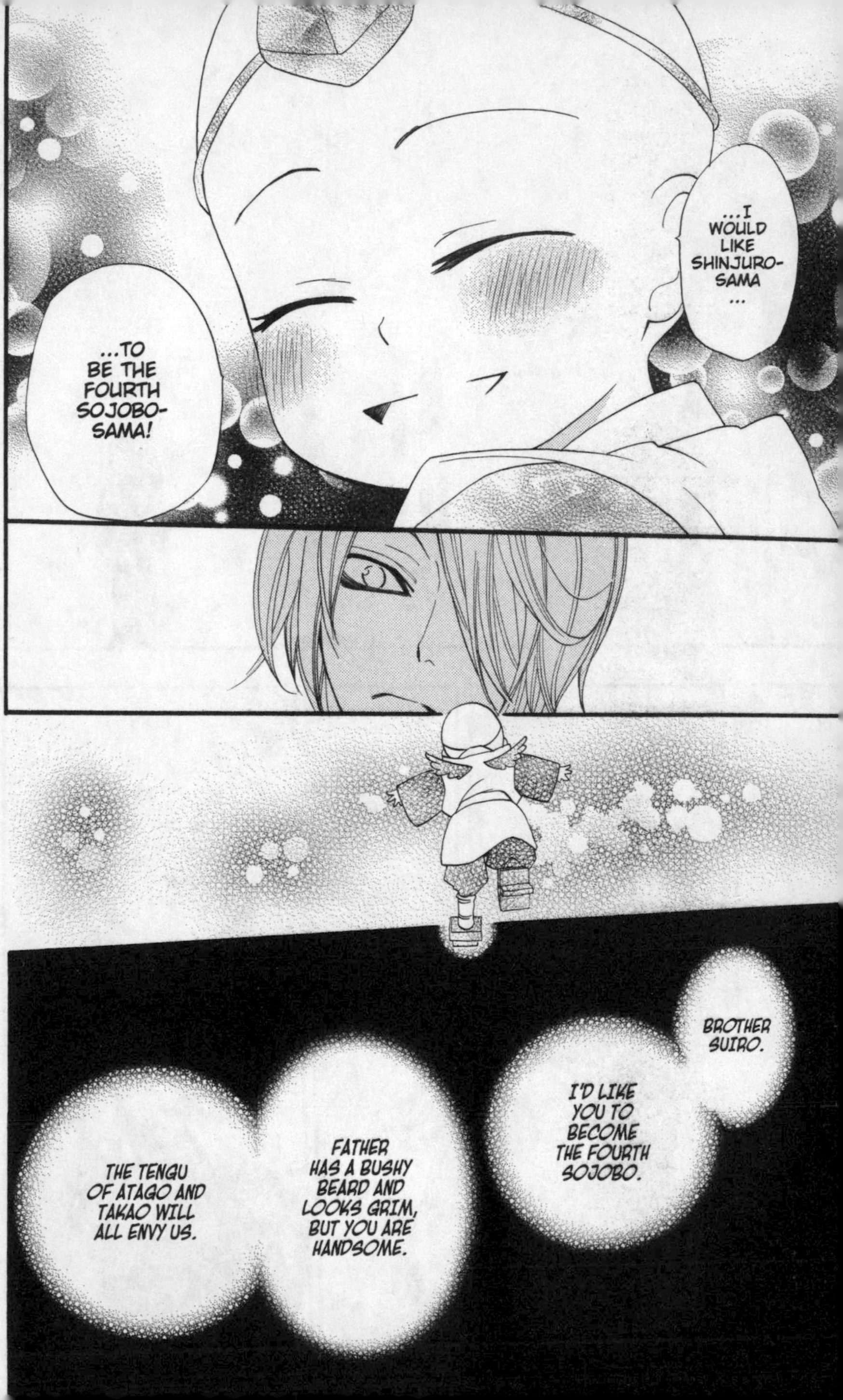
...I WOULD LIKE SHINJURO-SAMA ...
...TO BE THE FOURTH SOJOBO-SAMA!
BROTHER SUIRO.
I'D LIKE YOU TO BECOME THE FOURTH SOJOBO.
FATHER HAS A BUSHY BEARD AND LOOKS GRIM, BUT YOU ARE HANDSOME.
THE TENGU OF ATAGO AND TAKAO WILL ALL ENVY US.

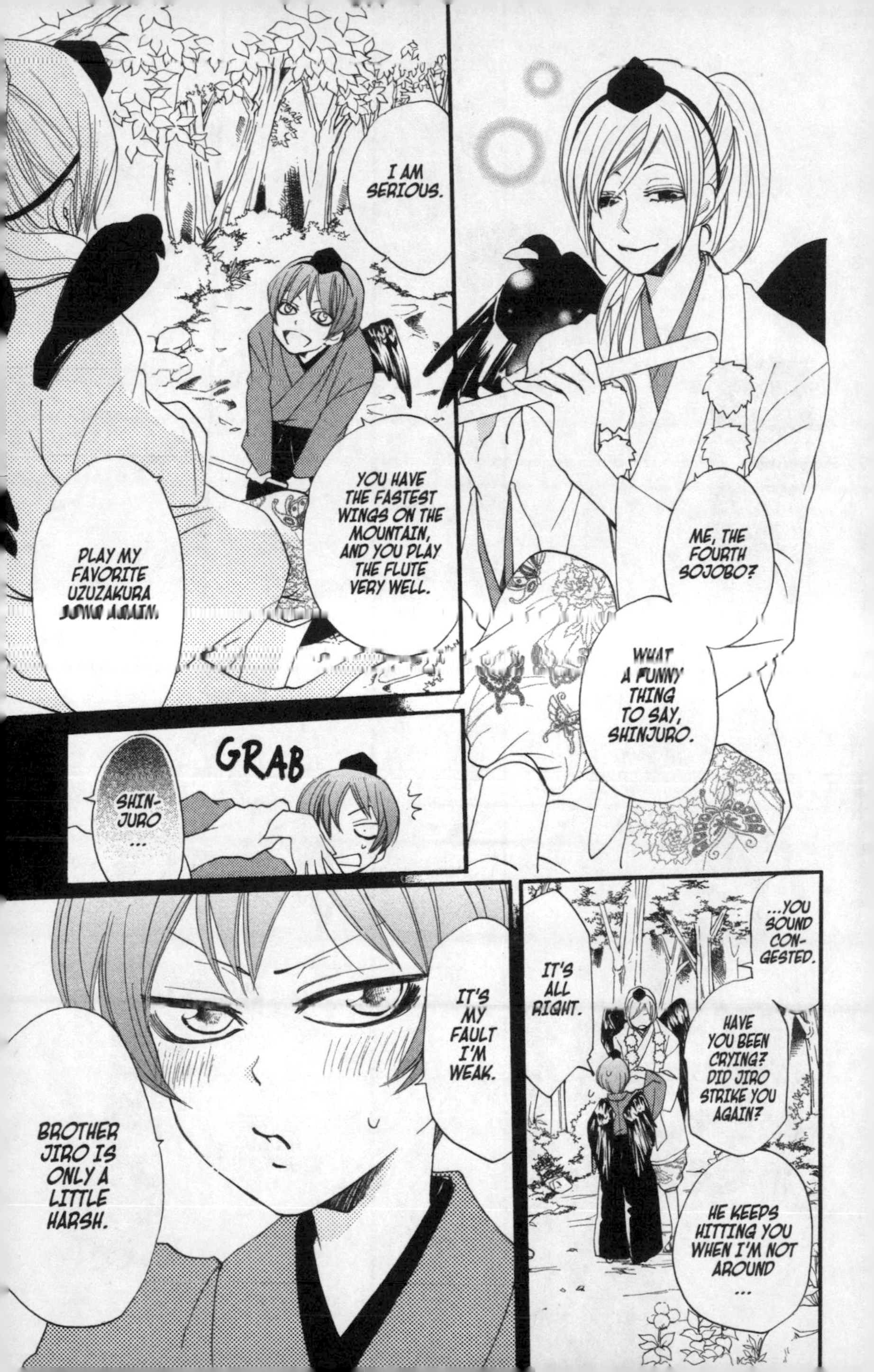
ME, THE FOURTH SOJOBO?
WHAT A FUNNY THING TO SAY, SHINJURO.
I AM SERIOUS.
YOU HAVE THE FASTEST WINGS ON THE MOUNTAIN, AND YOU PLAY THE FLUTE VERY WELL.
PLAY MY FAVORITE UZUZAKURA
GRAB
SHIN-JURO ...
...YOU SOUND CON-GESTED.
HAVE YOU BEEN CRYING? DID JIRO STRIKE YOU AGAIN?
IT'S ALL RIGHT.
HE KEEPS HITTING YOU WHEN I'M NOT AROUND ...
IT'S MY FAULT I'M WEAK.
BROTHER JIRO IS ONLY A LITTLE HARSH.

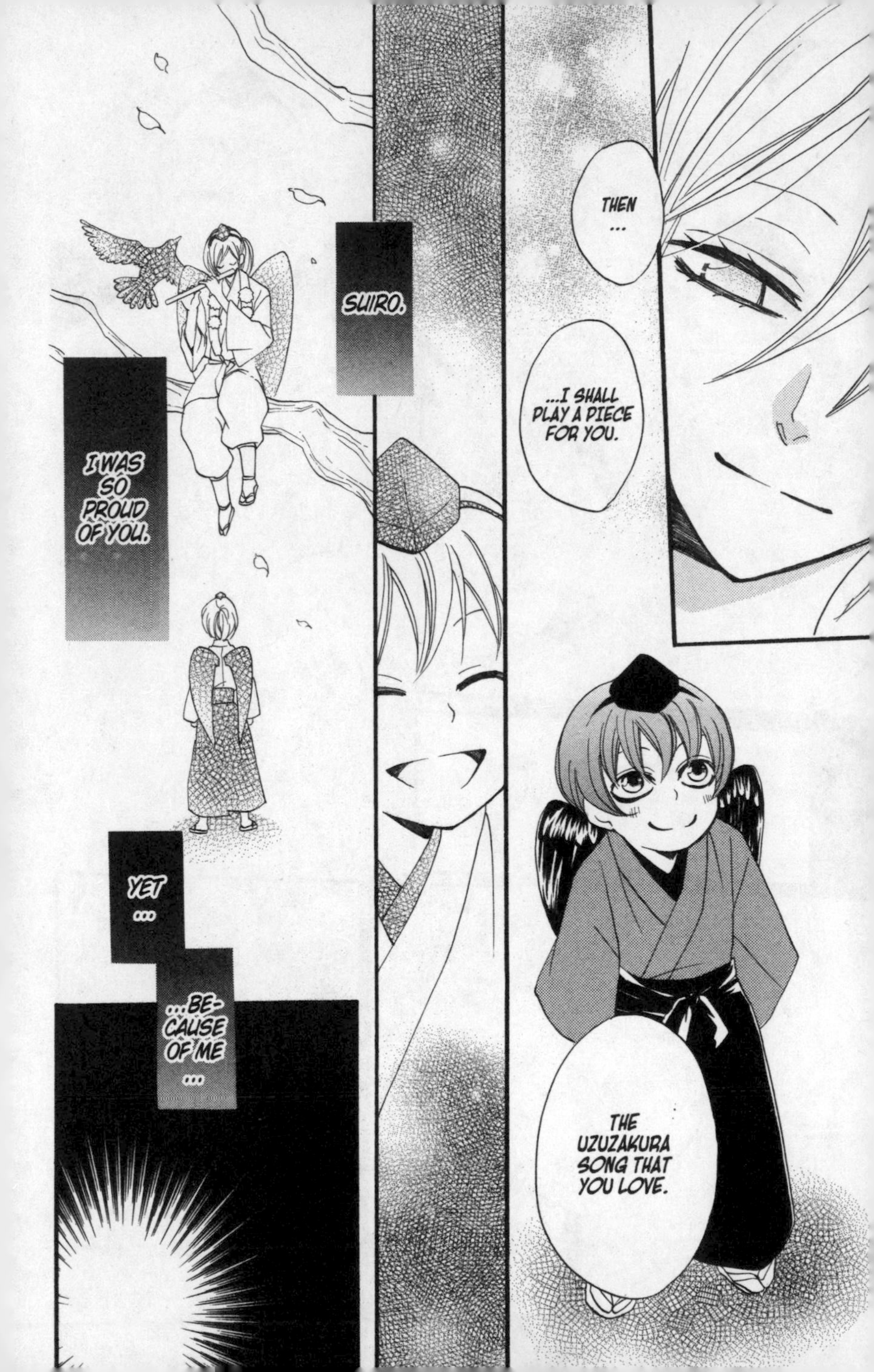
THEN ...
...I SHALL PLAY A PIECE FOR YOU.
THE UZUZAKURA SONG THAT YOU LOVE.
SUIRO.
I WAS SO PROUD OF YOU.
YET ...
...BE-CAUSE OF ME ...

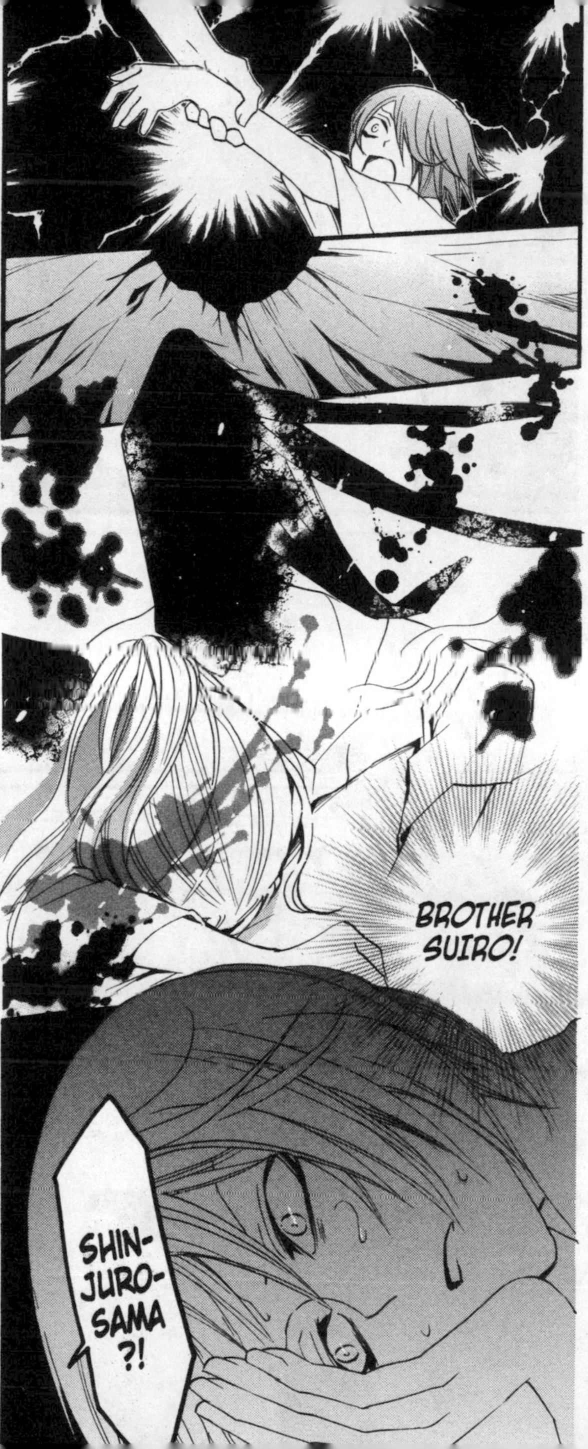
BROTHER SUIRO!
SHIN-JURO-SAMA?!

4

I went to Mount Kurama because I'm doing a story about tengu.

I've been saying since volume 3 that I've got to draw about Kurama, and I was finally able to.

This was my second time climbing Mount Kurama, and my legs were so tired I need to exercise more.

I saw a man in a suit climbing while carrying a suitcase.

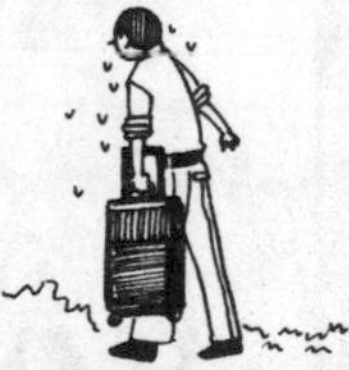

I saw a woman climbing in high heels!

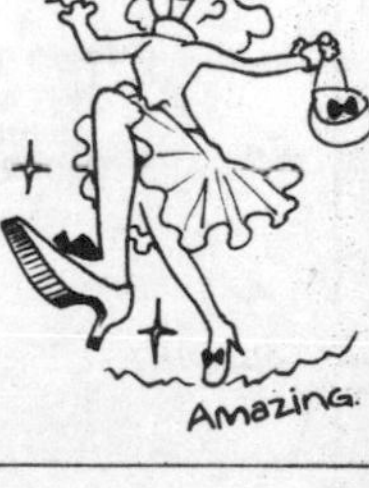
Amazing.

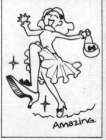

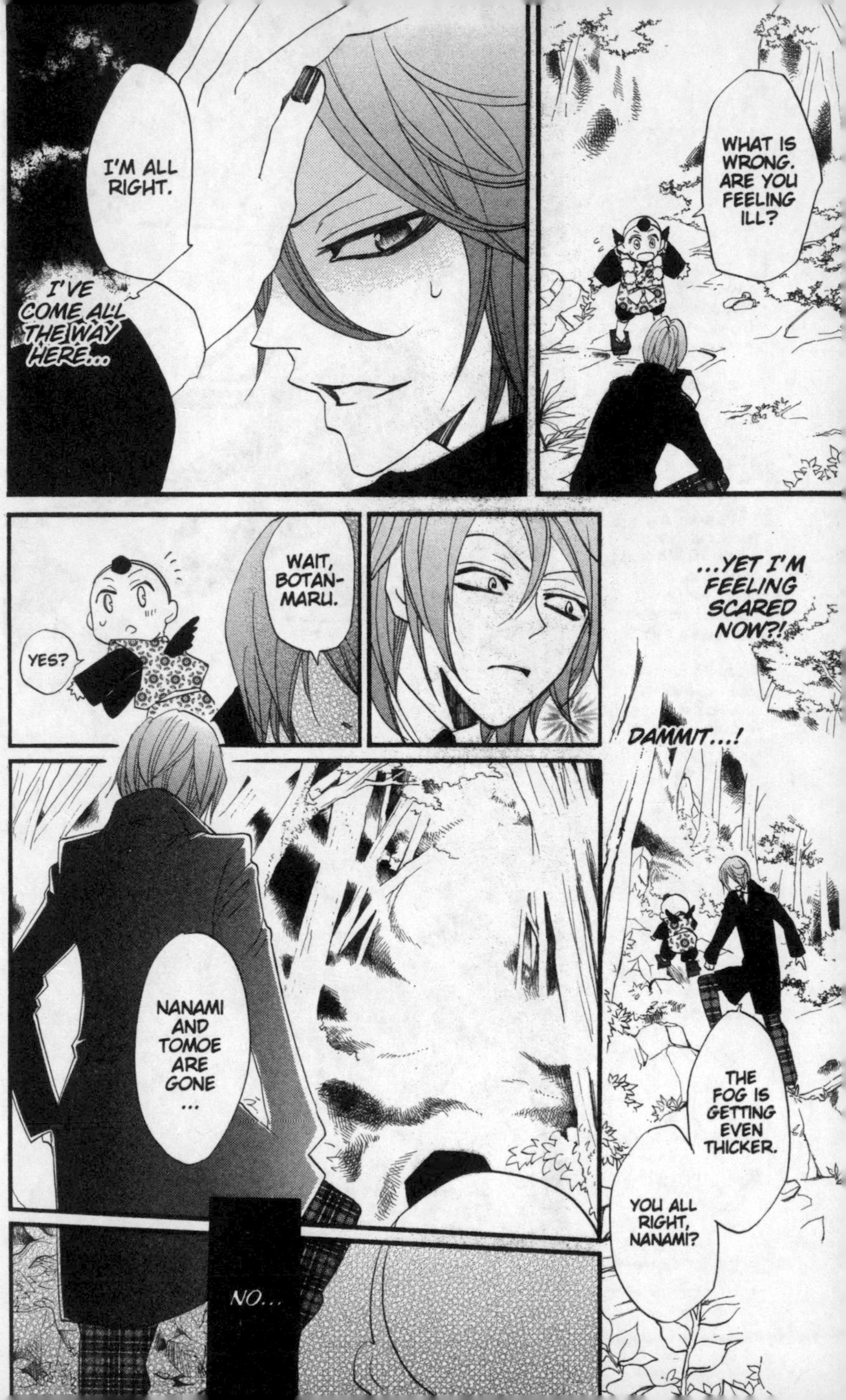
WHAT IS WRONG. ARE YOU FEELING ILL?
I'M ALL RIGHT.
I'VE COME ALL THE WAY HERE...
...YET I'M FEELING SCARED NOW?!
WAIT, BOTAN-MARU.
YES?
DAMMIT...!
THE FOG IS GETTING EVEN THICKER.
YOU ALL RIGHT, NANAMI?
NANAMI AND TOMOE ARE GONE ...
NO...

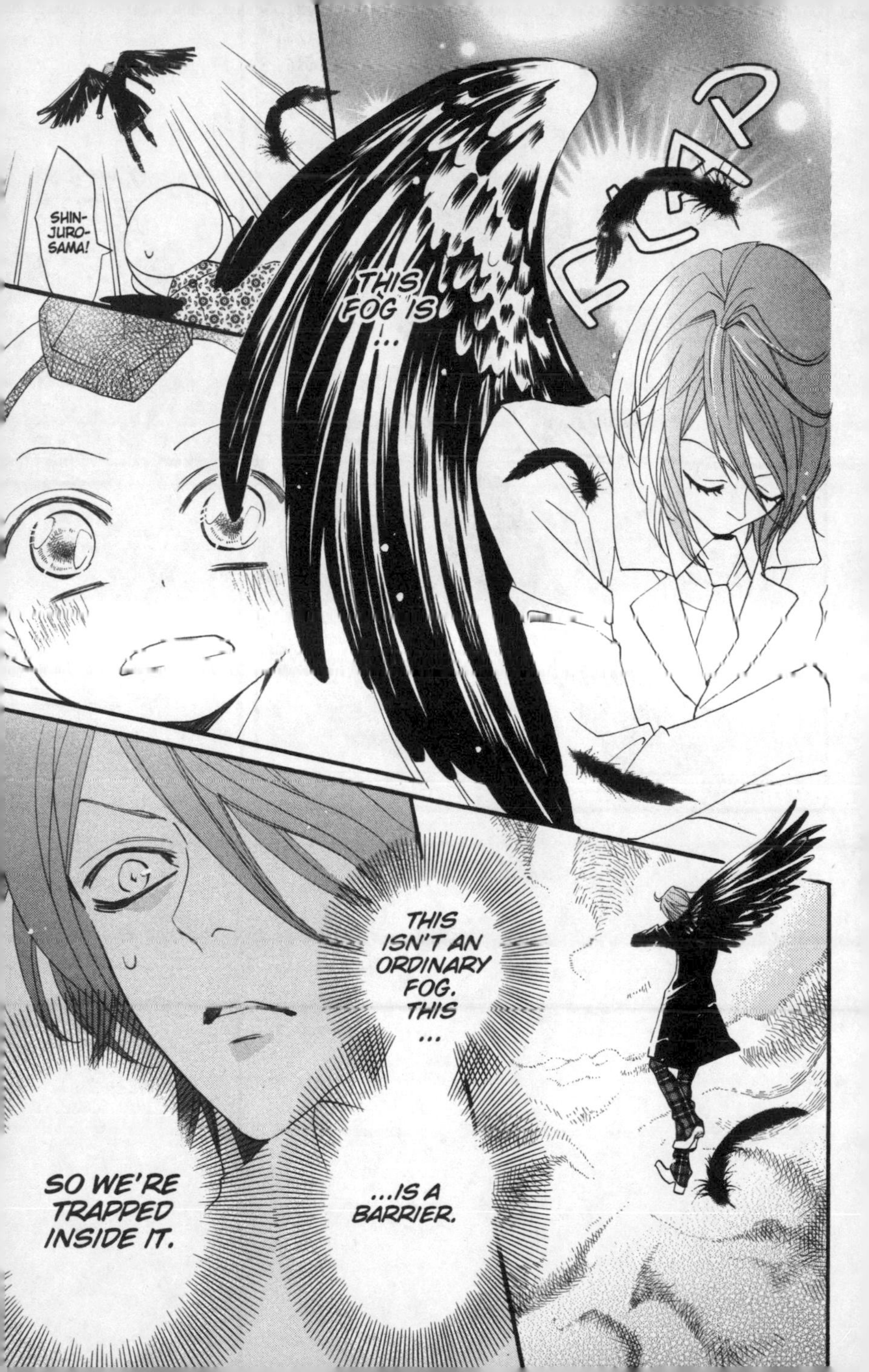
THIS FOG IS ...
SHIN-JURO-SAMA!
THIS ISN'T AN ORDINARY FOG. THIS ...
...IS A BARRIER.
SO WE'RE TRAPPED INSIDE IT.

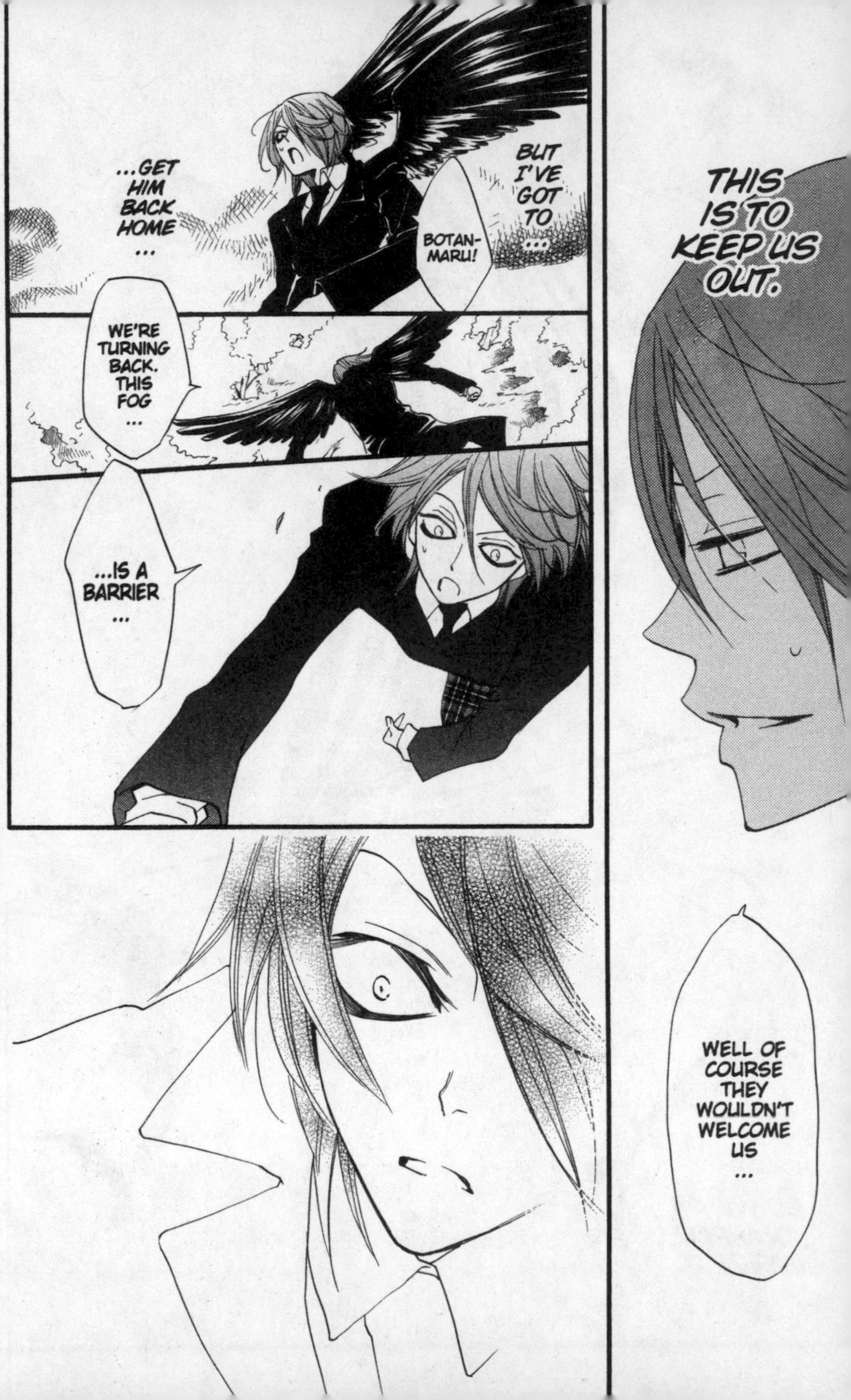
BUT I'VE GOT TO ...
BOTAN-MARU!
...GET HIM BACK HOME ...
WE'RE TURNING BACK. THIS FOG ...
...IS A BARRIER ...
THIS IS TO KEEP US OUT.
WELL OF COURSE THEY WOULDN'T WELCOME US ...

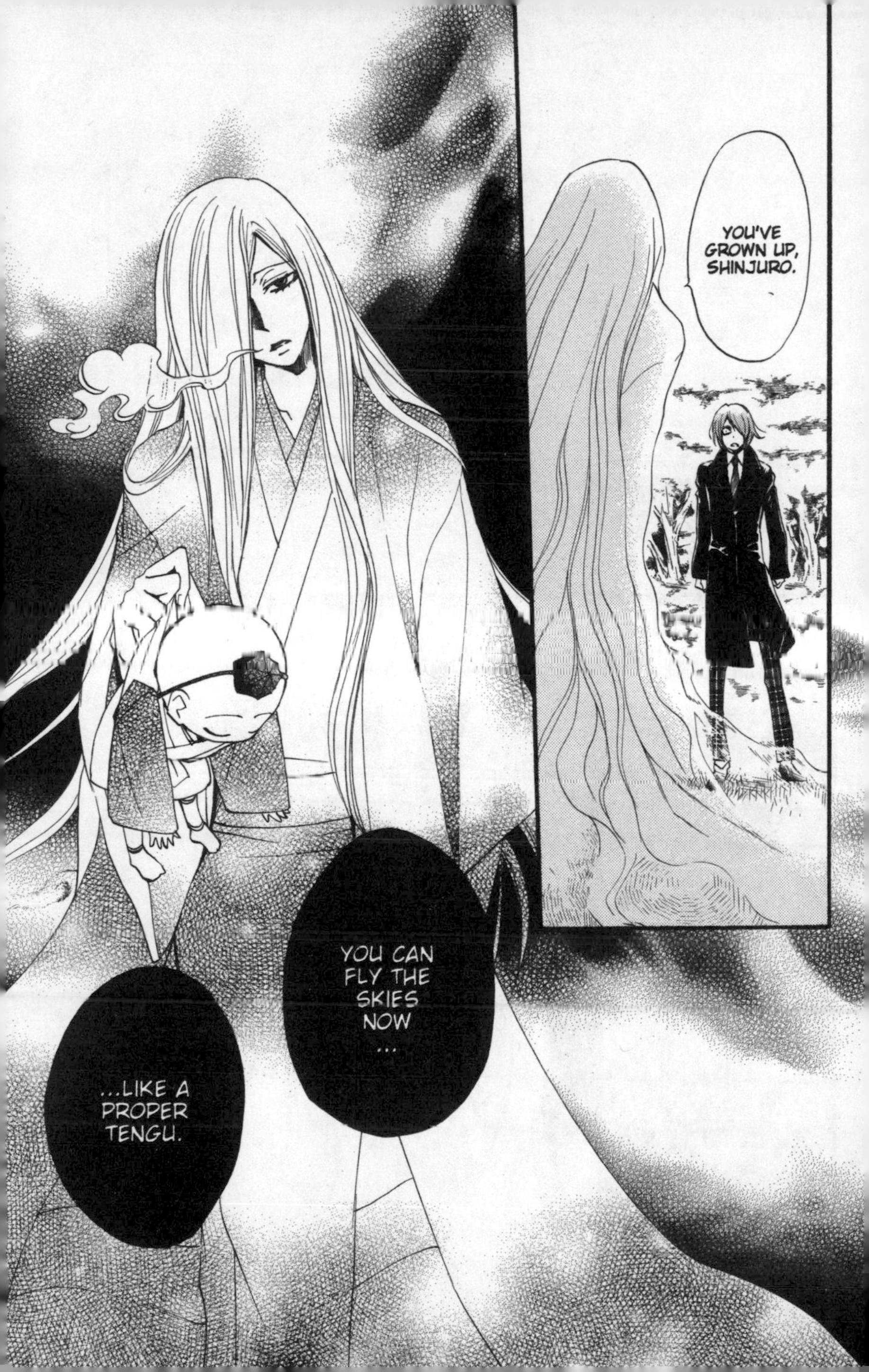
YOU'VE GROWN UP, SHINJURO.
YOU CAN FLY THE SKIES NOW ...
...LIKE A PROPER TENGU.

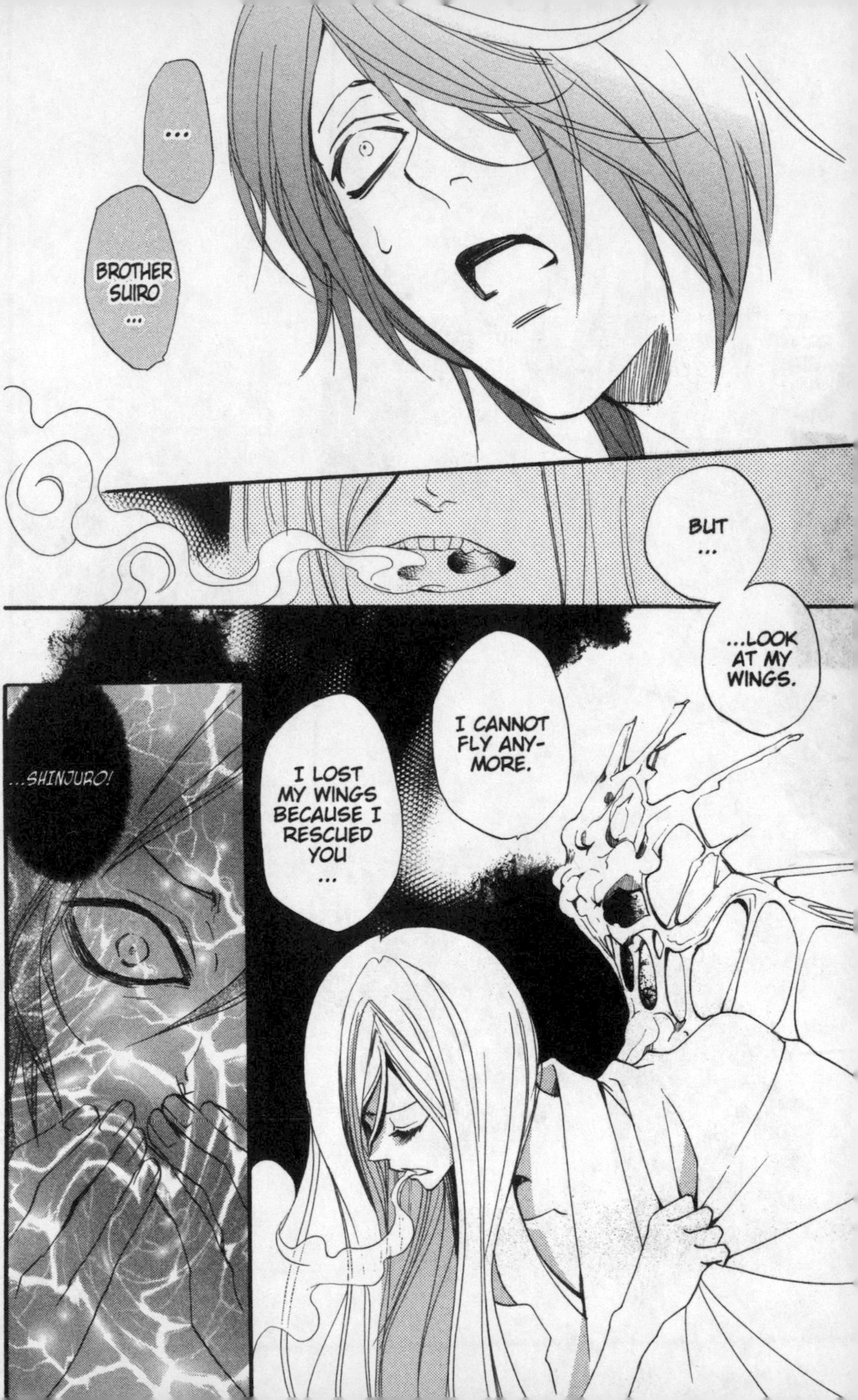
...
BROTHER SUIRO ...
BUT ...
...LOOK AT MY WINGS.
I CANNOT FLY ANY-MORE.
I LOST MY WINGS BECAUSE I RESCUED YOU ...
...SHINJURO!

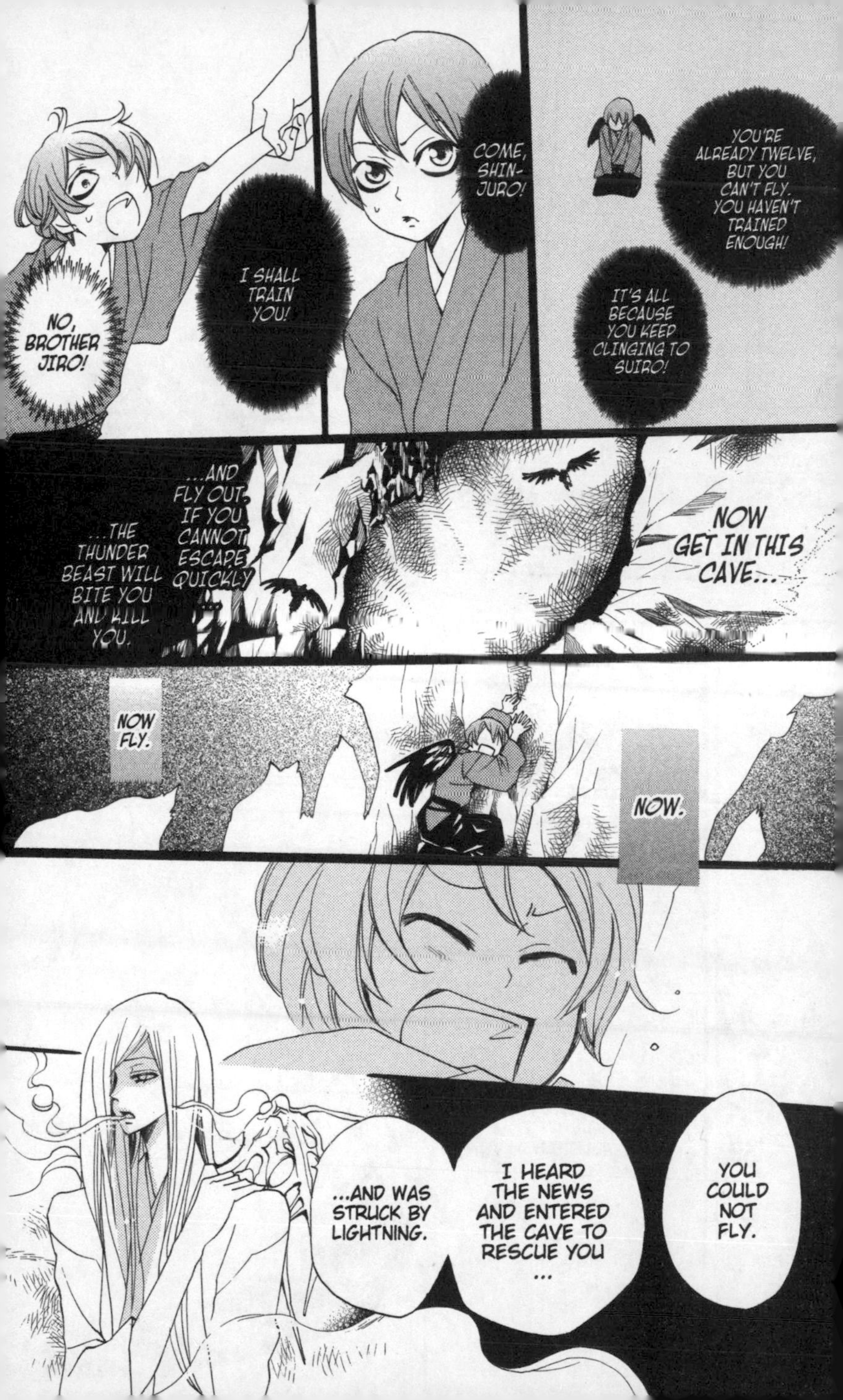

YOU'RE ALREADY TWELVE, BUT YOU CAN'T FLY. YOU HAVEN'T TRAINED ENOUGH!
IT'S ALL BECAUSE YOU KEEP CLINGING TO SUIRO!
COME, SHIN-JURO!
I SHALL TRAIN YOU!
NO, BROTHER JIRO!
NOW GET IN THIS CAVE...
...AND FLY OUT IF YOU CANNOT ESCAPE QUICKLY
...THE THUNDER BEAST WILL BITE YOU AND KILL YOU.
NOW.
NOW FLY.
YOU COULD NOT FLY.
I HEARD THE NEWS AND ENTERED THE CAVE TO RESCUE YOU ...
...AND WAS STRUCK BY LIGHTNING.

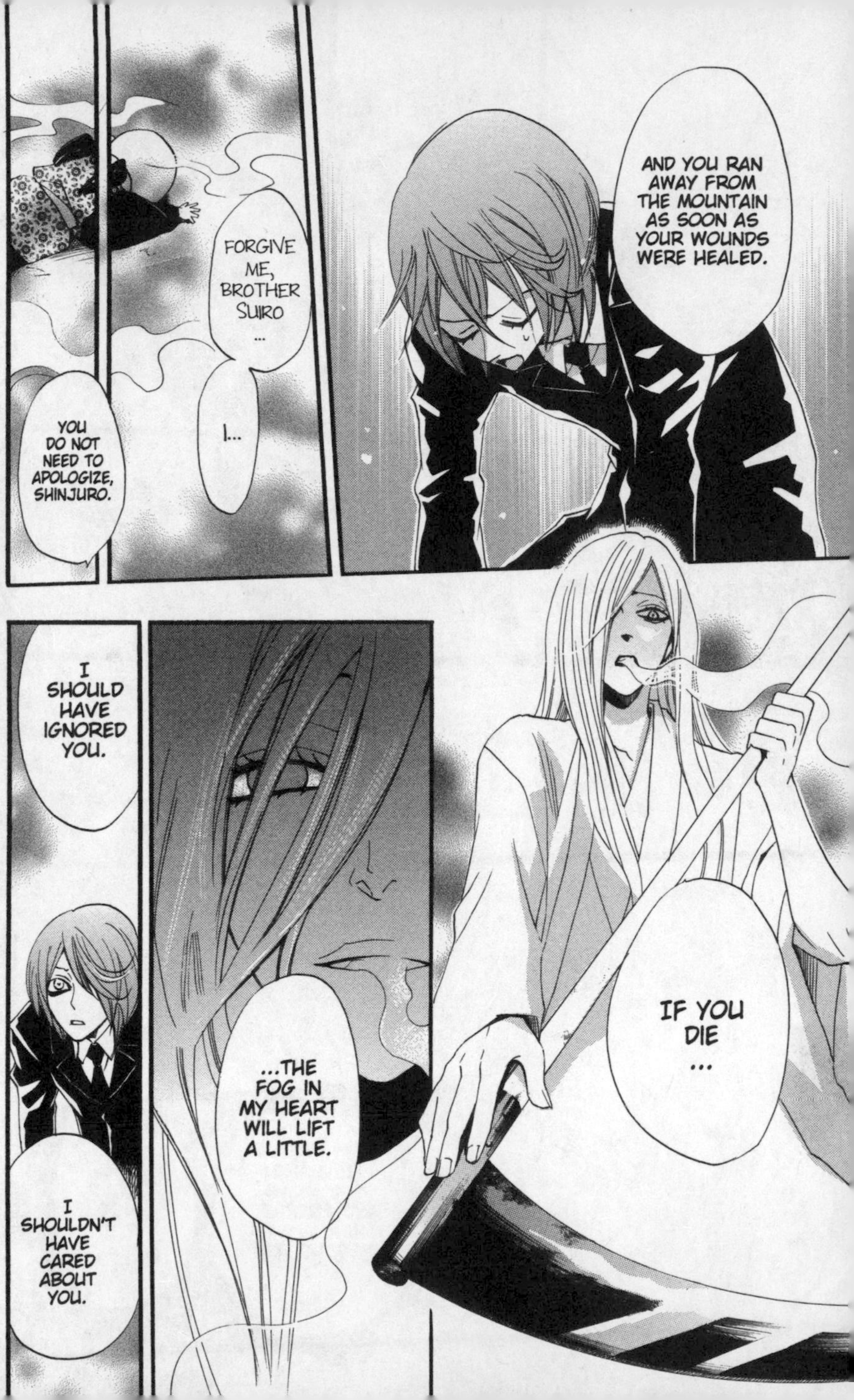
AND YOU RAN AWAY FROM THE MOUNTAIN AS SOON AS YOUR WOUNDS WERE HEALED.
FORGIVE ME, BROTHER SUIRO ...
I...
YOU DO NOT NEED TO APOLOGIZE, SHINJURO.
IF YOU DIE ...
...THE FOG IN MY HEART WILL LIFT A LITTLE.
I SHOULD HAVE IGNORED YOU.
I SHOULDN'T HAVE CARED ABOUT YOU.

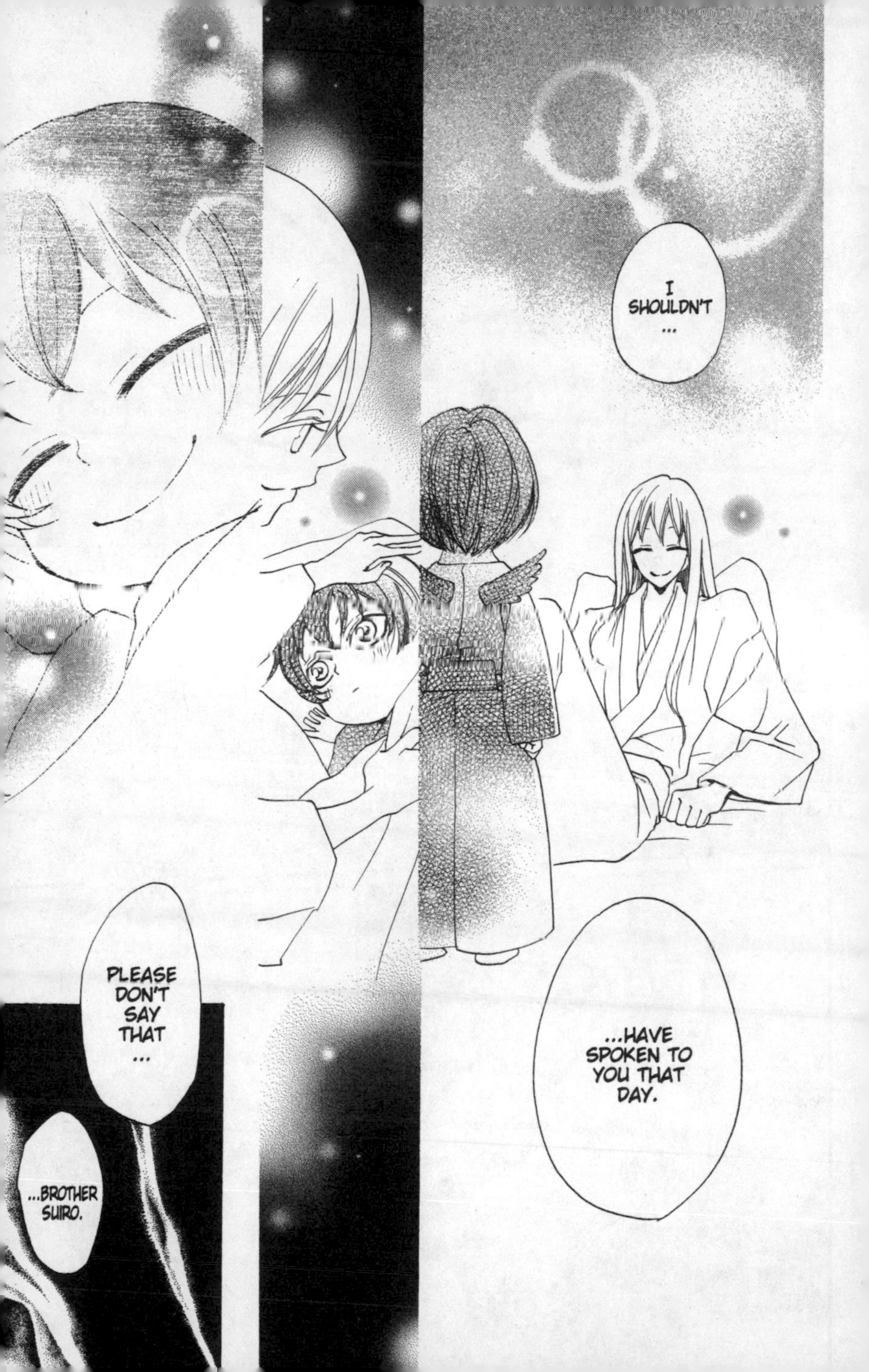
I SHOULDN'T ...
...HAVE SPOKEN TO YOU THAT DAY.
PLEASE DON'T SAY THAT ...
...BROTHER SUIRO.

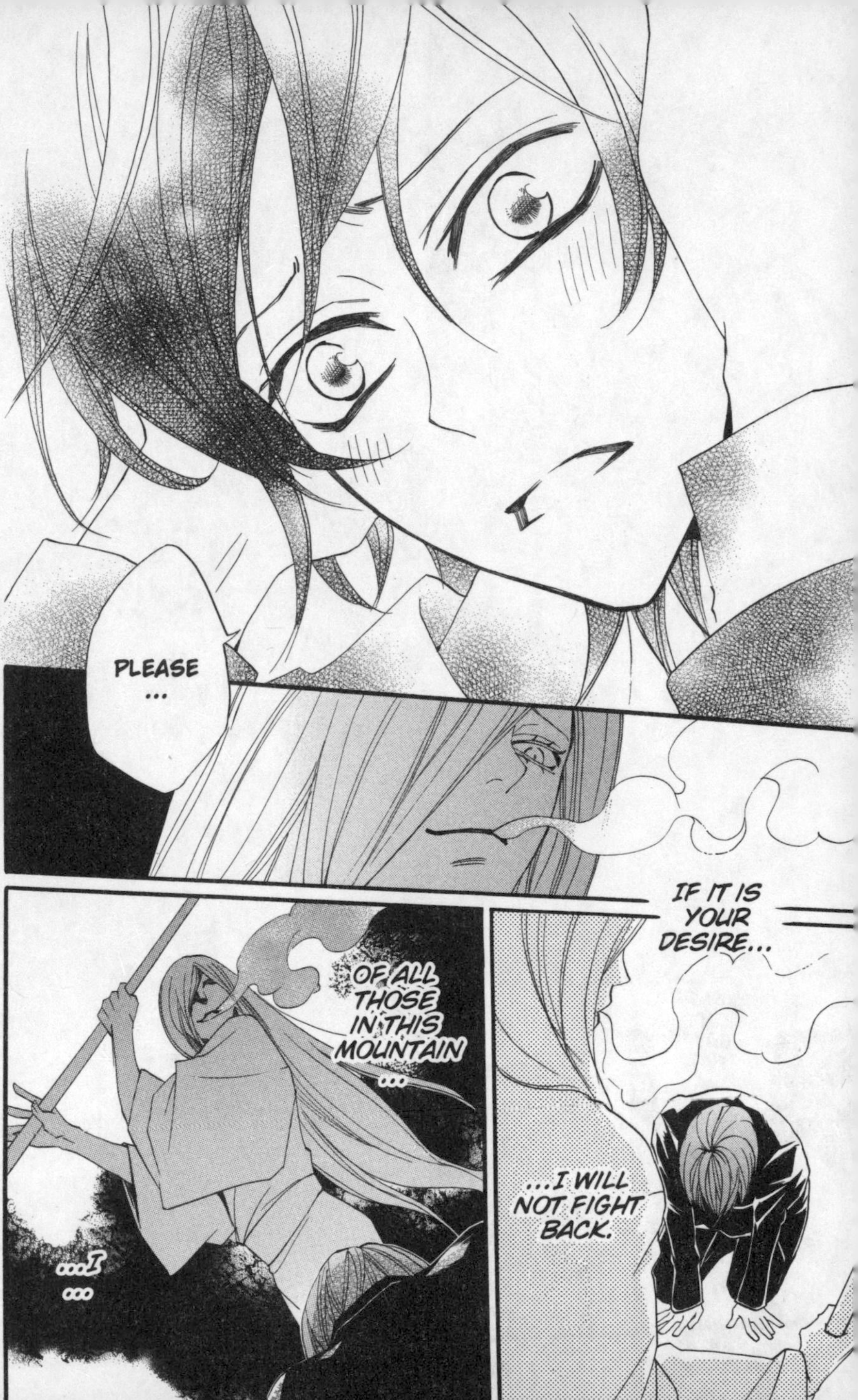
PLEASE ...
IF IT IS YOUR DESIRE...
...I WILL NOT FIGHT BACK.
OF ALL THOSE IN THIS MOUNTAIN ...
...I ...

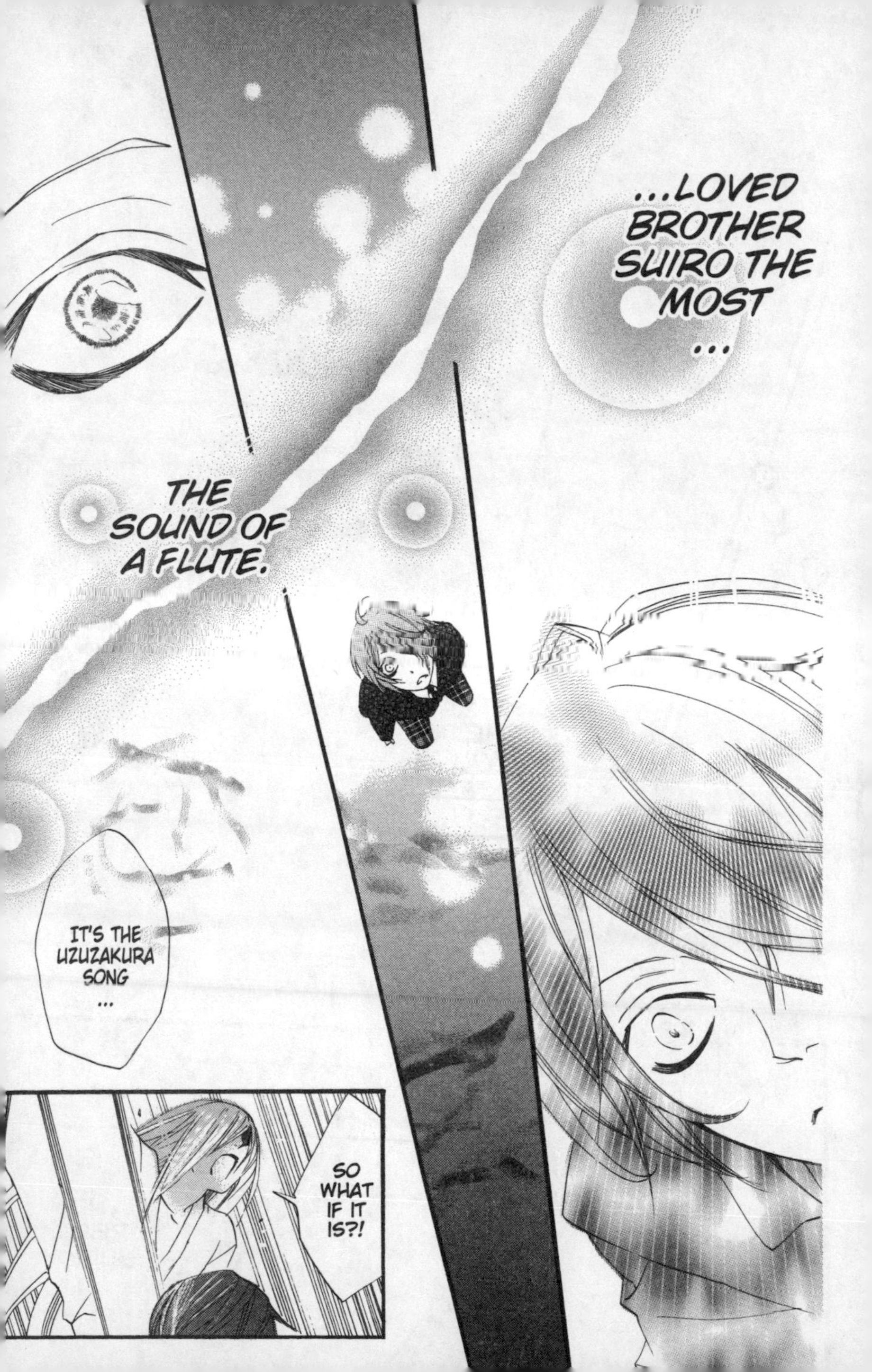
...LOVED BROTHER SUIRO THE MOST ...
THE SOUND OF A FLUTE.
IT'S THE UZUZAKURA SONG ...
SO WHAT IF IT IS?!

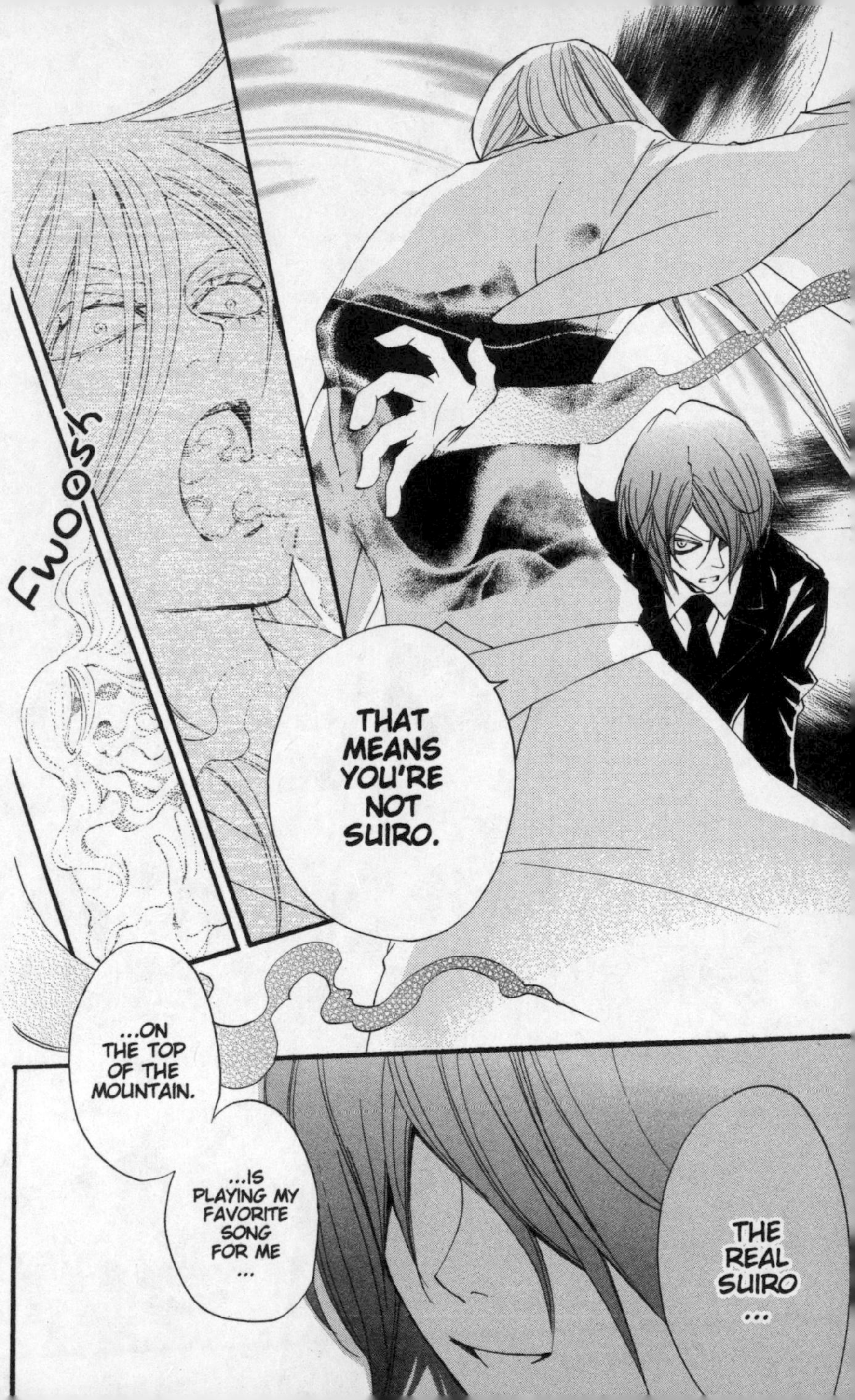
THAT MEANS YOU'RE NOT SUIRO.
Fwoosh
THE REAL SUIRO ...
...ON THE TOP OF THE MOUNTAIN.
...IS PLAYING MY FAVORITE SONG FOR ME ...

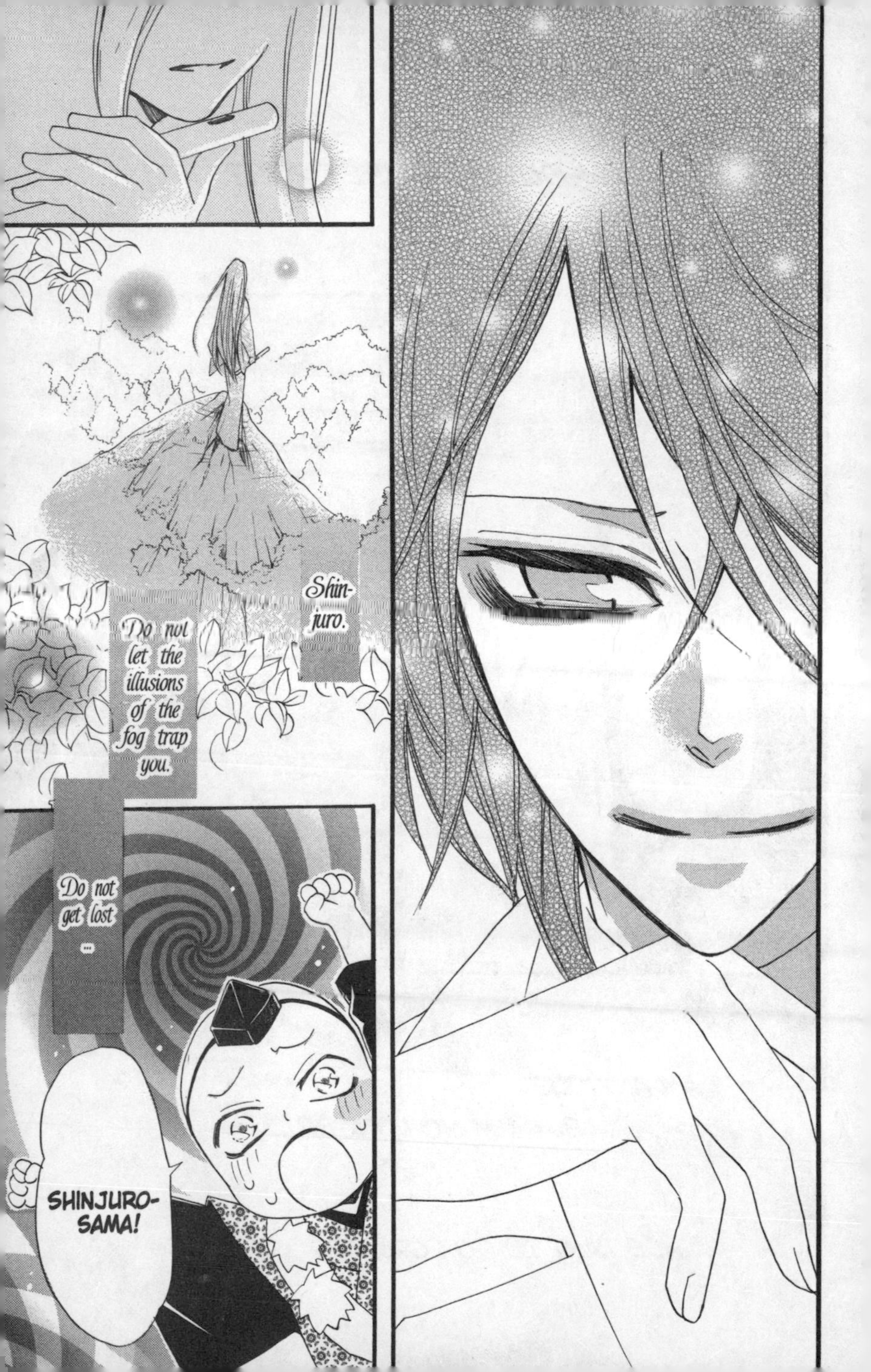

Shin-juro.
Do not let the illusions of the fog trap you.
Do not get lost ...
SHINJURO-SAMA!

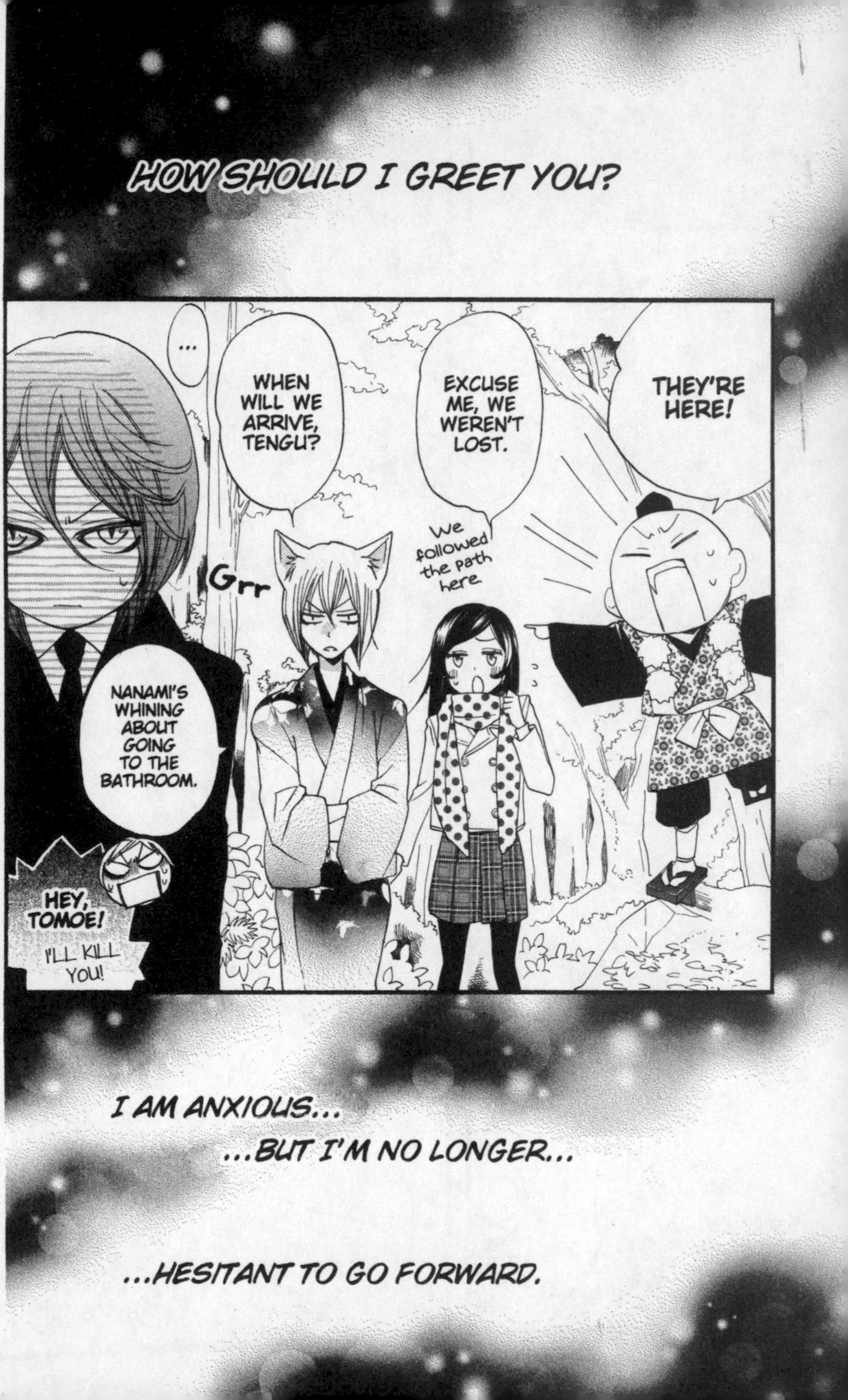
HOW SHOULD I GREET YOU?
THEY'RE HERE!
EXCUSE ME, WE WEREN'T LOST.
We followed the path here.
WHEN WILL WE ARRIVE, TENGU?
Grr
...
NANAMI'S WHINING ABOUT GOING TO THE BATHROOM.
HEY, TOMOE!
I'LL KILL YOU!
I AM ANXIOUS...
...BUT I'M NO LONGER...
...HESITANT TO GO FORWARD.

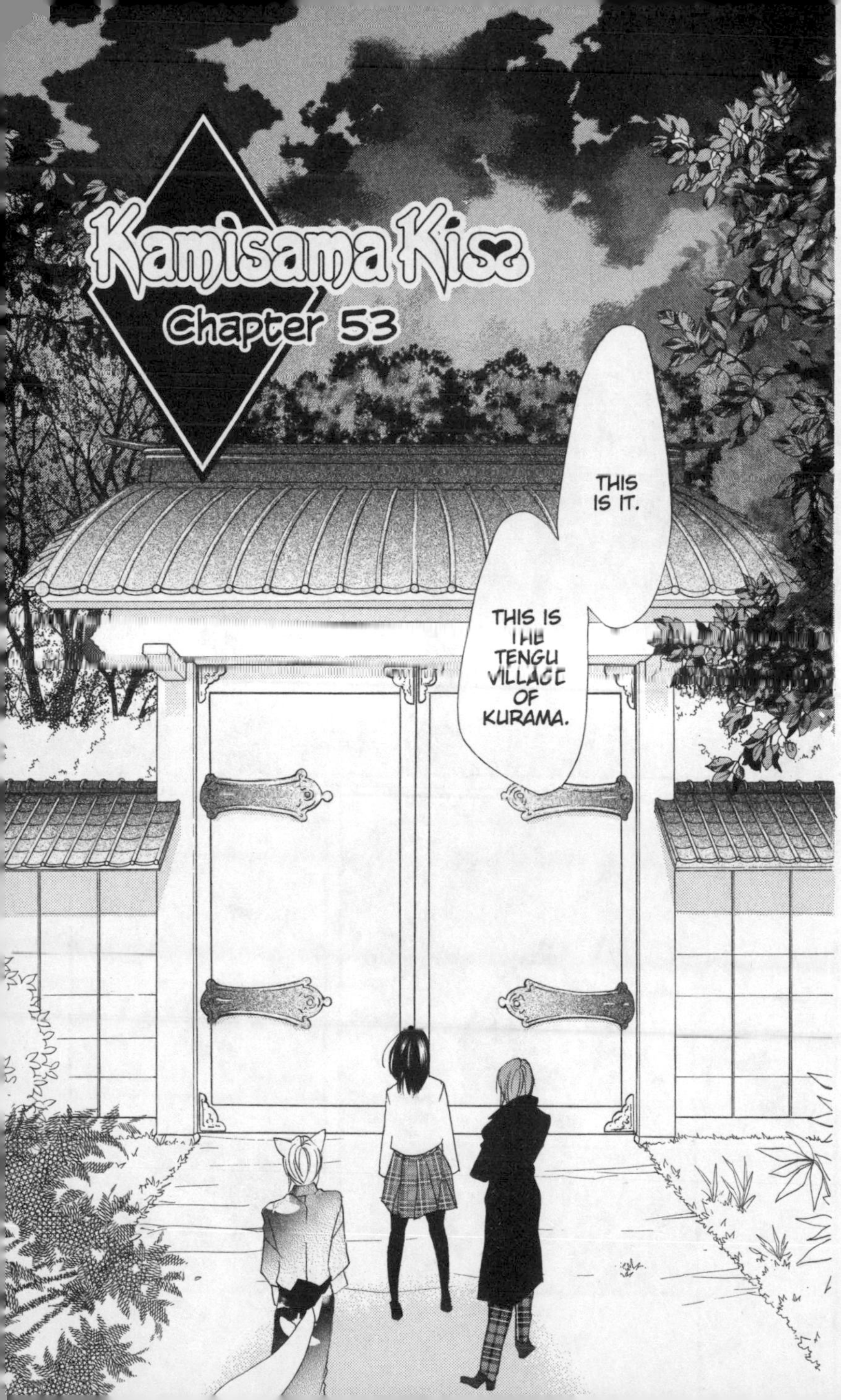
Kamisama Kiss
Chapter 53
THIS IS IT.
THIS IS THE TENGU VILLAGE OF KURAMA.

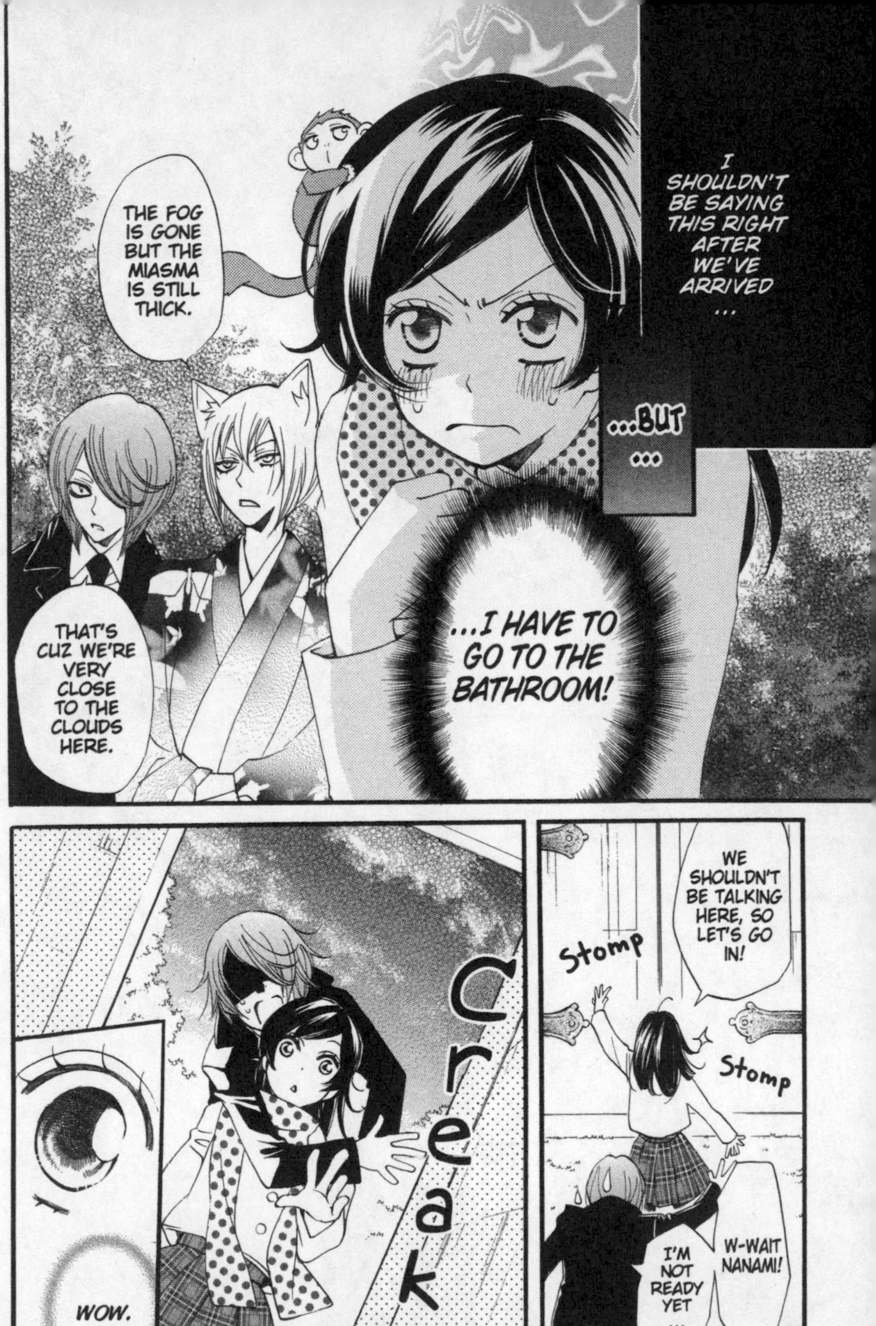
I SHOULDN'T BE SAYING THIS RIGHT AFTER WE'VE ARRIVED ...
THE FOG IS GONE BUT THE MIASMA IS STILL THICK.
...BUT ...
...I HAVE TO GO TO THE BATHROOM!
THAT'S CUZ WE'RE VERY CLOSE TO THE CLOUDS HERE.
WE SHOULDN'T BE TALKING HERE, SO LET'S GO IN!
Stomp
Stomp
W-WAIT NANAMI!
I'M NOT READY YET ...
creak
WOW.

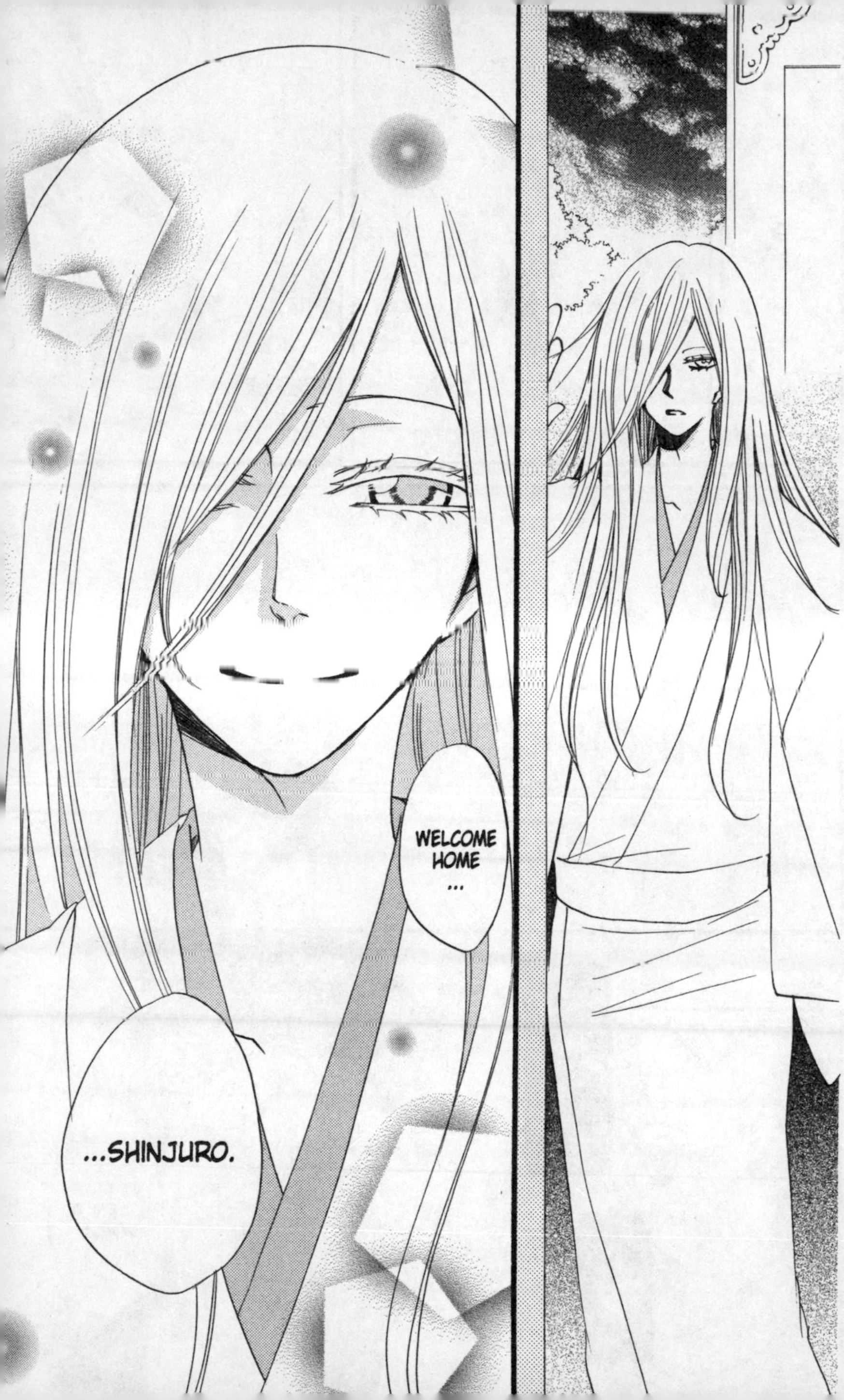
WELCOME HOME ...
...SHINJURO.

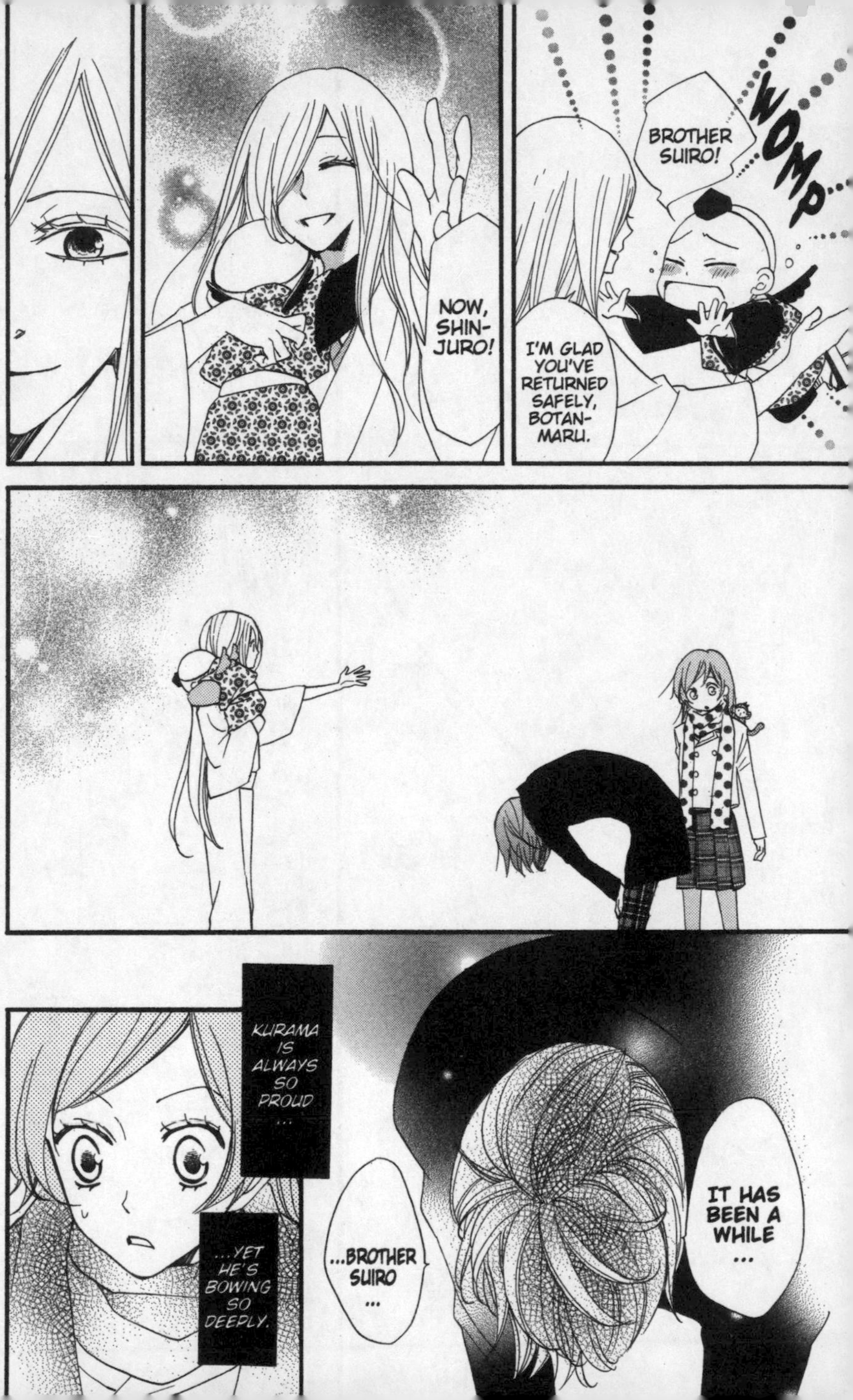
WOMP
BROTHER SUIRO!
I'M GLAD YOU'VE RETURNED SAFELY, BOTAN-MARU.
NOW, SHIN-JURO!
IT HAS BEEN A WHILE ...
...BROTHER SUIRO ...
KURAMA IS ALWAYS SO PROUD ...
...YET HE'S BOWING SO DEEPLY.

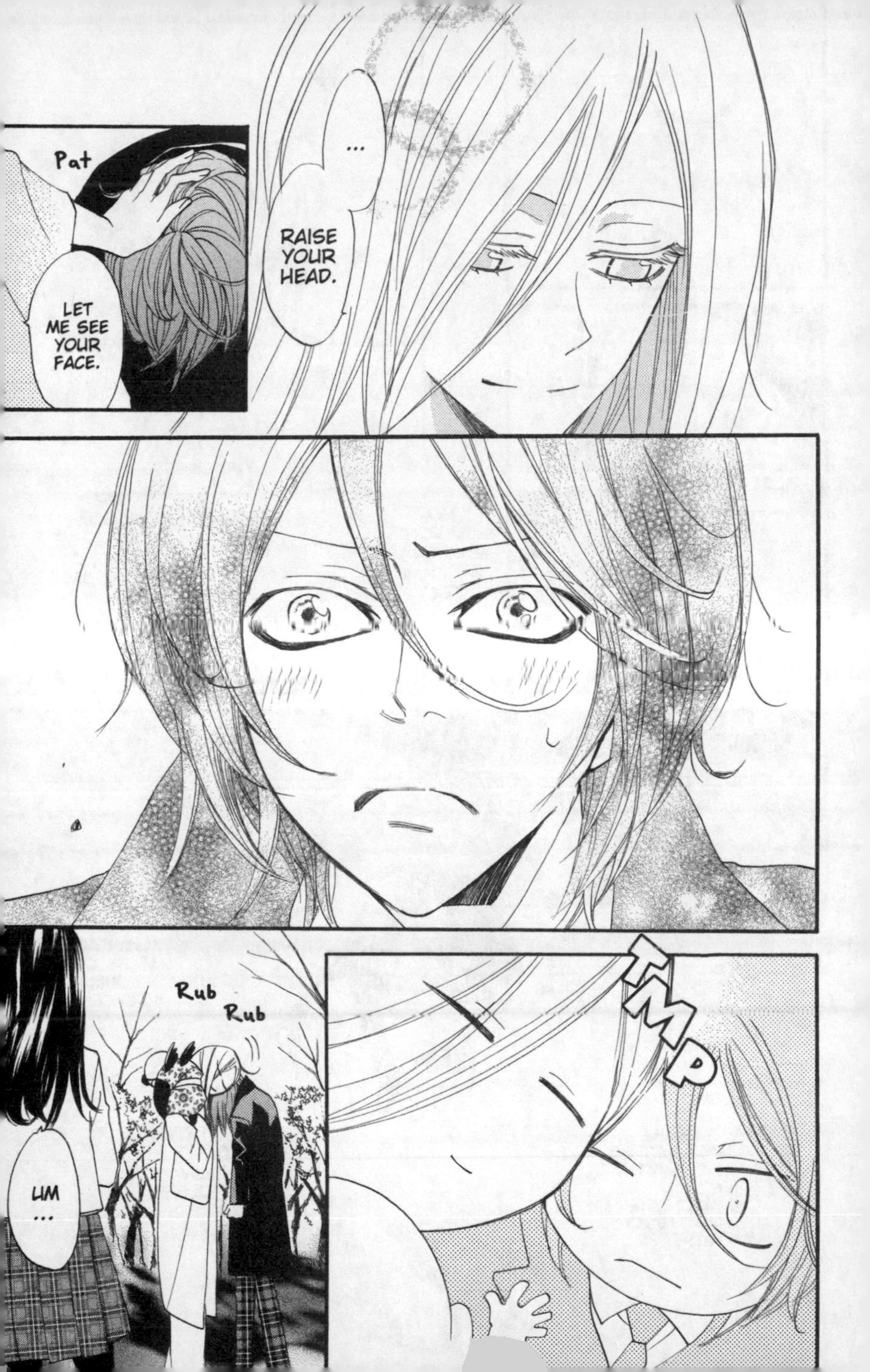
...
RAISE YOUR HEAD.
Pat
LET ME SEE YOUR FACE.
TMP
Rub
Rub
UM ...

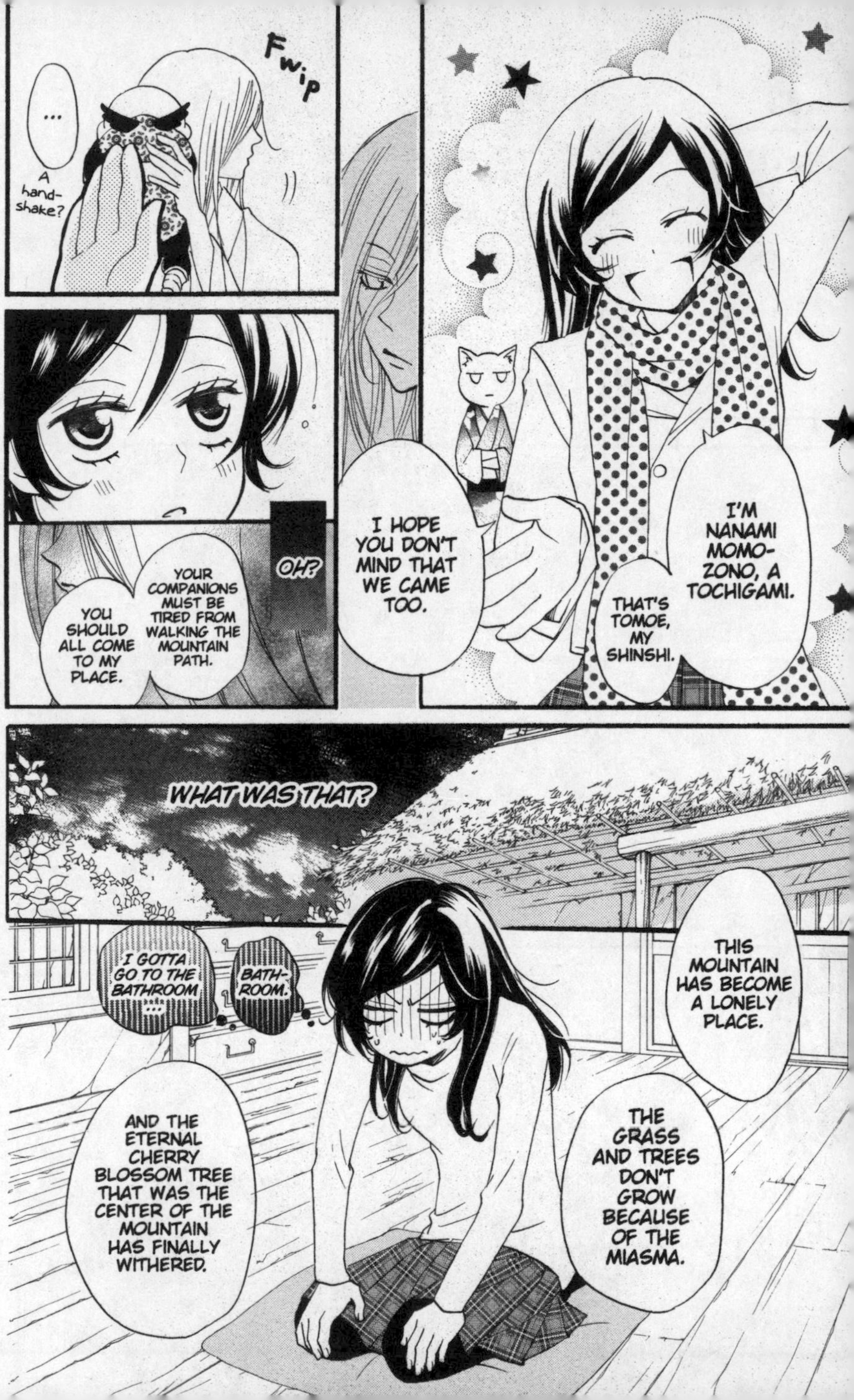
I'M NANAMI MOMOZONO, A TOCHIGAMI.
THAT'S TOMOE, MY SHINSHI.
I HOPE YOU DON'T MIND THAT WE CAME TOO.
Fwip
...
A hand-shake?
OH?
YOUR COMPANIONS MUST BE TIRED FROM WALKING THE MOUNTAIN PATH.
YOU SHOULD ALL COME TO MY PLACE.
WHAT WAS THAT?
THIS MOUNTAIN HAS BECOME A LONELY PLACE.
THE GRASS AND TREES DON'T GROW BECAUSE OF THE MIASMA.
AND THE ETERNAL CHERRY BLOSSOM TREE THAT WAS THE CENTER OF THE MOUNTAIN HAS FINALLY WITHERED.
BATH-ROOM.
I GOTTA GO TO THE BATHROOM ...

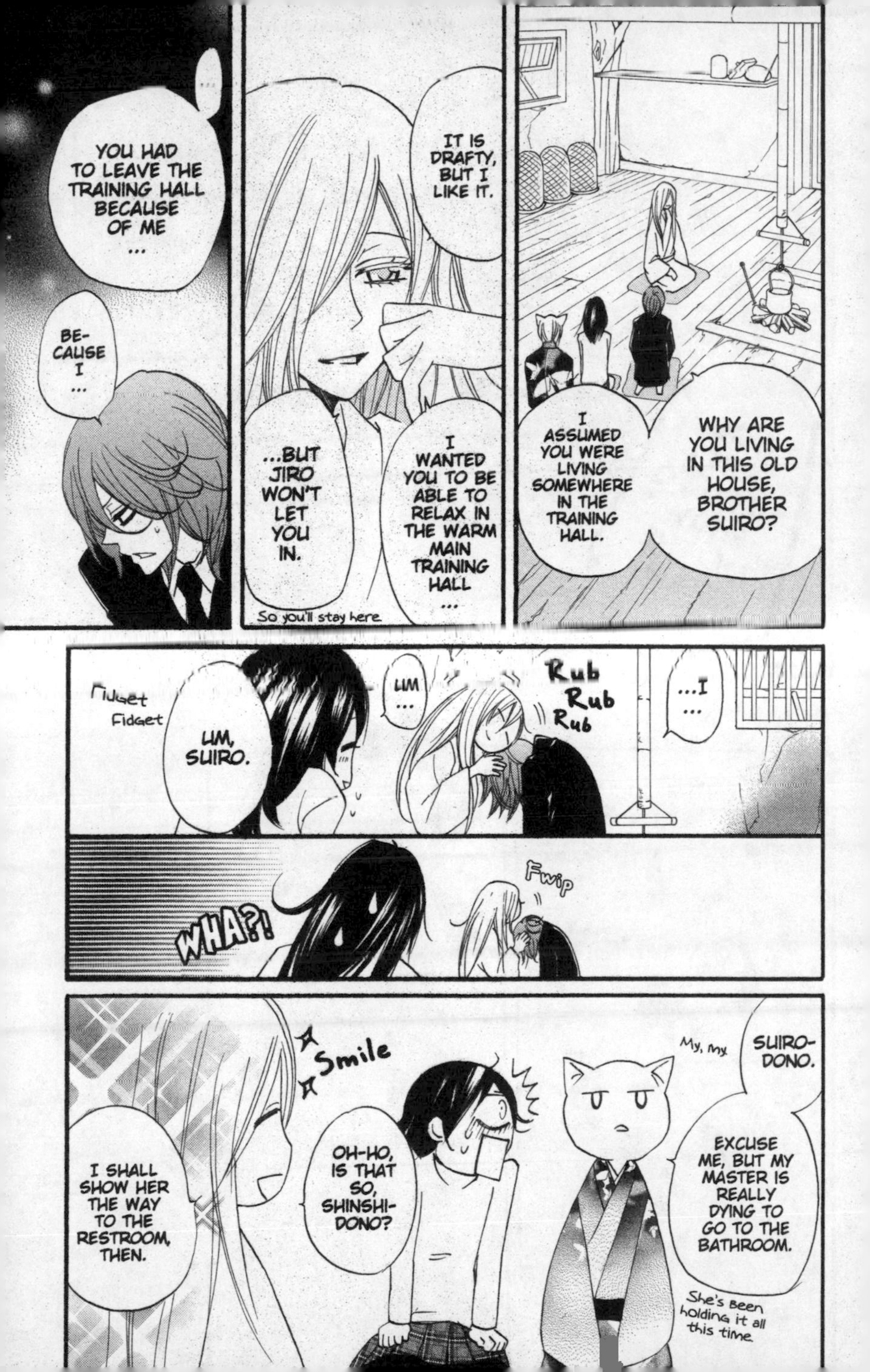
WHY ARE YOU LIVING IN THIS OLD HOUSE, BROTHER SUIRO?
I ASSUMED YOU WERE LIVING SOMEWHERE IN THE TRAINING HALL.
IT IS DRAFTY, BUT I LIKE IT.
I WANTED YOU TO BE ABLE TO RELAX IN THE WARM MAIN TRAINING HALL ...
...BUT JIRO WON'T LET YOU IN.
So you'll stay here.
...
YOU HAD TO LEAVE THE TRAINING HALL BECAUSE OF ME ...
BE-CAUSE I ...
...I ...
Rub Rub Rub
UM ...
UM, SUIRO.
Fidget Fidget
Fwip
WHA?!
SUIRO-DONO.
My, my.
EXCUSE ME, BUT MY MASTER IS REALLY DYING TO GO TO THE BATHROOM.
She's been holding it all this time.
OH-HO, IS THAT SO, SHINSHI-DONO?
Smile
I SHALL SHOW HER THE WAY TO THE RESTROOM, THEN.

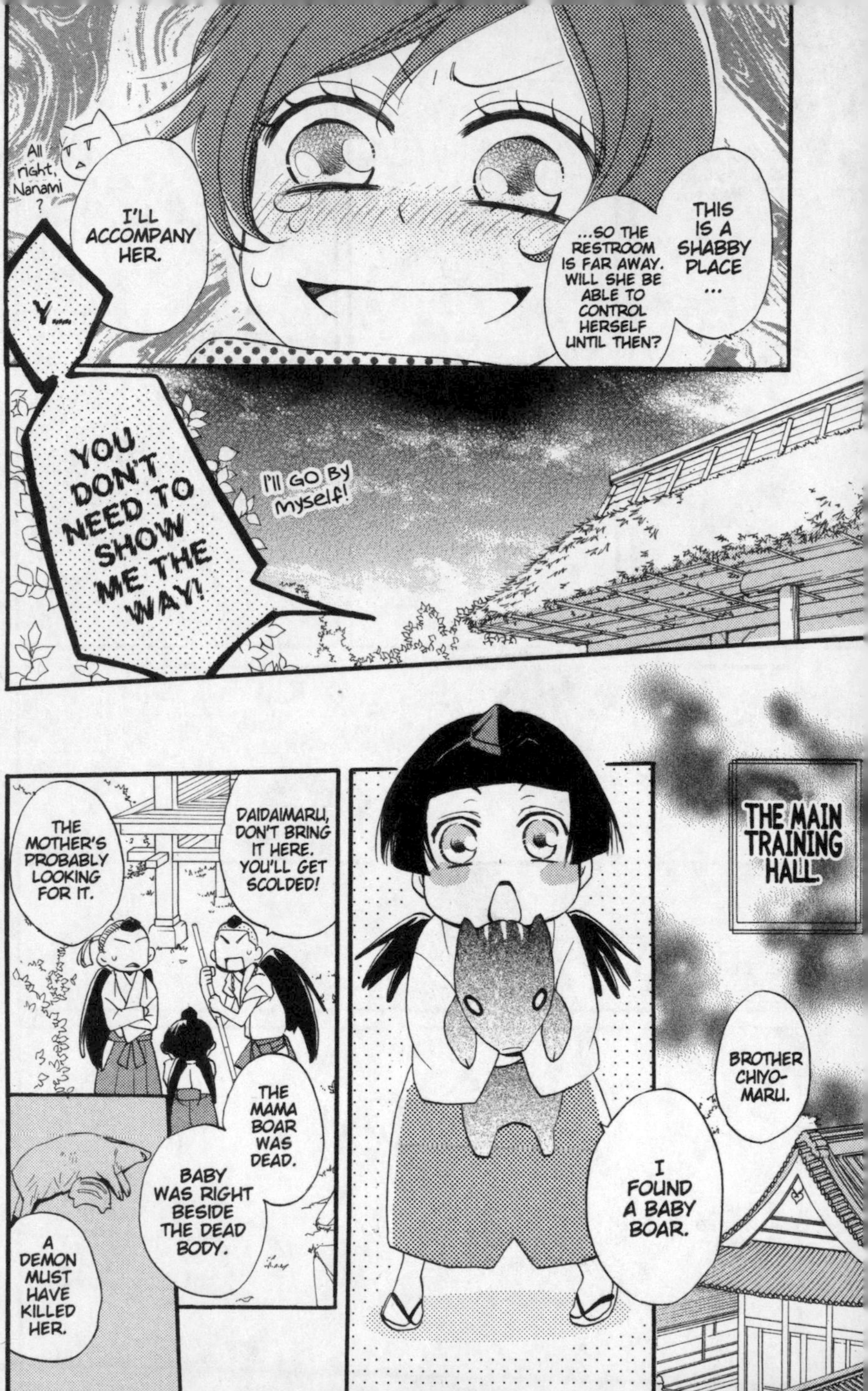
THIS IS A SHABBY PLACE ...
...SO THE RESTROOM IS FAR AWAY. WILL SHE BE ABLE TO CONTROL HERSELF UNTIL THEN?
I'LL ACCOMPANY HER.
All right, Nanami?
Y...
YOU DON'T NEED TO SHOW ME THE WAY!
I'll GO BY myself!
THE MAIN TRAINING HALL
BROTHER CHIYO-MARU.
I FOUND A BABY BOAR.
DAIDAIMARU, DON'T BRING IT HERE. YOU'LL GET SCOLDED!
THE MOTHER'S PROBABLY LOOKING FOR IT.
THE MAMA BOAR WAS DEAD.
BABY WAS RIGHT BESIDE THE DEAD BODY.
A DEMON MUST HAVE KILLED HER.

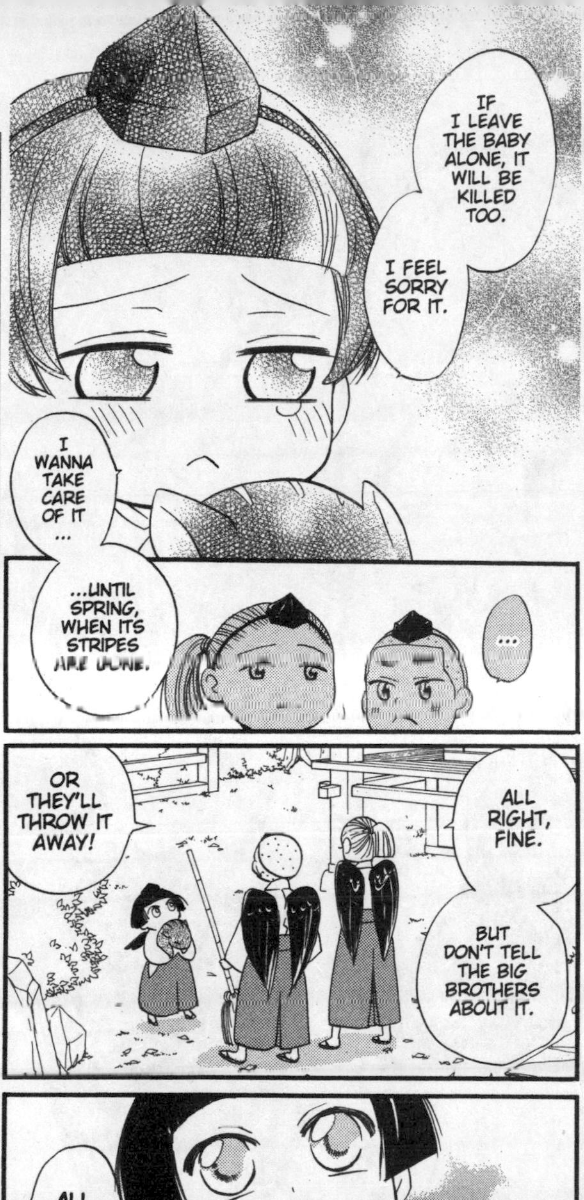
IF I LEAVE THE BABY ALONE, IT WILL BE KILLED TOO.
I FEEL SORRY FOR IT.
I WANNA TAKE CARE OF IT ...
...UNTIL SPRING, WHEN ITS STRIPES ARE GONE.
...
ALL RIGHT, FINE.
BUT DON'T TELL THE BIG BROTHERS ABOUT IT.
OR THEY'LL THROW IT AWAY!
ALL RIGHT!

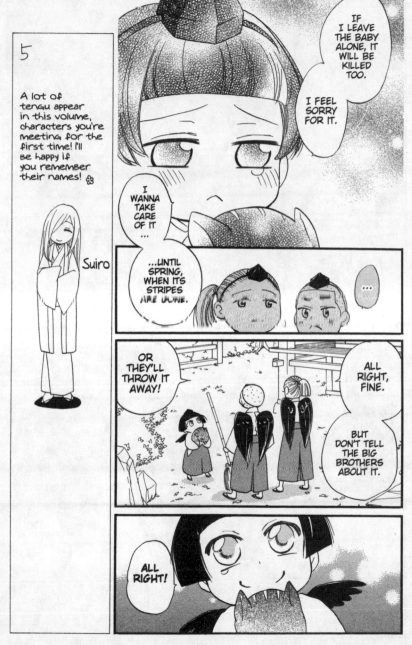

5

A lot of tengu appear in this volume, characters you're meeting for the first time! I'll be happy if you remember their names! ✿

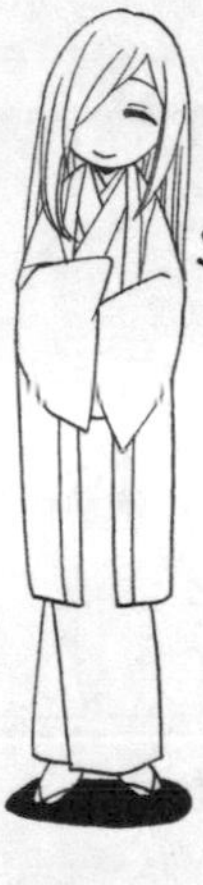

Suiro

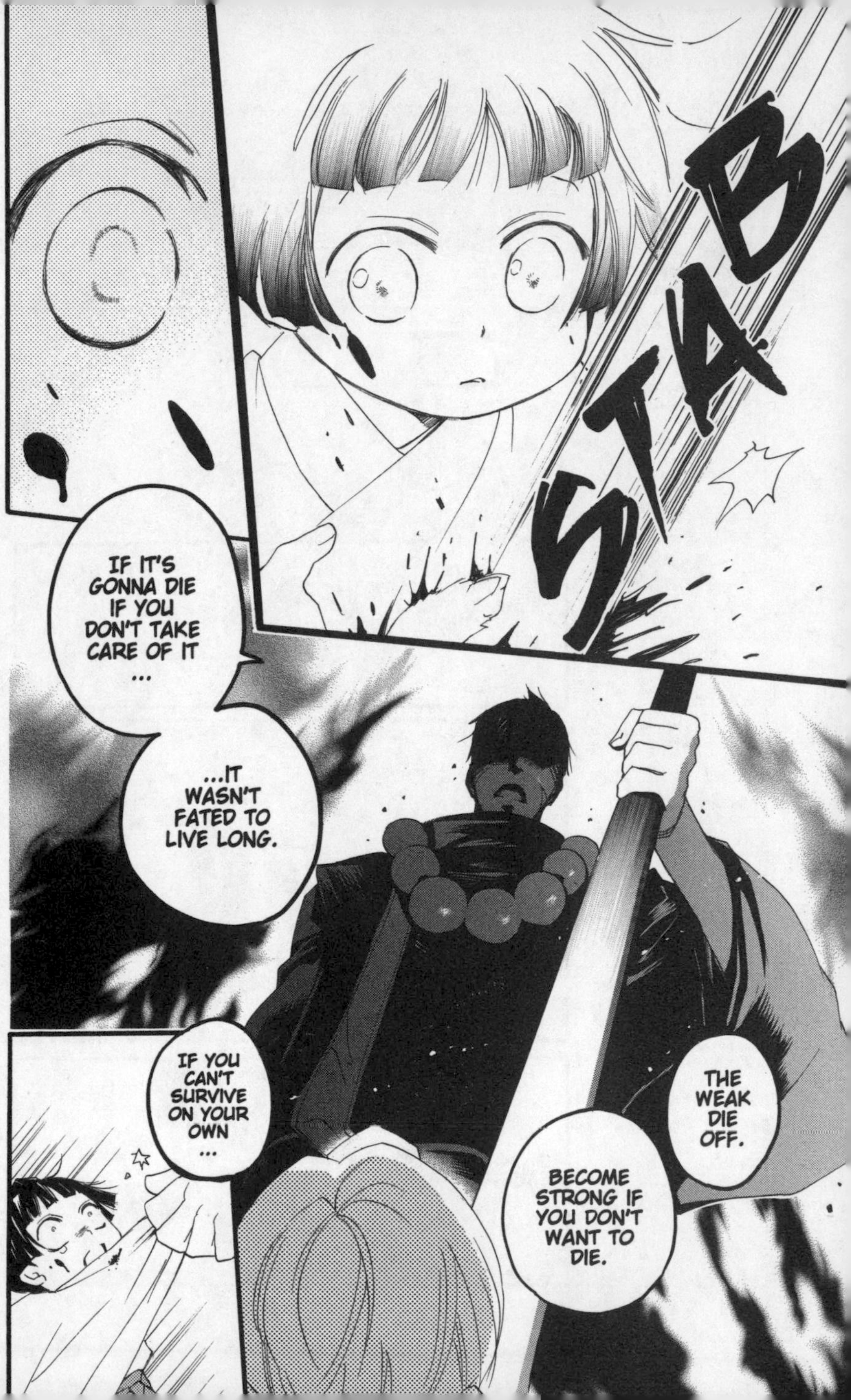
STAB
IF IT'S GONNA DIE IF YOU DON'T TAKE CARE OF IT ...
...IT WASN'T FATED TO LIVE LONG.
THE WEAK DIE OFF.
BECOME STRONG IF YOU DON'T WANT TO DIE.
IF YOU CAN'T SURVIVE ON YOUR OWN ...

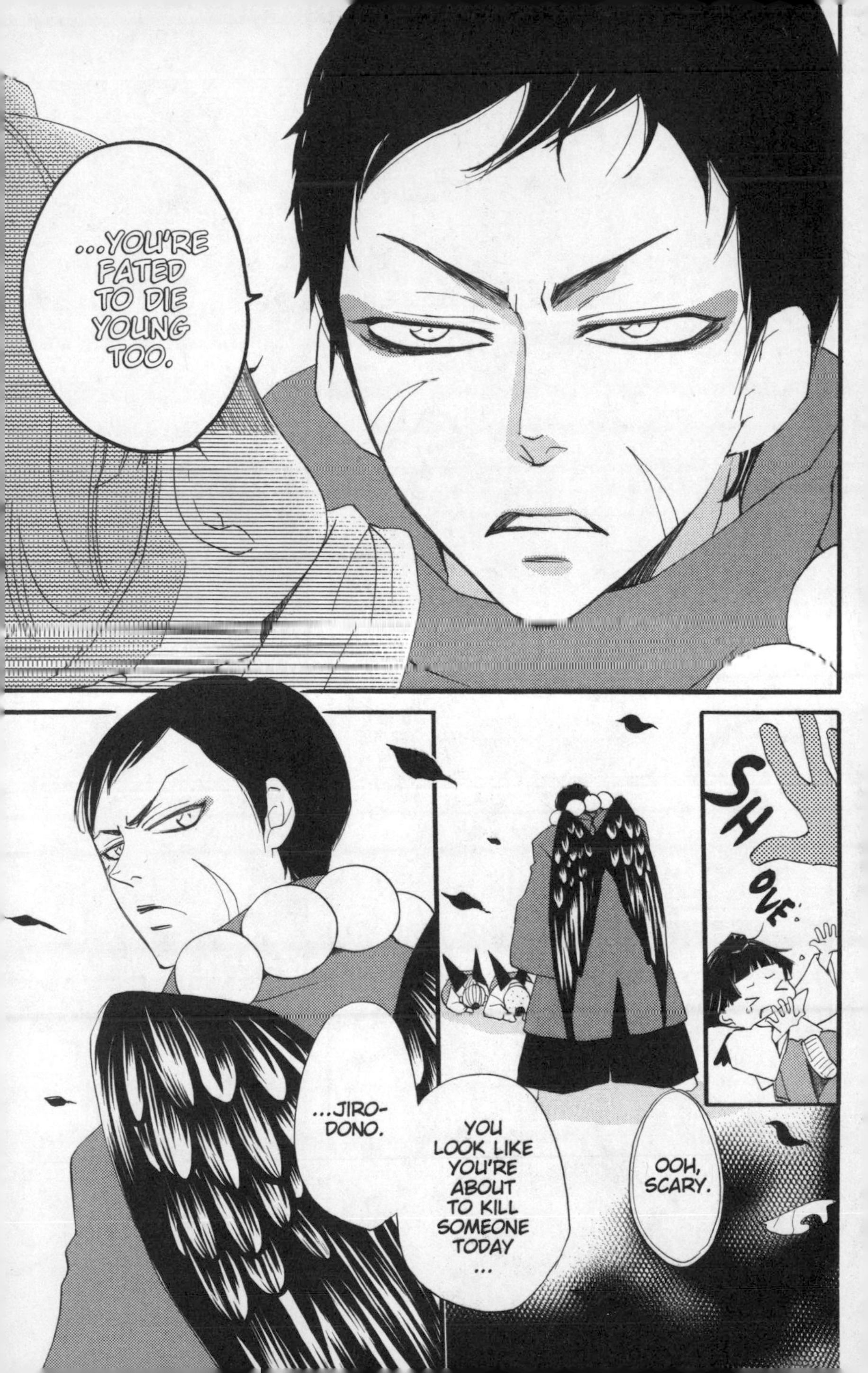
...YOU'RE FATED TO DIE YOUNG TOO.
SHOVE
OOH, SCARY.
YOU LOOK LIKE YOU'RE ABOUT TO KILL SOMEONE TODAY ...
...JIRO-DONO.

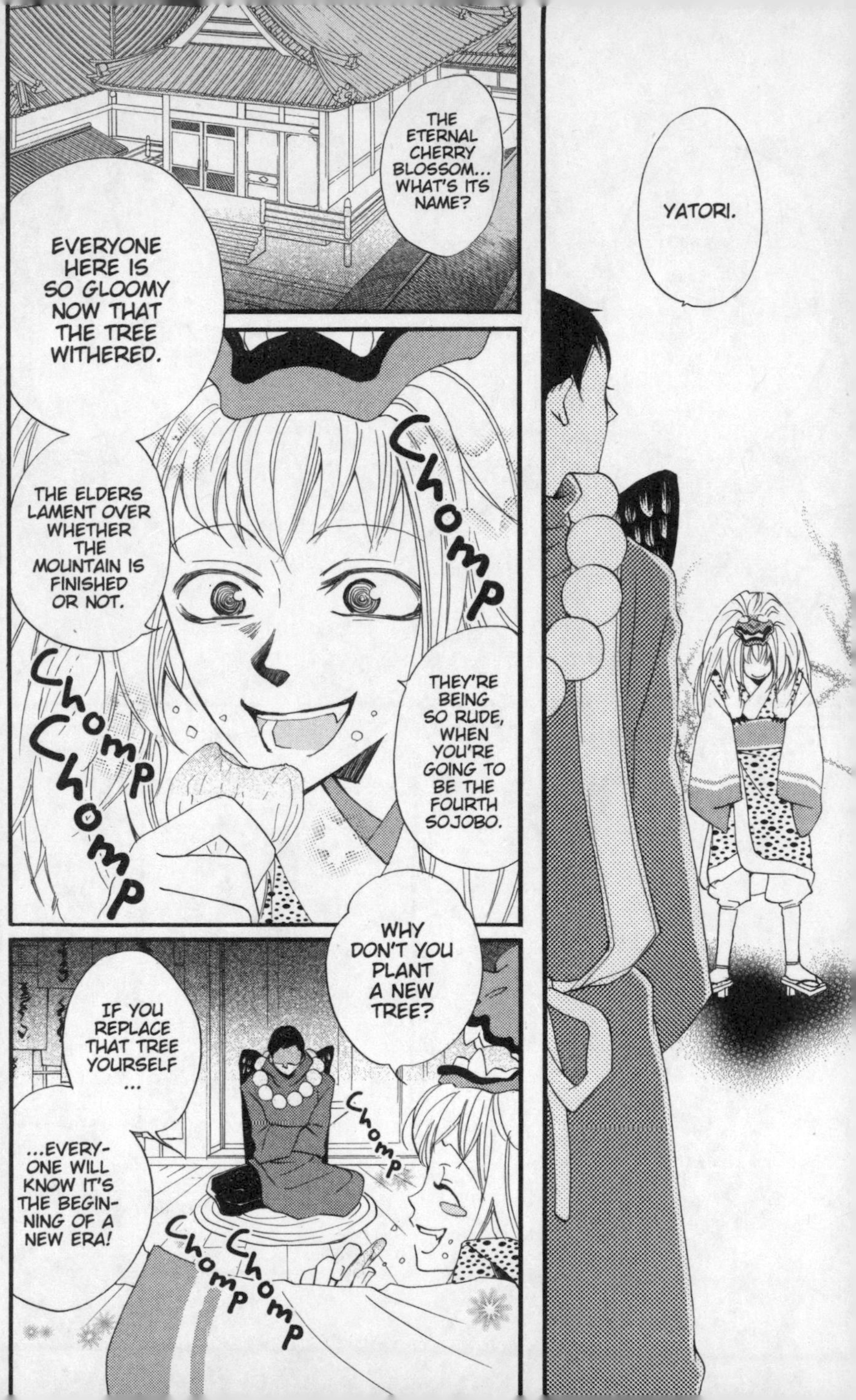
YATORI.
THE ETERNAL CHERRY BLOSSOM... WHAT'S ITS NAME?
EVERYONE HERE IS SO GLOOMY NOW THAT THE TREE WITHERED.
CHOMP
THE ELDERS LAMENT OVER WHETHER THE MOUNTAIN IS FINISHED OR NOT.
THEY'RE BEING SO RUDE, WHEN YOU'RE GOING TO BE THE FOURTH SOJOBO.
CHOMP CHOMP
WHY DON'T YOU PLANT A NEW TREE?
IF YOU REPLACE THAT TREE YOURSELF ...
...EVERY-ONE WILL KNOW IT'S THE BEGIN-NING OF A NEW ERA!
CHOMP
CHOMP CHOMP

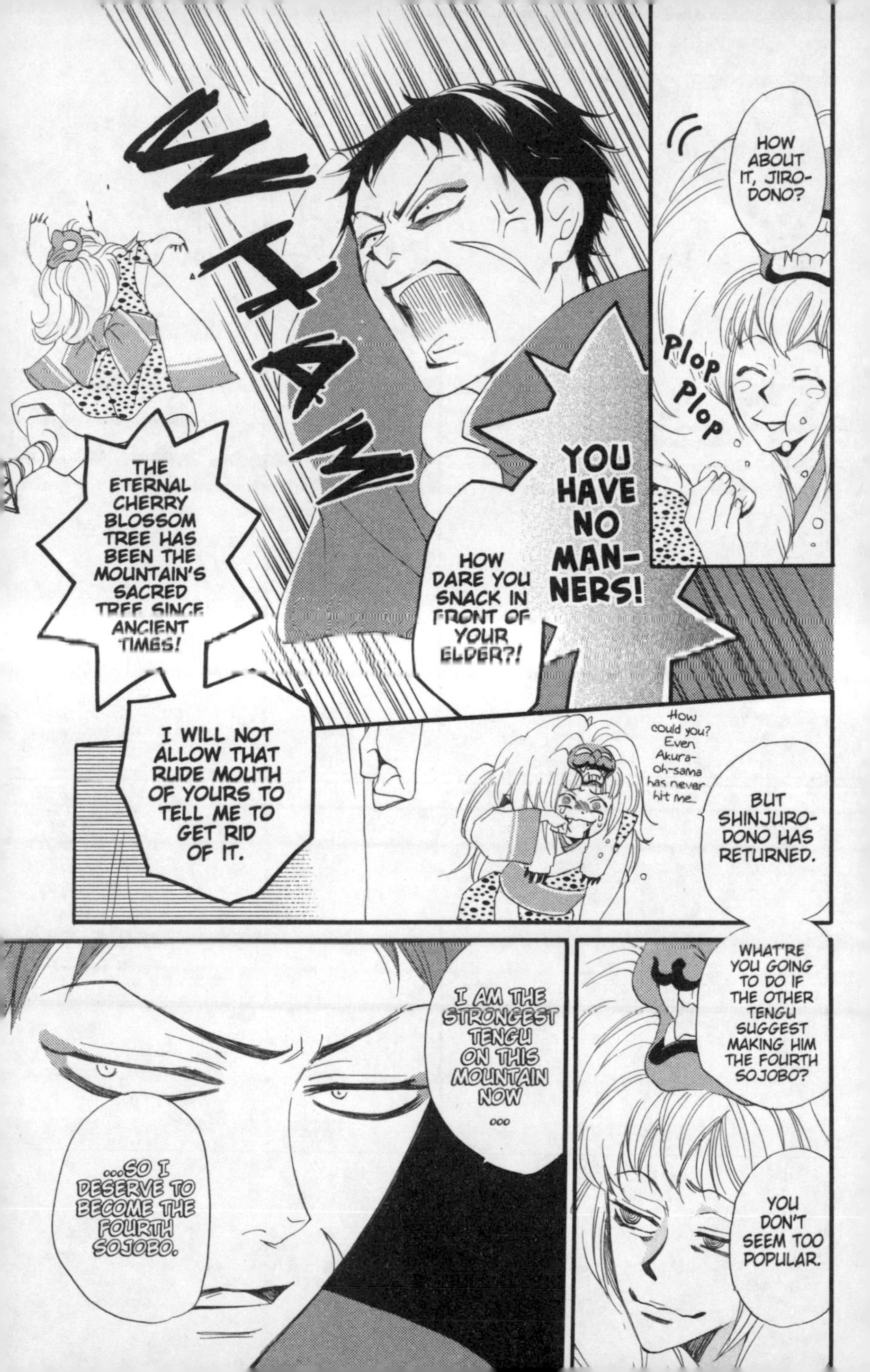
HOW ABOUT IT, JIRO-DONO?
Plop Plop
YOU HAVE NO MAN-NERS!
HOW DARE YOU SNACK IN FRONT OF YOUR ELDER?!
WHAM
THE ETERNAL CHERRY BLOSSOM TREE HAS BEEN THE MOUNTAIN'S SACRED TREE SINCE ANCIENT TIMES!
I WILL NOT ALLOW THAT RUDE MOUTH OF YOURS TO TELL ME TO GET RID OF IT.
How could you? Even Akura-oh-sama has never hit me...
BUT SHINJURO-DONO HAS RETURNED.
WHAT'RE YOU GOING TO DO IF THE OTHER TENGU SUGGEST MAKING HIM THE FOURTH SOJOBO?
YOU DON'T SEEM TOO POPULAR.
I AM THE STRONGEST TENGU ON THIS MOUNTAIN NOW ...
...SO I DESERVE TO BECOME THE FOURTH SOJOBO.

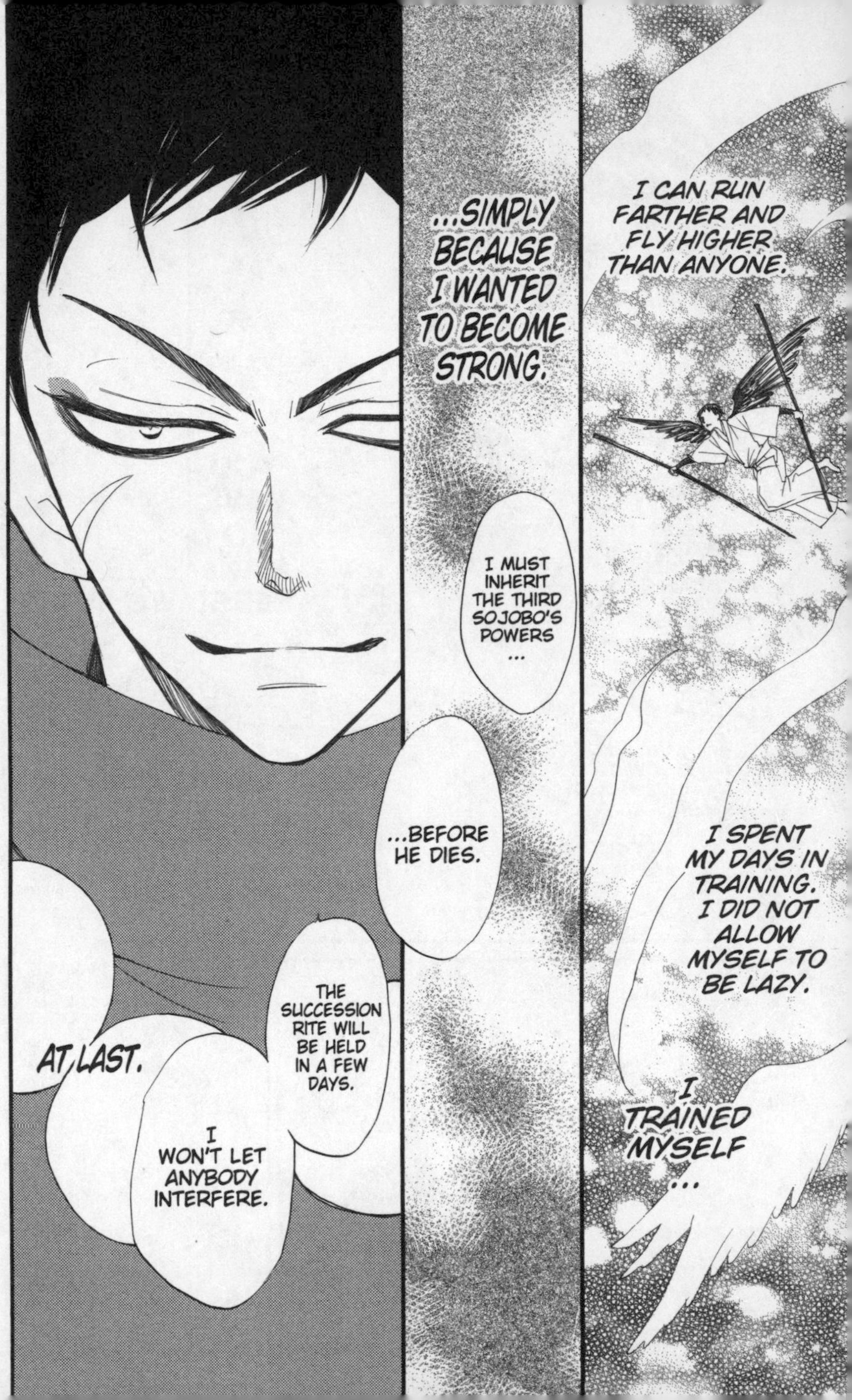
I CAN RUN FARTHER AND FLY HIGHER THAN ANYONE.
I SPENT MY DAYS IN TRAINING. I DID NOT ALLOW MYSELF TO BE LAZY.
I TRAINED MYSELF...
...SIMPLY BECAUSE I WANTED TO BECOME STRONG.
I MUST INHERIT THE THIRD SOJOBO'S POWERS...
...BEFORE HE DIES.
THE SUCCESSION RITE WILL BE HELD IN A FEW DAYS.
AT LAST.
I WON'T LET ANYBODY INTERFERE.

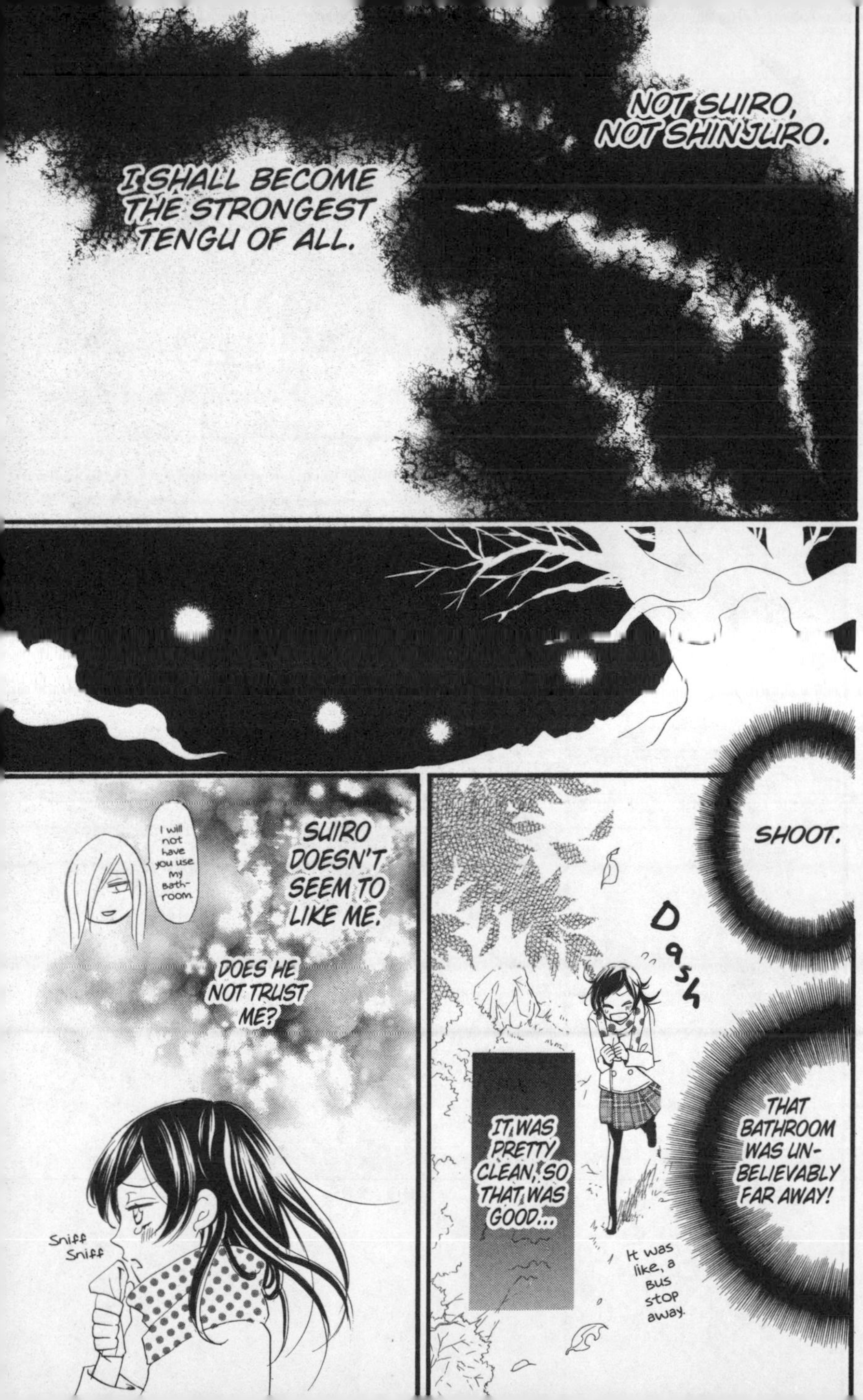
NOT SUIRO, NOT SHINJURO.
I SHALL BECOME THE STRONGEST TENGU OF ALL.
SHOOT.
Dash
THAT BATHROOM WAS UN-BELIEVABLY FAR AWAY!
IT WAS PRETTY CLEAN, SO THAT WAS GOOD...
It was like, a bus stop away.
SUIRO DOESN'T SEEM TO LIKE ME.
I will not have you use my bath-room.
DOES HE NOT TRUST ME?
Sniff Sniff

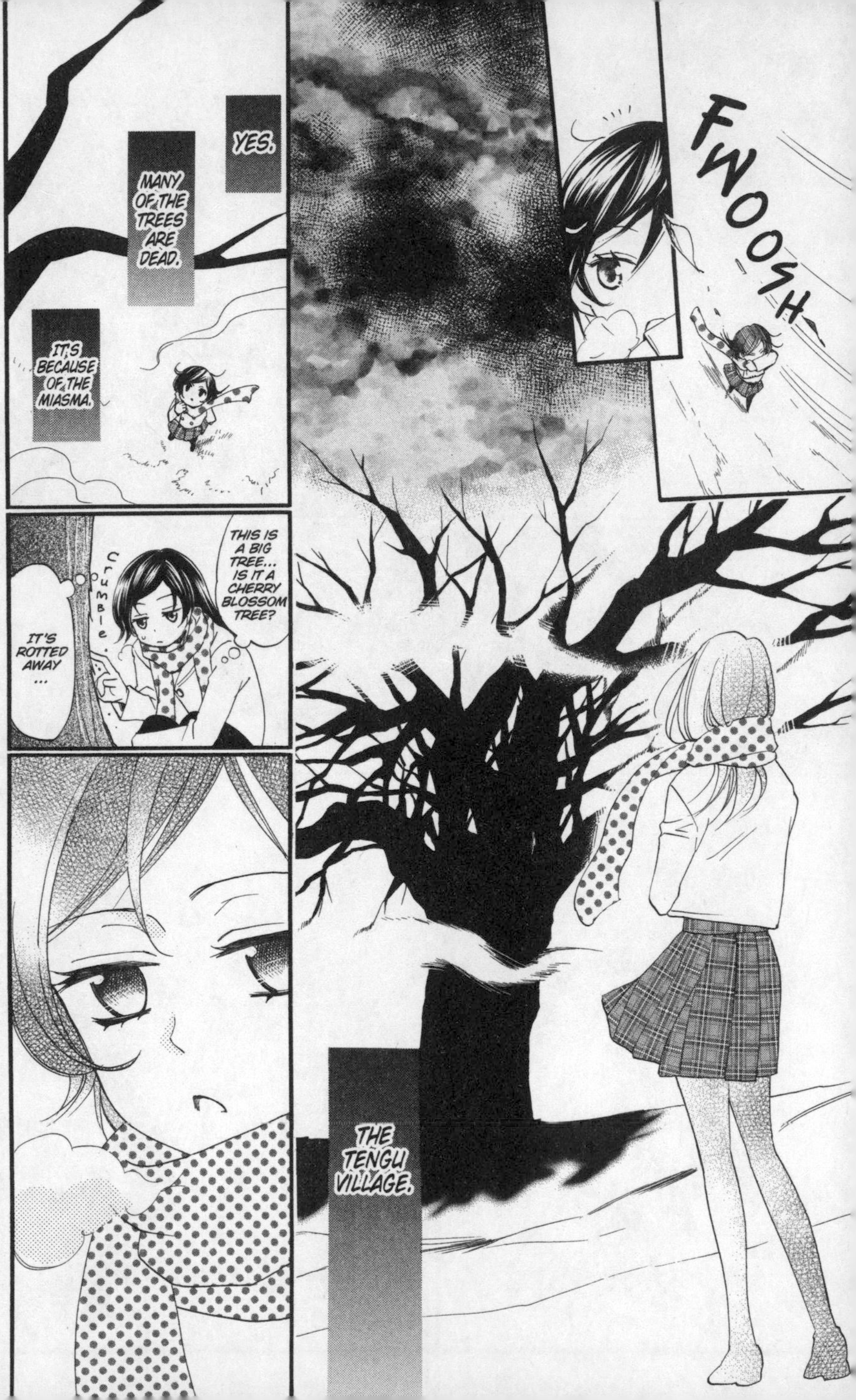
FWOOSH
THE TENGU VILLAGE.
YES.
MANY OF THE TREES ARE DEAD.
IT'S BECAUSE OF THE MIASMA.
THIS IS A BIG TREE... IS IT A CHERRY BLOSSOM TREE?
Crumble
IT'S ROTTED AWAY...

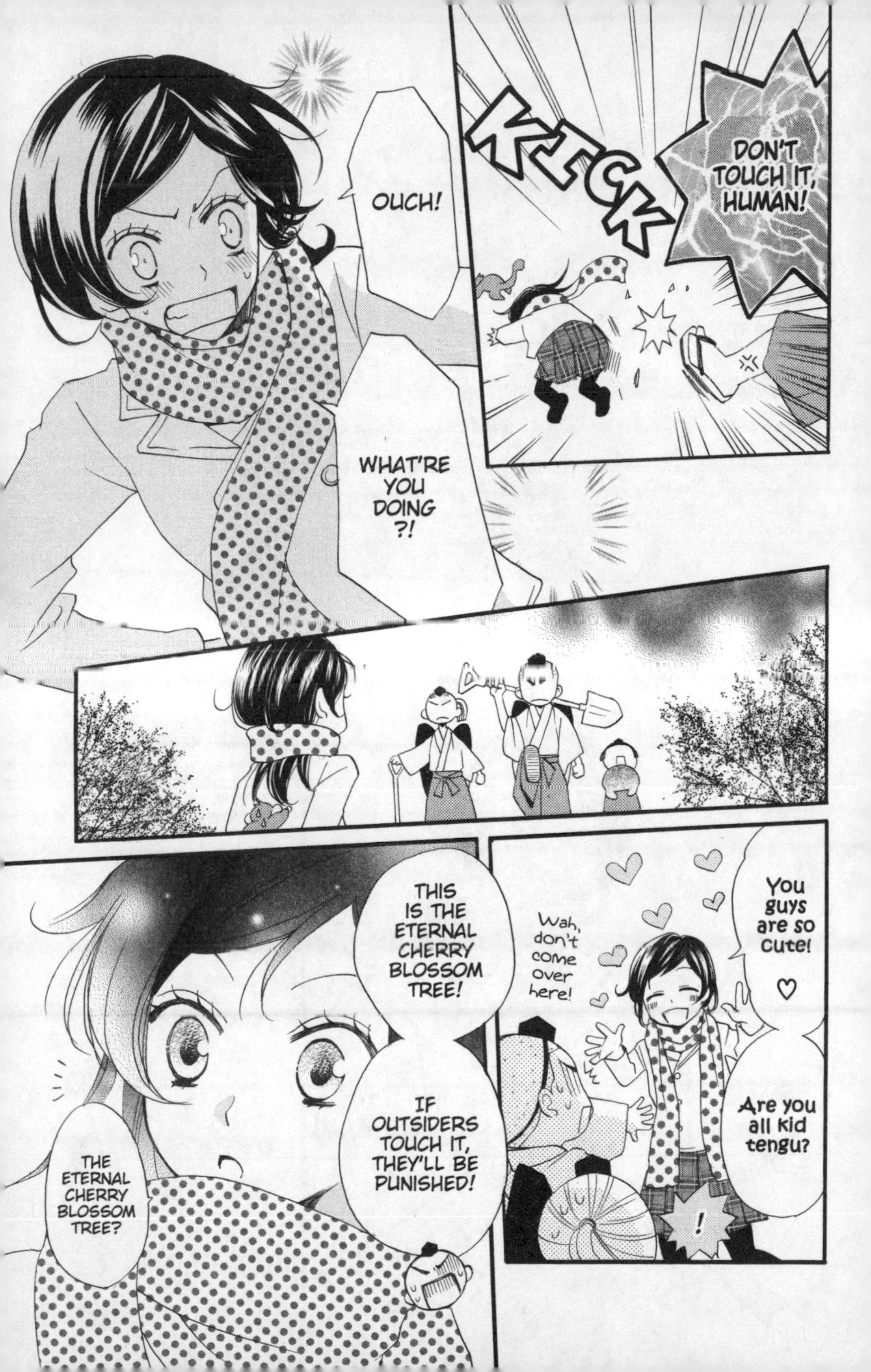
KICK
DON'T TOUCH IT, HUMAN!
OUCH!
WHAT'RE YOU DOING ?!
You guys are so cute! ♡
Wah, don't come over here!
Are you all kid tengu?
!
THIS IS THE ETERNAL CHERRY BLOSSOM TREE!
IF OUTSIDERS TOUCH IT, THEY'LL BE PUNISHED!
THE ETERNAL CHERRY BLOSSOM TREE?

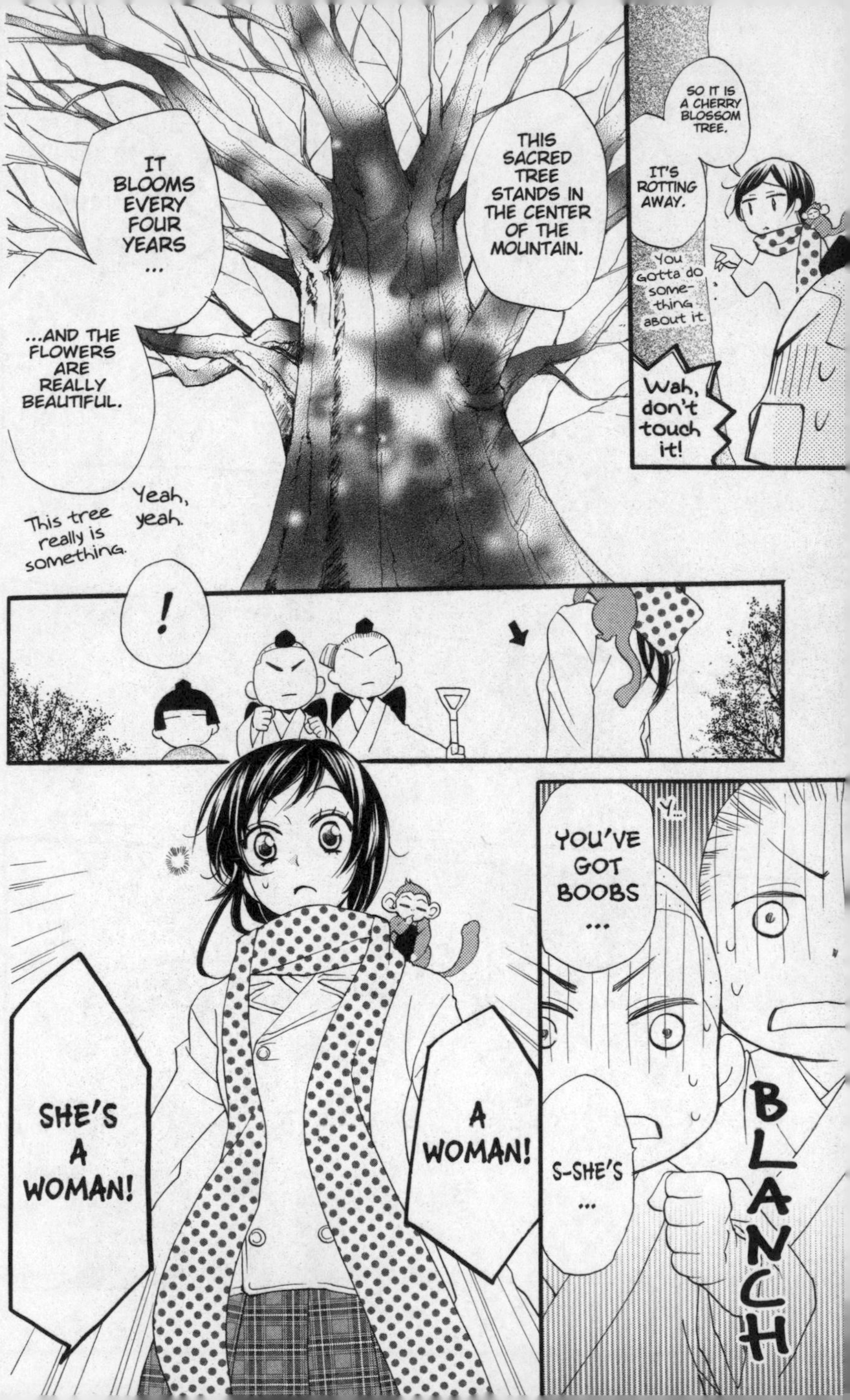

SO IT IS A CHERRY BLOSSOM TREE.
IT'S ROTTING AWAY.
You gotta do something about it.
Wah, don't touch it!
THIS SACRED TREE STANDS IN THE CENTER OF THE MOUNTAIN.
IT BLOOMS EVERY FOUR YEARS...
...AND THE FLOWERS ARE REALLY BEAUTIFUL.
Yeah, yeah.
This tree really is something.
!
Y...
YOU'VE GOT BOOBS...
S-SHE'S...
BLANCH
A WOMAN!
SHE'S A WOMAN!

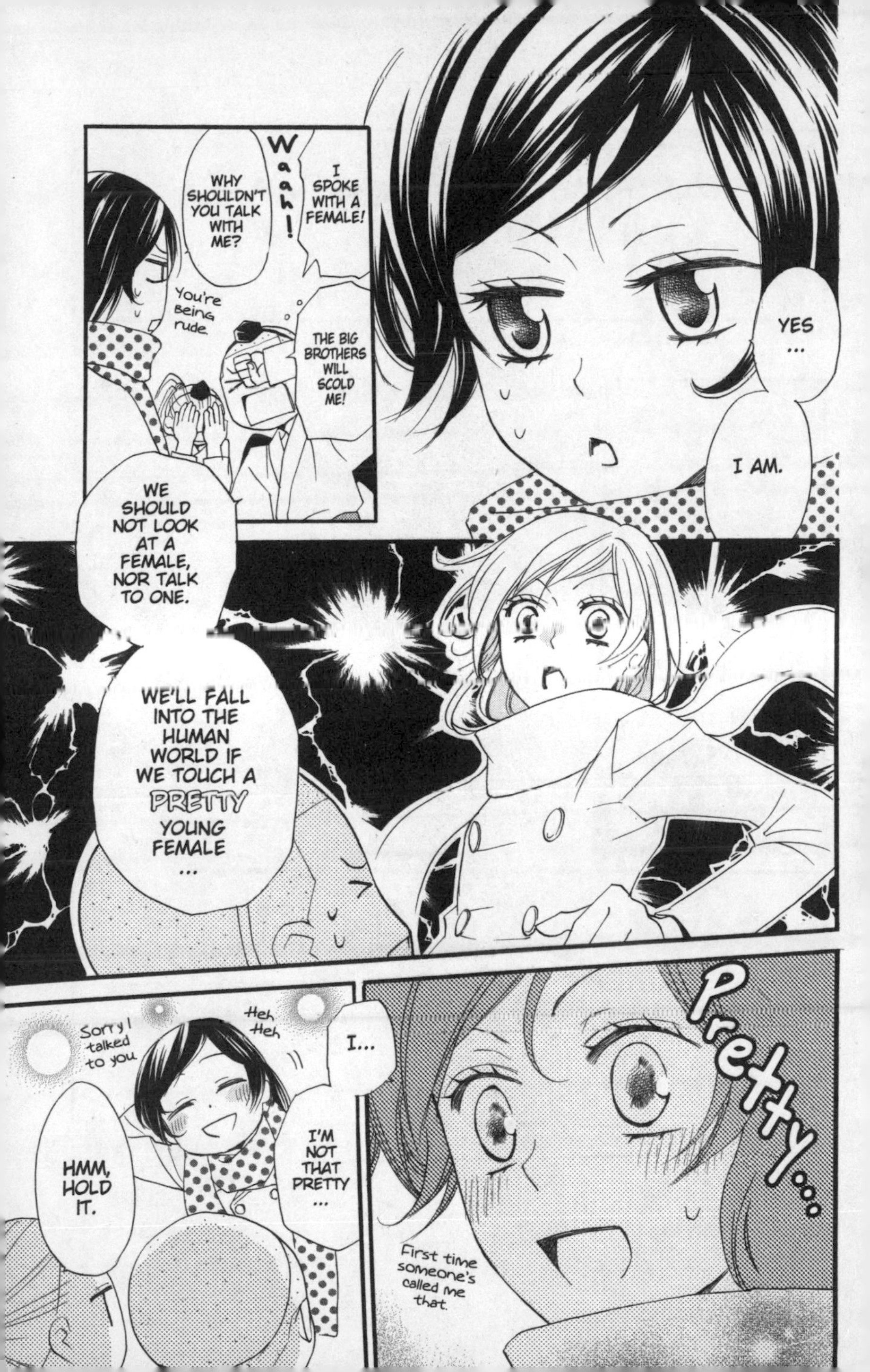
YES ...
I AM.
Waah!
I SPOKE WITH A FEMALE!
WHY SHOULDN'T YOU TALK WITH ME?
THE BIG BROTHERS WILL SCOLD ME!
You're being rude.
WE SHOULD NOT LOOK AT A FEMALE, NOR TALK TO ONE.
WE'LL FALL INTO THE HUMAN WORLD IF WE TOUCH A PRETTY YOUNG FEMALE ...
Pretty...
First time someone's called me that.
I...
Heh Heh
Sorry I talked to you
I'M NOT THAT PRETTY ...
HMM, HOLD IT.

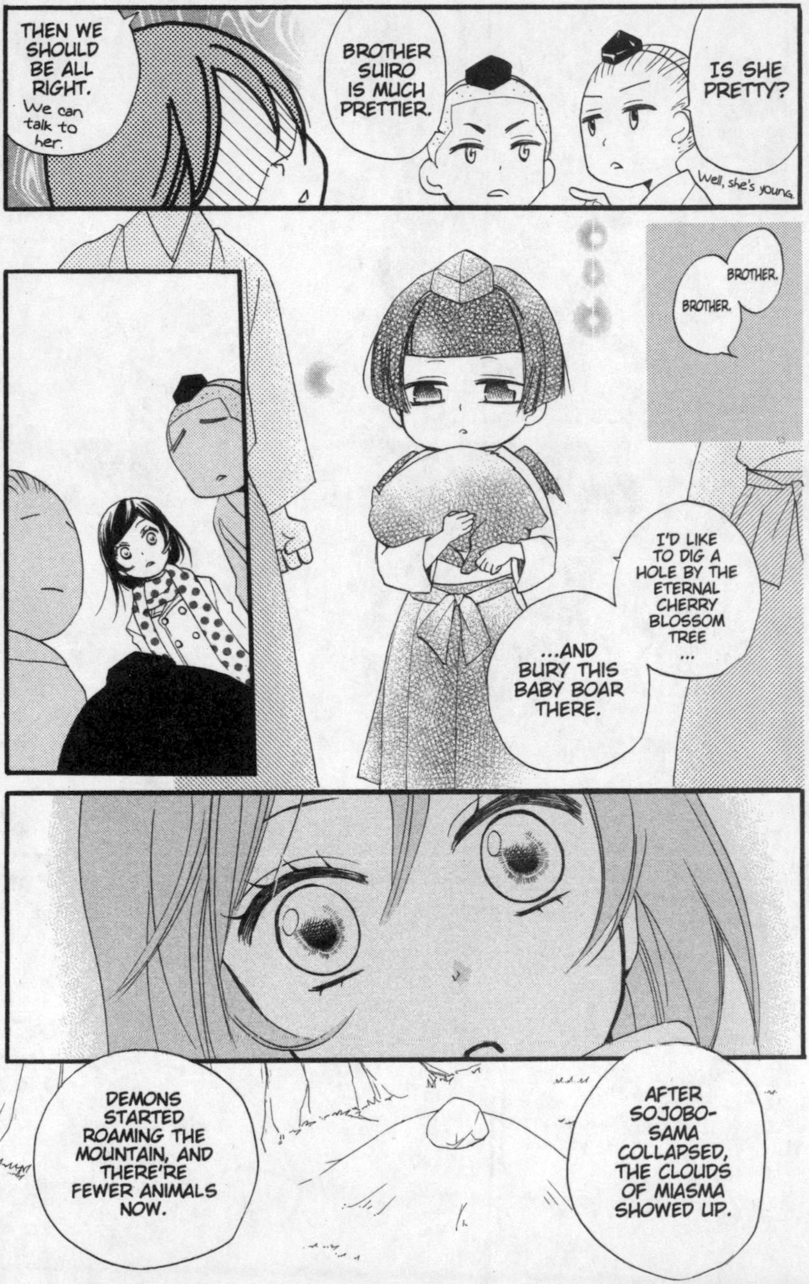
IS SHE PRETTY?
Well, she's young.
BROTHER SUIRO IS MUCH PRETTIER.
THEN WE SHOULD BE ALL RIGHT.
We can talk to her.
BROTHER.
BROTHER.
I'D LIKE TO DIG A HOLE BY THE ETERNAL CHERRY BLOSSOM TREE ...
...AND BURY THIS BABY BOAR THERE.
AFTER SOJOBO-SAMA COLLAPSED, THE CLOUDS OF MIASMA SHOWED UP.
DEMONS STARTED ROAMING THE MOUNTAIN, AND THERE'RE FEWER ANIMALS NOW.

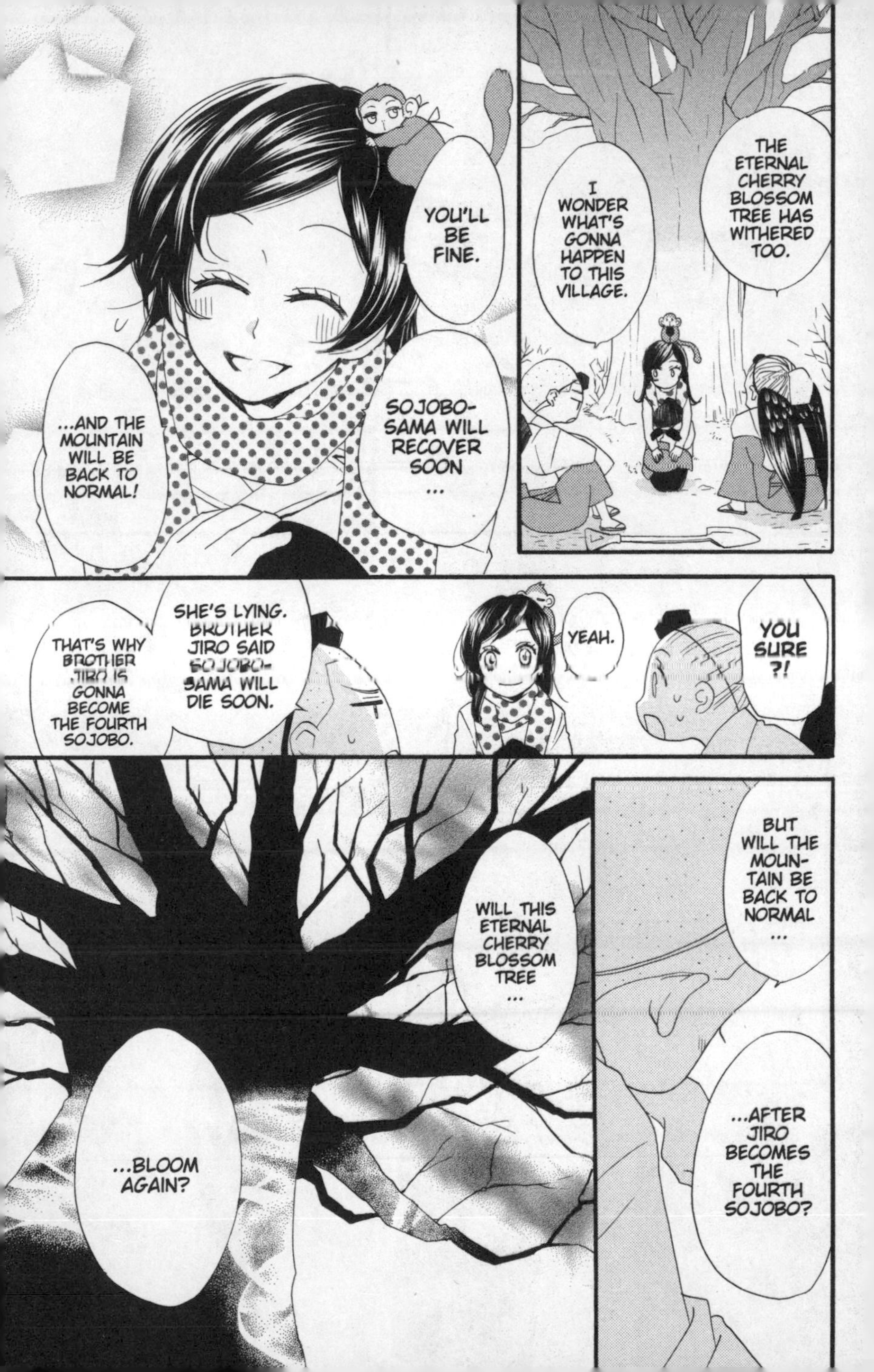
THE ETERNAL CHERRY BLOSSOM TREE HAS WITHERED TOO.
I WONDER WHAT'S GONNA HAPPEN TO THIS VILLAGE.
YOU'LL BE FINE.
SOJOBO-SAMA WILL RECOVER SOON ...
...AND THE MOUNTAIN WILL BE BACK TO NORMAL!
YOU SURE ?!
YEAH.
SHE'S LYING. BROTHER JIRO SAID SOJOBO-SAMA WILL DIE SOON.
THAT'S WHY BROTHER JIRO IS GONNA BECOME THE FOURTH SOJOBO.
BUT WILL THE MOUN-TAIN BE BACK TO NORMAL ...
...AFTER JIRO BECOMES THE FOURTH SOJOBO?
WILL THIS ETERNAL CHERRY BLOSSOM TREE ...
...BLOOM AGAIN?

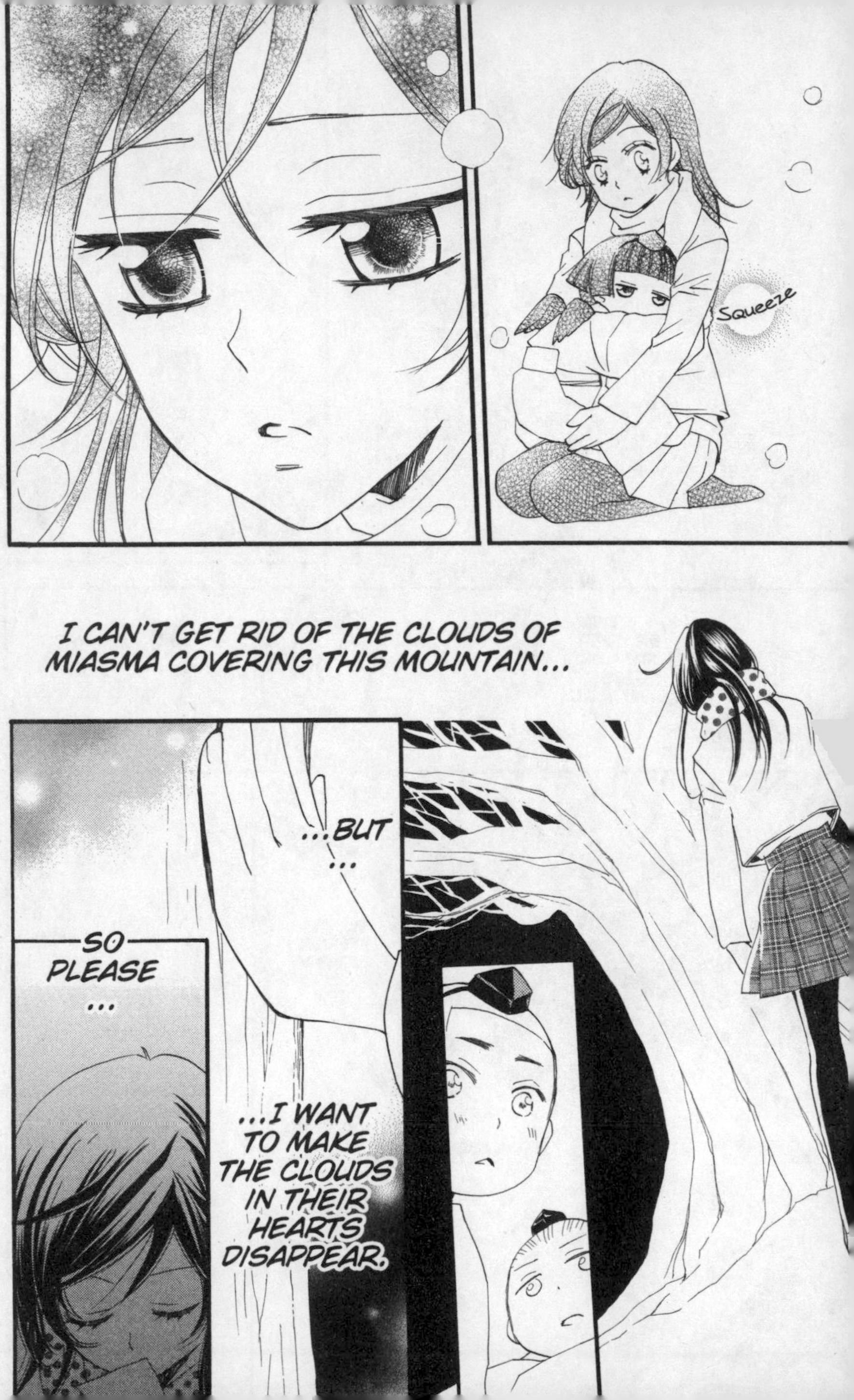
Squeeze
I CAN'T GET RID OF THE CLOUDS OF MIASMA COVERING THIS MOUNTAIN...
...BUT ...
SO PLEASE ...
...I WANT TO MAKE THE CLOUDS IN THEIR HEARTS DISAPPEAR.

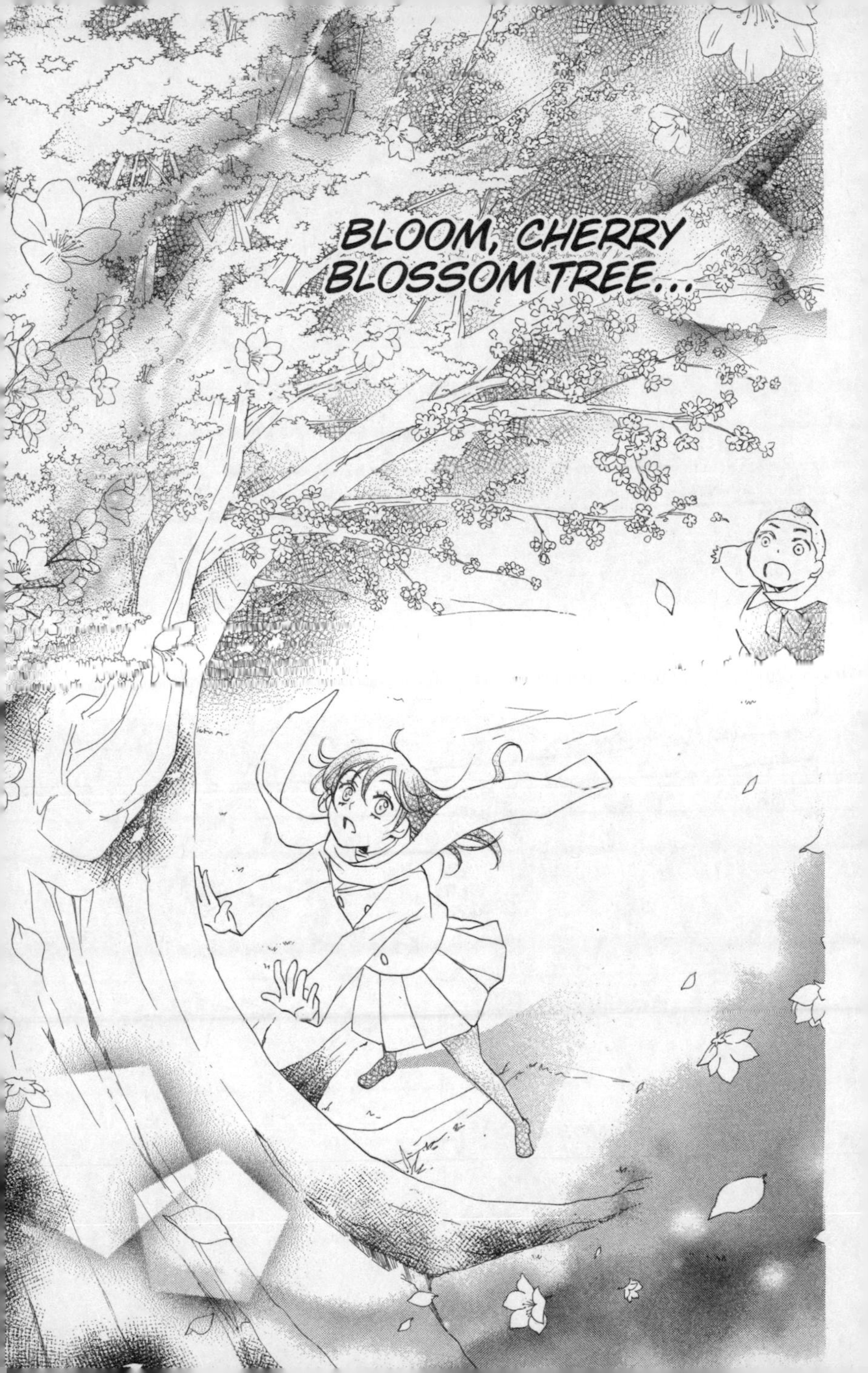
BLOOM, CHERRY
BLOSSOM TREE...

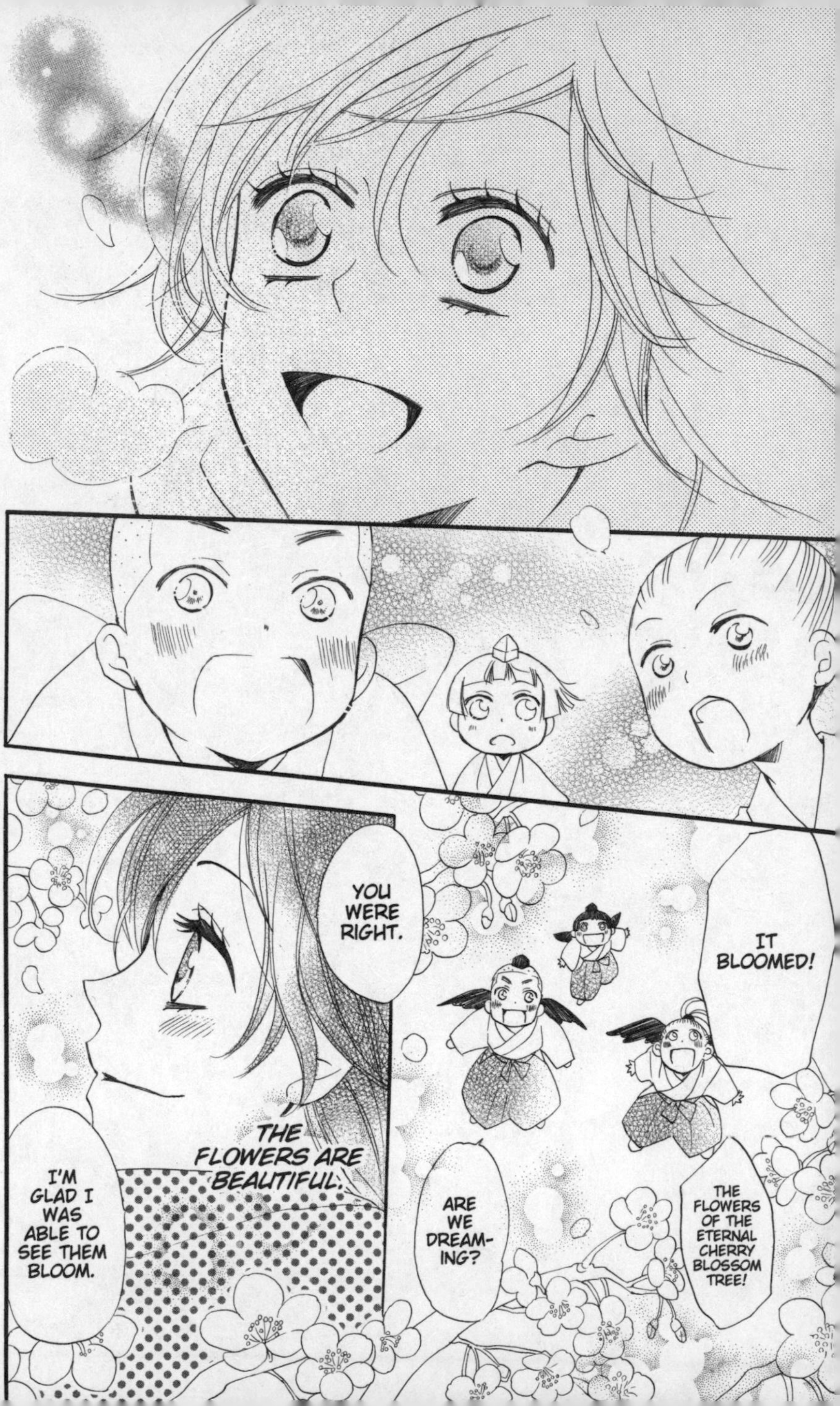
IT BLOOMED!
THE FLOWERS OF THE ETERNAL CHERRY BLOSSOM TREE!
ARE WE DREAMING?
YOU WERE RIGHT.
THE FLOWERS ARE BEAUTIFUL.
I'M GLAD I WAS ABLE TO SEE THEM BLOOM.

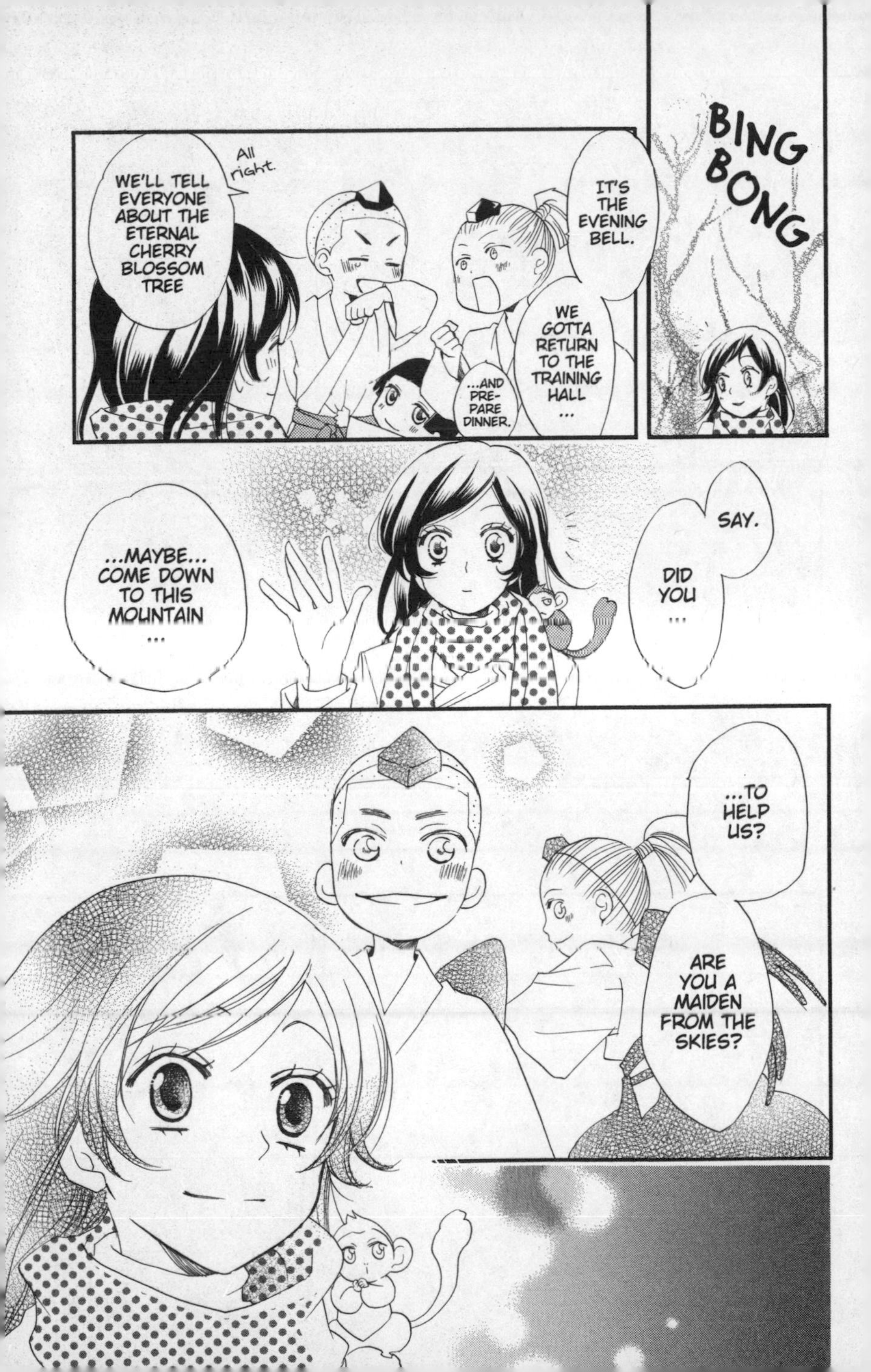
BING BONG
IT'S THE EVENING BELL.
WE GOTTA RETURN TO THE TRAINING HALL...
...AND PREPARE DINNER.
All right.
WE'LL TELL EVERYONE ABOUT THE ETERNAL CHERRY BLOSSOM TREE
SAY.
DID YOU...
...MAYBE... COME DOWN TO THIS MOUNTAIN...
...TO HELP US?
ARE YOU A MAIDEN FROM THE SKIES?

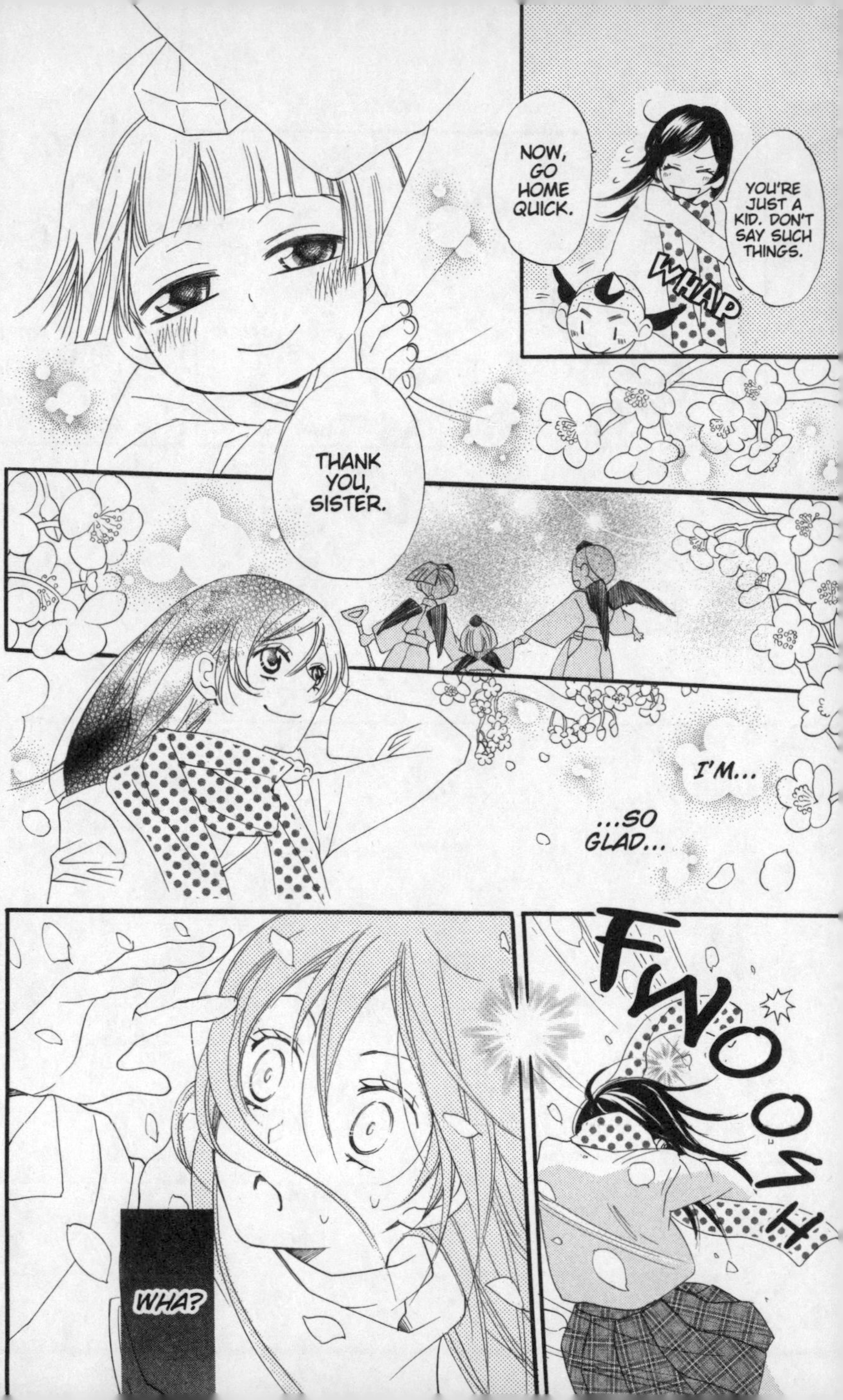
YOU'RE JUST A KID. DON'T SAY SUCH THINGS.
NOW, GO HOME QUICK.
WHAP
THANK YOU, SISTER.
I'M...
...SO GLAD...
FWOOSH
WHA?

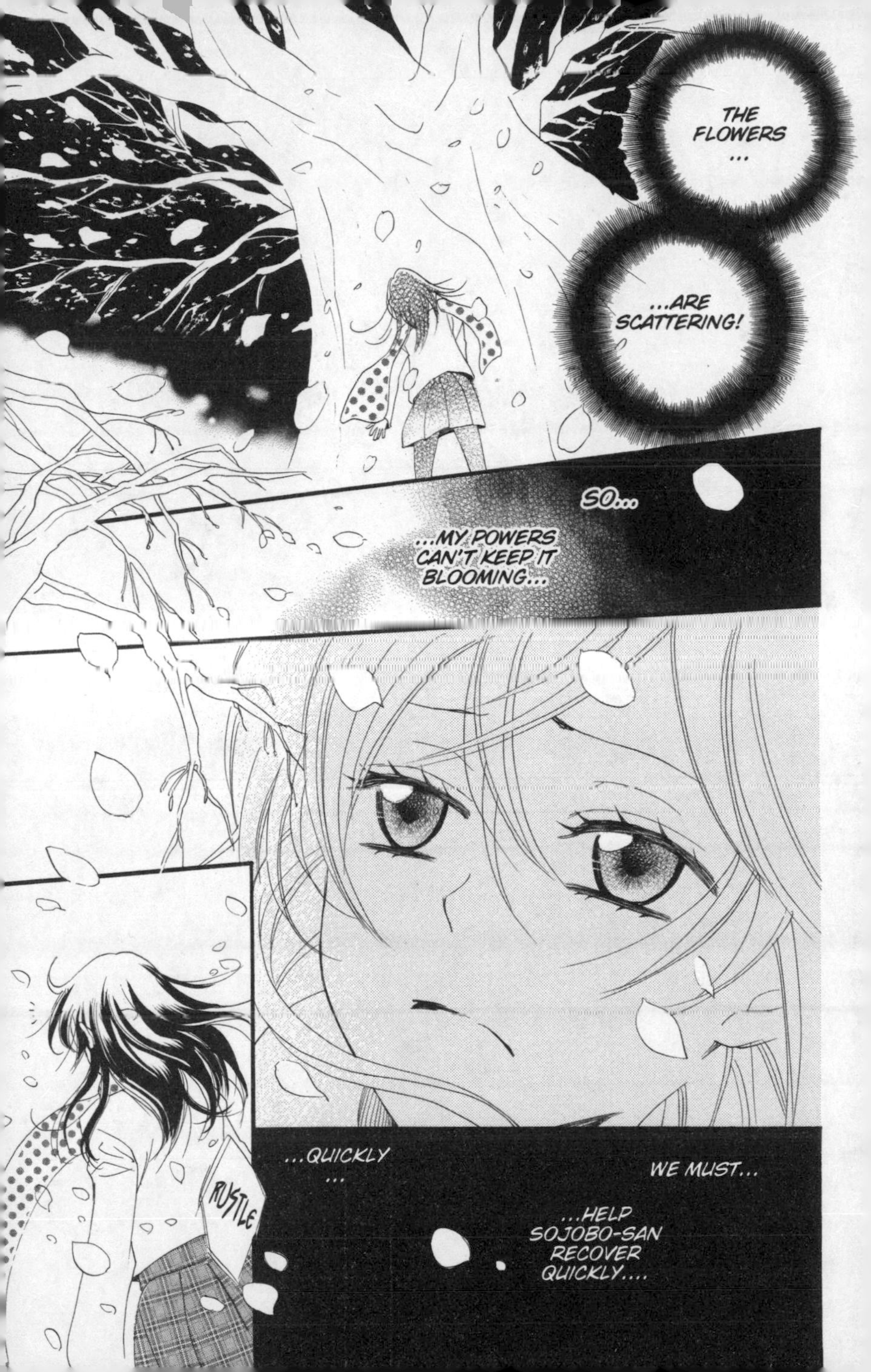
THE FLOWERS ...
...ARE SCATTERING!
SO...
...MY POWERS CAN'T KEEP IT BLOOMING...
WE MUST...
...HELP SOJOBO-SAN RECOVER QUICKLY....
...QUICKLY ...
RUSTLE

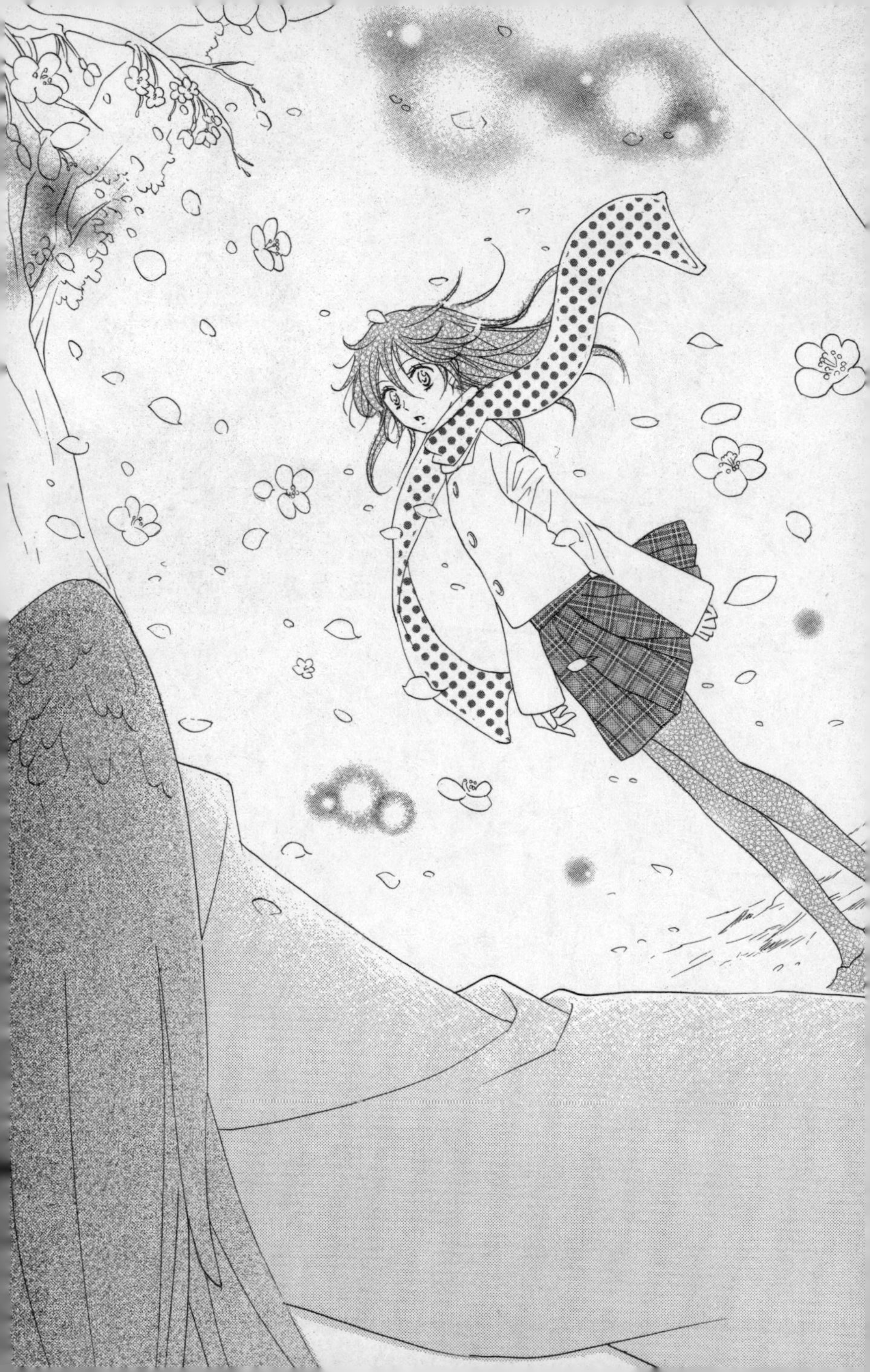

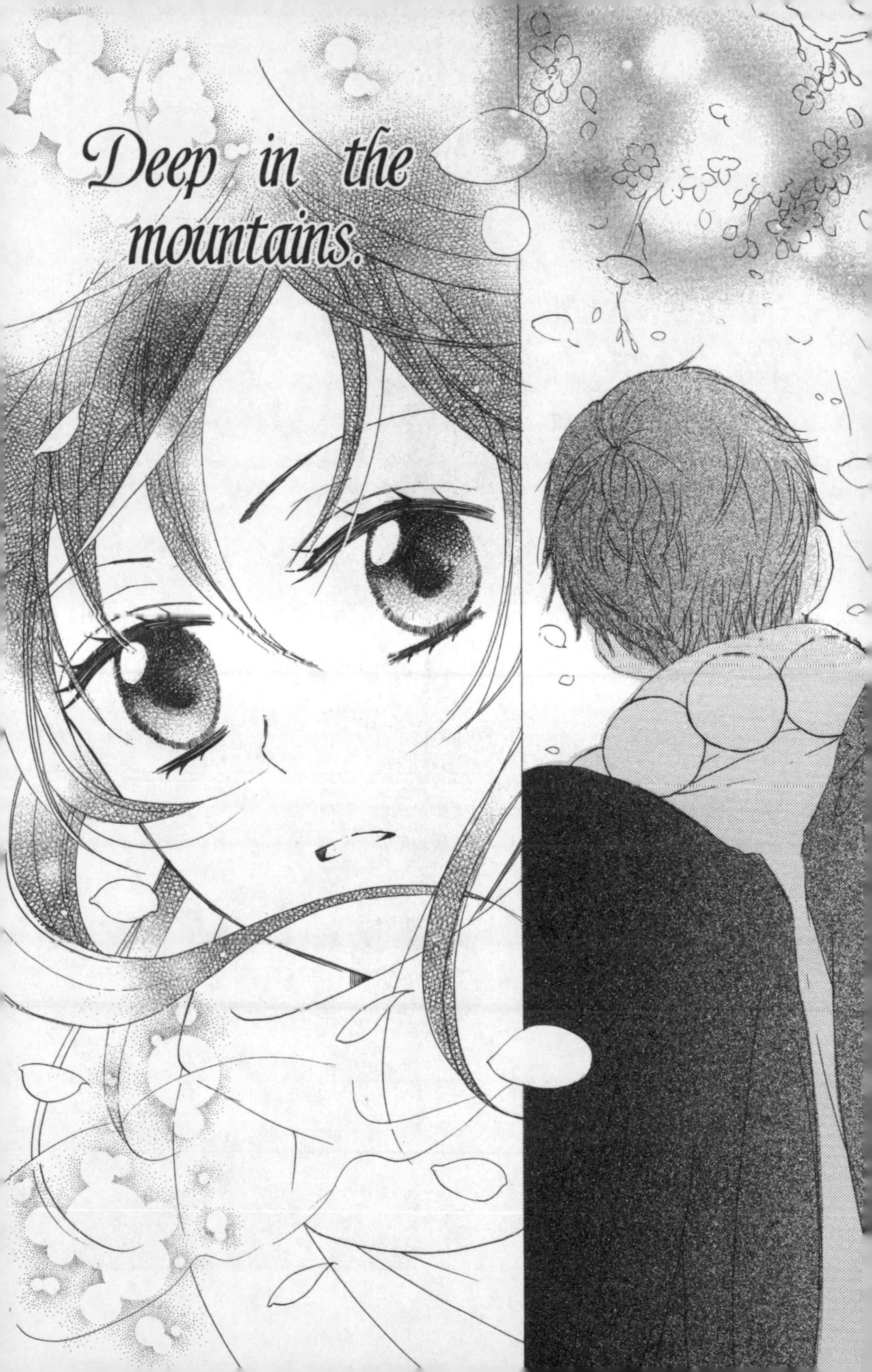
Deep in the mountains.

In the Kurama village where females are forbidden entry...

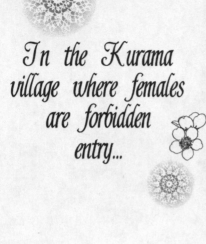

...a man met a maiden from the skies.

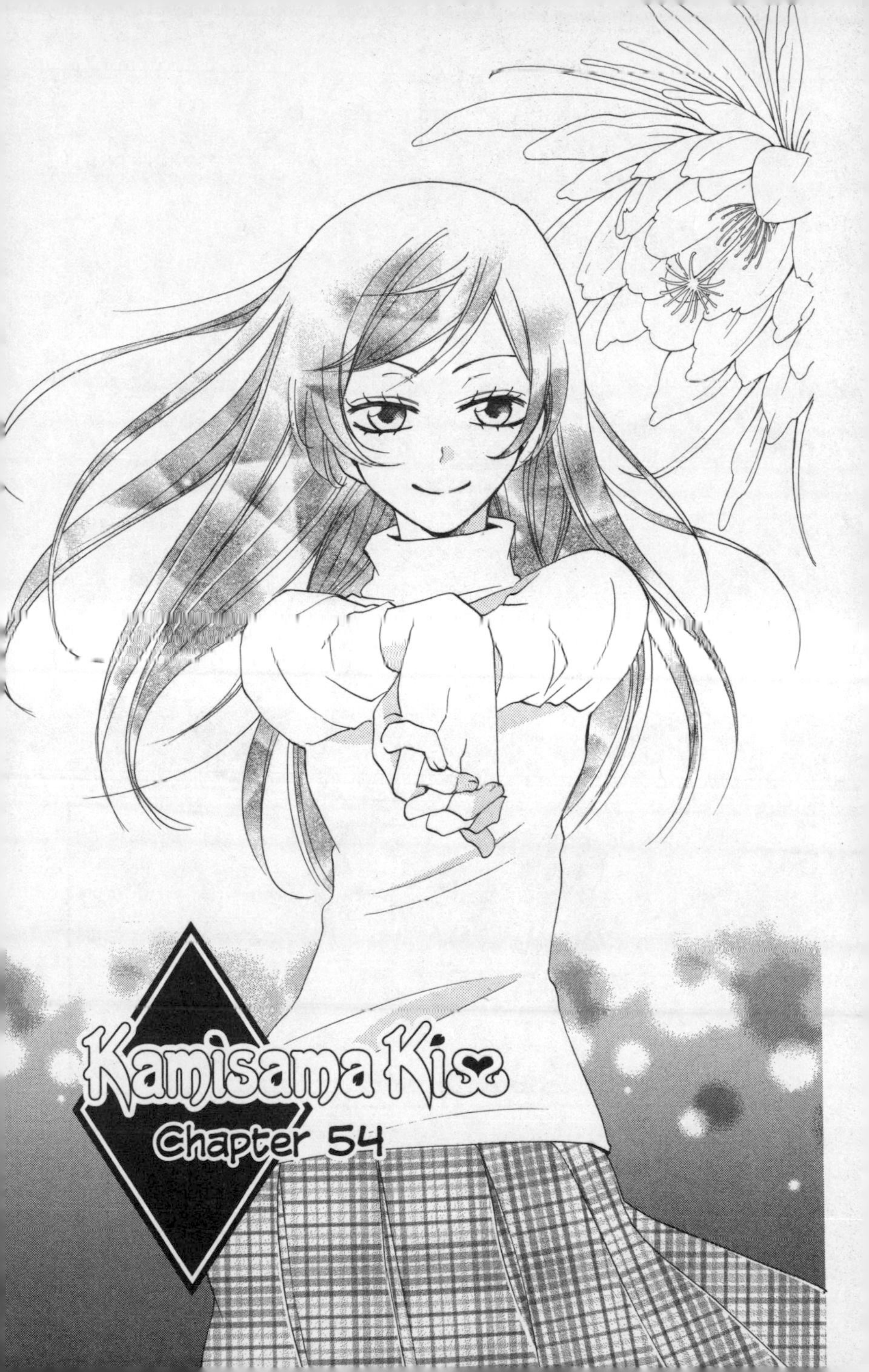
Kamisama Kiss
Chapter 54

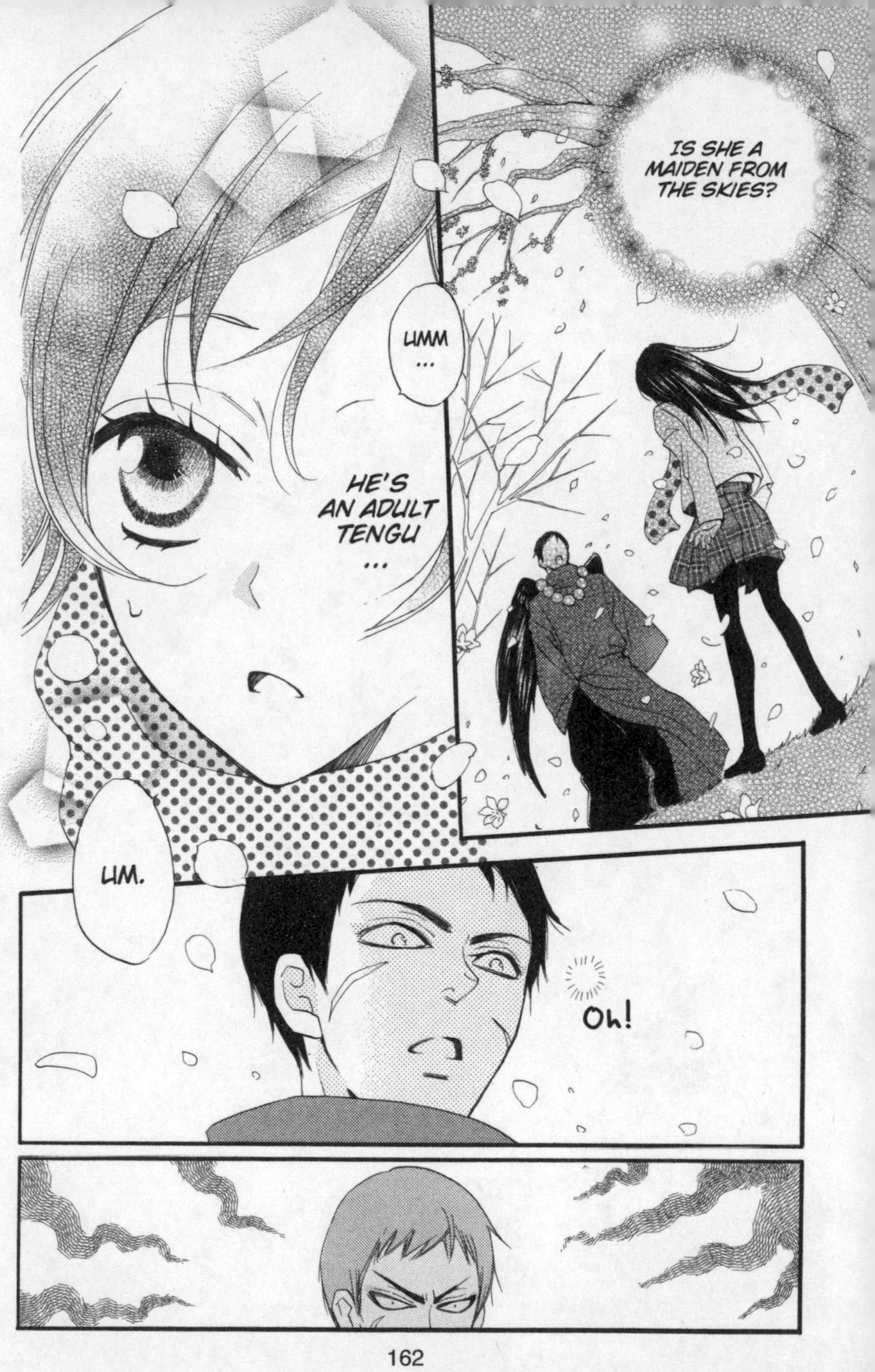
IS SHE A MAIDEN FROM THE SKIES?
UMM ...
HE'S AN ADULT TENGU ...
UM.
Oh!

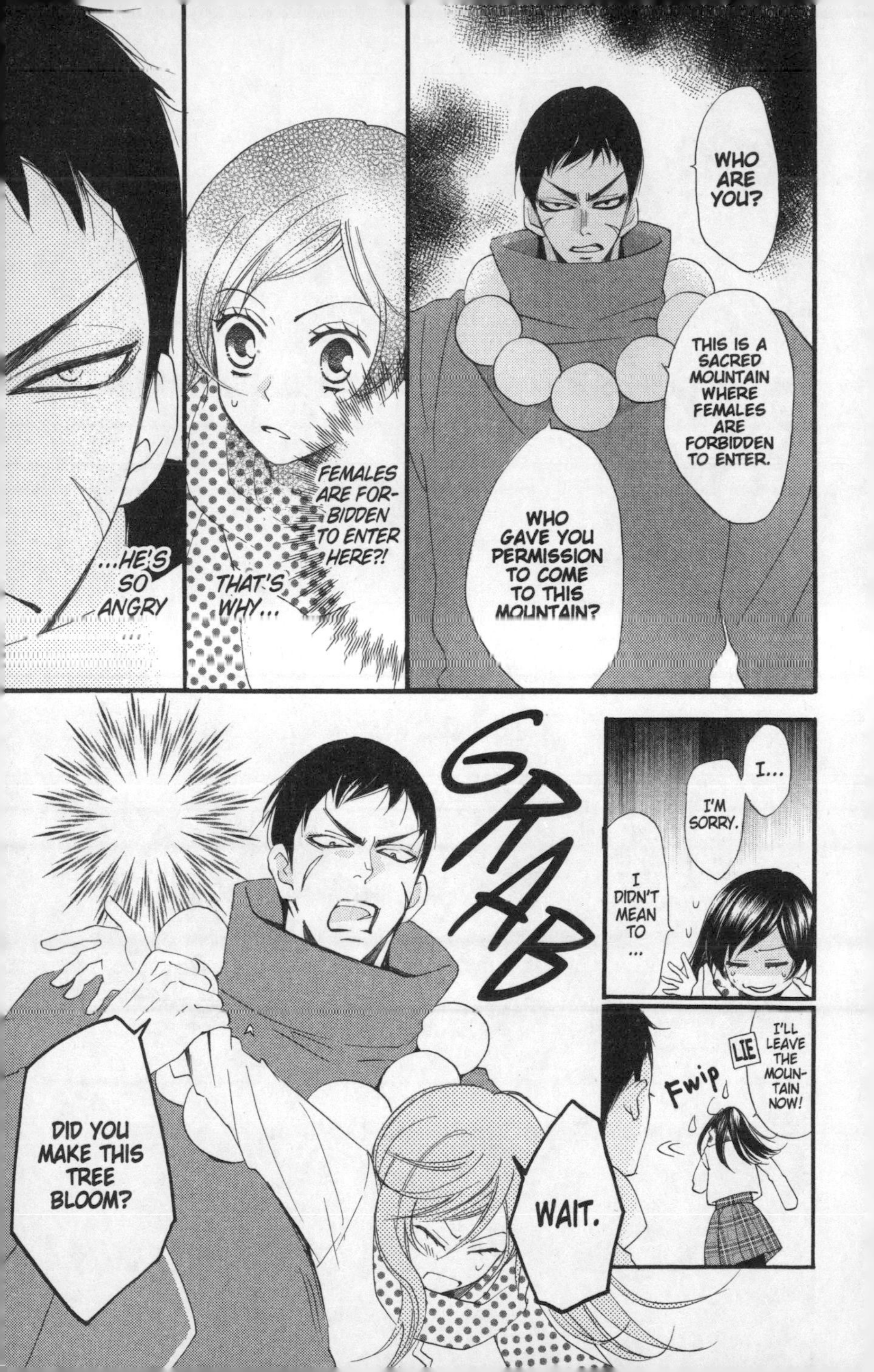
WHO ARE YOU?
THIS IS A SACRED MOUNTAIN WHERE FEMALES ARE FORBIDDEN TO ENTER.
WHO GAVE YOU PERMISSION TO COME TO THIS MOUNTAIN?
FEMALES ARE FOR-BIDDEN TO ENTER HERE?!
THAT'S WHY...
...HE'S SO ANGRY ...
I...
I'M SORRY.
I DIDN'T MEAN TO ...
I'LL LEAVE THE MOUN-TAIN NOW!
LIE
Fwip
GRAB
WAIT.
DID YOU MAKE THIS TREE BLOOM?

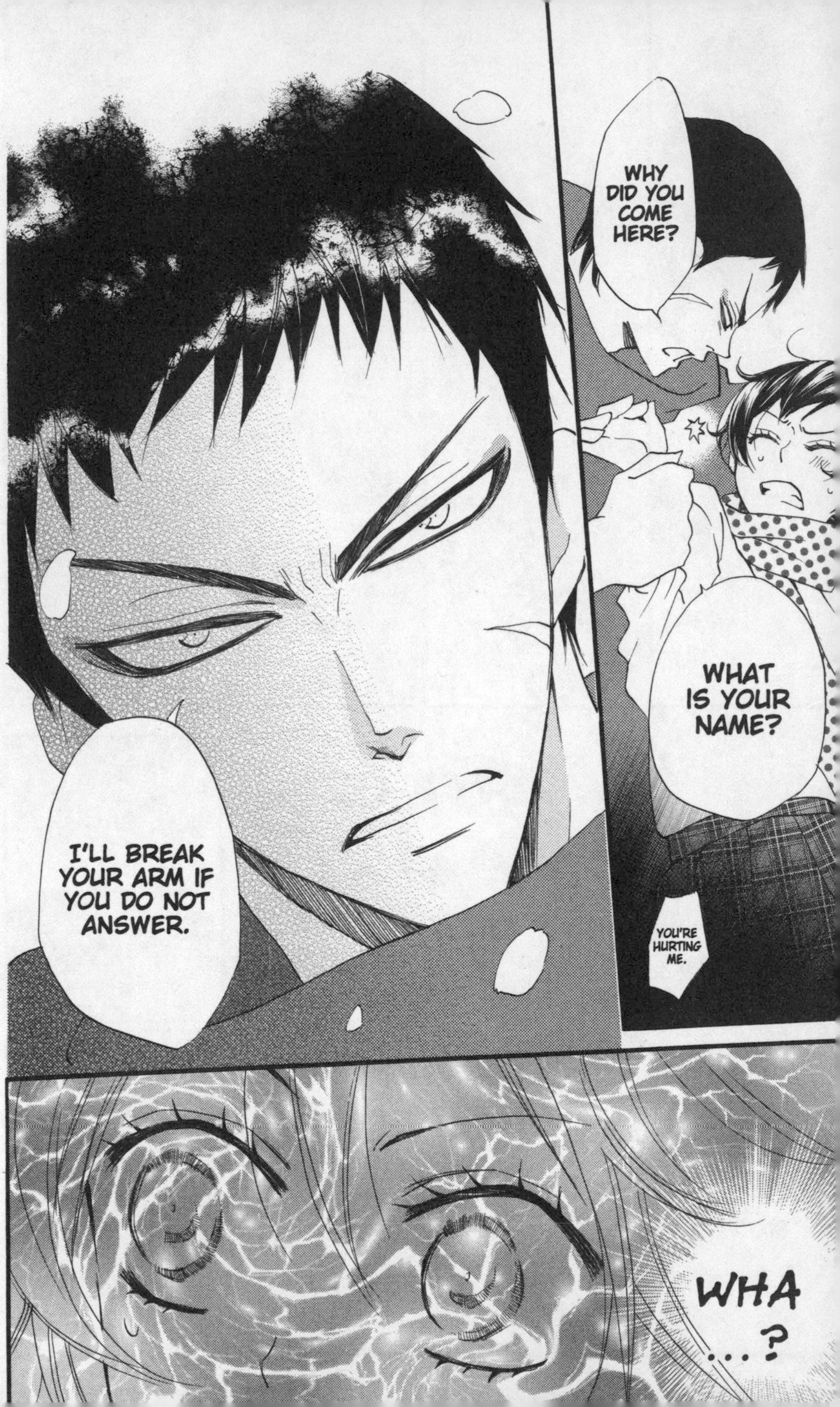
WHY DID YOU COME HERE?
WHAT IS YOUR NAME?
YOU'RE HURTING ME.
I'LL BREAK YOUR ARM IF YOU DO NOT ANSWER.
WHA...?

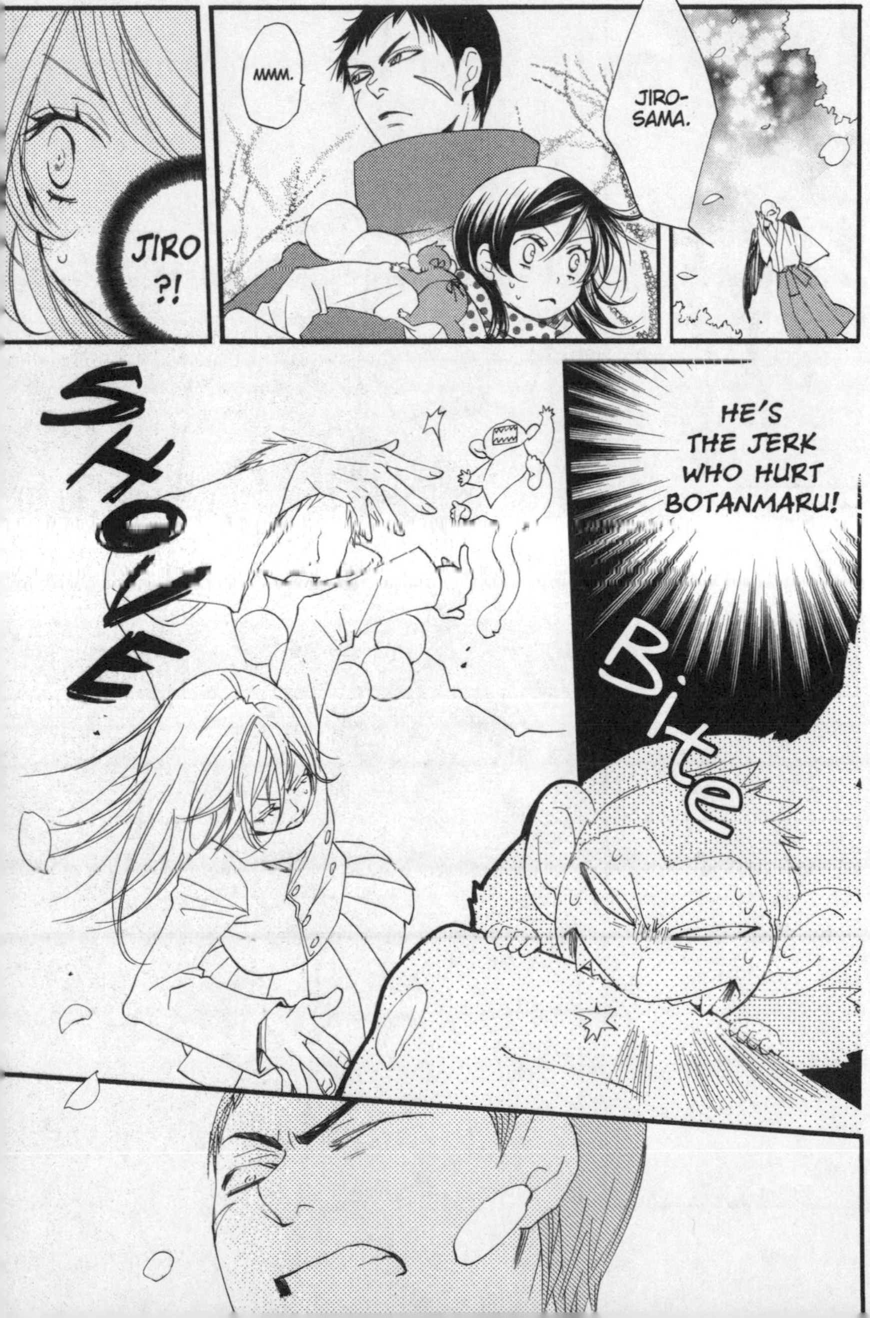
JIRO-SAMA.
MMM.
JIRO ?!
HE'S THE JERK WHO HURT BOTANMARU!
Bite
SHOVE

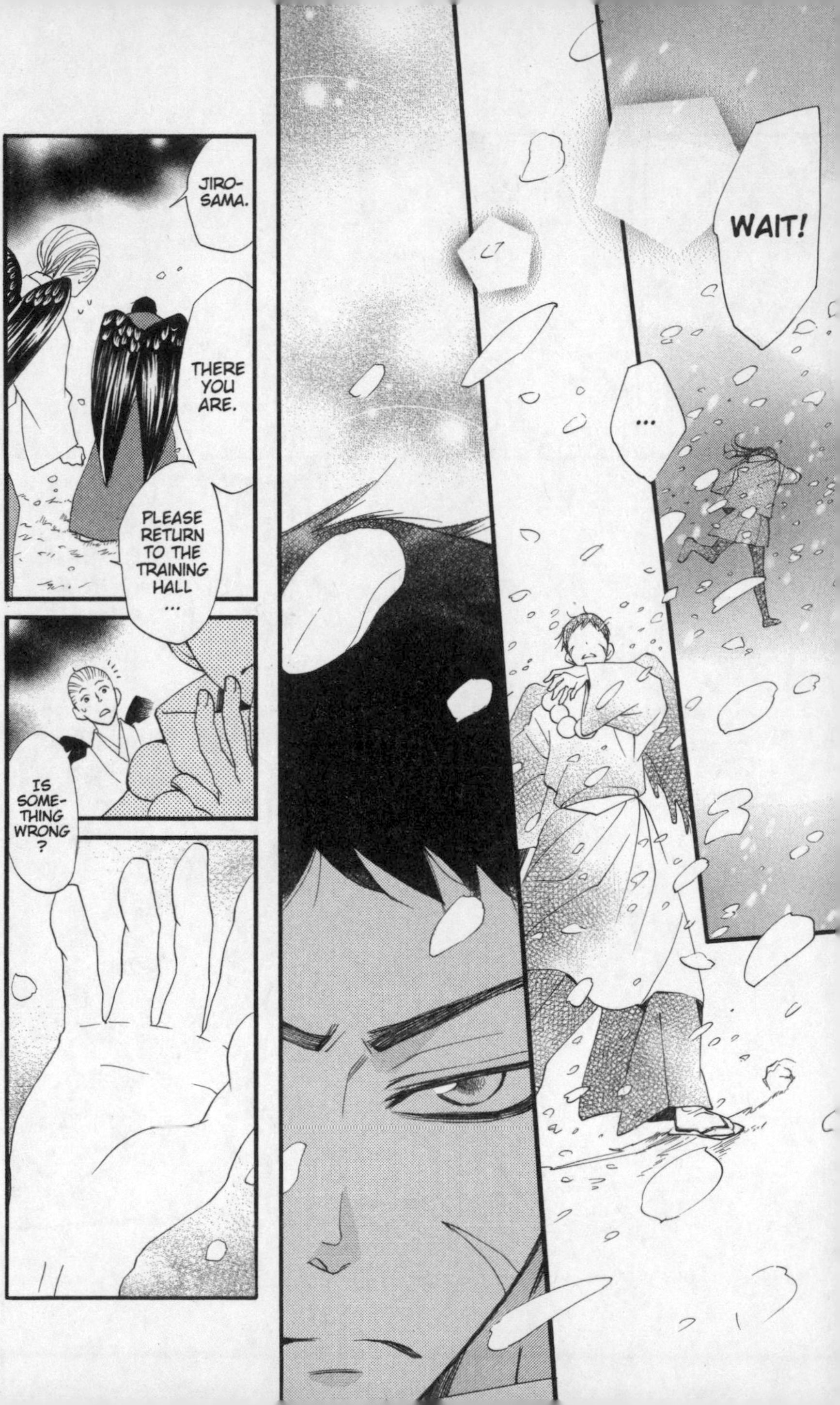
WAIT!
...
JIRO-SAMA.
THERE YOU ARE.
PLEASE RETURN TO THE TRAINING HALL ...
IS SOMETHING WRONG?

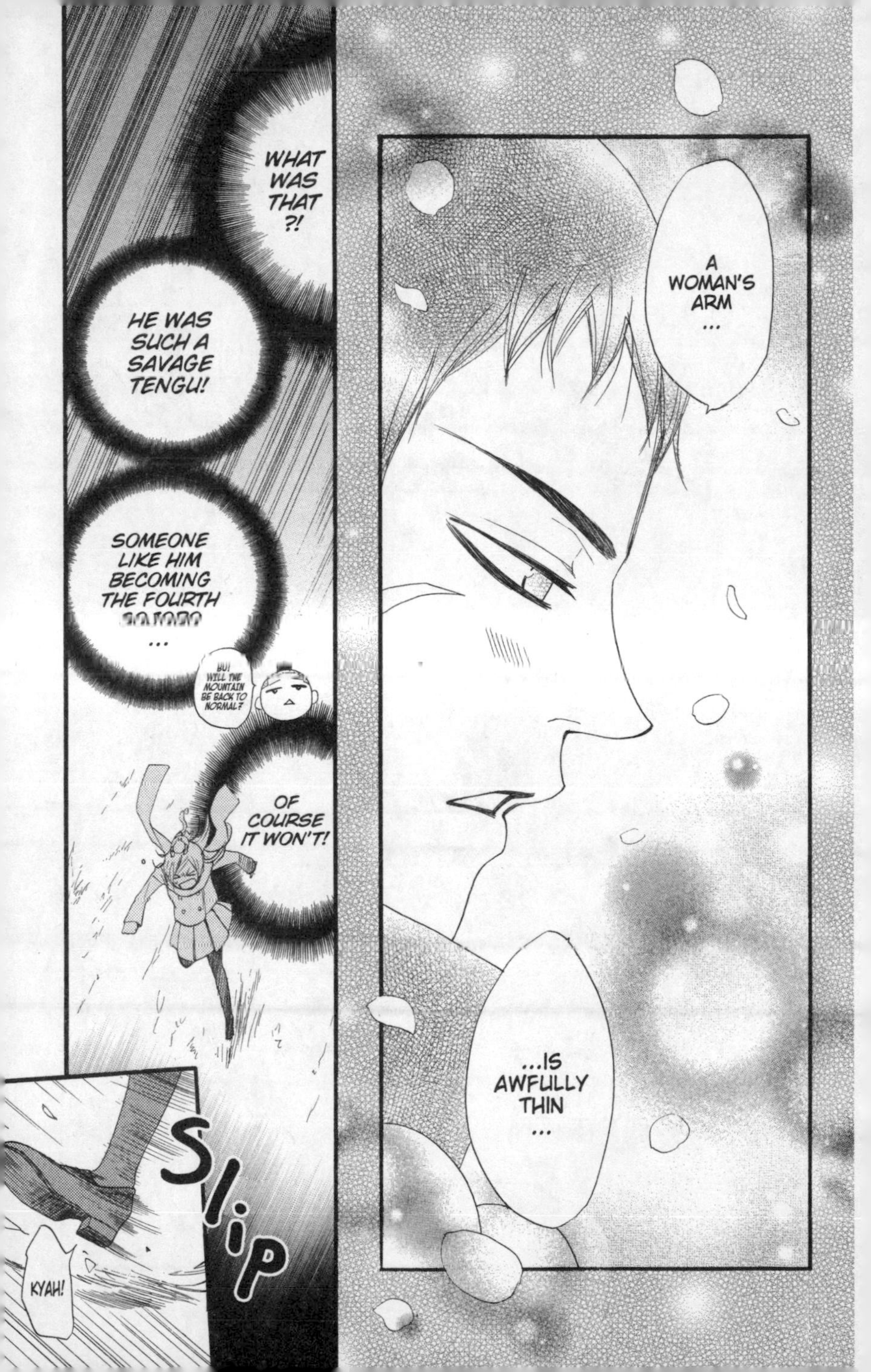
A WOMAN'S ARM ...
...IS AWFULLY THIN ...
WHAT WAS THAT?!
HE WAS SUCH A SAVAGE TENGU!
SOMEONE LIKE HIM BECOMING THE FOURTH
...
BUT WILL THE MOUNTAIN BE BACK TO NORMAL?
OF COURSE IT WON'T!
SLIP
KYAH!

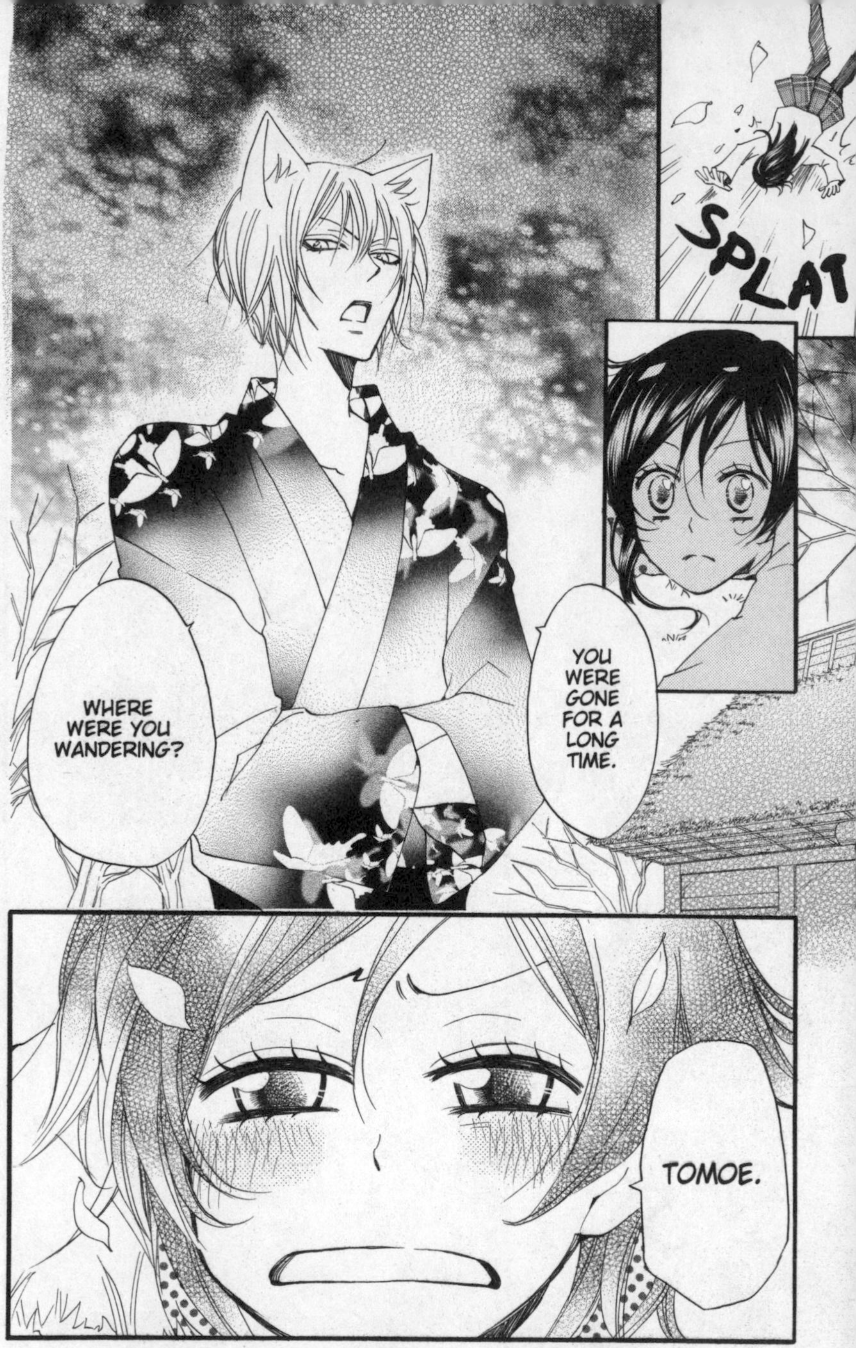
SPLAT
YOU WERE GONE FOR A LONG TIME.
WHERE WERE YOU WANDERING?
TOMOE.

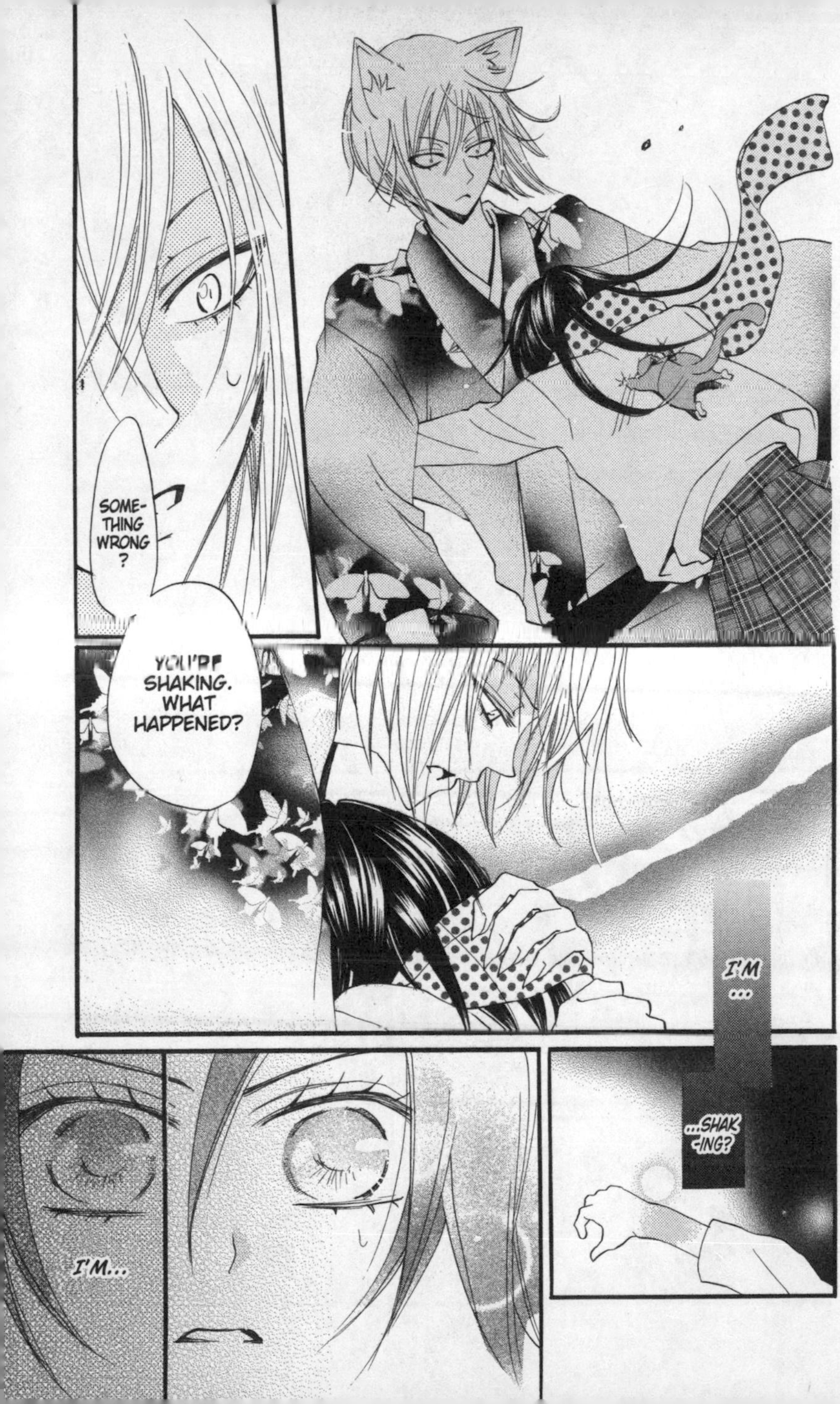
SOMETHING WRONG?
YOU'RE SHAKING. WHAT HAPPENED?
I'M ...
...SHAK-ING?
I'M...

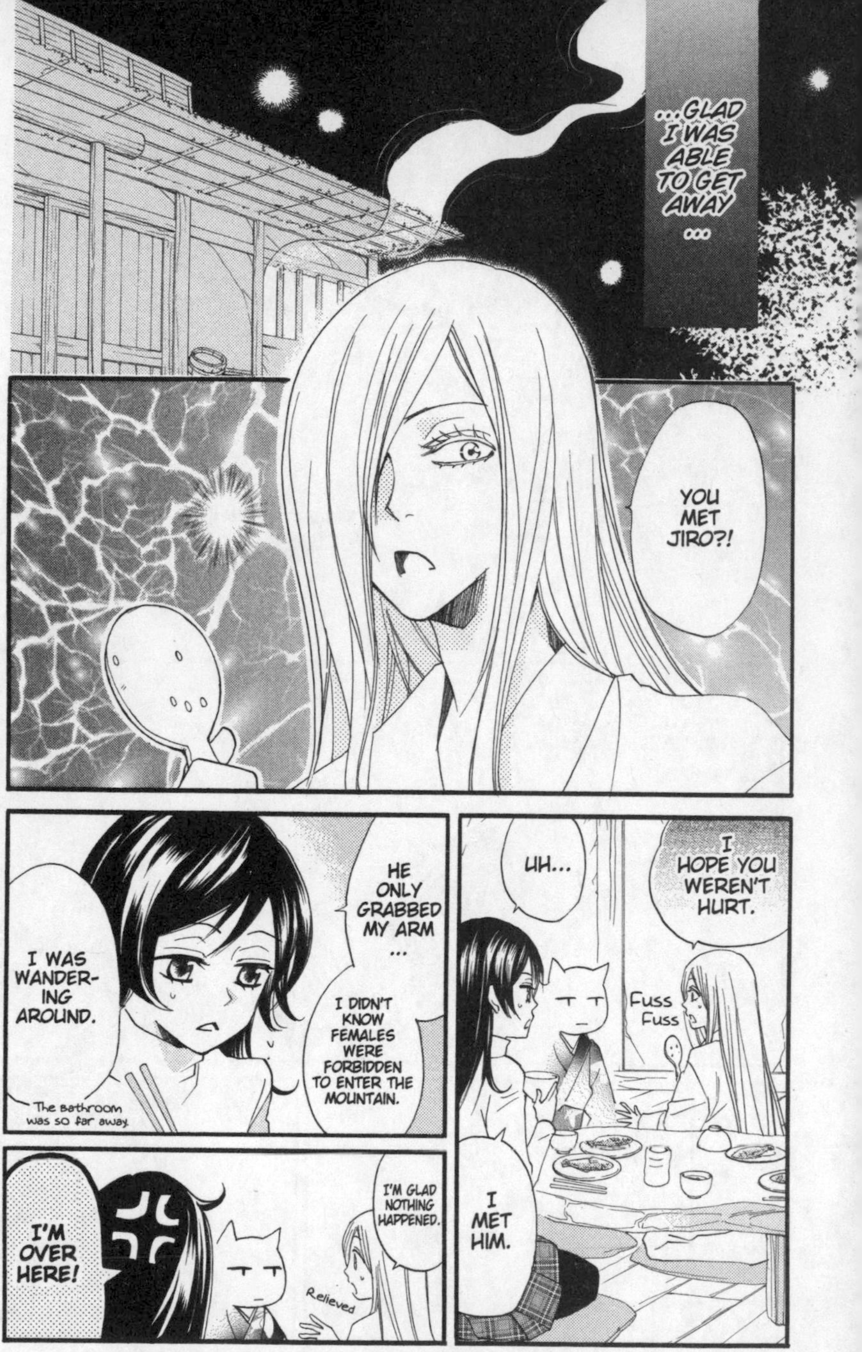
...GLAD I WAS ABLE TO GET AWAY ...
YOU MET JIRO?!
I HOPE YOU WEREN'T HURT.
UH...
Fuss Fuss
I MET HIM.
HE ONLY GRABBED MY ARM ...
I WAS WANDER-ING AROUND.
I DIDN'T KNOW FEMALES WERE FORBIDDEN TO ENTER THE MOUNTAIN.
The bathroom was so far away.
I'M GLAD NOTHING HAPPENED.
Relieved
I'M OVER HERE!

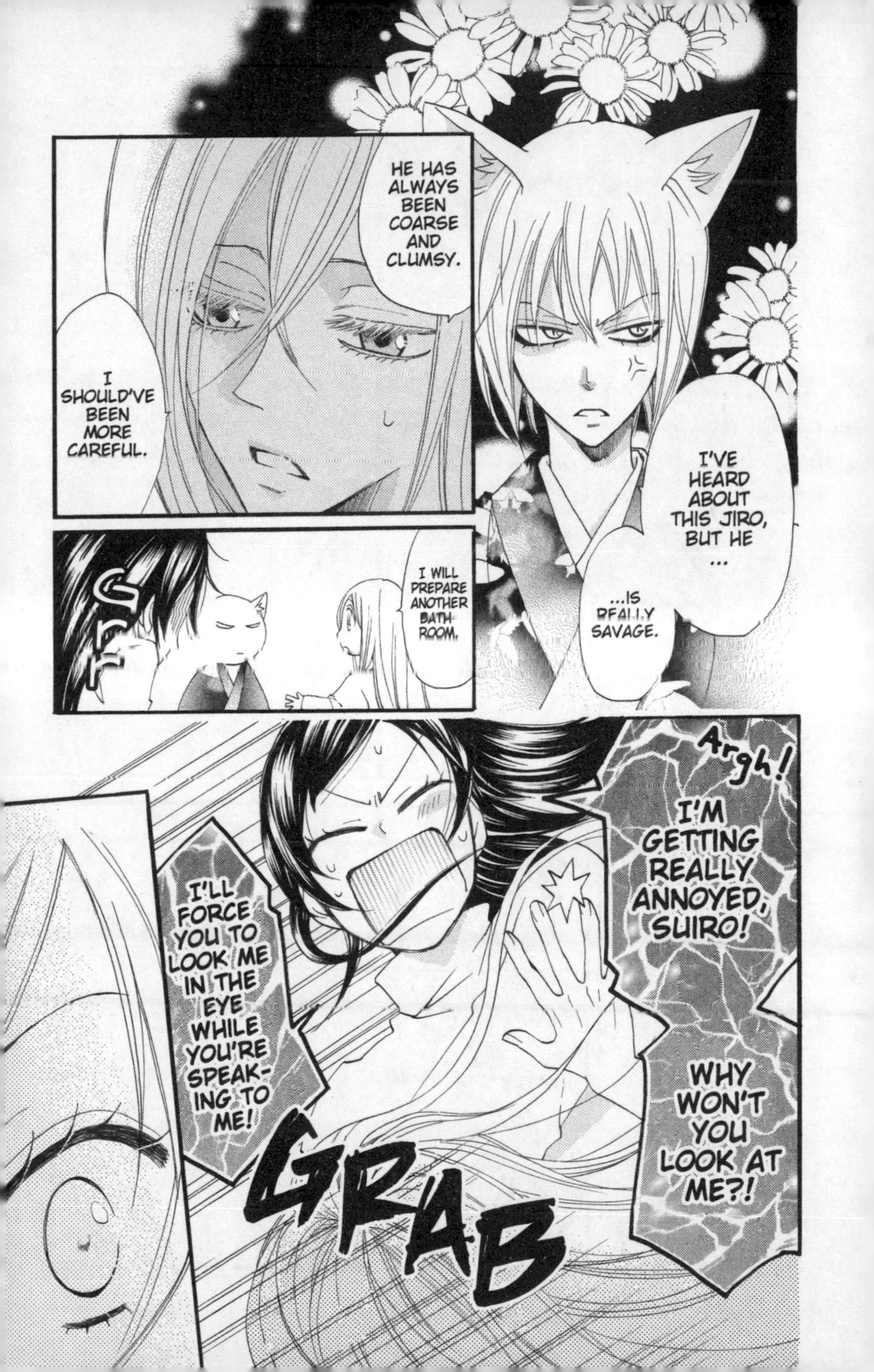
I'VE HEARD ABOUT THIS JIRO, BUT HE ...
...IS REALLY SAVAGE.
HE HAS ALWAYS BEEN COARSE AND CLUMSY.
I SHOULD'VE BEEN MORE CAREFUL.
I WILL PREPARE ANOTHER BATH ROOM.
Grr
Argh!
I'M GETTING REALLY ANNOYED, SUIRO!
WHY WON'T YOU LOOK AT ME?!
I'LL FORCE YOU TO LOOK ME IN THE EYE WHILE YOU'RE SPEAK-ING TO ME!
GRAB

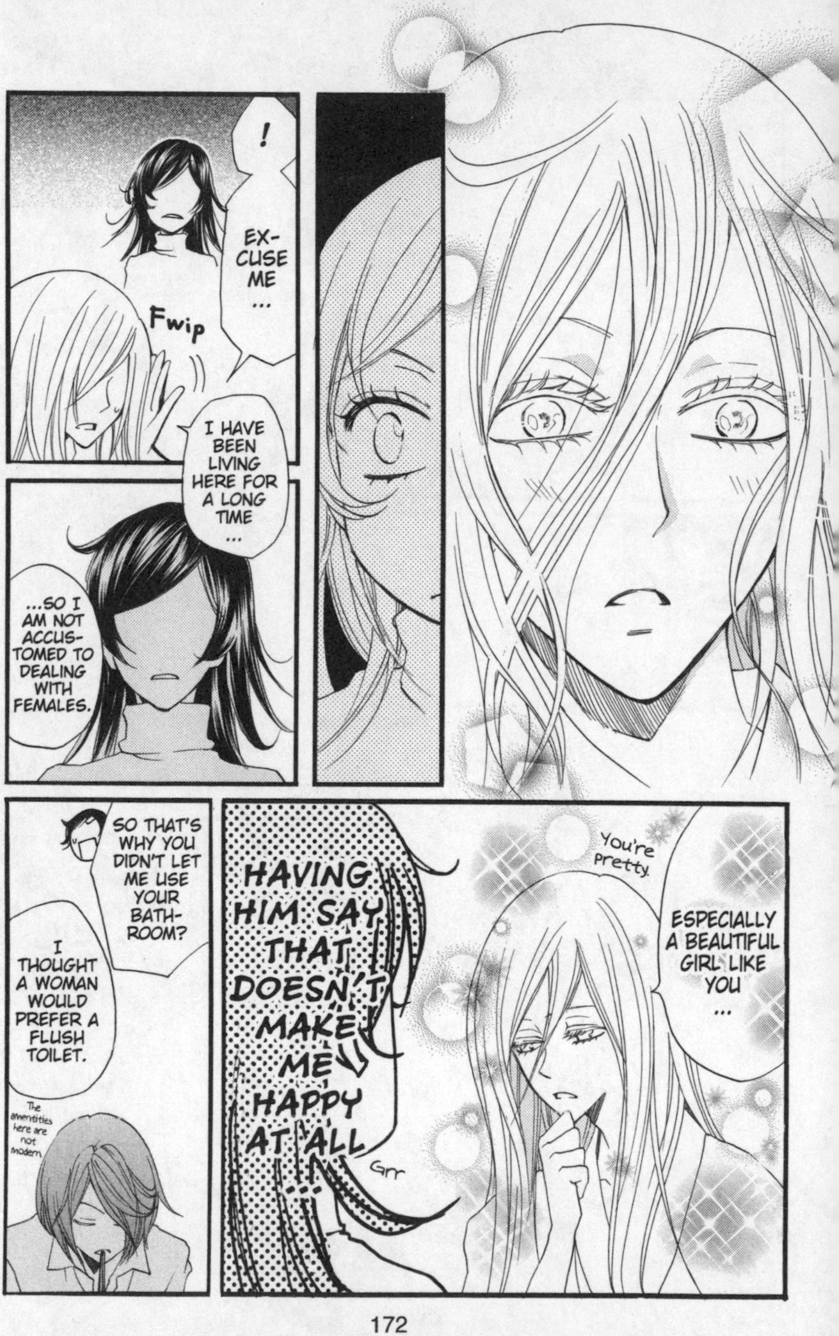
!
EX-CUSE ME ...
Fwip
I HAVE BEEN LIVING HERE FOR A LONG TIME ...
...SO I AM NOT ACCUS-TOMED TO DEALING WITH FEMALES.
You're pretty.
ESPECIALLY A BEAUTIFUL GIRL LIKE YOU ...
HAVING HIM SAY THAT DOESN'T MAKE ME HAPPY AT ALL ...!
Grr
SO THAT'S WHY YOU DIDN'T LET ME USE YOUR BATH-ROOM?
I THOUGHT A WOMAN WOULD PREFER A FLUSH TOILET.
The amentities here are not modern.

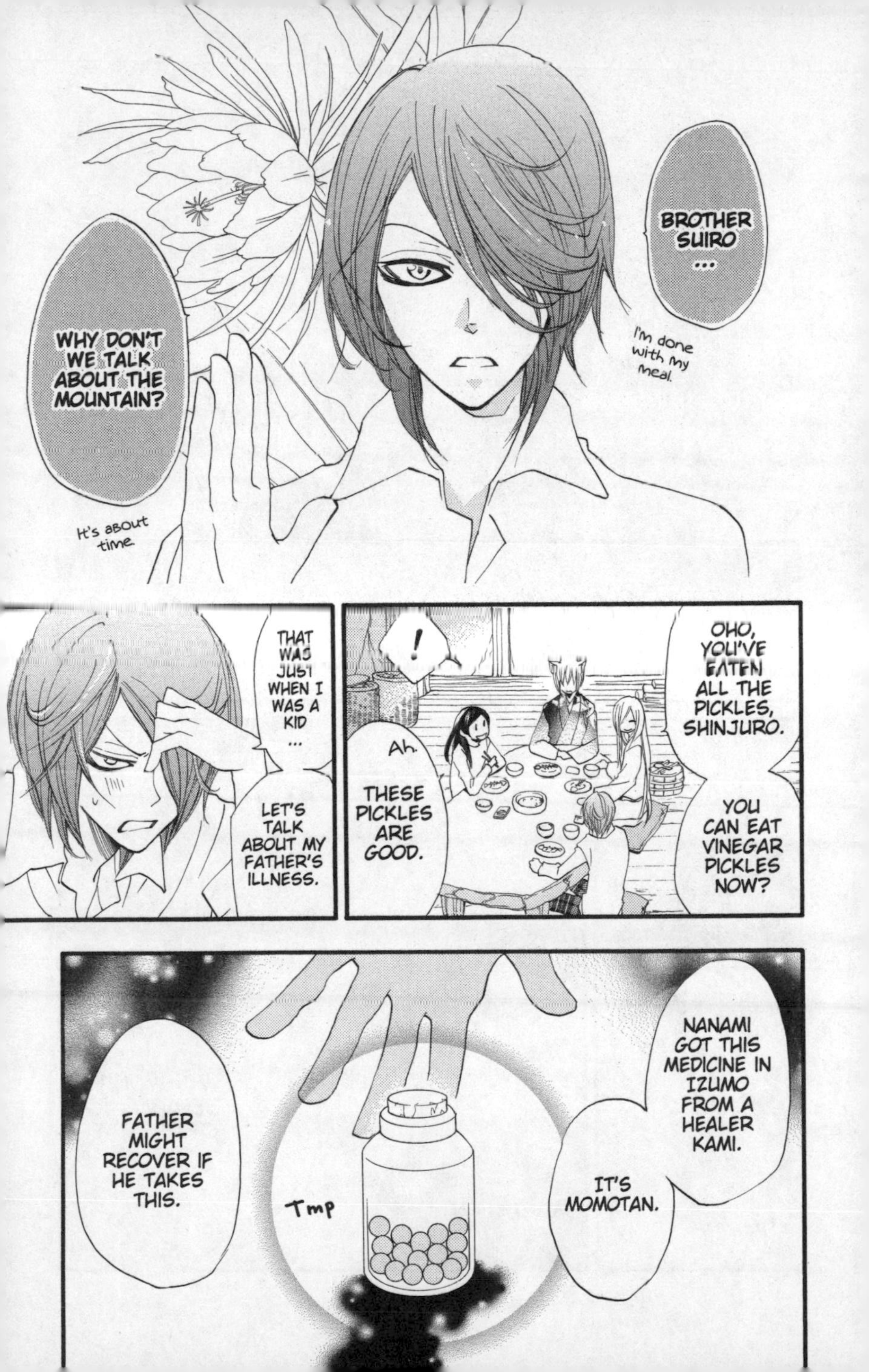
BROTHER SUIRO ...
I'm done with my meal.
WHY DON'T WE TALK ABOUT THE MOUNTAIN?
It's about time.
OHO, YOU'VE EATEN ALL THE PICKLES, SHINJURO.
YOU CAN EAT VINEGAR PICKLES NOW?
!
Ah.
THESE PICKLES ARE GOOD.
THAT WAS JUST WHEN I WAS A KID ...
LET'S TALK ABOUT MY FATHER'S ILLNESS.
NANAMI GOT THIS MEDICINE IN IZUMO FROM A HEALER KAMI.
IT'S MOMOTAN.
Tmp
FATHER MIGHT RECOVER IF HE TAKES THIS.

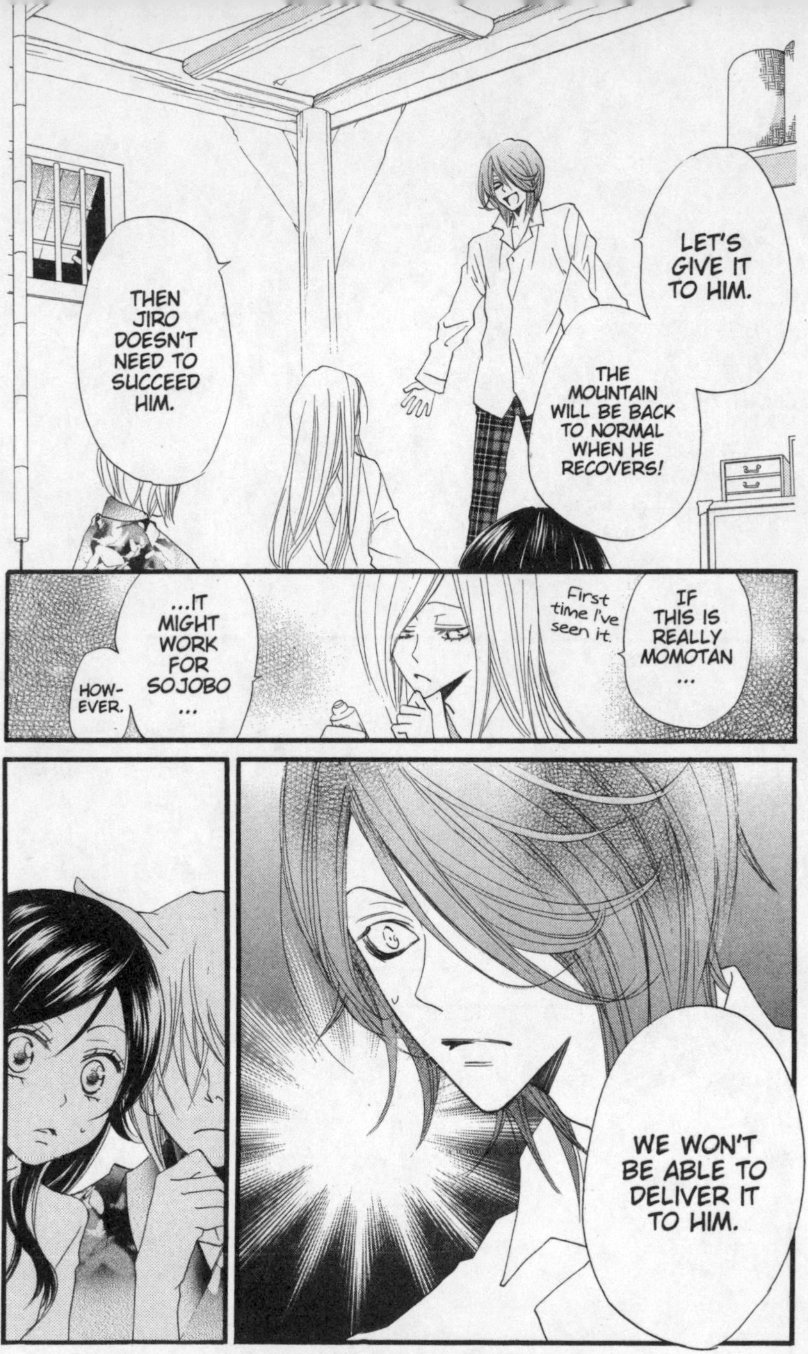
LET'S GIVE IT TO HIM.
THE MOUNTAIN WILL BE BACK TO NORMAL WHEN HE RECOVERS!
THEN JIRO DOESN'T NEED TO SUCCEED HIM.
IF THIS IS REALLY MOMOTAN ...
First time I've seen it.
...IT MIGHT WORK FOR SOJOBO ...
HOW-EVER.
WE WON'T BE ABLE TO DELIVER IT TO HIM.

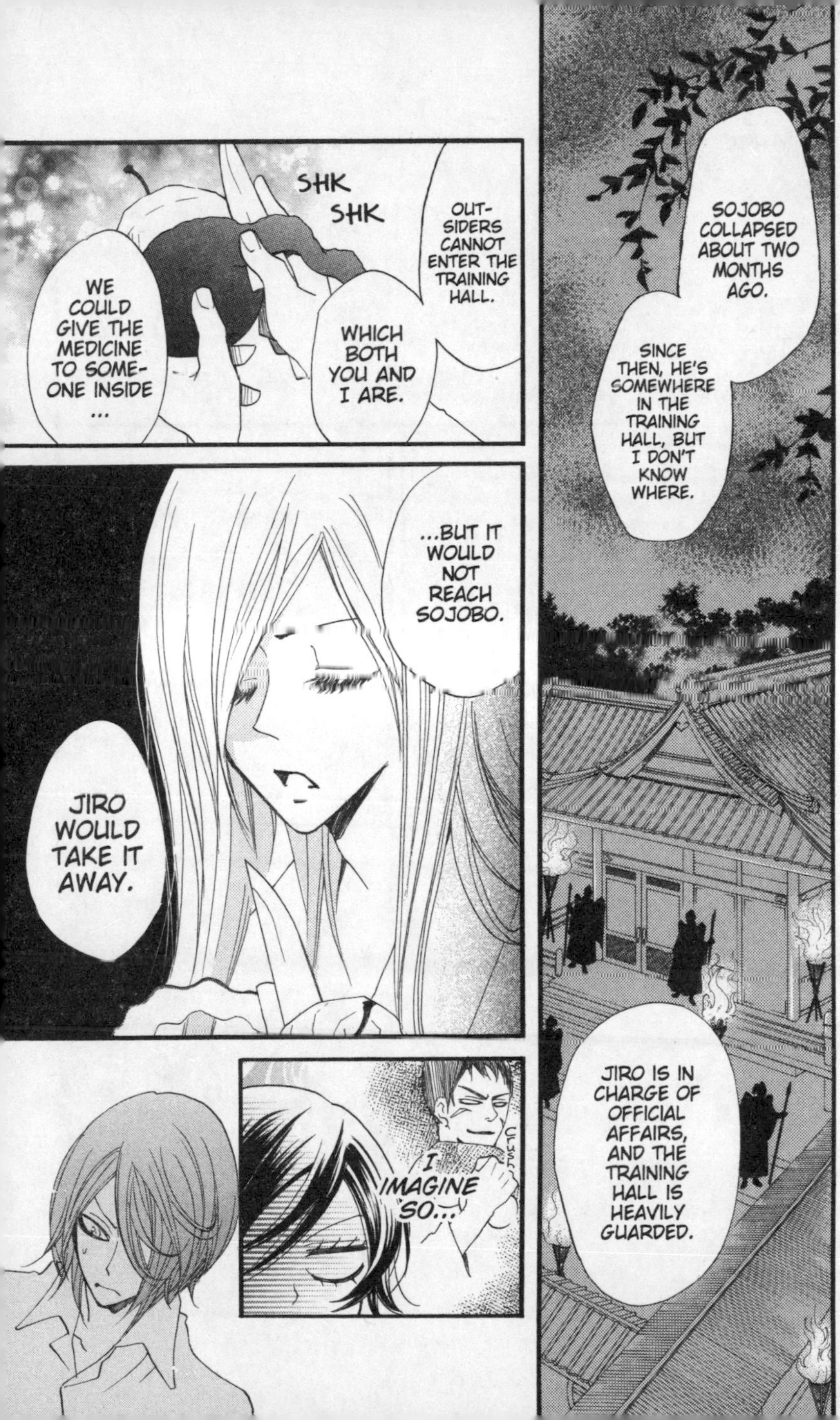
SOJOBO COLLAPSED ABOUT TWO MONTHS AGO.
SINCE THEN, HE'S SOMEWHERE IN THE TRAINING HALL, BUT I DON'T KNOW WHERE.
JIRO IS IN CHARGE OF OFFICIAL AFFAIRS, AND THE TRAINING HALL IS HEAVILY GUARDED.
OUT-SIDERS CANNOT ENTER THE TRAINING HALL.
SHK SHK
WHICH BOTH YOU AND I ARE.
WE COULD GIVE THE MEDICINE TO SOME-ONE INSIDE ...
...BUT IT WOULD NOT REACH SOJOBO.
JIRO WOULD TAKE IT AWAY.
I IMAGINE SO...

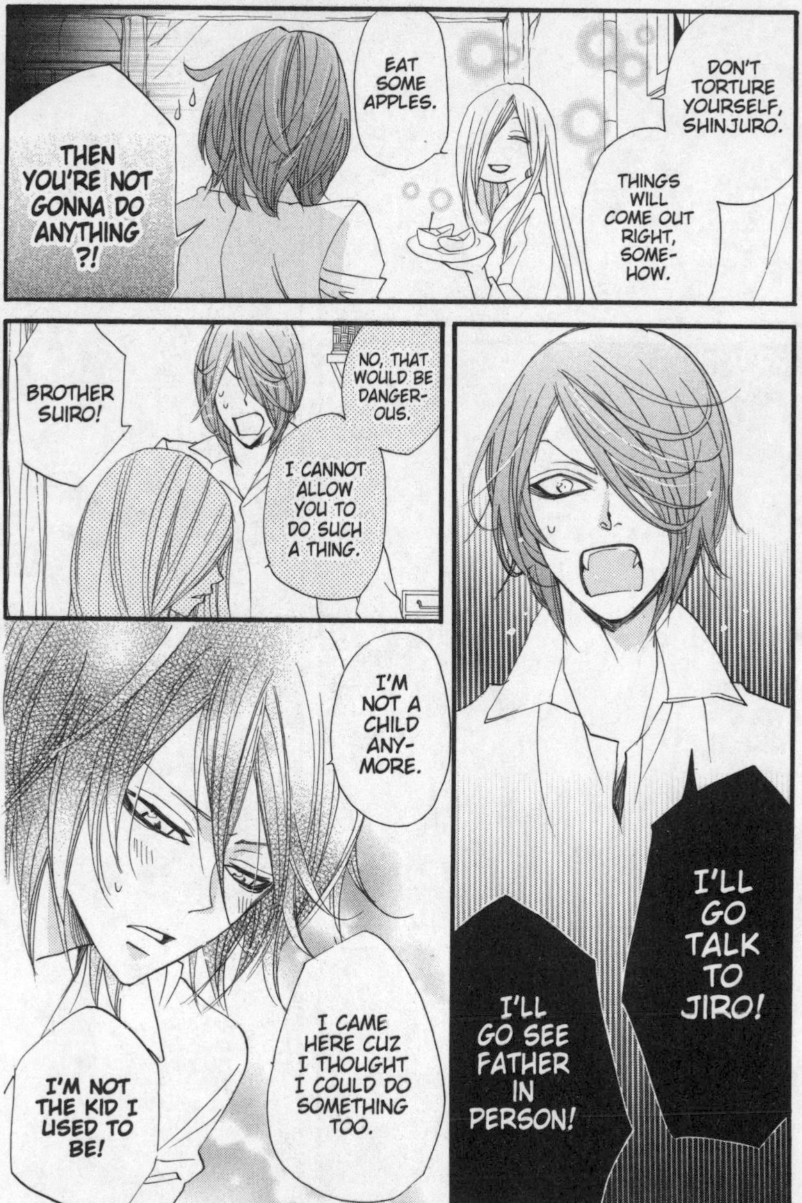
DON'T TORTURE YOURSELF, SHINJURO.
THINGS WILL COME OUT RIGHT, SOME-HOW.
EAT SOME APPLES.
THEN YOU'RE NOT GONNA DO ANYTHING ?!
I'LL GO TALK TO JIRO!
I'LL GO SEE FATHER IN PERSON!
NO, THAT WOULD BE DANGER-OUS.
I CANNOT ALLOW YOU TO DO SUCH A THING.
BROTHER SUIRO!
I'M NOT A CHILD ANY-MORE.
I CAME HERE CUZ I THOUGHT I COULD DO SOMETHING TOO.
I'M NOT THE KID I USED TO BE!

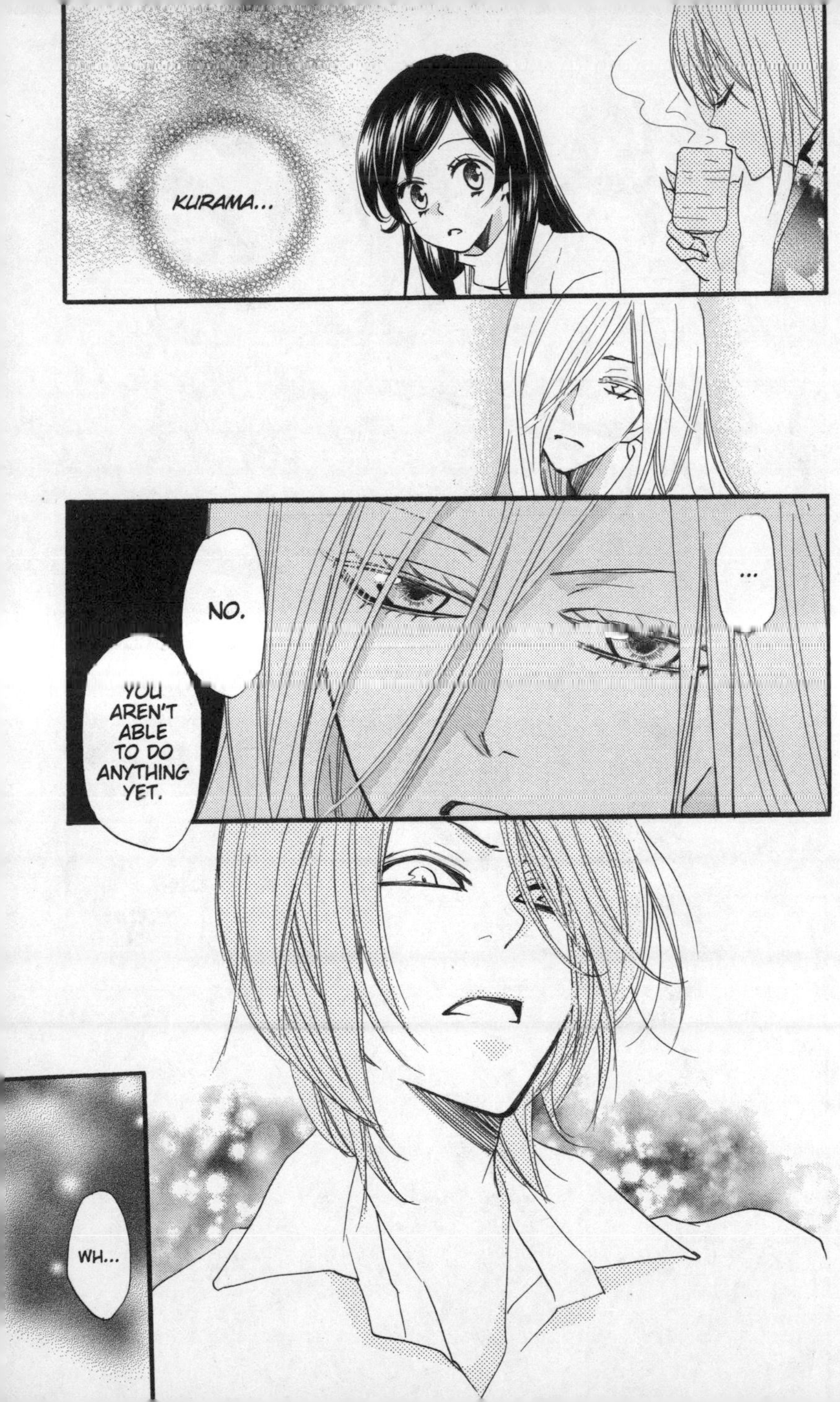
KURAMA...
...
NO.
YOU AREN'T ABLE TO DO ANYTHING YET.
WH...

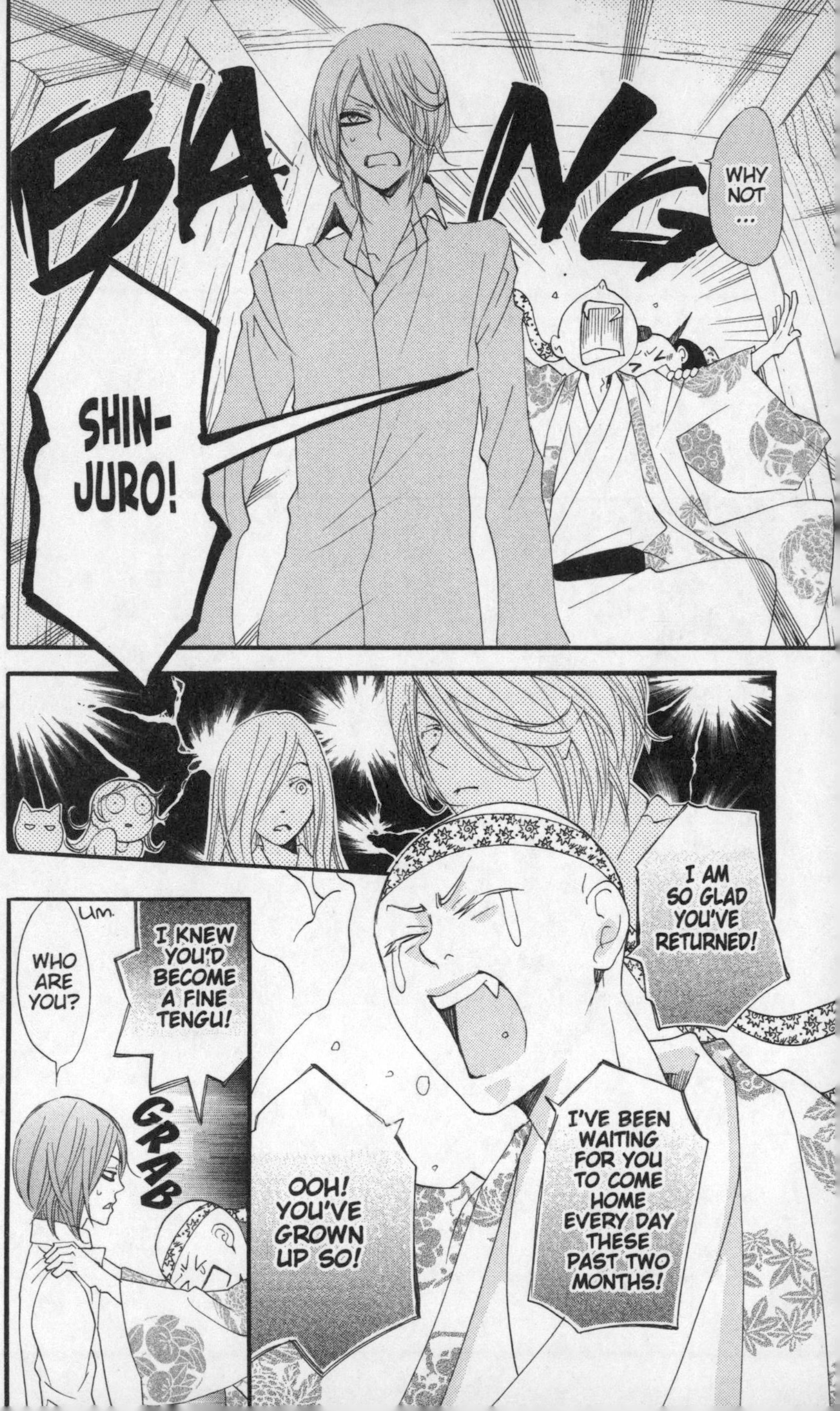
WHY NOT ...
BANG
SHIN-JURO!
I AM SO GLAD YOU'VE RETURNED!
I'VE BEEN WAITING FOR YOU TO COME HOME EVERY DAY THESE PAST TWO MONTHS!
OOH! YOU'VE GROWN UP SO!
I KNEW YOU'D BECOME A FINE TENGU!
GRAB
UM.
WHO ARE YOU?

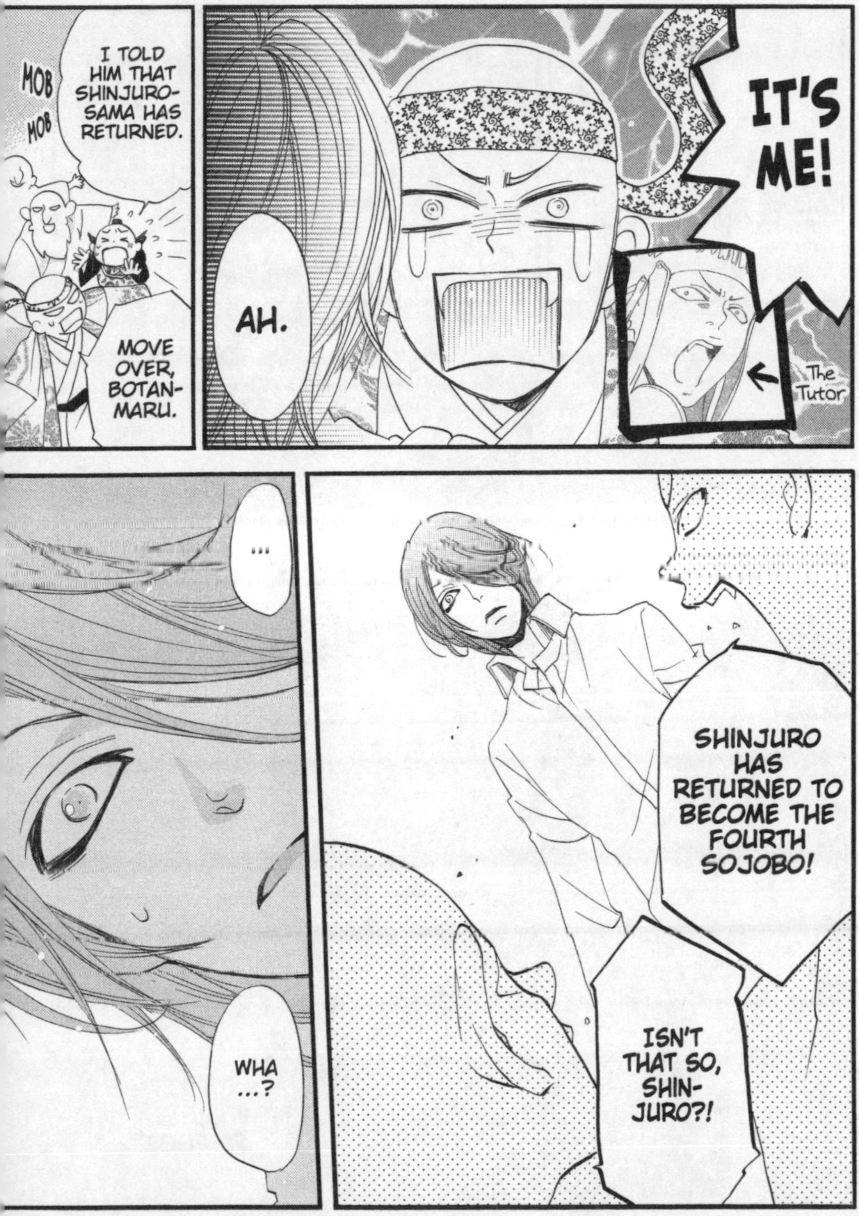
IT'S ME!
The Tutor
AH.
I TOLD HIM THAT SHINJURO-SAMA HAS RETURNED.
MOB MOB
MOVE OVER, BOTAN-MARU.
SHINJURO HAS RETURNED TO BECOME THE FOURTH SOJOBO!
ISN'T THAT SO, SHIN-JURO?!
...
WHA ...?

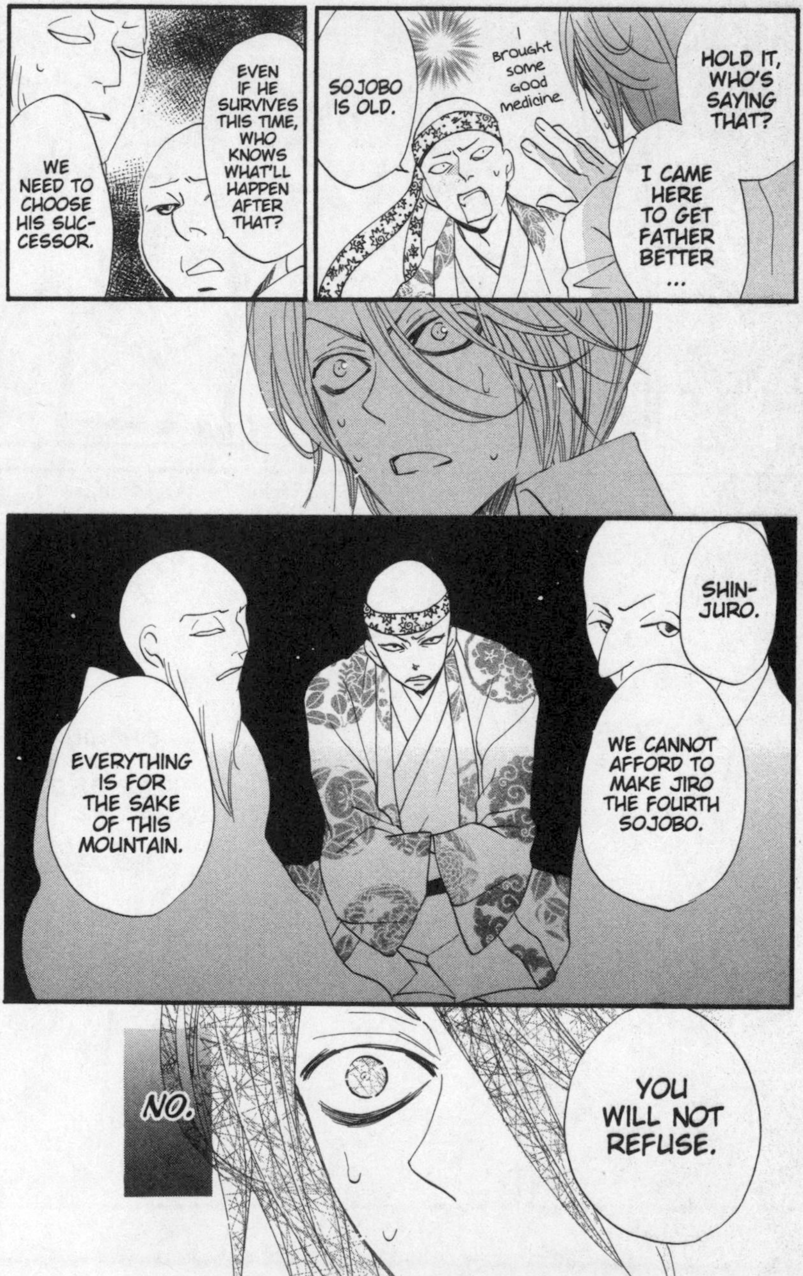
HOLD IT, WHO'S SAYING THAT?
I CAME HERE TO GET FATHER BETTER ...
I brought some good medicine
SOJOBO IS OLD.
EVEN IF HE SURVIVES THIS TIME, WHO KNOWS WHAT'LL HAPPEN AFTER THAT?
WE NEED TO CHOOSE HIS SUCCESSOR.
SHIN-JURO.
WE CANNOT AFFORD TO MAKE JIRO THE FOURTH SOJOBO.
EVERYTHING IS FOR THE SAKE OF THIS MOUNTAIN.
YOU WILL NOT REFUSE.
NO.

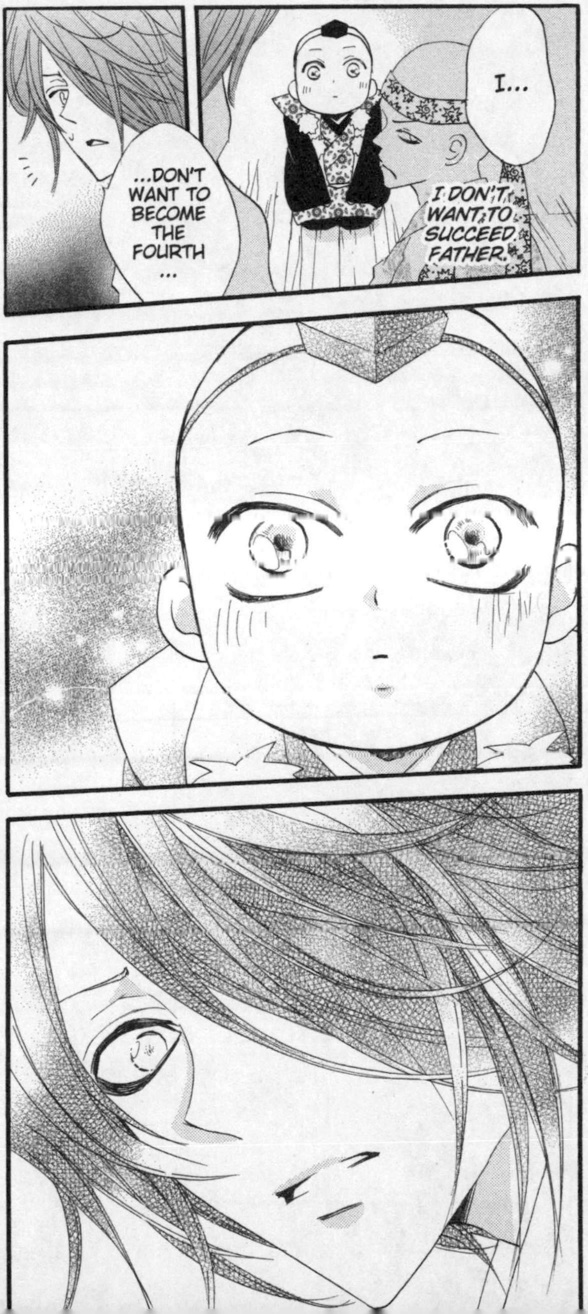

I...
I DON'T WANT TO SUCCEED FATHER.
...DON'T WANT TO BECOME THE FOURTH ...

6

This is the last sidebar. Thank you for reading this far.

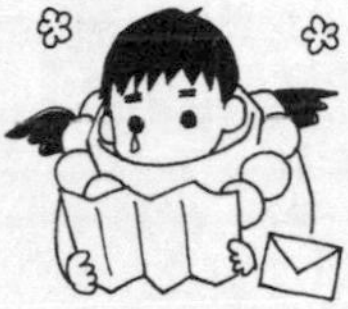

Thank you for your letters. They always cheer me up.

If you have any comments about this volume, please send your letters to the following address...

P.O. Box 77010
San Francisco, CA
94107

Please

Thank you.

Then!

I pray from my heart that we'll be able to meet again in volume 10 as well.

-Julietta Suzuki

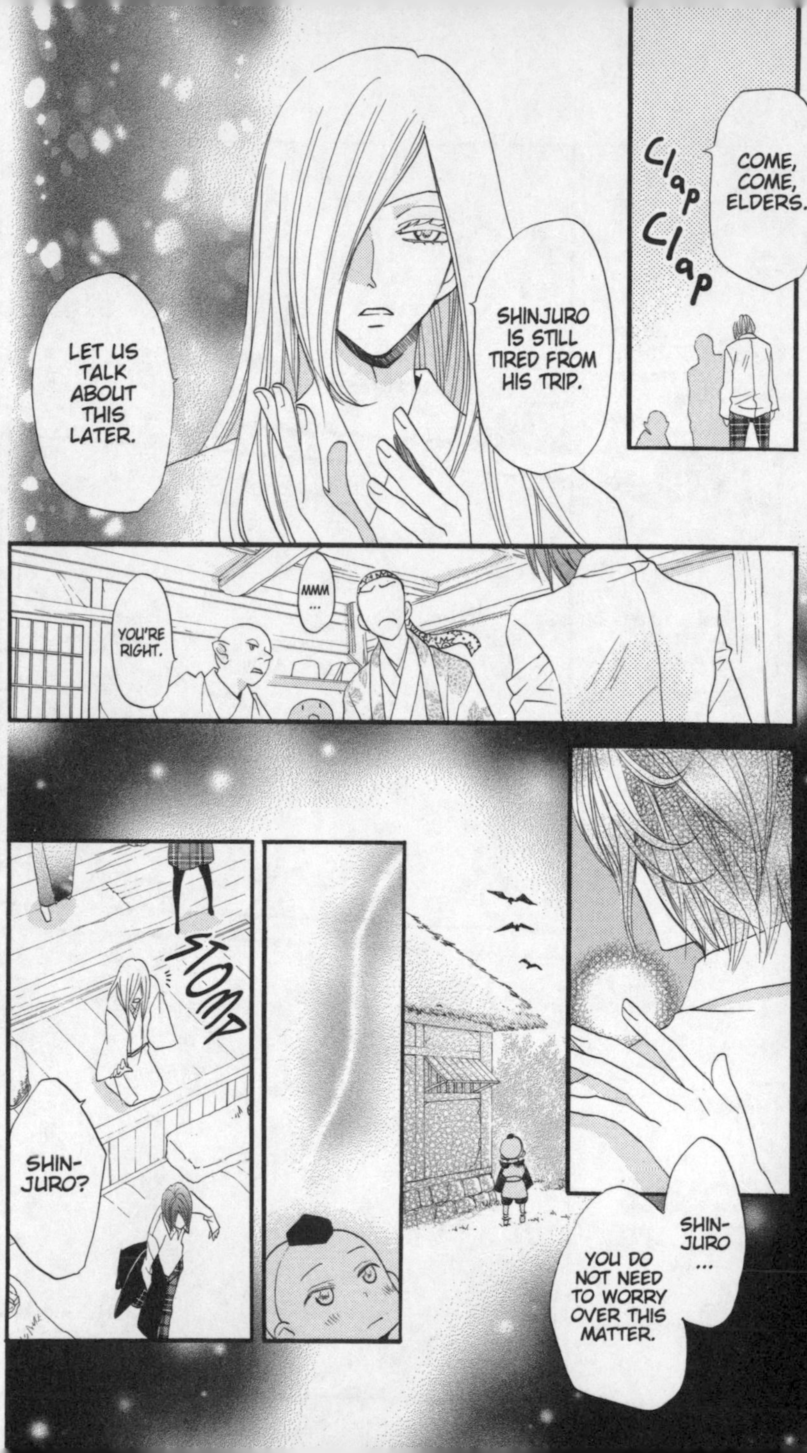
COME, COME, ELDERS.
Clap Clap
SHINJURO IS STILL TIRED FROM HIS TRIP.
LET US TALK ABOUT THIS LATER.
MMM...
YOU'RE RIGHT.
SHIN-JURO...
YOU DO NOT NEED TO WORRY OVER THIS MATTER.
STOMP
SHIN-JURO?

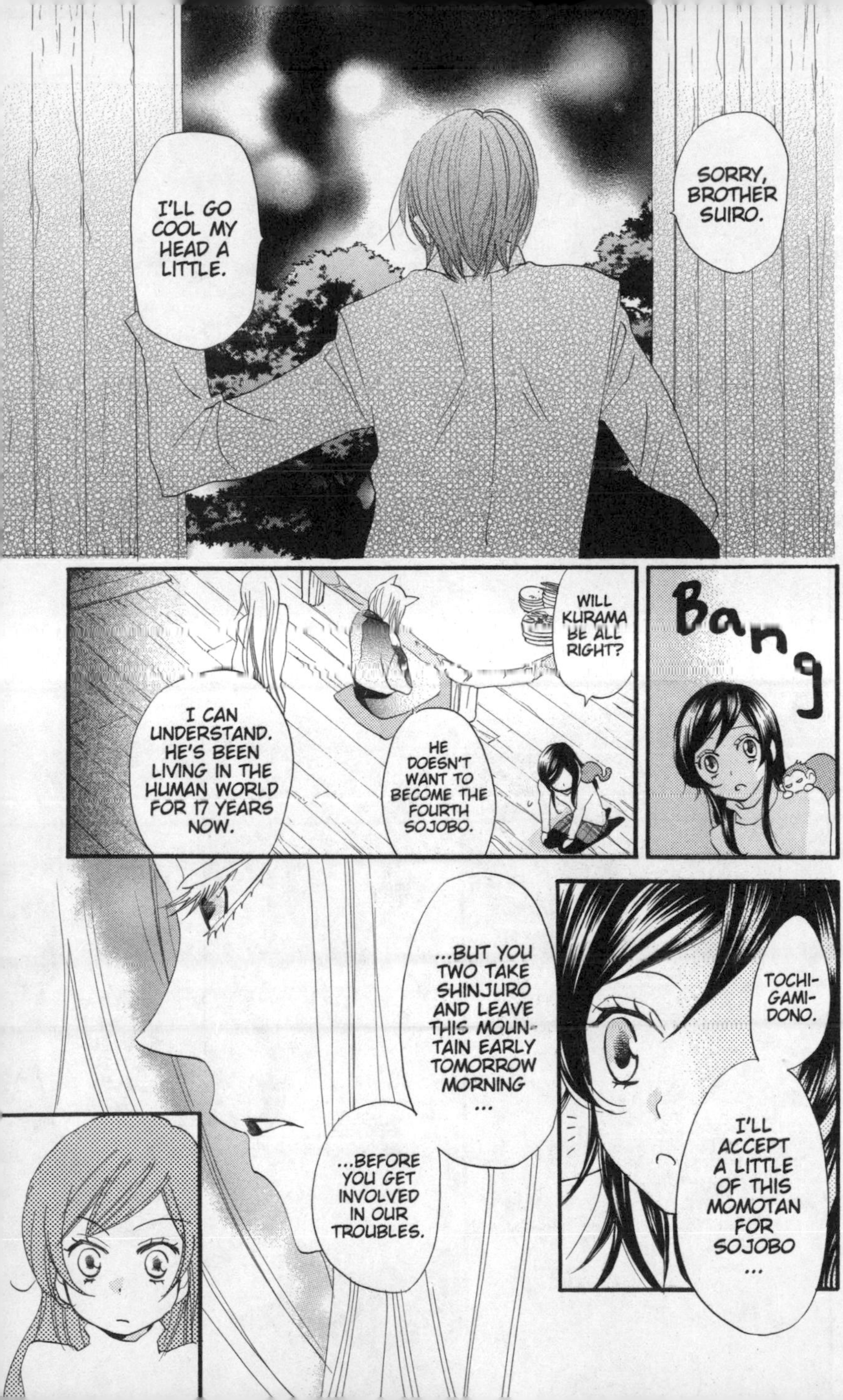
SORRY, BROTHER SUIRO.
I'LL GO COOL MY HEAD A LITTLE.
Bang
WILL KURAMA BE ALL RIGHT?
HE DOESN'T WANT TO BECOME THE FOURTH SOJOBO.
I CAN UNDERSTAND. HE'S BEEN LIVING IN THE HUMAN WORLD FOR 17 YEARS NOW.
TOCHI-GAMI-DONO.
I'LL ACCEPT A LITTLE OF THIS MOMOTAN FOR SOJOBO ...
...BUT YOU TWO TAKE SHINJURO AND LEAVE THIS MOUNTAIN EARLY TOMORROW MORNING ...
...BEFORE YOU GET INVOLVED IN OUR TROUBLES.

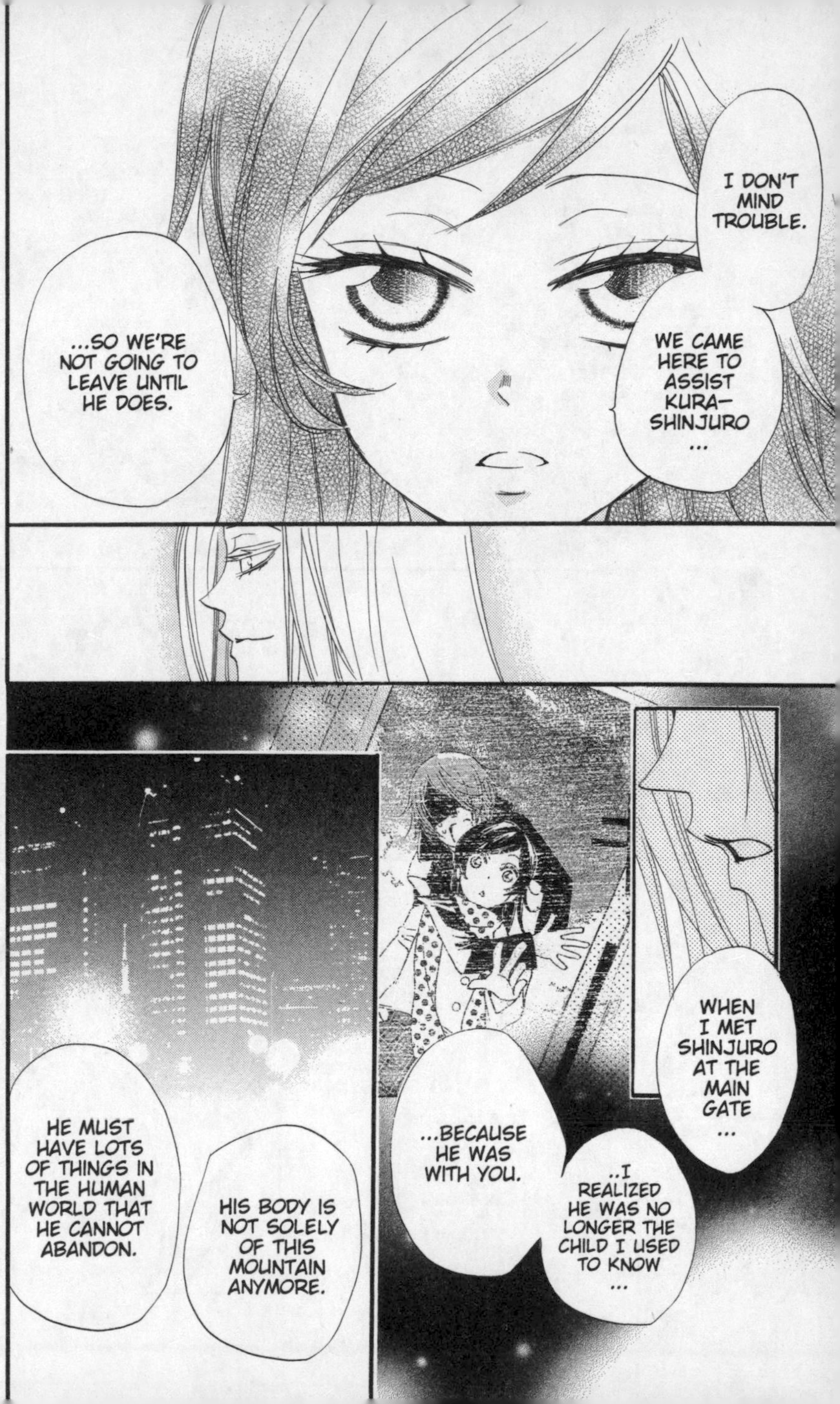
I DON'T MIND TROUBLE.
WE CAME HERE TO ASSIST KURA-SHINJURO ...
...SO WE'RE NOT GOING TO LEAVE UNTIL HE DOES.
WHEN I MET SHINJURO AT THE MAIN GATE ...
..I REALIZED HE WAS NO LONGER THE CHILD I USED TO KNOW ...
...BECAUSE HE WAS WITH YOU.
HIS BODY IS NOT SOLELY OF THIS MOUNTAIN ANYMORE.
HE MUST HAVE LOTS OF THINGS IN THE HUMAN WORLD THAT HE CANNOT ABANDON.

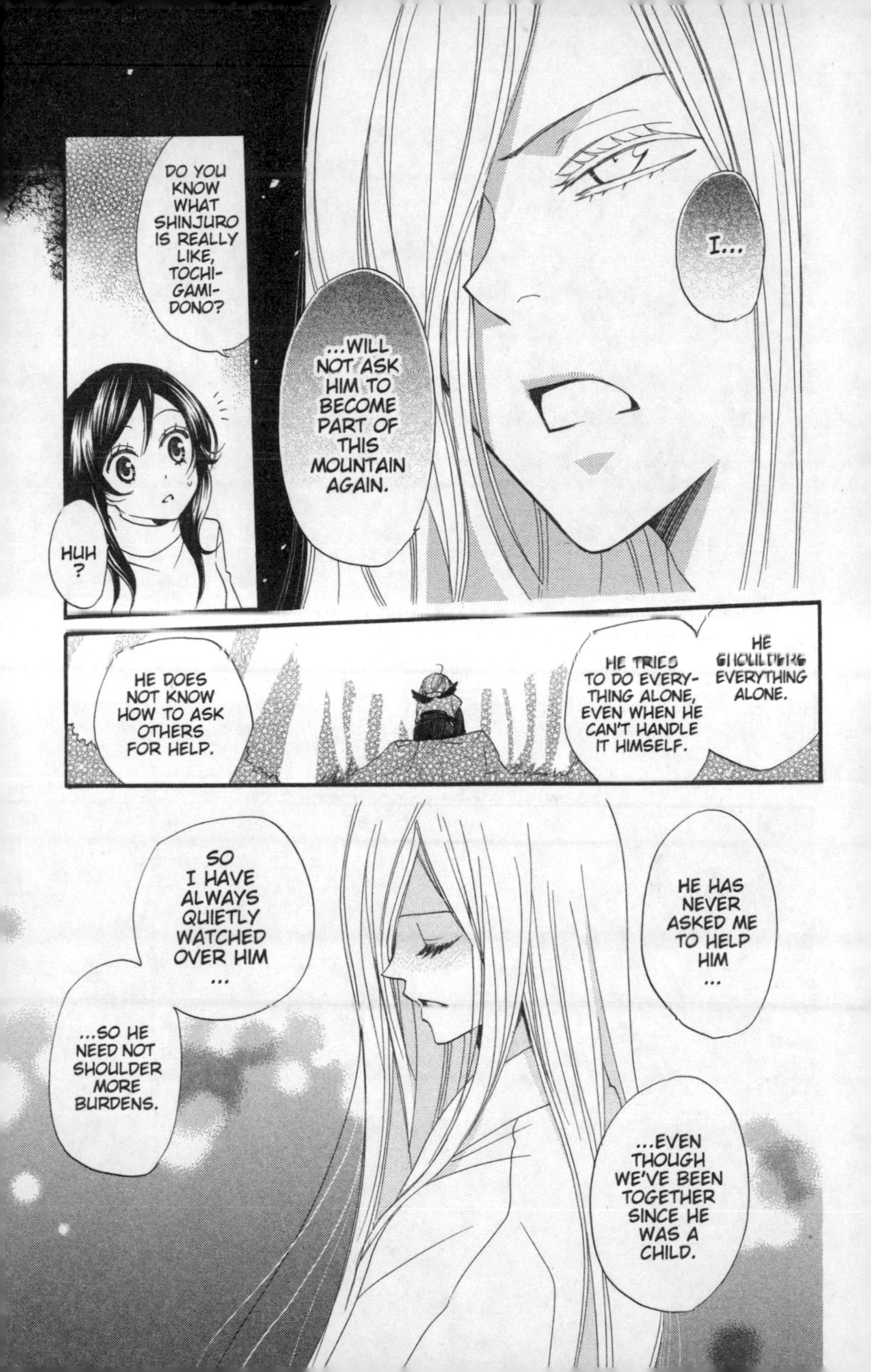
I...
...WILL NOT ASK HIM TO BECOME PART OF THIS MOUNTAIN AGAIN.
DO YOU KNOW WHAT SHINJURO IS REALLY LIKE, TOCHI-GAMI-DONO?
HUH?
HE SHOULDERS EVERYTHING ALONE.
HE TRIES TO DO EVERY-THING ALONE, EVEN WHEN HE CAN'T HANDLE IT HIMSELF.
HE DOES NOT KNOW HOW TO ASK OTHERS FOR HELP.
HE HAS NEVER ASKED ME TO HELP HIM...
...EVEN THOUGH WE'VE BEEN TOGETHER SINCE HE WAS A CHILD.
SO I HAVE ALWAYS QUIETLY WATCHED OVER HIM...
...SO HE NEED NOT SHOULDER MORE BURDENS.

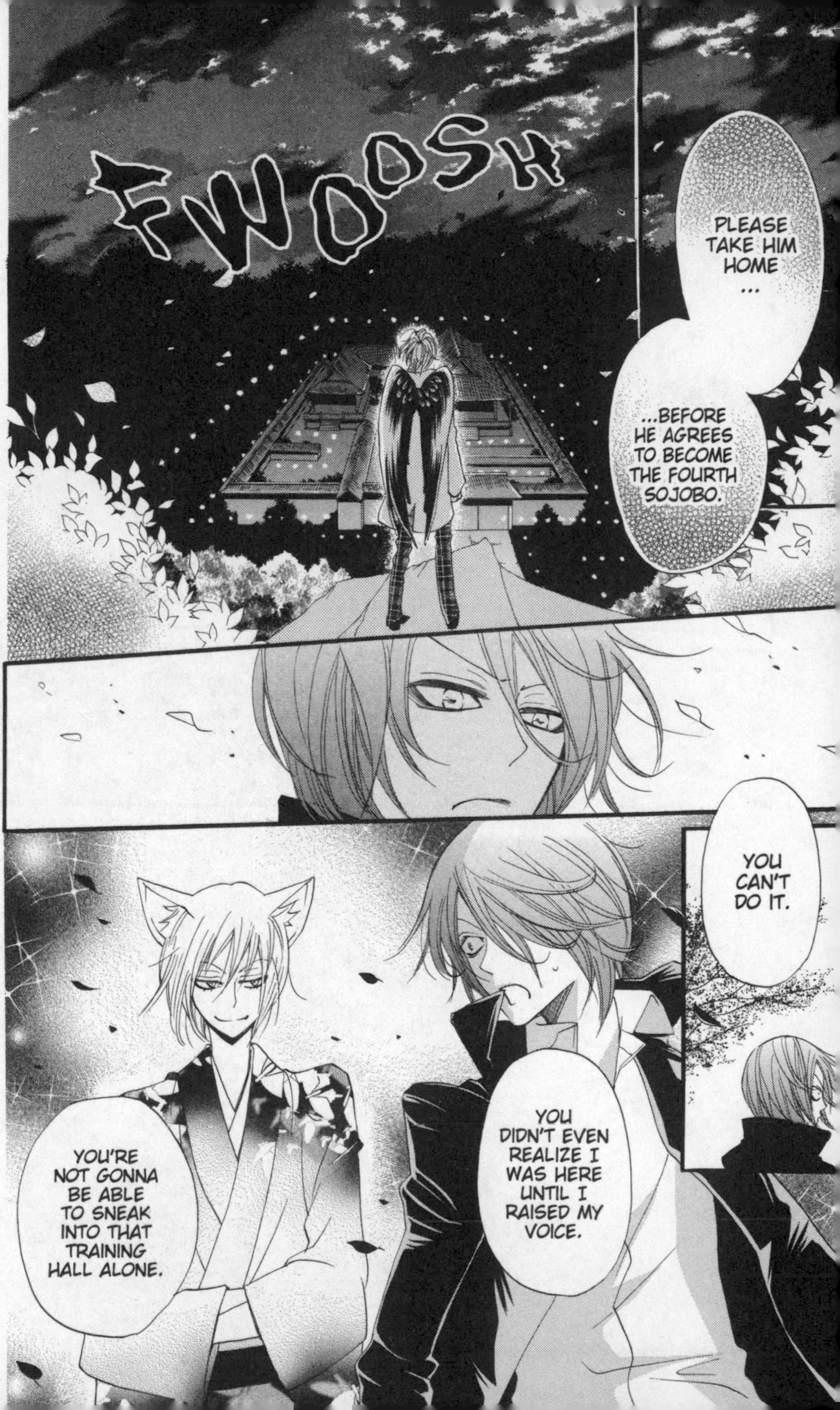
PLEASE TAKE HIM HOME ...
...BEFORE HE AGREES TO BECOME THE FOURTH SOJOBO.
FWOOSH
YOU CAN'T DO IT.
YOU DIDN'T EVEN REALIZE I WAS HERE UNTIL I RAISED MY VOICE.
YOU'RE NOT GONNA BE ABLE TO SNEAK INTO THAT TRAINING HALL ALONE.

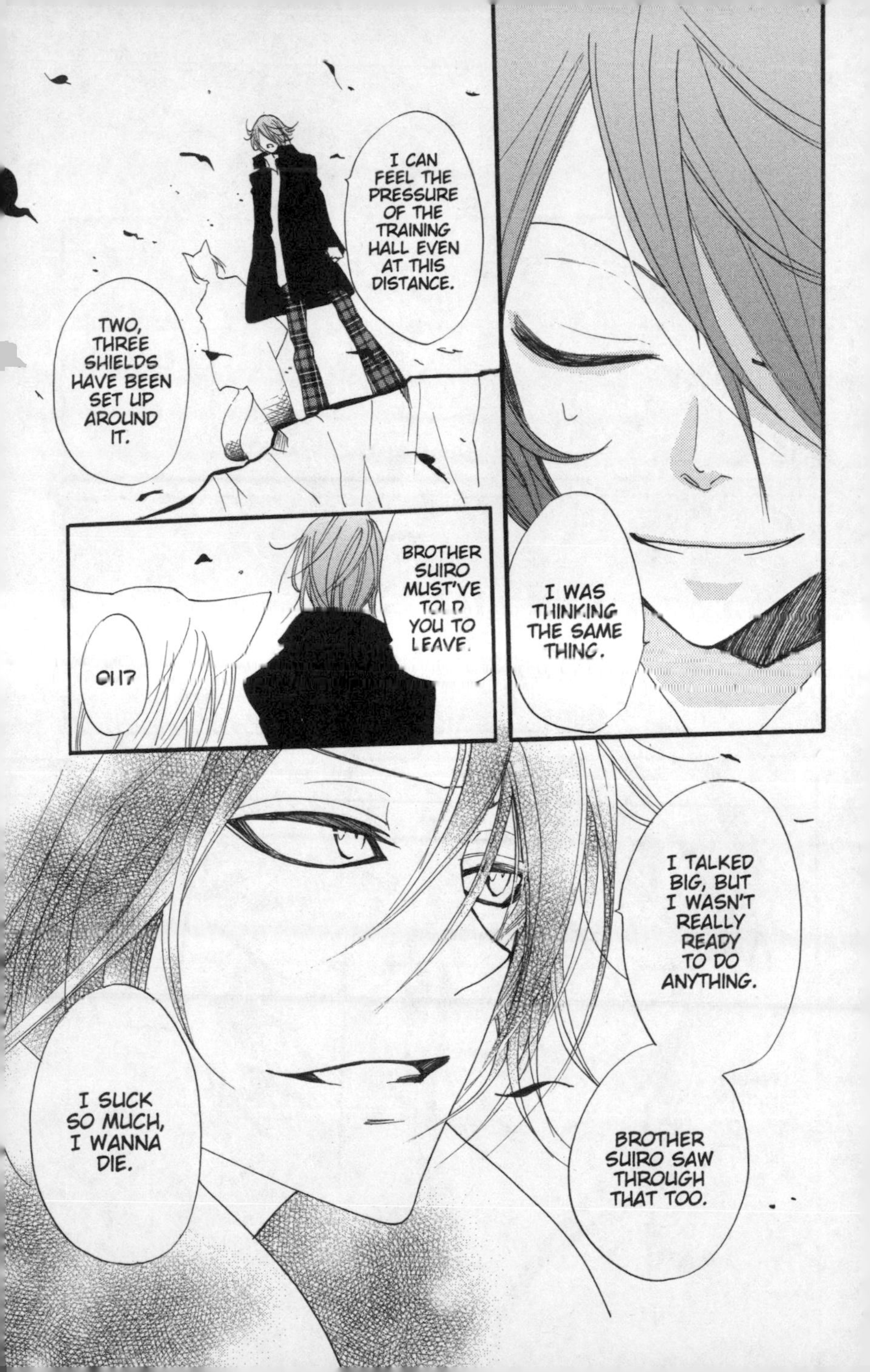
I WAS THINKING THE SAME THING.
I CAN FEEL THE PRESSURE OF THE TRAINING HALL EVEN AT THIS DISTANCE.
TWO, THREE SHIELDS HAVE BEEN SET UP AROUND IT.
BROTHER SUIRO MUST'VE TOLD YOU TO LEAVE.
OI!?
I TALKED BIG, BUT I WASN'T REALLY READY TO DO ANYTHING.
BROTHER SUIRO SAW THROUGH THAT TOO.
I SUCK SO MUCH, I WANNA DIE.

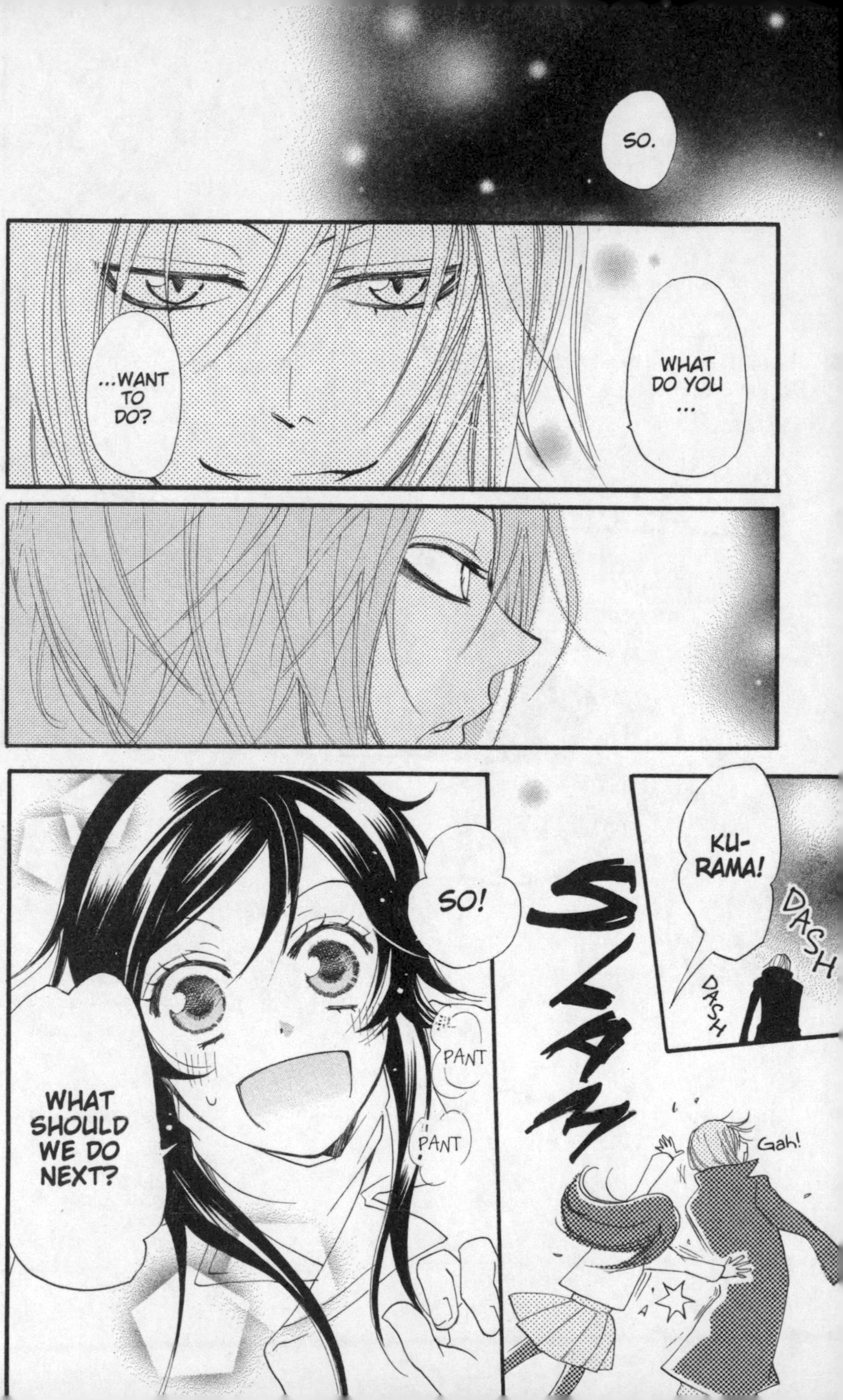
SO.
WHAT DO YOU ...
...WANT TO DO?
KU-RAMA!
DASH
DASH
SLAM
Gah!
SO!
PANT
PANT
WHAT SHOULD WE DO NEXT?

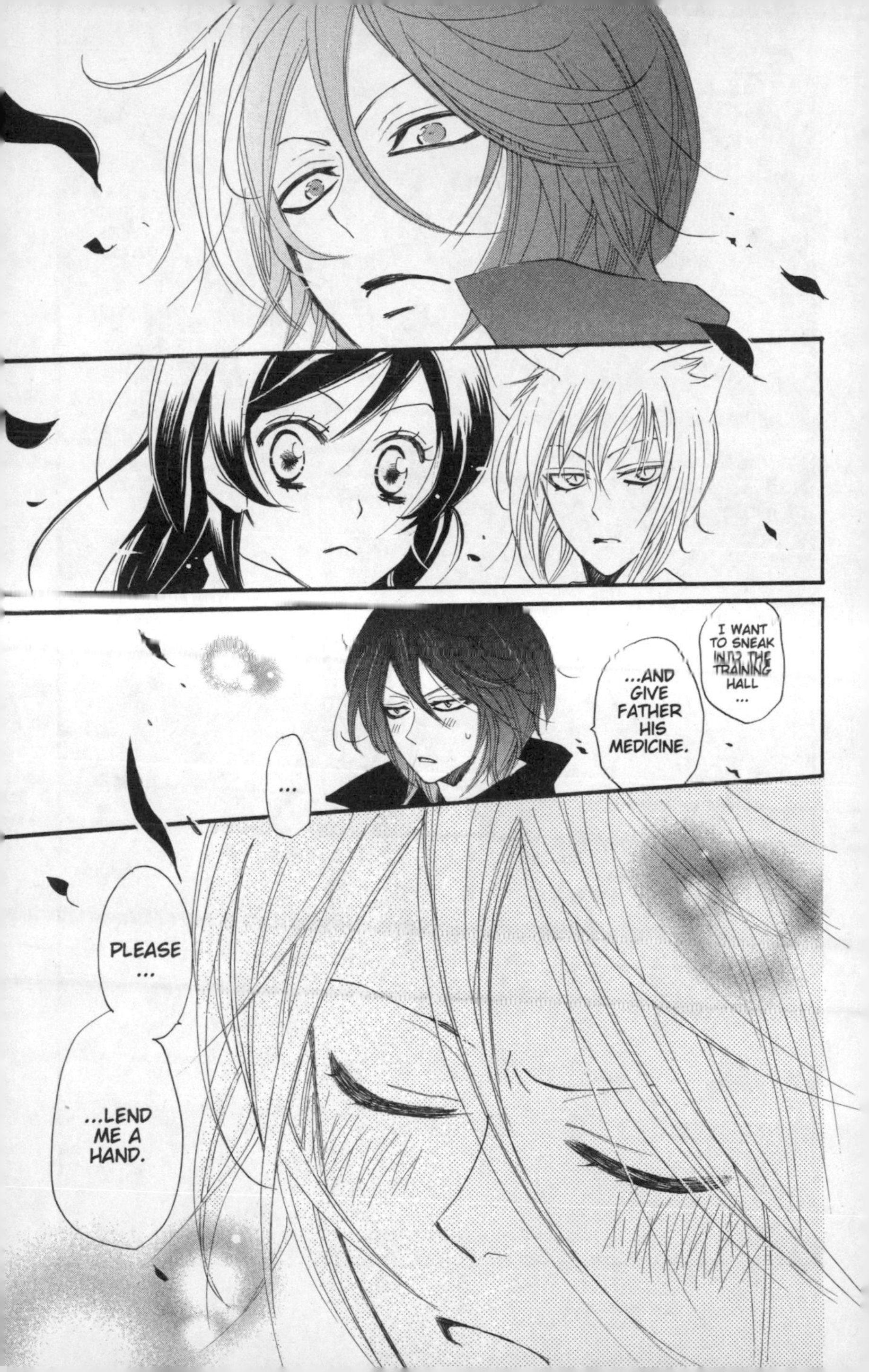
I WANT TO SNEAK INTO THE TRAINING HALL ...
...AND GIVE FATHER HIS MEDICINE.
...
PLEASE ...
...LEND ME A HAND.

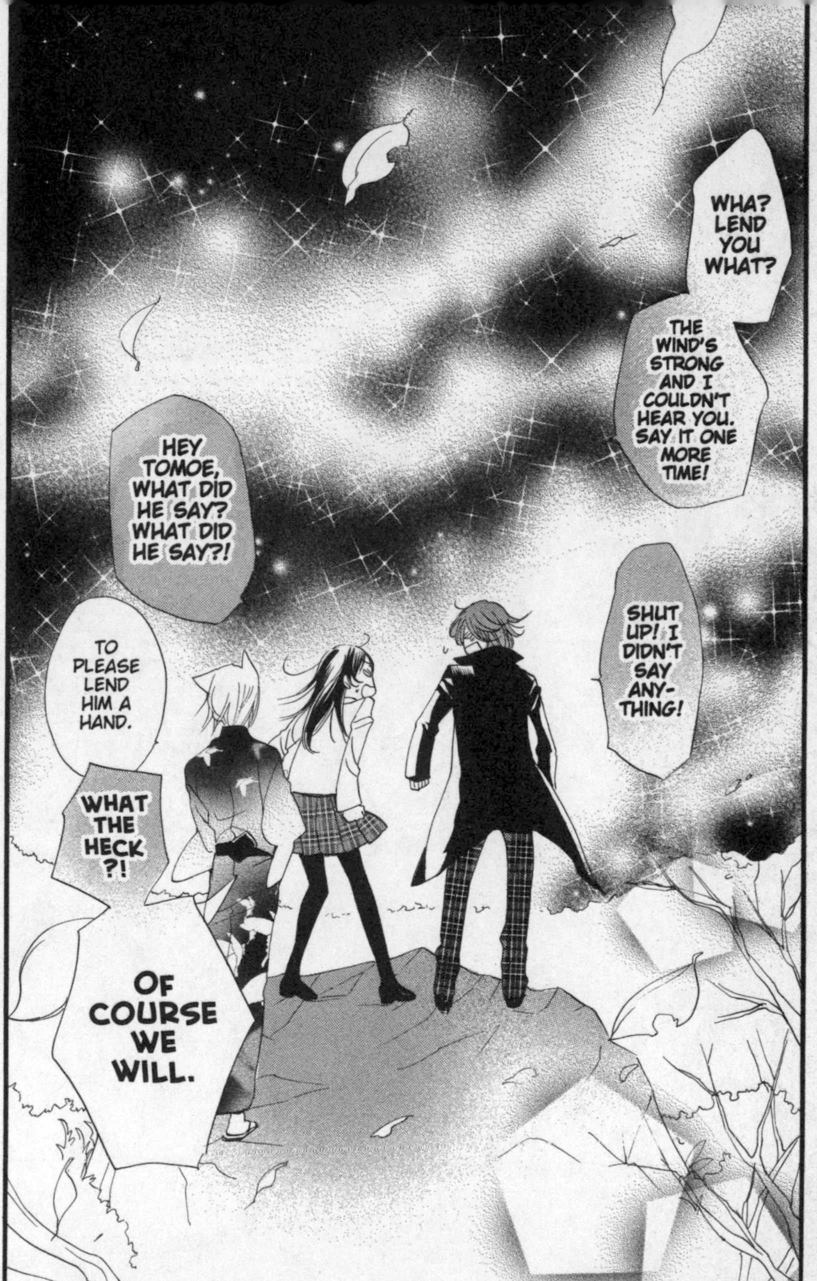
WHA? LEND YOU WHAT?
THE WIND'S STRONG AND I COULDN'T HEAR YOU. SAY IT ONE MORE TIME!
HEY TOMOE, WHAT DID HE SAY? WHAT DID HE SAY?!
SHUT UP! I DIDN'T SAY ANY-THING!
TO PLEASE LEND HIM A HAND.
WHAT THE HECK?!
OF COURSE WE WILL.

The Otherworld

Ayakashi is an archaic term for yokai.

Kami are Shinto deities or spirits. The word can be used for a range of creatures, from nature spirits to strong and dangerous gods.

Kamuhakari is the weeklong convocation of kami at Izumo Oyashiro shrine in October of the lunar calendar. Therefore in the lunar calendar, October is called Kamiarizuki (month-with-kami) in Izumo, and Kannazuki (month-without-kami) in other regions. Festivals are held at Izumo Oyashiro during the Kamuhakari.

Onibi-warashi are like will-o'-the-wisps.

Shikigami are spirits that are summoned and employed by *onmyoji* (Yin-Yang sorcerers).

Shinshi are birds, beasts, insects or fish that have a special relationship with a kami.

Tochigami (or *jinushigami*) are deities of a specific area of land.

Tsuriki is a kami's power and becomes stronger the more it is used.

Honorifics

-chan is a diminutive most often used with babies, children or teenage girls.

-dono roughly means "my lord," although not in the aristocratic sense.

-hime means princess, although a Japanese princess is not the same as a Western one and isn't necessarily the daughter of a king.

-san is a standard honorific similar to Mr., Mrs., Miss, or Ms.

-sama is used with people of much higher rank.

Notes

Page 23, panel 5: Ikebana
Traditional Japanese flower arranging.

Page 40, panel 2: Waratte Iikamo
Spoofing a Japanese TV show called *Waratte Iitomo* that is broadcast at noon on weekdays.

Page 41, panel 1: Go-kon
A group dating event where the same number of males and females gather for activities like karaoke.

Page 79, panel 1: Mount Takao
A mountain about an hour away from Tokyo where, according to folklore, tengu live.

Page 104, panel 2: Futon
Traditional Japanese bedding. Japanese futon are much lighter than Western ones, and are designed to be folded and stored during the day.

Page 104, panel 3: Tatami
Straw mats that make up traditional Japanese flooring.

Page 111, panel 1: Sojogadani Valley
An actual valley northwest of Mount Kurama.

Page 111, panel 2: Negative ions
Negatively charged ions are released by bodies of water and green areas such as forests. Negative ions are said to have health benefits, including making you feel energized and invigorated.

Page 114, panel 4: Atago, Takao
One of the eight great tengu (*hachi daitengu*) is said to live on Mount Atago. Another of the eight great tengu, Naigubu, is said to live on Mount Takao.

Page 115, panel 2: Uzuzakura
Cherry blossoms that bloom on Mount Kurama.

Julietta Suzuki's debut manga *Hoshi ni Naru Hi* (The Day One Becomes a Star) appeared in the 2004 *Hana to Yume Plus*. Her other books include *Akuma to Dolce* (The Devil and Sweets) and *Karakuri Odette*. Born in December in Fukuoka Prefecture, she enjoys having movies play in the background while she works on her manga.

KAMISAMA KISS
VOL. 9
Shojo Beat Edition

STORY AND ART BY
Julietta Suzuki

English Translation & Adaptation/Tomo Kimura
Touch-up Art & Lettering/Joanna Estep
Design/Yukiko Whitley
Editor/Pancha Diaz

KAMISAMA HAJIMEMASHITA by Julietta Suzuki
© Julietta Suzuki 2011
All rights reserved.
First published in Japan in 2011 by HAKUSENSHA, Inc., Tokyo.
English language translation rights arranged with
HAKUSENSHA, Inc., Tokyo.

The stories, characters and incidents mentioned
in this publication are entirely fictional.

Printed in Italy

Published by VIZ Media, LLC
P.O. Box 77010
San Francisco, CA 94107

10 9 8
First printing, June 2012
Eighth printing, March 2024

viz.com   shojobeat.com

PARENTAL ADVISORY
KAMISAMA KISS is rated T for Teen
and is recommended for ages
13 and up. This volume contains
fantasy violence.

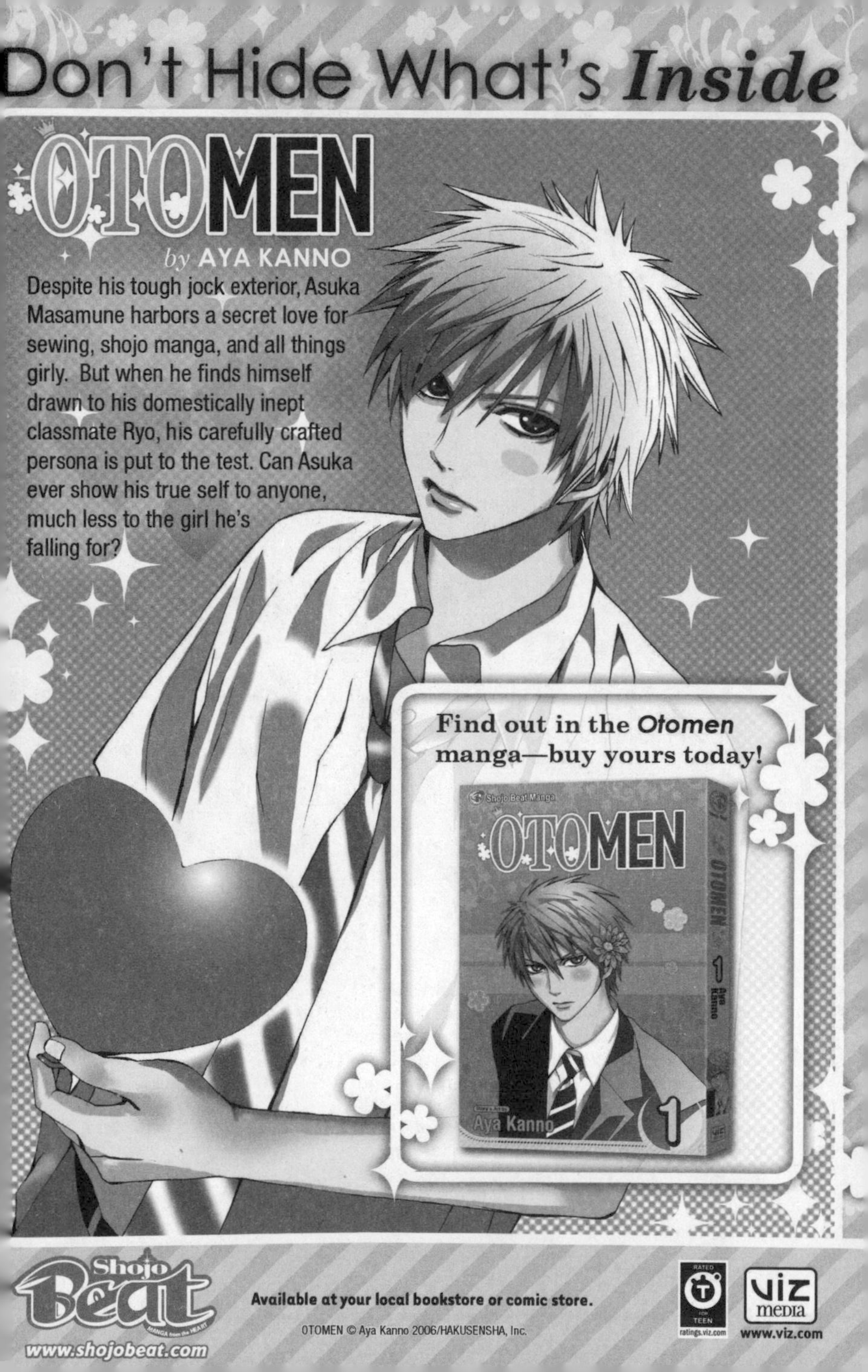
Don't Hide What's Inside
OTOMEN
by AYA KANNO
Despite his tough jock exterior, Asuka Masamune harbors a secret love for sewing, shojo manga, and all things girly. But when he finds himself drawn to his domestically inept classmate Ryo, his carefully crafted persona is put to the test. Can Asuka ever show his true self to anyone, much less to the girl he's falling for?
Find out in the Otomen manga—buy yours today!
Shojo Beat Manga
OTOMEN
Aya Kanno
1
Shojo Beat
MANGA from the HEART
www.shojobeat.com
Available at your local bookstore or comic store.
OTOMEN © Aya Kanno 2006/HAKUSENSHA, Inc.
RATED T FOR TEEN
ratings.viz.com
VIZ MEDIA
www.viz.com

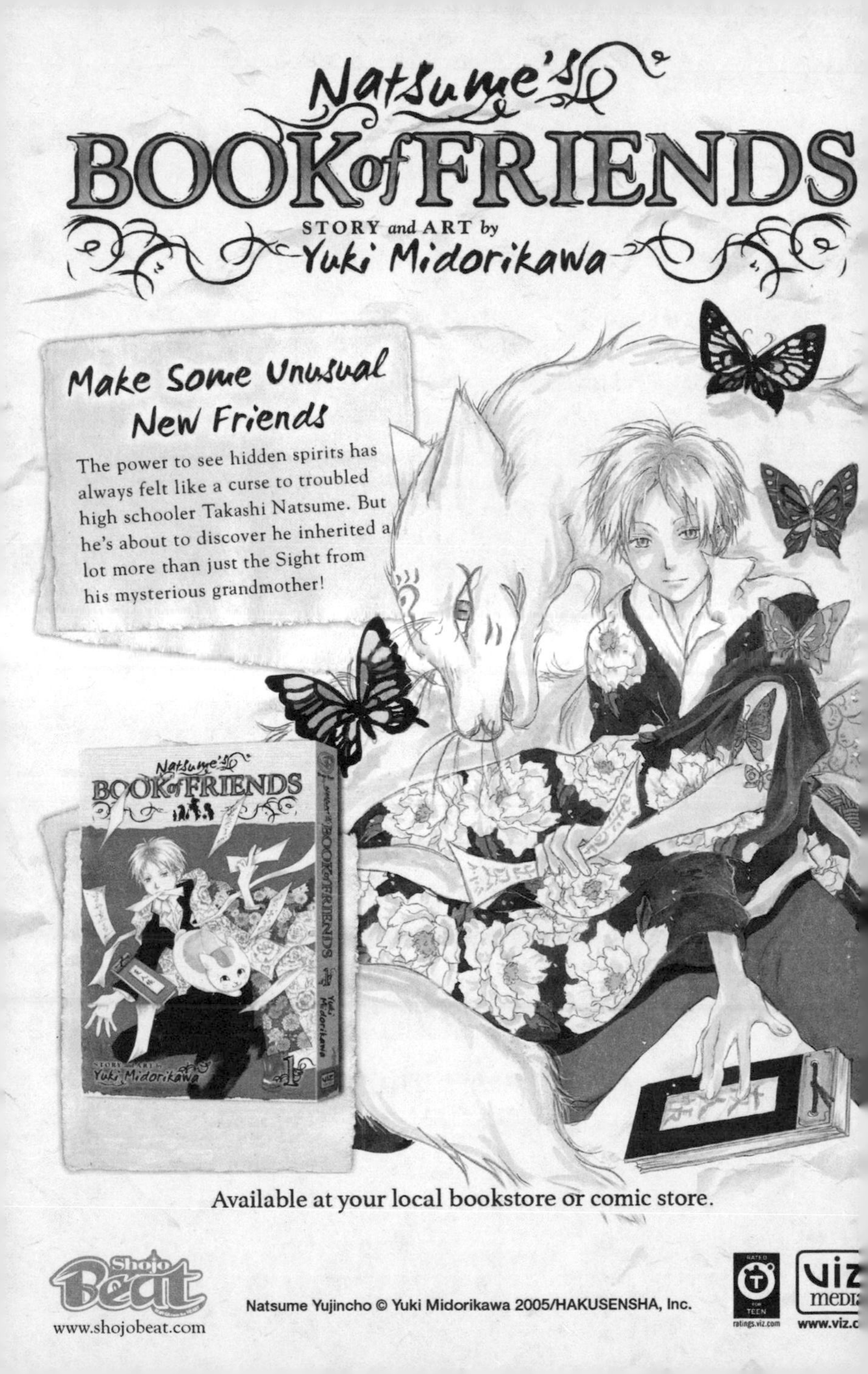

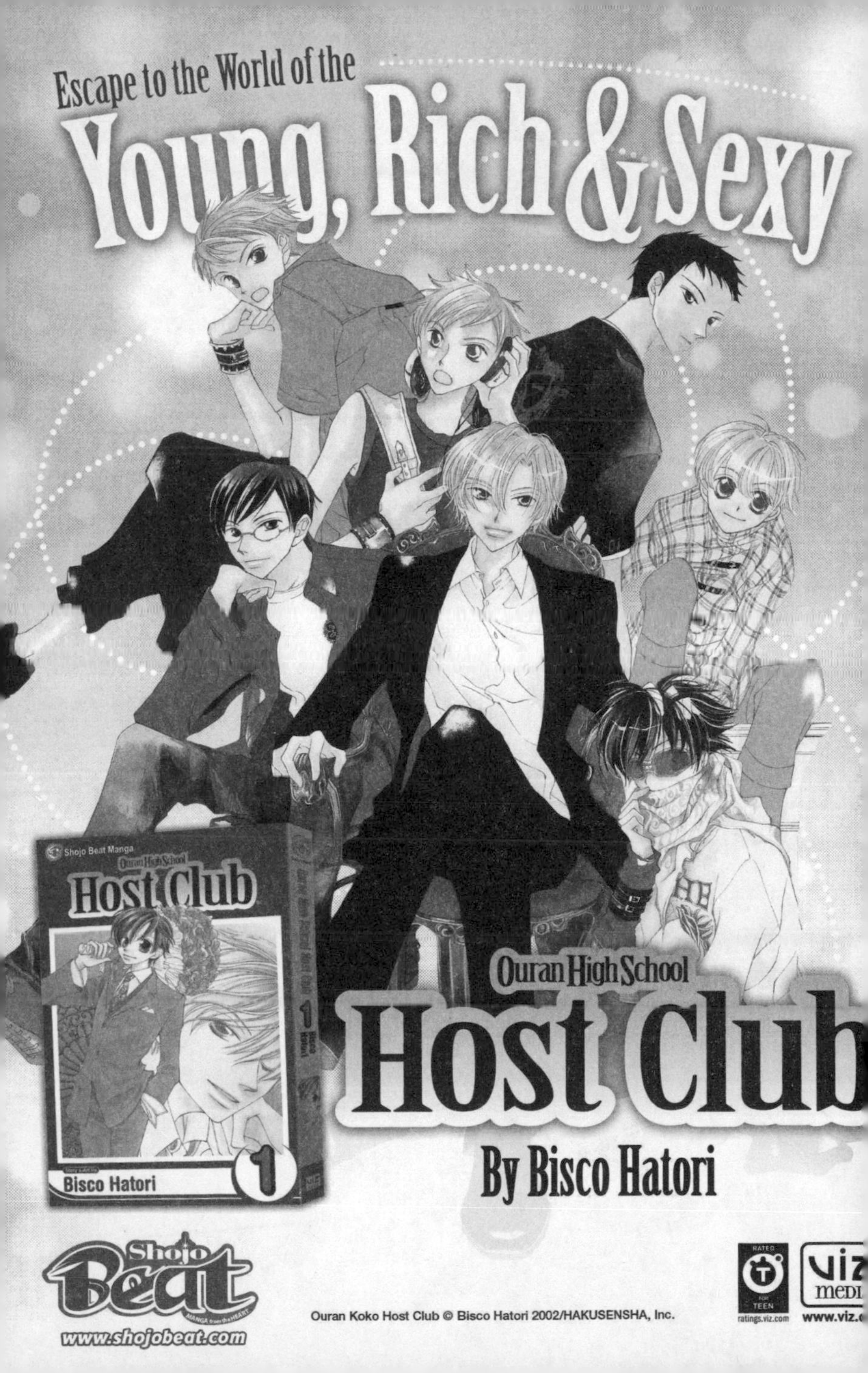
Escape to the World of the
Young, Rich & Sexy
Shojo Beat Manga
Ouran High School
Host Club
Bisco Hatori
1
Ouran High School
Host Club
By Bisco Hatori
Shojo Beat
www.shojobeat.com
Ouran Koko Host Club © Bisco Hatori 2002/HAKUSENSHA, Inc.
RATED
T
FOR
TEEN
ratings.viz.com

This is the last page.

In keeping with the original Japanese comic format, this book reads from right to left—so action, sound effects, and word balloons are completely reversed. This preserves the orientation of the original artwork—plus, it's fun! Check out the diagram shown here to get the hang of things, and then turn to the other side of the book to get started!